A PHENOMENOLOGY OF CHRISTIAN LIFE

INDIANA SERIES IN THE
PHILOSOPHY OF RELIGION

Merold Westphal, *editor*

A PHENOMENOLOGY OF CHRISTIAN LIFE

Glory and Night

Felix Ó Murchadha

Indiana University Press

Bloomington and Indianapolis

This book is a publication of

Indiana University Press
Office of Scholarly Publishing
Herman B Wells Library 350
1320 East 10th Street
Bloomington, Indiana 47405 USA

iupress.indiana.edu

Telephone orders   800-842-6796
Fax orders   812-855-7931

Manufactured in the United States of America

Library of Congress Cataloging-in-Publication Data

Ó Murchadha, Felix.
  A phenomenology of Christian life : glory and night /
Felix Ó Murchadha.
     pages cm— (Indiana series in the philosophy of religion)
  Includes bibliographical references and index.
  ISBN 978-0-253-01000-1 (cloth : alkaline paper) —
ISBN 978-0-253-01009-4 (ebook) 1. Christian philosophy.
2. Phenomenology. 3. Life —Religious aspects —Christianity.
4. Christian life. 5. Philosophy. 6. Philosophical theology.
I. Title.
  BR100 .O23 2013
  248—dc23
                                          2013008816

1 2 3 4 5 18 17 16 15 14 13

In Memory of my Father
Aibhistín Ó Murchadha (1927–2008)

Contents

Preface

Pʜɪʟᴏsᴏᴘʜɪᴄᴀʟ ʀᴇꜰʟᴇᴄᴛɪᴏɴ ʙᴇɢɪɴs with what is given. However, philosophical beginnings are uncertain and deeply ambiguous: philosophy begins with that
which has already begun and yet attempts to incorporate all other origins into
itself. Historically, philosophy arose 'out of' a Greek way of being-in-the-world,
informed by Homer and Hesiod. It attempted to find in the logos a way of justification to which such being-in-the-world would by an inner necessity need to sub-
mit itself. Philosophy, however, began again, in the sense here understood, with
Christianity. Again, it sought to incorporate a prior beginning, this time that of
the being-in-the-world of scripture. This attempt left a residue, which led eventually to a disciplinary break (unthinkable in classical Greek philosophy) between
philosophy and theology, just as the first beginning of philosophy had resulted,
as Nietzsche shows in the *Birth of Tragedy*, in a break between philosophy and
poetry. Certain phenomena, essential to the Christian being-in-the-world, remained philosophically unjustifiable, that is, unrecognizable and unaccountable,
and hence only valid under the auspices of faith and religion. This book attempts
to explore that residue, to think that which disrupts and disturbs philosophy and
leads philosophy beyond its Greek beginning.

If philosophy began again in reflecting upon the Christian way of being-in-
the-world, this beginning did not mark any radical break with its Greek origins.
This failure had fundamental and paradoxical effects: there has been no originally
Christian philosophy in the past two millennia—at most Christian trappings on
Greek thought, as Max Scheler puts it. Many of the foremost Christian thinkers
have been anti-philosophers, para-philosophers, snipping so to speak from the
sidelines. In certain moods Paul, Origen, Tertullian, Augustine, Luther, Pascal,
and Kierkegaard form a necessarily eclectic tradition of such para-philosophy.
This place of Christian thought in the European tradition should make us pause.
For all the undoubted influence of Christianity on that history, the paradigmatic
place of Greek conceptuality remained for long periods unshaken. Greek conceptuality is fundamentally Platonic. Despite the influence of Aristotle, the Stoics,
and other strands of Greek thought, at the core of all metaphysics worthy of the
name is Plato, such that for Greek philosophy Whitehead's oft quoted remark
about philosophy being a series of footnotes to Plato is justified. As I will show
in this book, there are fundamental reasons concerning the self-understanding
of the early Christian church fathers for the fact that Christianity did not es-

sentially disturb Platonism, but rather incorporated it and by consequence was incorporated into it. The concern of this book is not to argue the merits or faults of such incorporation. Rather, in the para-philosophical tradition to which I have alluded, this book seeks to explore those themes in Christianity—revolving around the figures of glory and night—which fundamentally disrupt Platonism and Greek philosophy from Plato to Heidegger.

The crisis of Greek thought is not confined to the ontological. Emmanuel Levinas brought to the fore an encounter with Greek thought, which the para-philosophical tradition represents: the vanity of ontology and the centrality of the ethical relation. Since his groundbreaking work, it has become a commonplace to set the difference between Greek and Judeo-Christian thought along the fault line between ethics and ontology. To do this, however, threatens to reinforce the marginality of the tradition of para-philosophy. What we find in Judeo-Christianity, what we find in the extreme phenomena outlined in the New Testament, is an account of the phenomenality of phenomena that is deeply ontological at the same time as it is deeply ethical. The key term here, as Urs von Balthasar has shown, is 'love' (*agápe*), which defines the being of God as much as his action in the Christian scriptures.

It is essential to note here that the term 'Judeo-Christian' is anything but harmless. The differences obscured by the hyphen in this term are not thematically dealt with here as they are beyond the scope of this book, but they are ever-present, particularly when the discussion turns to incarnation, creation, and time. This book is concerned specifically with a phenomenology of Christian life, but it is important to recognize that Judaism also disrupts Greek philosophy.

This book attempts to position those phenomena around a fundamental double structure of phenomenon which is expressed in the Christian tradition as glory and night. Glory here is to be understood neither principally aesthetically (von Balthasar) nor principally politically (as Agamben has recently done), but phenomenologically. Glory is understood here as a structure of appearance which in its double relation with night expresses a specifically Judeo-Christian experience of phenomenon. Furthermore this experience can only be understood in terms of ontology *and* ethics. From that basis glory and night are viewed as both aesthetic and political, however problematic any conjunction of Christianity and politics may be. 'Glory' and 'night' refer to the being of phenomena to which the Christian way of being-in-the-world responds. One of the crucial elements of Christianity is the central place of faith. Since Kierkegaard we have become used to thinking in terms of a 'leap of faith' and the decision without ultimate rational justification to take that leap. But without denying the pertinence of Kierkegaard's account, if we look to Paul for our bearings, we find that faith is first and foremost a *response* that has its own logic. If the Christian way of being is a way of faith, it is one which understands existence from the basis of response.

Response in this sense is not a specific, but a fundamental experience. Glory and night are both modes of appearance *for* that being whose being begins in response. The form of that response is prayer and worship. Here language functions not to describe or bring about effects, but to give articulation to its own limits and those of the world. The true response to god's love is pure worship (see John 4:24, 9:38), a glorifying thanksgiving (see Matthew 15:36, Romans 1:8). An entity whose being begins in response is a creature, whose self-understanding leads her back to utter passivity in relation to the origins in love of her being.

The pertinence of that response, the place of Christianity in human society, is in the West at least far from self-evident. The increasingly marginal place of Christianity in today's world gives added resonance to the Pauline formula for defining the Christian as "in the world, but not of the world." 'Glory' and 'night' express that liminal moment articulated in Paul's formula. They communicate an experience of god which paradoxically subverts the conditions of experience, or put more cautiously, subverts the worldly conditions of experience. They challenge the worldliness of appearance and of experience. This amounts to a challenge to Platonism. One of the central theses of this book is that Platonic philosophy is *worldly* philosophy. This thesis is not pursued as a historical claim, although it does rely on certain historical claims about Plato and the appropriation of Platonic philosophy by the church fathers. The concern rather is with contemporary debates and with the Platonic inheritance as it continues to influence our understanding of both Christianity and philosophy. The incorporation of Christianity into Platonism required a supra-cosmic reinterpretation of Plato. But I will argue that for Plato there is nothing more ultimate than the cosmos. The world of forms is not a separate world, but is the world as it really is. 'Glory' and 'night' express an intrusion into the world, which is not of the world. These terms indicate light and dark, but in a manner which subverts the Platonic schema. For Plato the world is light and the earth is dark: the dark of the cave against the light of the sun. In the Christian understanding, that which is beyond the world reveals the darkness of the world, but does so precisely by becoming earthlike: as the Prologue to John's Gospel tells us: "the Word became flesh." Suddenly the ordered universe of Plato is overturned. In its place is a dynamic relation between entities in flux, which goes well beyond anything we read in Heraclitus. Something in the world, something fleshy and earthly in the world, promises a transformation of all worldly relations in terms of that which is beyond the world.

My concern in this book is philosophical rather than historical. Methodologically, my question is: what in Christianity resists Greek metaphysics? When I speak of Christianity, that is the limit of my interest. There are many Christianities and there have been since the very first accounts of the life and death of Jesus of Nazareth. Philosophically, the task is not so much to mediate between these different accounts as to find in them what is new, what expands the possibilities for thought, possibilities which lie outside Platonism. Furthermore, my concern is philosophical also as distinct from theological. Specifically, the Christological question of the divinity of Jesus of Nazareth, as a question of theological truth, lies outside the domain both of my competence and the book's concerns. The philosophical issue is rather this: what can it *mean* for someone to be in the world and yet not of the world; what can it be for flesh, earthiness, to contain within itself in the form of the incarnate god the ultimate meaning of things? What, if anything, do the phenomena recounted in the Christian scriptures disclose or reveal about our being-in-the-world and the world in which we are?

This book is an experiment. Philosophical books fit roughly into one of the following categories: doctrinal tracts (e.g., Spinoza's *Ethics*), investigations/explorations (e.g., Plato's *Phaedo,* Husserl's *Ideas I*), propaedeutic texts (e.g., *Discourse on Method*), and experiments (e.g., Levinas's *Otherwise than Being*). Doctrinal texts elaborate and defend basic theses, as solving or clarifying outstanding ontological, epistemological, or ethical issues. Exploratory, investigatory texts, while in part elaborating and defending basic theses, are primarily concerned not so much to argue a position as to examine certain ideas and phenomena. Propaedeutic texts are generally methodological in orientation, attempting to elaborate the proper mode of thinking about things before either defending theses or exploring phenomena. These categories are not mutually exclusive, and there are passages, for example, in the *Critique of Pure Reason,* which are more like explorations and others which are propaedeutic. But it is possible to pick out the principal orientation in a philosophical text in terms of these different categories. Experimental texts are not experimental in the natural scientific sense; they do not go about proving a hypothesis. Rather, they are experimental more in the artistic sense of trying out something, taking it to the limit to which the artist is capable of going, in order to see what, if anything, it can communicate. This book is an experiment in that sense. It is not an attempt to defend Judeo-Christianity or its philosophical relevance; rather it takes up the challenge of contemporary thought and pursues the philosophical articulation of the key—and philosophically most difficult—Christian phenomena as far as it can.

The title of this book declares it to be a phenomenology. I understand this work to come out of the tradition of philosophy which has its roots in that movement in philosophy initiated by Edmund Husserl. Phenomenology's simple principle of *zu den Sachen selbst,* to the things themselves, calls philosophy back to its beginning in the mode of appearance of things appearing. Philosophical thinking begins and ends with appearance, with the self-giving of that which is to be thought. To engage in such thinking without presuppositions is to allow for no unexamined distinctions between genuine and inauthentic appearances, between objective and subjective modes of apprehending appearance.

Phenomenology's claim to be 'first philosophy'—a claim made by Husserl and reaffirmed more recently by Marion—is a claim to understand appearance in its appearing, the phenomenality of phenomena prior and foundational to any and all disciplinary distinctions. For this reason the traditional opposition between philosophy and theology is relativized in phenomenology, despite Heidegger's claims to the contrary. Nonetheless, my indebtedness to Heidegger is evident in the title, a 'phenomenology of Christian life.' Heidegger in the early 1920s engaged in a similar task—a phenomenology of *religious* life; the published version of his lecture course on this theme has been a constant inspiration to this work. The implication of this approach is that those modes of appearance which form the basis of theology must themselves be open to philosophical investigation. This idea has been seen within French phenomenology by such thinkers as Levinas, Marion, Henry, and Chrétien, amongst others. What these thinkers share is not a "theological turn," as Dominique Janicaud claimed, but rather a phenomenology which poses a philosophical challenge to theology. Theology as a discipline developed out of the tensions arising from the marrying of Platonism and scriptural revelation. Phenomenology, by investigating the phenomenal basis of scriptural revelation, threatens to philosophically challenge theological assumptions regarding the mode of understanding such revelation. Approaching scripture without regard for its 'authority,' phenomenology allows the phenomenality of revelation to be disclosed anew; refusing the claim of the ultimacy of Platonic categories, it allows these phenomena to gain renewed philosophical import.

Nonetheless, as Janicaud's polemic made finally inescapable, the challenge here cuts both ways, and within the phenomenological tradition the growing concentration on revelation has not gone uncontested. The fundamental issue concerns the limits of phenomenology. The objection raises the issue that if phenomenology is concerned with appearances, it is paradoxical for it to end up in investigations of the non-apparent. More specifically, the phenomenologies of Husserl and Heidegger seem to agree at least on this: that phenomenology concerns the world, that appearances are worldly, and that the non-appearance of appearance is a mode of appearance of worldly things. Once phenomenology goes beyond the world, beyond worldly appearance, it has broken with the correlational a priori of Husserl and has left the realm of 'science.'

Against this, however, one must affirm again the phenomenological starting point: if there is a mode of appearance which breaks with the worldliness of appearance, then phenomenology cannot declare that mode of appearance as out of bounds. Levinas discovered such a mode of appearance in the Other, Marion in the icon, Chrétien in the call, Henry in auto-affection. In this work, I wish to argue that at the core of Christianity is a recognition of such a breaking with the worldliness of appearance, that indeed the very notion of the Incarnation expresses such a break.

To think, as phenomenology attempts to do, without presuppositions is also to think the possibility of the impossibility of philosophy. In thinking the possibility of its own impossibility phenomenology is at its most philosophical: Philosophy always begins and ends in the impossibility of securing its own possibility. This lack of security is philosophy's vulnerability to violence. As such, philosophy is radically open to the potential for being silenced by the other; indeed such a silencing is its constant experience and preoccupation. Such a silence does not, however, mark the end of philosophy (either as fulfillment or failure). Silence lies at the heart of thinking itself, always present in thinking's response to the other and its horrified wonder in the strange regions where it finds itself. Philosophy names this possibility. What thinking is, how thinking is possible—these questions are implicit in every act of thinking, and they form a subtext of this book. Thinking always leaves itself in question. For this reason it is in its negative voice that theology is at its most philosophical. By showing the limits of speech and thought, theology challenges philosophy to encounter its own limits. In undertaking a phenomenology of Christian life I am attempting to explore these limits by aiming toward them.

Acknowledgments

THE IDEA FOR this work developed slowly over the past decade and more. It began out of my undergraduate lecture courses in the Philosophy of Religion at the National University of Ireland, Galway, and I would like to begin by thanking all the students who attended those lectures and who challenged and prodded me along the way.

As with any work of this nature, the contents of these pages have been distilled from many conversations and discussions with many colleagues. It would be impossible to trace all these influences, but I would like to specially acknowledge Richard Kearney, Markus Wörner, William Desmond, Donn Welton, Klaus Held, Ricca Edmondson, László Tengelyi, Merold Westphal, Bruce Ellis Benson, and Len Lawlor.

In recent years I have had the opportunity to discuss these themes with graduate students and have benefited greatly from these discussions. In this respect I would like to acknowledge in particular Daniel Bradley, Aengus Daly, Erin Flynn, Miles Kennedy, Pat O'Connor, Davy Walsh, Veronica O'Neill, Roisin Lally-Bradley, Pearce Johnson, Pierre-Yves Fioraso, Sabine Müller, and David Beirne.

For their friendship and encouragement over many years, and specifically their comments and observations concerning the present project, I am indebted to Marty Fairbairn, Anthony Jenkins, and Maricarmen Jenkins.

I have presented some of the ideas which form the basis of this book at various fora, and would like to thank the audiences at these discussions in particular in the philosophy departments at SUNY at Stonybrook, KU Leuven (Belgium), Bergische Universität Wuppertal (Germany), St. Thomas More College, Saskatoon (Canada), University College Dublin, Mary Immaculate College, Limerick, Mater Dei Institute, Dublin and NUI, Galway (Ireland), and the participants at the annual conferences of the *Society for Phenomenology and Existential Philosophy*, the *Society for European Philosophy*, the *Nordic Society of Phenomenology*, the *Canadian Society for Continental Philosophy*, and the *British Society for Phenomenology*.

I would like to thank my editor at Indiana University Press, Dee Mortensen, for all her help, and the referees appointed by the Press for their constructive and insightful comments.

Much of the research for this book was conducted using the Western Theological Trust Collection at the Galway Mayo Institute of Technology (GMIT) Library. I gratefully acknowledge both the Western Theological Institute, which owns the collection, and the GMIT Library, which curates it.

For their patience during my long absences—even at times when I was physically in their presence—as I worked on this project, I am as always grateful to my wife Anne and my son Felix Alexander, without whose help and encouragement this book could not have been written.

A PHENOMENOLOGY OF CHRISTIAN LIFE

Introduction
Christianity and Philosophy

Philosophy and the Supra-cosmic

A phenomenology of Christian life is a Christian phenomenology of life. Not a phenomenology committed to the veracity of Christianity, but rather one which addresses phenomena in those terms in which Christianity addresses them. Such a phenomenology takes those accounts under epoché, which is to say, accepts the phenomenality accounted within them as authentic attempts at truth, perhaps incommensurable with non-Christian accounts. The phenomenality indicated here is one which can be characterized as an appearing *in* the world in embodied form, but a manifestation of that which is not *of* the world. This is a phenomenality of rupture, an appearance of that which is both apparent and breaks with the order of appearance—a break, namely, with that which makes it possible as appearance. This is neither the phenomenality of everyday appearance, nor of the evidence of science, nor of the ordered, coherent world of metaphysics. The rupture in the phenomenality of those realms (the everyday, the scientific, the metaphysical) cannot be seen except through a singular sensitivity. This sensitivity has throughout Christian thinking been called faith. Faith sees, but sees that which the 'world' does not see; faith hears, but hears that which the world does not hear. This paradoxical seeing and hearing is of a transcendence of the world in the world, of an appearing which gives its own conditions of appearing within the conditionality of worldly appearance. 'Glory' and 'night' are expressions of appearing in the world: of a god who appeared in the world, but whose 'glory' was unrecognizable to the world; glory understood in terms of sight and of light, but only by means of a radical 'perversion' of light and sight—a turning from their worldly place. Such 'perversion' of light and sight takes place within their worldly relations: light which is enlightening, which gives sight, also has the capacity to blind sight, to destroy, to turn the luminous into night.

To be in the world is to be orientated within the world, but that is the world of daylight, the world in which we look toward the horizon at that which the sun illuminates, in the order of its relation to the sun and to the order of the sun. In glory light blinds, day becomes night, the soul sees only due to its incapacity to see. Without orientation in such a night, hierarchies are undone, the gulf between human and divine opens up as abysmal. Yet, in that night, one point of orientation remains, namely, the call of that which the world fails to see or hear.

'Glory' and 'night' name the phenomenality of phenomena characterizing a way of being-in-the-world, which breaks with the world. This way of being allows the specifically Christian phenomena of creation, incarnation, resurrection, *kairos,* love (*agápe*), and faith to appear. They do so paradoxically and disruptively, radically disturbing the relation of being-in-the-world. St. Paul expresses this disruption at the heart of such a being-in-the-world when he states that the Christian 'is in the world as if not of the world.'[1] This 'as if' is not a hypothetical projection, but a response to that which Paul perceived—and exhorted others to perceive—as an existent which was in the world and not of the world, namely Jesus the Messiah (Christ). In such an understanding Jesus Christ radicalizes almost to breaking point the mode of appearance of the divine, namely, glory. The brightness of the world darkens in the light of that which is not of the world. But that light, the divine light, is itself a dark night in which only the eyes of faith can see.

Such a discourse, however, arouses suspicion. At its mildest, it is a suspicion of regionality, and this suspicion may be expanded rather than diminished by reference to such 'phenomena' as creation, resurrection, or even faith. But it is precisely the foreignness of these phenomena which allows us to bracket such suspicion. These phenomena remain incompatible, non-integrable into Greek thought. They cannot even be rendered regional; they can only be excluded. This is not to deny the possibilities of translating Christian phenomena into Greek terms, nor is it to deny the richness and variety of Greek thought from Anaximander to Plotinus and beyond, but only to claim that such a translation always leaves a residue, and in Greek terms always threatens to fall into incoherence. Furthermore, the Christian claim to universality does not simply repeat that of Greek philosophy, but is a rival claim, a claim to a universality of human kind and arguably of all creation in relation to a supra-cosmic instance. This claim has brought Christianity into conflict with Greek thought from St. Paul through Luther to the more contemporary critique of metaphysics beginning with Kierkegaard and Nietzsche and finding resonance in the work of Marion, Henry, Chrétien, and Lacoste. This Christian claim to universality is the claim to a phenomenality which finds no place in Greek thought. This is not to deny the Christianity of those integrations of Greek thinking from Origen through Augustine to Aquinas. It is rather to point out—as is acknowledged by each of these great Christian thinkers—that any such integration was incomplete. This incompletion, however, must not—so it will be argued here—be understood simply in terms of the difference between faith and reason, but rather points to a phenomenality which radically escapes any category that relies on the coherence of the world (*cosmos*), as the categories of Greek thought inevitably do.

It is striking that despite its many rebuttals, the notion of 'Christian philosophy' constantly recurs. Most recently we find this in the work of Michel Henry and Jean-Luc Marion.[2] This suggests that the *question* of the relation of philosophy and Christianity is an inescapable one. What makes it inescapable is the challenge Christianity poses to philosophy, a challenge which is real only because it concerns a central issue of philosophy, namely, the issue of world. Philosophy begins in cosmology and through its many manifestations it has remained a logos concerning cosmos. The ultimate philosophical question, why is there something rather than nothing, assumes a pre-understanding of that 'something' as world. Yet, St. Paul understands cosmos as the realm of human affairs, which he opposes not to the perfect rhythms of the heavenly bodies, but to the saving grace of Christ. In this case the logos of the cosmos is ultimately a vain discourse because it concerns not eternal immutable being, but that which is fallen and which will come to an end in a transformation brought by that which is as nothing in the world. As Karl Barth tells us, Christianity has no cosmology.[3]

Without deciding anything regarding the intrinsicism/extrinsicism debate in contemporary theology, it seems clear that Christianity challenges philosophy by placing the source of significance and goodness beyond the world. At least in this limited sense, Christianity can be said to be an acosmic discourse and as such challenges philosophy and does so with respect to the very goal philosophy sets itself, namely, the 'good life.' Put in the starkest terms, while philosophy offers the way to the good life as being in conformity with the world, Christianity claims that the way to the good life is through Christ, that is, through the one who did not conform with the world, a measure which is not of the world. Conformity with the world here does not mean with the merely worldly: clearly the philosopher can rarely conform to that, as is shown by the exemplary philosophers from Socrates to Seneca to Boethius and beyond. But this refusal of conformity with the worldly is founded on a free and thoughtful conformity with the world in its rational and immutable being. The Christian aim for a good life, as that which welcomes the end of the world, which furthermore understands that 'end' as having its source beyond the world (both in terms of beginning and end, *alpha* and *omega*), is radically incommensurate with the Greek ideal.

It is remarkable how this incommensurability has been faced and overcome throughout the intellectual history of the West. Central to Christianity's dissociation from Greek philosophy is the question as to the relation of the human being, of the nature of that being, to the salvation promised by Christ. Such a question concerns the human being-in-the-world: is that being already directed toward god, is there in the world that which leads to god, *or* is salvation purely from beyond the world, is the world indifferent to salvation? If one takes the first approach then there is a possibility of synthesis between Christianity and philosophy, at least up to a point: the logos of the cosmos is of that order which contains traces of the divine, albeit traces which can only be properly understood retrospectively in terms of revelation. The second approach understands the world as fallen from god and that only through a mortification of human nature, a *via crucis,* is salvation possible.[4]

But between these two extremes, the possibility of a phenomenology—hence a philosophy—of Christian life opens up: between natural and supernatural desire, between worldliness and radical alterity, between night and glory. In this 'between' philosophy meets theology, and in the pages that follow the names of Heidegger, Levinas, and Marion mix with those of Barth, von Balthasar, and de Lubac.

My interest in these issues is philosophical rather than theological. In other words, my question is what these rival accounts of world can bring to an account of the phenomenality of phenomena that assumes nothing of the 'truth,' but affirms the meaning, of Christianity. That such a pursuit involves an interrogation of theological themes is not surprising: theology is nothing other than the place of arbitration between philosophy and Christianity. But my concern is whether philosophy can remain unscathed by this encounter.

Thinking after Greece

Platonism and Christianity

To think Christianity is—directly or indirectly—to confront Platonism. The latter term is a difficult one: it can denote the philosophy of Plato, the Platonic schools of the ancient world (including Neo-Platonism), a way of doing philosophy which was the object of critique by Nietzsche and then Heidegger (in the context of his critique of onto-theology). In relation to the concerns of this book, I am using the term in the latter sense. Nevertheless, in taking seriously the Nietzschean/ Heideggerian (and also, in a different key, Kierkegaardian and Levinasian) account of Western philosophy as both Greek and Platonic, I am implicitly making a certain historical claim about Greek philosophy and its historical legacy. In both respects the relation of Platonism and Aristotelianism is crucial. For the early Christians and their contemporaries an account of Aristotle's relation to Plato as one of an unrelenting critic, the claim that one could not coherently follow Aristotle in crucial elements of his metaphysics and still remain a Platonist, would have seemed strange: the philosophies of the two thinkers were generally considered complementary and harmonious. A thorough examination of this question would need to examine the developmentalist thesis—most associated with Werner Jaeger—according to which Aristotle's thought developed from an early Platonism to a later anti-Platonic position. Such an examination is beyond the reach of this book. What does need to be claimed here, however, is this: that Aristotle shared with Plato a fundamental belief in the intelligibility of the world, a hierarchical account of being which was deeply imbued with a cosmological vision of inner harmony of all beings in the world, and a belief in the teleological aim of human existence toward wisdom—wisdom which could be attained through contemplation of the unchanging rational structure of the world (cosmos). It is precisely this view of the cosmos as a self-sufficient eternal whole, one which is orientated toward its divine principle in the demiurge or the unmoved mover, in each case divinities which manifest the intrinsic intelligibility and purpose of the world, which Christianity disrupts.[5]

The importance of Platonism for early Christianity was in some manner an accident of history: in the world of early Christianity, Platonism, or more correctly an eclectic mixture of Platonism and Stoicism, prevailed. But more than that—and as we will see this historical accident could not be understood as accidental by the early Christians[6]—Platonic thought seemed to give articulation to the *movement* of Christian life from below to above, from matter to spirit, from sin to salvation. In our own day, the Platonic concept of participation (*methexis*) has been understood by the proponents of the 'Radical Orthodoxy' movement as a concept in systematic agreement with that of Christian incarnation.[7] For Catherine Pickstock, who is such a proponent, what we find in Plato is an affirmation of world, of embodiment, and of temporality. This is so because through the structure of participation the transcendence of the good acts as a kind of contagion, such that its plenitude spills over into immanence, "in such a way that the good is revealed in the beauty of physical particulars."[8] Materiality and temporal order is affirmed in Plato because the transcendent is manifest in the immanent. There is a good deal of plausibility in this account, and I will defend an interpretation of Plato which tends in a similar direction in chapter 2. It breaks with the otherworldly interpretations of Plato, which commit the latter to a dualism that seems at odds with his concern for coherence and unity—the guiding principle of the theory of forms. Plato is not urging a withdrawal from the world; only the Christian interpretations of Plato have led us to imagine otherwise. The irony is that Pickstock, in aiming to show the commonality of Plato and Christianity, in fact undermines the traditional interpretation of Plato rooted in the church fathers.[9] More importantly, Pickstock goes too far in her re-reading of Plato, particularly in claiming a 'contagion' of immaterial and material. The coherence between material and immaterial is for Plato premised on an order of clear delineations and structured relations. This coherence is of a world in which the soul has fallen into the body, but in which the possibility exists—if only by recourse to a discourse which is mythological because it aims beyond the limits of experience—of pure intellectual existence and apprehension. What this points to is the absence of any notion of creation in Plato:[10] once we speak in terms of creation—specifically in the radical sense of *creatio ex nihilo* (to which I will return in chapter 6)—the unity of soul and body finds its source at the very origin of the world. As James K. Smith concludes:

> A participatory ontology only affirms materiality and embodiment as a kind of 'necessary evil' based on a prior determination of embodiment as already constituted by a fall. In contrast, an incarnational ontology is based on a prior affirmation of the goodness of creation (Gen. 1:27) as an affirmation of the primordial and necessary goodness of materiality.[11]

The irony here—and this is an irony with which we will need to grapple throughout this work—is that the affirmation of the goodness of materiality is premised on the finitude of the world, i.e., on seeing the world as being in a relation of utter dependence on an acosmic source. Participation in a Platonic model functions not to hold together two worlds, but rather as the unifying structure of one world. It is only with Christianity that one might think differently, because there the problem arises of the relation of world to that which is not of the world, but which is simultaneously in the world, namely, Jesus of Nazareth as son of the one transcendent god. In that case, all at once, worldly hierarchies are undermined: the Word has become flesh, the immortal dies, the most high is as a slave. Such an incarnational logic is precisely a logic not just of contagion but of contamination, indeed of profanation. It stands opposed to a sacred logic, which still governs Plato's texts.[12] Such a logic is one of separation and protection from contamination. It is a logic which abhors mixture and maintains hierarchy through prohibitions inscribed in law. This logic animates Greek philosophy especially in its Platonic form. Christianity is profane precisely in its refusal of that logic. Those things which are kept separate and apart in Platonic thought—matter and form, divine and human, life and death, being and becoming—are mixed and allowed to mutually contaminate each other in Christian life. This is not to say that Platonically these oppositions are dualistic; on the contrary, Platonic thought derives its coherence precisely by its careful articulation of the means of mutual relation between all these oppositions. But such a mutual relation does not amount to mingling; that which participates remains the same and can again be separated.[13] It is for this reason that the figure of Christ is Platonically an ultimately impossible thought. It thinks the contradictory; it thinks divine and human at the same time and in the same respect.[14] What we find here is a fundamental refusal of the sacred, which is more radical than that found in philosophy. At the heart of Christian revelation is the thought of contamination rooted in a refusal of the ultimacy of the world, a refusal of worldly, sacred order.

Socrates and the Platonism of the People

Over practically the past two centuries we can witness a concerted effort to think 'after Greece' or at least 'after Plato.' This attempt has from the beginning involved an encounter with Judeo-Christianity: hostile in the case of Nietzsche and Heidegger who sought a proto-Greek, non-Platonic thought, which was not so susceptible to 'Christianization' as Platonism was; friendly in the case of Kierkegaard, Levinas, Henry, and Marion who sought to find a Judeo-Christian thought which was not captured in Greek terms, even if in each case the ghost of a certain Platonism is to be found. But through these different forms a thinking after Greece/Plato meant a thinking which was alive to the ambiguity of the world: the world as fallen and as redeemed, the world as illusion and as reality, the world as a strange land and as home.[15]

While Kierkegaard opposed Christianity to Platonism (in the figure of Socrates), and Nietzsche identified them in his characterization of Christianity as the "Platonism of the people," crucially for both the critique of Platonism was inseparable from an engagement in and evaluation of Christianity. For both, the task of philosophy was to think 'after Greece'—for Nietzsche such a thought was possible only through a rethinking of the proto-Greek, the Greece of the heroic age, for Kierkegaard through a rethinking of Christianity as subjectivity. In both cases philosophy is historical reflection and such reflection encounters inescapably both Platonism and Christianity.

It is true that both these terms 'Platonism' and 'Christianity' mean different things for Nietzsche and Kierkegaard, and arguably their respective meanings are more related to the philosophical tasks both thinkers set themselves than to historical accuracy. It would nonetheless be a mistake to see them as mere place-holders. Christianity and Platonism are real possibilities of being and of thought with which both Kierkegaard and Nietzsche see human beings as confronted, not simply intellectually but also, and more fundamentally, existentially. What we find in both thinkers is an acknowledgment that thinking is historical in the sense of being both an expression of, and a molding influence on, existence.

For Kierkegaard, Jesus of Nazareth and Socrates differ fundamentally not so much in terms of the content of their thought but in the mode of their teaching.[16] While Socrates awakens a reminiscence of ideas already present and as such serves only the occasion of his disciples' knowledge of them, Jesus of Nazareth is the content of his own teaching. His life discloses that which without him would never have been known. This difference is significant in two fundamental respects: firstly, understanding is related to the event of truth, which is a historical event in the sense that it refigures both past and future. The event of Jesus of Nazareth refigures the past by giving it a radically new focus and the future through the 'rebirth' of the one who hears it. In this sense the relation of time and eternity which we find in Plato is inverted: no longer is time a mere image of eternity, but eternity acts on and in time to transform both the perception of time and existence within such time. Secondly, Jesus of Nazareth becomes an example, an exemplary existence, in a manner impossible to conceive of Platonically. His life as that of the incarnate Messiah is understood not simply as an example of a way of being toward the eternal, but *is* the eternal in human form. This means that the eternal takes on an incarnate and personal presence which can be exemplified in the incarnate and personal life of the disciple. While the Socratic disciple understands Socrates, and as such himself too, as a mere occasion of knowledge, the Christian disciple understands his own unique existence as being a singular imitation of the singular existence of Christ.

For Nietzsche, on the other hand, Christianity is Platonic, and conversely Plato himself is a Hebraized Greek, the viaduct of Hebrew thought into Greece. The fundamental issue here for Nietzsche is the substitution of the real world, the incarnate world of experience, with an ideal world, the world of Platonic forms or the redeemed world of Pauline Christianity. Christianity is the highest expression of humanity, because it expresses morality in its most refined form and does so—paradoxically—because it reveals the fundamental impurity of morality. The 'Overman' (*Übermensch*) is for Nietzsche without defined content because he is a not-yet-realized future, a future which Nietzsche attempts to write in the form of an anti-Apocalypse: a new heaven and a new earth, one though not of the Christian god, but of other gods and other men.

This 'anti-Apocalypse' repeats a prior transvaluation of values brought about by Christianity, which amounts to a transformation of the very notion of divinity—a transformation in fact to the ultimate godlessness, the ultimate atheism.[17] The gods in a pre-Christian sense represent overwhelming power. The will to power is a will to command, but to command it is necessary to obey. Obedience to the gods is an obedience to those drives in nature which the 'master' brings to expression. The principal gods in this respect are Dionysus and Apollo, and Nietzsche's first major work, *The Birth of Tragedy,* is an extended reflection on the mode of expression of these gods in music and art. Nature is manifest in the human otherwise than in any other entity. The double drive of wild intoxication and calm serenity are drives of nature, which come to expression aesthetically as the Apollonian and the Dionysian. Nietzsche goes so far here as to talk of the drive to art in nature (*Kunsttriebe der Natur*),[18] which precedes any mediation on the part of human artists. Taking the artist's activity as the original human activity itself, one can say that the divine is not that which the human creates, but rather *that* in nature which he seeks to represent in visual and aural forms. Art in such an understanding is nothing other than a bringing to expression of forces and drives which the human being experiences as influencing him from without or rather enveloping and penetrating him to the exclusion of all else. In Nietzsche the Olympian gods far from being the projections of human consciousness were born out of a drive of nature to artistic expression, which is doubled between Apollo and Dionysus.[19] The creation of the Olympian gods makes sense only in respect to a prior intuition of a deeper, more penetrating divinity in nature itself.

The transvaluation of values which Christianity brings about is based, according to Nietzsche, on a splitting of the divine from nature, which reflects the human splitting of himself from nature. But in both the same feeling of power is being divinized, except in the latter the feeling of power is of power turned inward and in the process covered over and distorted. Power can be turned inward only with great effort and at great expense. The tendencies of conquest and exploitation experienced in the master are also experienced—but now with poignancy—by the priest and even more so by the slave. The latter shares these tendencies but can give them no outlet. Instead of adapting himself to his particular range of power, the slave, under the leadership of the priest, transforms these tendencies into evil. The Christian—already Platonic—transvaluation of values is exemplified by the notion of evil. Evil is an unnatural predicate: nothing in nature is evil. Rather, the judgment of evil is a judgment against nature, a judgment which places the human against nature. So by tyrannizing that part of himself, the slave places himself over against nature, against his corporeality, against instinct. All of this is done in the name of a higher destiny, a destiny above and beyond nature, a destiny in the hands of god who does not participate in the plurality of nature, but rather for whom nature is all one corrupt materiality. That god is the Judeo-Christian god, the god who stands against nature and, far from manifesting the human destiny of superiority within nature, promises to redeem the human *from* nature. This amounts to an undoing of what is, a revision of what was. In place of what has occurred, the redeeming god presents a double of subjective will and responsibility. This amounts to a radical turning of the will against its own true redemption, which would be to state in the face of the contingency of the past: "thus I willed it!"[20]

Common to both Kierkegaard and Nietzsche is a confrontation between Christianity and Greece. Out of this confrontation comes the possibility of the new: the new world beyond reminiscence or the new world of the Overman. The new is beyond reminiscence for Kierkegaard because it comes from elsewhere; for Nietzsche the Overman comes from within, through a radical forgetting which opens up a future. The move beyond Plato in both is a move to an ecstatic temporality, one which opens up the possibilities—the non-chronological potentialities—of past, present, and future.

Destruktion *and Heidegger's World*

Heidegger's appropriation of both Kierkegaard and Nietzsche is of fundamental importance to his philosophical project from the beginning.[21] Similar to both,

Heidegger rejects the Platonic notion of world. But he does so neither to affirm faith as a subjective truth (Kierkegaard) nor to herald a new world of the body as the great reason (Nietzsche), but rather to answer the question allegedly forgotten since Plato, namely, the question of being, the forgetting of which is at the same time a forgetting of the question of world. Heidegger's first philosophical breakthroughs in the 1920s arose in no small part from his readings of Kierkegaard and Nietzsche, specifically in his appropriation of their rethinking of time in an avowedly anti-Platonic way.

Heidegger drew on these two thinkers to give substance to his early rejection of scholasticism, especially of Thomism.[22] Despite, or perhaps because of, the revival of Thomism in the Catholic Church in the late nineteenth and early twentieth centuries, not only Heidegger but the mainstream of phenomenology has been anti-Thomistic.[23] Specifically, any concept of *analogia entis* has been consistently denied from Heidegger to Marion. This denial entails a clear separation of discourse on god and discourse on the world, a discourse on god without being. In this respect phenomenology parallels—and these parallels were at least in part facilitated by some cross-fertilization—the theology of Karl Barth and his followers. It was Barth who first brought Kierkegaard to the fore of theological discourse and from Heidegger through Levinas to Derrida and Marion the commonalities of his thought and phenomenology are profound.[24] Central to Barth's work is his insistence on the absolute otherness of god. Inherent in Barth's account is the claim that theology, if it has any value or substance, must be in a position to tell the world that which the world itself could never know. Starting from the world it is impossible to reach god. In such a view there are in the world no phenomena of god, only religious phenomena which are the work of human beings. To find god in the world is to mistake the worldly for the divine; it is to worship idols. Such a view evacuates the world of all divine reference, leaving the task of filling in that reference in a manner without reference either to the world or the worldly. Furthermore, it is to understand the finitude of human beings in terms of their *incapacity* to reach the infinite.

Barth's understanding of the world as without god reaffirmed a 'pathos of distance,' an emphasis on the radical otherness of god. It will be instructive, however, to us as we work through the thesis of this book—the philosophical as opposed to theological understanding of Christian life—that Barth modifies his early account of this distance through his later Christology. It is through his Christological reflections that Barth comes again to speak of the humanity and—by extension—the worldliness of god. This will be significant for us as we go on.

Initially, however, Heidegger and Barth both were engaged—independently of each other—in re-appropriations of Luther, in particular of the *theologica crucis*.[25] The effects of this rethinking of Luther can be seen in Heidegger's key methodological concept of *Destruktion*.

The term 'Destruktion' itself can be traced back to Luther's use of the term *destruere* (to destroy). Such destruction Luther applied to Scholastic philosophy, the goal of which was to liberate the Christian experiences hidden beneath Greek philosophical terms. Heidegger employs this method in line with a Kierkegaardian insight into the event character of truth and a Nietzschean strategy of genealogical critique, in order to liberate experience from the history of ontology. An early use of the term 'Destruktion' is to be found in the context of his interpretation of Paul's letters in which Heidegger states that the history of religion is only fruitful for phenomenology when it is subjected to phenomenological Destruktion.[26] What this entails is an understanding of Paul's letters in terms of the 'situation' in which Paul finds himself. The phenomenological explication is one which begins with existence within a historical situation. This, though, is not merely a methodological principle; the very theme under consideration—the original Christianity of Paul and his followers—itself characterizes an understanding of existence which the approach of Destruktion assumes. Christian religiosity *lives* temporality, according to Heidegger. It is a time in which the "when can in no manner be fixed objectively."[27] This is the case because the time of the world is not the ultimate time. Time regulated by the pure movements of the heavenly bodies is a time which governs everything and everyone in the world. But Christ being not of the world cannot be governed by that time. Hence, for Paul the time of Christ cannot be a *chronos,* but rather a *kairos,* an unworldly time, which comes in the worldlessness of the world—night. If that which is central to Christianity is an experience of worldless time—one full of surprise and uncertainty—that cannot be fixed objectively, then every attempt at such fixing, every attempt, namely, to hand on into the future—an attempt made problematic by that very temporal experience—must be viewed with great suspicion. For this reason the witness in Christianity is both fundamental and problematic: fundamental because the experience cannot be transmitted objectively but only subjectively, problematic because the witness must always be newly interpreted in the life of the present.[28] It is this problem which Heidegger sets out more formally in section 6 of *Being and Time.*

The fundamentally Christian assumption underlying the project of Destruktion is that thought—including philosophical thought—is essentially historical. Destruktion is made necessary because of the ambiguous nature of such historicity. '*Dasein*' for Heidegger can be so ensnared—fallen—in what has been handed on from the past (tradition) that it cannot perceive it anymore. In this way tradition "deprives Dasein of its own leadership in questioning and choosing."[29] Dasein's concern here is one with its own subjectivity, that is, with the event of its own apprehension of the truth as being constitutive of that truth itself. The forgetting of historicity is only an issue if the event of truth is constitutive of that truth. This is the case for Jesus of Nazareth, but not for Socrates. In this sense the concern underlying Destruktion is radically un-Socratic. The forgetting which is at issue is not to be overcome by a reminiscence of a pre-existing past, but rather by a taking up of responsibility on the part of Dasein in the present. The relating of ancient ontology to the original experiences from which it emerged is not done primarily in order to better understand ancient philosophy; it aims rather to loosen the traditional reification of such philosophy. In that sense Destruktion concerns not the past but "the 'today'" (*das 'Heute'*).[30] This 'today' is the present of our own experience; only by uncovering the experience underlying the history of philosophy can I 'repeat' that experience in full self-responsibility. In that sense, to read the history of philosophy responsibly is to engage in its Destruktion. The opening of eyes which can arise out of this is not that of the slave boy in the *Meno,* but of the men on the road to Emmaus, who have their worldly wisdom 'destroyed' by a teacher who de-structures their understanding of history (scripture).

The whole section on Destruktion in *Being and Time* seems at first strangely out of place, as it concerns the methodology of the final section of that work which was never written. Of the parts of that work which were written it seems only to concern directly the sections in the penultimate chapter on historicity. But once we grasp the historicity of Dasein in terms of Destruktion, then we can understand that the analyses of Dasein in *Being and Time* involve an uncovering of Dasein's historicity—in the specific sense of relating to the history of ontology.[31] Accepting the claim to phenomenological method at the heart of these analyses, what one must understand from Heidegger is that phenomenology is an act of historical Destruktion. While one of the sources of Heidegger's account of Destruktion is Husserl's concept of *Abbau,* more fundamentally, the analyses of Dasein are of a historically specific happening of the ontological difference. Phenomenology is the discourse about that happening as it concerns the historical existence of today's Dasein. Historicity for Heidegger is not a mere fact of being historical, but is a responsibility to be historical in the form of a resolute taking up of the heritage in which Dasein finds itself.[32] Phenomenology is for Heidegger such a resolute taking up of heritage in the sense that it allows that heritage to appear in terms of its originary experiences.

Phenomenology is historical because history is not a matter of positive science alone. Historical science does not reach the historicity of Dasein; indeed through its objectifications it alienates Dasein from that historicity.[33] Phenomenology reaches the historicity of Dasein not through a direct analysis of that history but through an analysis of present Dasein in its temporal and spatial constitution. What makes that constitution possible transcends anything to be found within time and space—namely, being (*Sein*). The event of being is an event which happens in Dasein, in the movement of being-in-the-world, but is nothing which appears in the world. Being is disclosed in Dasein's understanding, but disclosed precisely as that which is not of that understanding, rather as the making possible of that understanding. In that way being discloses Dasein to itself in its difference from entities (*Seiende*). This difference it finds within itself as both being and entity, both possibility and actuality (present and possible actuality). Thus, what it finds is that which can be disclosed only as hiddenness, as a withdrawal from presence.

But such a withdrawal from presence is constitutive of world. The ontological difference is a difference of world, a difference between entities and world. But being in the world is one side of the Pauline injunction. It speaks also of being not *of* the world. Ultimately, what is not of the world is god. For Luther sin is defined as not letting god be god or wanting to be god. This, for Luther, is Adam's sin. *Being and Time* makes a fundamental theological decision by excluding the question of that which is not of the world. It is a decision to understand Dasein as 'godforsaken.'[34] Seen in this light Heidegger's methodological atheism is an atheism of the world: the world is atheistic, is without god. This is not to affirm that there is no god, simply that there is nothing in the world of god. Living in the world and living not of the world are two modes of being separated fundamentally from one another. Before ever raising the question of faith, Dasein needs to freely take up its own being-in-the-world.[35] In so doing Dasein understands itself as a self-responsible being. Such a self-responsible being is responsible to itself not as an inner-worldly entity, but as that for which there is world. In that sense Dasein must gather itself together in the fullness of its own self-capacity, not in order to deny any limit to that capacity, but precisely to make such a limit clearer.

The question of being—implicitly in *Being and Time* and more clearly after the *Kehre*—leads phenomenology to the question of the hiddenness of phenomena. Phenomenology concerns precisely not that which appears, the entity, but rather that which conceals itself in this disclosure, being. That which Heidegger later calls the phenomenology of the inapparent[36] is already operative in *Being and Time*. But it is operative precisely because the question of being for Heidegger concerns the intersection of the existing entity and the questioning unmotivated by any entity. The question of being is unmotivated by any entity, but rather lies hidden in any question concerning an entity. Every sentence contains an understanding of being, the concealment of which is constitutive for all dealings with entities. The concern with entities involves a turning away from being; the concern with being means a con-version in our dealing with entities. The question of being requires a way of being toward entities, which resists being enraptured by those entities.

Nothing in the world, no inner-worldly entity, can motivate such resistance to enrapture. All that can motivate it is being. But being is precisely that which remains concealed, that which withdraws so that entities can be. It is this which Heidegger refers to as the "clear night [*hellen Nacht*] of the nothing."[37] Only in this night can entities be disclosed. But there are no gradations between the light of entities and the dark of being. Rather, what is required is a leap: "Philosophy gets under way only through a unique leap of Dasein's own existence into the basic possibilities of Dasein as a whole."[38] This leap is a leap toward the inapparent, that which nothing appears able to motivate, but which is rooted in the being of Dasein precisely as that being for whom being is a question. The leap beyond entities is a leap beyond the inner-worldly toward being. Being is nothing, but rather the event of things: *Ereignis*. "That is the essential swaying of be-ing [*Seyn*] itself. We call it enowning [*Ereignis*]."[39] The leap to Ereignis is one of dispossession; it is a renouncing of any expectations from entities.[40] This leap is one which responds to a historical situation—responds, that is, to the historicity of the present and does so through a resolute taking up of a heritage, namely, that of the first beginning. The other beginning, though, that which is prepared for in this taking up, is one in which "all entities are sacrificed to be-ing [*Seyn*]."[41] Such a sacrifice renounces the cosmology of Greek philosophy for an event which can be prepared for without expectation. It is the event which gives space to the 'last god,' a god without name, and it is in preparation for this last god that we should not allow history up to now "to terminate [*verenden*], but rather must be brought to its end."[42]

Heidegger strongly resists any 'Christian' interpretation of these passages on the last god, indeed the epigraph to the section reads, "the totally other against the having been, especially the Christian." In these discussions of the 'last god' we can hear a Nietzschean tone working through Hölderlin-like motifs. But at the same time this is a thinking of history, of that event in the world which transforms the world, which makes all things new. In thinking such an event Heidegger hints at a Christological model when he traces the—at least biographical—roots of his question concerning the relation of being and language to that between logos in the New Testament and speculative theology.[43] But if this does mark a turn to Christology, it is one which remains ultimately Greek. The Christ who appears here is an entity governed by the ontological difference: an entity appearing in the light of being. In this respect Heidegger remains Platonic. There is a worldlessness in Heidegger, but it is the worldlessness of the world itself. The world is worldless because the world is nothing—what *is* is in the world, but the "world worlds." For Heidegger the phenomenology of the inapparent is in the end a phenomenology of world. It is not by accident that in stating that the Greeks did not have concepts and as such lived in the phenomenology of the inapparent he singles out *horismos* as not being a concept.[44]

Heidegger takes up the Pauline injunction as an injunction to releasement from entities in the world. This is a theme which we find in Heidegger from his early to late writings and is explicit in the phenomenology of the inapparent. To live in the world as if not of the world is for Heidegger to live precisely in relation to the world as the event of worldliness: what happens in the world in that case can be set aside; responsibility consists in listening to the worlding of the world in and through that which happens in the world. But such a way of being tends toward an indifference to the world, against which Paul warned the Corinthians.

Heidegger's critique of metaphysics remains Greek. It is a critique in terms of the ontological difference, a difference which is of the world. To think beyond Greece is to think beyond the ontological difference, beyond being.[45] Thinking beyond the ontological difference is a thinking which refuses that difference, or rather refuses to accept its purported ultimacy. The new French phenomenology (starting with Levinas) can be understood as operating within such a refusal.

It is important here to note the extent to which Levinas shares Heidegger's account of world. For Levinas, too, the question of god is not a question which concerns the world. While Heidegger speaks of methodological atheism, Levinas shows more clearly the stakes by affirming the atheism of the world. Clearly Levinas saw this, too, as a commentary on Heidegger. He terms egoism—that which characterizes Dasein—atheistic. Its atheism does not consist in an affirmation or denial of god's existence, but rather in a being separated. Such a separation is life, or rather love of life. It consists of being in the world as enjoyment. Enjoying the world, the existent experiences it as that which is appropriable to itself. This, for Levinas, is the root experience of ontology: the submission of the other to the same—consumption.

Heidegger, according to Levinas, subordinates the other to ontology.[46] However, in Levinasian terms to be true this would mean that Heidegger would subordinate god—the wholly other—to ontology. But this he explicitly does not do. He does not do so for Barthian reasons, as indeed Levinas reflects Barth in some ways.[47] Certainly Heidegger does understand the other ontologically. But he does not confine the understanding of the other to ontology. Rather, he understands the other as that other who appears in the world in relation to worldly concerns—at work (*bei der Arbeit*), for example.[48] The point of rupture is not that of the other or of ethics, but rather the manner of appearance of transcendence. Heidegger understands transcendence strictly in terms of immanence: transcendence is always transcendence *in the world;* Levinas understands transcendence as an interruption of the world.

World and Worldlessness after Heidegger

It is important to distinguish Levinas's attempt to think transcendence in the world from Heidegger's accounts of the holy and the divine. Heidegger understands the divine in terms of the thing as that which is in the relation of the fourfold. The being of the thing is only in this totality of relations which Heidegger terms 'world.' This forms a line of continuity from his account of the ready-to-hand in *Being and Time* to his later descriptions of the fourfold. The divine is that message of the gods which is received in the world. It forms so to speak a pre-Christian (in the structural not historical sense) mode of being, which prefigures any encounter with the divine. The world is god-forsaken, but by that same token the human being can sense the absence of the divine in the world. That absence is experienced in the indicative messages (*winkende Boten*) of the gods. There is, though, no thinking in Heidegger of the singular presence of the worldless, of an entity which ruptures rather than confirms the fourfold mirror play of world. Levinas's means of pursuing that which breaks with the fourfold is through discourse, through that which establishes the social relation.

Heidegger uses the German term *Rede* to translate 'logos'—and distinguishes it sharply from *Sprache* (language).[49] He defines Rede as "the articulation of intelligibility."[50] Rede can thus be understood as the basic linguistic articulatability of things, i.e., insofar as they can be articulated intelligibly. Rede can be translated as 'discourse' (as it normally is) but—as the reference to logos suggests—it is the discursivity of things, their being intelligible, which is at issue. To speak, Heidegger states, is always to speak about something (*Worüber*). This 'speaking about' is a bringing to speech of the intelligibility of things in the world. Such a relation of intelligibility between the world and speech is the condition of possibility of language for Heidegger. This relation of intelligibility is neither in things (reference) nor in natural languages such as German or English (sense), but rather is that which holds both sense and reference together. There is for Heidegger nothing to talk about outside or beyond such a relation of intelligibility, because meaning is always mediated by the understanding (*Verstehen*). "In the understanding of the world the being-in is always also understood. Understanding of existence as such is always an understanding of world."[51] This understanding of the world is conditioned by discursivity, or the relations of intelligibility fundamental to language. Discourse in this understanding is about things and about things in the world.

Levinas, in denying this primacy of world to discourse, begins with the "divine word":

> To hear the divine word does not amount to knowing an object; it is to be in relation with a substance overflowing its own idea in me. . . . When simply known, thematized, the substance no longer is 'according to itself.' Discourse, in which it is at the same time foreign and present, suspends participation and, beyond object cognition, institutes the pure experience of the social relation.[52]

The divine word is that word which traces god in the world, specifically in the scriptures. But the divine word is by no means confined to this. On the contrary, the divine word is an expression of the absolute to the atheist, a relation of welcome to the absolute unmediated by the "violence of the sacred." The divine word is that word which is heard above the din of the world, a word irreducible to the economy of the world. But this 'epiphany' is inseparable from my neighbor: god is close by. Reflecting St. John in his first letter, Levinas states: "There can be no 'knowledge' of god separated from the relationship with men."[53]

Levinas denies the possibility of rational theology at least with respect to the god of the Bible. Such a theology can only think god horizontally and escapes the embarrassment of this thought by understanding god as the highest being.[54] But this should not be interpreted as an appeal to faith. Faith he puts on a level with opinion, both of which speak the language of being.[55] In saying this he denies the "formal opposition established by Yehouda Halévi and revived by Pascal" between the god of faith and the god of philosophy.[56] In denying this difference Levinas opens up an avenue beyond Heidegger.[57] He pursues this further by stating "that philosophy is not only understanding of immanence, it is immanence itself."[58] In other words, philosophy—understood as Greek philosophy—is worldly by definition, or better defines worldliness. It is for this reason that Levinas suggests that we need to question whether experience is the source of meaning.[59] Experience is understood here as experience of that which is manifest in the world. In opposition to philosophy rooted in worldly experience, Levinas places revelation. But it is not enough simply to invoke revelation, not because of its 'irrational' or unverifiable nature, but rather because it all too quickly becomes assimilated into dialectical theology. The task is rather to think and to speak of that which is irreducible to experience "in terms of being, of presence and of immanence."[60] To do so is to speak of that which does not signify a theme.

Levinas's thinking is a thinking of the unthematic, of that which is irreducible to philosophical discourse, but philosophical discourse can only follow behind, accounting for it at the limits of its articulations. This is so for a fundamental reason: "before transcendence the ego is passive, indeed is more passive than all passivity . . . the passivity of the created."[61] The ego finds itself in this passivity in relation to the infinite. It is this "relation without relation," as Levinas calls it, which surprises the ego in the immanence of the world. The ego does not experience the infinite as an object in the world, but rather encounters it in its desire. Desire is for the infinite, for that which transcends satisfaction and interest: "Desire without end, of the beyond of being: disinterest, transcendence—desire for the good."[62] This Levinas understands as a "love without eros,"[63] a love which does not appropriate. Levinas's concern is not so much with ethics as with transcendence. As such it concerns the problem of god most profoundly; indeed it can be said to begin and end with that problem—namely, how can that which is not of the world be given philosophical if not phenomenological articulation? This problem leads him to the question of glory.

The issue here is the possibility of worldlessness. Heidegger guards phenomenology from the worldless: the inapparent is itself constitutive of world. But Levinas, in opening philosophy up to the worldless, does so by accepting

Heidegger's immanentist understanding of world. The discourse which breaks through that immanent world is the infinite discourse which cannot be confined to the said. It is a discourse of glory. We might pause here to consider this term 'glory.' 'Glory' translates *doxa* which in the Septuagint renders the Hebrew term *kabod*. This term has the connotation of weightiness. When used in reference to god, kabod refers to that which makes god apparent; it is the manifestation of the invisible god, while maintaining his invisibility.

Levinas is drawing on this notion of kabod semantic history when he speaks of the 'glory of the infinite.' This glory, which characterizes transcendence, disallows all synthesis. In the face of such glory we can only speak of a diachronic truth, a truth without possible synthesis. This is the only truth we can have of god, whose place here wavers between the exemplary and the exceptional.[64] A diachronic truth is one which breaks with traditional understanding. Truth, for Aristotle, is by definition synthetical and, if one understands truth propositionally, this follows by necessity. What Levinas is pointing to, however, is a truth that is not experienced as such, but which surprises, comes from elsewhere, and which calls not for rational assent, but for ethical responsibility. In such surprise the ego is exposed in its vulnerability before the other.[65] The glory of the other reveals the ego in its total exposure, which Levinas terms its sincerity or veracity.[66] This sincerity is made possible by the saying which responds to the other, which expresses the excess of passivity before the other. This excess of passivity responds to an an-archy, a privation of origin and of rule, which characterizes the other, the transcendence that is without any currency and as such inconvertible to immanence. Here we are "beyond reminiscence, separated by the night of the interval from all presence."[67] The luminous time of the day, the time in which knowledge shines forth, is interrupted in its luminosity by an interval which is the time of night because it has no worldly source. This time is a Cartesian time, an unworldly time, a time of continuous creation where the self experiences itself as creature.

The creaturehood of the self cannot be spoken, for Heidegger, because to do so would be to return to a Scholastic natural theology. For Levinas we can speak this creaturehood once we attend to the vulnerability and passivity of the self in the face of the other. Such vulnerability is irreducible to worldly experience. It is an 'experience' rather of that which transcends all experience. However, can it for that reason be beyond the world? It is surely the case that all experience—even if in this case we may need to cross out experience—is of that which is in the world, namely, the face of the other. "The face [of the Other] speaks."[68] The meaning of this sentence depends on some reference to a face which appears, to something which is recognizably a face: something physical, something in the world. This is implicitly acknowledged by Levinas in the effort he makes to disassociate the face from physical form. This is not to say that such disassociation fails; it is rather to point to the necessary movement from thing to person which we find also in Husserl. As with Husserl, in Levinas too this movement is not an inference. To see the face as face is to see it as that which is in excess of its mere physicality. But must we go further and follow Levinas when he states: "The Other is not the incarnation of God, but precisely by his face, in which he is disincarnate, it is the manifestation of the height in which God is revealed"?[69] The Other in its speech withdraws so thoroughly from the world here that it manifests a height beyond incarnate being. Derrida, in commenting on the "height of the most high," states that it "does not belong to space . . . not because it is foreign to space, but because (within) space it is the origin of space, orientating space through speech and glance."[70] This goes to the core of Levinas's thought, specifically his understanding of exteriority. As Derrida points out, for Levinas (in *Totality and Infinity*) exteriority is non-spatial. But such non-spatial exteriority is ultimately unthinkable:

> to neutralize space within the description of the other, in order thereby to lib-erate positive infinity—is this not to neutralize the essential finitude of a face (glance-speech) which *is a body*, and not, as Levinas continually insists, the corporeal metaphor of etherealized thought? Body: that is, *also* exteriority, lo-cality in the fully spatial, literally spatial, meaning of the word; a zero point, the origin of space certainly, but an origin which has no meaning before the *of*.[71]

The face is a body, in other words, the face, though not of the world, is and must be *in* the world. But to be in the world and not of the world means to be original to the world. Such an origin cannot be without relation to the world. If the face is not of the world in the objective genitive sense, it is of the world in the subjective genitive, in the generative, sense: of the world in the sense of being original to the world. This origin within is a recurring theme in Derrida's interrogation of Levi-nas. The tensions here are evident when he turns to the place of war in Levinas:

> in a world in which the face would be fully respected (as that which is not of this world), there would no longer be war. In a world where the face no longer would be absolutely respected, where there no longer would be a face, there would be no more cause for war. God, therefore, is implicated in war.[72]

In other words, if "polemos is the father of all" (Heraclitus) and if this is the basic principle of world, then this is so because of the face: the face is that which lets the world be world. Derrida shows how this polemos begins with the face which *speaks*. In speaking, the face is already complicit in the same, in language. The peace of which Levinas speaks is an eschatological peace, a peace beyond history. But discourse is only possible in the finite language(s) of history. As such, "there is war only after the opening of discourse, and war dies out only at the end of discourse. Peace, like silence, is the strange vocation of a language called outside of itself by itself."[73] From this Derrida concludes against Levinas that the phi-losopher cannot escape history. But history is not totality, as Levinas claims, but rather "the history of the departures from totality, history as the very movement of transcendence, of the excess over the totality without which no totality would appear as such. . . . History is transcendence itself."[74]

This claim entails further that metaphysics (in Levinas's sense) cannot escape light and hence phenomenology, i.e., world. This is so because the appearance of the other as other requires light, requires a horizon of light in which to appear. If it did not, then we would be left with nothing of which to speak. Furthermore, Husserl in his understanding of the horizon stresses the very inadequation to that horizon which for Levinas is characteristic of the infinity of the Other. Indeed, Derrida goes so far as to say:

> Is not intentionality respect itself? The eternal irreducibility of the other to the same, but of the other appearing as other for the same. For without the phenomenon of other as other no respect would be possible. The phenomenon of respect supposes the respect of phenomenality.[75]

He goes on to say: "In this sense phenomenology is respect itself."[76] Furthermore, phenomenology "is profoundly foreign to all hierarchies."[77] Precisely because phenomenology lets the other appear in an infinite horizon, in a horizon which makes all constitution possible, it has a profoundly ethical gesture, which can tolerate no pre-given hierarchies, no order which does not come from the other itself. But such a movement of respect requires that the other appear as other. It is this which "gives Husserl the right to speak of the infinitely other."[78] This is so because as Derrida does not cease to emphasize: "the other cannot be absolutely exterior to the same without ceasing to be other . . . consequently, the same is not a totality closed in upon itself."[79]

Through his long dialogue with Levinas, Derrida never ceased to insist on the irreducible worldliness of alterity. In doing so he pursued phenomenology as respect precisely in bringing to appearance the transgression of same and other: a transgression whereby the same is always being undermined by the other. All hierarchies rooted in clear identifications are undone in this process. In this sense the phenomenology of respect which Derrida pursues is a deconstruction as "radical profanation."[80] Such profanation is one in which sacred prohibitions are not so much undermined as they are shown to undermine themselves. In this way deconstruction not alone thinks phenomenology through, but it thinks in a manner which is after Greece through a rejection of the sacred logic which animates Greek thought.

Christian Phenomenology—Henry and Marion

If deconstruction is avowedly secular in its orientation, Henry and Marion are explicit in defending a notion of Christian philosophy and do so within their phenomenologies of life and givenness respectively. They do so each in a conscious effort to think Christianity after Greece.

Henry is clear that Christianity is a practice rather than a philosophy. None-theless, it incorporates intuitions and affirmations which are susceptible to philo-sophical reflection.[81] One of those affirmations which Henry highlights is the fol-lowing: "He who loves his life will lose it, he who hates his life in this world will keep it for eternal life" (John 12:25). What is interesting here is that Henry chooses John's version, which differs from those of the Synoptics. The latter accounts do not speak of hating life in this world. Rather, they speak of losing their lives for Christ's sake. They go on to speak of gaining the whole world and losing one's life. What is striking here is the manner in which Henry stresses the tension to the point of dichotomy between life and world. For Henry, the Christian affirmation of life is no longer meaningful for us, because since Galileo we no longer think life. In distinguishing between primary and secondary qualities, Galileo makes it impossible to think life. Galileo reduced the world in which human beings live to "its physical substructure, to geometric reality."[82] To this point Henry repeats the main thrust of Husserl's critique. But what is lost for Henry is not the Life-*world* but life. For this reason he can call on Descartes as a counter-voice: instead of leaving to one side the sensible qualities, Descartes carried out a "counter-reduction" and retained them.[83]

Henry sees this very counter-reduction manifest in Christ. In a critical chap-ter of his book *I Am the Truth,* titled "The Phenomenology of Christ," Henry aims to set out the phenomenological significance of Christ. He begins from his over-riding premise, "in the world and in the externality of its 'outside,' no 'Living' is possible—and consequently no livings either."[84] The Barthian denial of the truth of the external world is here brought to a fundamental conclusion: there is noth-ing of god in the world because there is no life in the world (and god is life). Hence, to live in the world is strictly impossible; the Pauline injunction is an injunction to be true to the reality of life, that it is not of the world. World here designates an answer—the Greek answer—to the question of truth: "The World is not a set of things, of beings, but the horizon of light where things show themselves in their quality as phenomena."[85] What Henry emphasizes here is the indifference of the world: the world is the self-showing of things, qualitatively different from that which shows itself. Although not stated in these terms, what Henry is describing is the ontological difference, and he—rightly—points out its worldliness. What characterizes world in this difference is externality: things appear in the world as external, as facing toward. Characteristic of the world is ecstasis, temporality: the world is that self-externality of things, whereby things face outward, constituting the temporal horizons in which things appear. Time, Henry states—reflecting a traditional thesis—is the agent of destruction, of death.[86]

For Henry the self-externalization of things is their conversion into two-dimensionality, into mere surface without depth. But is the self-externalization not a movement which shows itself in the world? In other words, does the movement to appearance not show the thing in the withdrawal of its own self behind that of itself which makes it manifest? And if this is the case, do not destruction and death point toward something other than the world, in the world? These questions become all the more pressing when Henry comes to state the "truth of Christianity." This truth is not a historical truth, is not a worldly truth at all, rather it "*differs in essence from the truth of the world.*"[87] It does so because in Christianity the difference between truth and what is true, between being and entity, no longer exists. What we have in Christianity is revelation in which "*God reveals Himself.*"[88] This doctrine, for Henry, points to a totally different, non-Greek, phenomenality. God's self-revelation owes nothing to the phenomenality of the world.

Henry is faced here with a similar problem to that faced by Levinas: if revelation owes nothing to the phenomenality of the world, how then can we have access to it?[89] Henry's answer to this question bears structural similarities to Levinas as well: our access is through an immediate experience of that which is non-worldly. But this access is not to be found in the exterior—however construed—but in the interior, in life. Life cannot be known through the mediation of the world—so not through time, the agent of death and destruction—but through itself alone. In this way Henry defines the immanent as the realm of tautology: life is life. This immanent, tautological sphere is not the sphere of moral judgment: "in Christianity, the ethical is subordinated to the order of things."[90] Christianity is not a call to ethical action, but rather a manifestation of that which we find within ourselves, namely, life. But if that is the case, then why would we need Christianity? Or to put the question more succinctly: is Christ for Henry a teacher or a practitioner of Socratic maieutics? In Levinasian terms, is the Christian not living a "separate existence"? This seems all the more probable when Henry states that "experiencing oneself as Life does is to enjoy oneself."[91] The reality of this self-enjoyment, the reality of sensation, is lost in worldliness for Henry. This is clearly true in the sciences of life, and we can agree with Henry that Christianity is a plea for life as that which the 'I' senses in itself. Greek philosophy culminating in Galilean science dissimulates life by reducing it to the world.[92] Christianity makes manifest the self-experience of life, which the world can dissimulate but not abolish ("Life, which does not cease in its 'Living' to experience itself"[93]). But again, what is the role of Christianity here—simply to make manifest the already apparent self-experience of life? This question goes to the core of the notion of revelation: what gets revealed in revelation?

To understand Henry's answer to these questions we must grasp his idea of life as self-generation. What is striking is the manner in which Henry opposes the 'believer' and the non-believer: the 'believer' has no 'rigorous knowledge' of what Christianity takes as life, and thus can only hear enigmatic propositions without understanding them. On the other hand, "for someone who penetrates the interior essence of Life . . . the enigmatic content of Christianity is suddenly illuminated."[94] The atheist, the one who is in the world, is worldly, can find nothing of Christianity there except the enigmatic pronouncements of 'believers.' But *once* he has penetrated life, *then* the content of Christianity is suddenly illuminated. In other words, Christianity is not an event at all, but a content which requires a prior penetration into life. Christianity is only accessed through life. But in that case what is prior is a phenomenology of life. This is a phenomenology without being, a phenomenology which is not of the world. "Life 'is' not. Rather, it occurs and does not cease occurring. . . . Life continuously engenders itself."[95] Such self-generation is the essence of ipseity. Ipseity is nothing in the world, because in the world the self simply externalizes itself. Rather, it is 'transcendental,' but in the very particular sense of immanent. A fundamental consequence of this is a rethinking of birth. For Henry it is a false understanding of birth as coming into being or existence. For Christianity—but we must insist first and foremost for a phenomenology of life—"in the world . . . no birth is possible."[96] Birth is not a coming into the world, but a coming into life. Coming into life is a coming from life to life; in that sense life is self-revelation: "absolute Life experiences itself in actualized Ipseity."[97] This relation is expressed in the sonship of Christ. It is this relation, this relation of Jesus to his heavenly father, which for Henry is decisive in the Gospel story.

We return, however, to the question of revelation: what is revealed in Christ? Or more specifically, what in the person of Christ in the world is revealed? The essential content of Christianity is "Christ's discourse about himself."[98] But we may ask, is it not rather the testimony of those who *heard* Christ's discourse about himself? Are the Gospels not a testimony of those who witnessed an existent, a being in the world, who spoke about himself—that being in the world? This Henry will not deny, but for him that testimony needs to be read in the light of a prior penetration into life. Indeed, Henry implies that this penetration existed in antiquity as a precondition of hearing the discourse of Christ—a precondition we have lost since Galileo. Without such precondition Christianity becomes meaningless.

But in offering this reading, Henry is calling to remembrance: "the coming of Christ into this world . . . aims to make the Father manifest to . . . those who have forgotten their true father and true Life."[99] Revelation then is a reminder of that which is at the origins of the world—Life—but which cannot appear in the world. But in that case, what does it mean to speak of the "coming of Christ into the world"? This does not refer to birth, as birth is not a coming into the world. If life is invisible, how can it be made manifest?

Henry responds to this potential contradiction by reference to key passages in John's Gospel and First Letter. The first is from John's prologue: "The word became flesh and made his dwelling among us. We have seen his glory" (John 1:14).

Glory means here the same thing as truth or revelation, Henry tells us. This glory is that god has as the only son "his own revelation as God's self-revelation."[100] But this glory cannot be seen in the world. The invisible can only be made known within the invisible. "The *mere* visible appearance of a man, even if he be Christ, is actually incapable of revealing that he is Christ."[101] Henry is certainly correct that this is a situation "constantly reproduced in the Gospels," but in what sense can Christ reveal himself if constitutive of that appearance is not also, indeed at once, his visible appearance? This seems confirmed precisely by a text Henry quotes in this context: "anyone who has *seen* me has *seen* the Father" (John 14:9, my emphasis).[102] It is difficult to understand how we go from seeing to believing in Henry. Believing, he says, is a substitution of one mode of manifestation for another, but what in that worldly mode of manifestation 'motivates' such a substitution? *There must be in the visible some trace of the invisible, to lead beyond it.* Life reveals itself in the Word, for Henry. But this notion simply displaces the problem, because the language of this Word is not the phenomenal language of the world, but rather a language of life. The problem still remains: what motivates this movement from world to life? The revelation of Christ reminds us of that forgotten life, but what in the appearance of Christ, in Christ in the world, can trigger such a reminiscence? In Plato it is participation, through which the unity of the world is established. But in Henry it is precisely the dichotomy of life and world which is being claimed.

Henry speaks rather of inversion: "Christianity inverts the phenomenological concepts."[103] A paradigmatic example of this is the concept of light. The Greek equivalent of light, truth, and world is inverted in John's prologue once it is claimed that Christ is the true light that has come into the world. This light, which cannot be recognized in the world, turns the light of the world into darkness. This inversion is complete and is fundamental to any phenomenology of Christian life in the sense that it *relativizes* the light of the world. But again, how does this inversion occur? First the light must appear in the world, and this Henry tells us is only possible through *kenosis,* through emptying.[104] Through such an emptying Christ is recognizable as a man. But as such he is not recognizable as god. In terms of the world, he is "a man among others."[105] In terms of the 'truth of life' the "Son's generation co-belongs to Life's self-generation as what this self-generation accomplishes, as the essential ipseity in which Life, in its self-embrace, becomes Life."[106] But in that case, it remains mysterious how kenosis should function: divesting himself of his equality with god allows Christ to come into the world, but his worldly being leads away not toward the truth of his revelation. For Henry, central to this distinction is a difference in glories.

While the glory of the world is one of seeking prestige, of a struggle of self-affirmation and self-manifestation, the glory of Revelation consists in the interior relation of Father and Son, what Henry calls their "reciprocal interiority." The glory of the Father and the glory of the Son consist in their reciprocal relation in which Father and Son reveal themselves in the other. This glory is one of Life, of Life's self-revelation. To illustrate this point, Henry quotes "Christ's final prayer": "I have brought you glory on earth by completing the work you gave me to do. And now, Father, glorify me in your presence with the glory *I had with you before the world began*" (John 17:4–5, emphasis in Henry).[107] But this passage does not so much speak the language of dichotomy as of harmonious tension: the glory which the Son had before the world began can be brought to earth through the completion of work (*ergon teleiosas*), which is itself worldly: "I say these things *in the world* to share my joy with them to the full" (John 17:13, my emphasis). The work done in the world, the work of a mission which goes out toward others, is that of teaching that they are not of the world: "They do not belong to the world any more than I belong to the world" (John 17:16). The phenomenology of Christ must resolve the issue of how the latter message can be heard in the world, how in other words that which is not of the world can appear in the world. This "phenomenological aporia" can only be resolved for Henry by a conversion, a change in perception, to an understanding of the human being as not being in the world.

Henry echoes Barth—consciously or not—when he states that "far from understanding Christ . . . on the basis of man and his condition, it is man who must be understood on the basis of Christ."[108] That is to say, the human being is not a natural being but the "son of God." This is the case because the "appearing out of which my phenomenological flesh is made . . . is not the appearing of the world."[109] It is only in this realization that Christ is revealed as the self-revelation of Life. Henry explains this appearing in terms of auto-affection, in terms of a phenomenality which is not of the world. But what he does not show is how one can disclose the other, how from that which is in the world we can be led back to that in ourselves which is not of the world. This notion alone does not make the revelation of Christ problematic, but it impoverishes in a crucial respect the significance of that revelation.

Henry stresses the references Christ makes to being before the world, as such, breaking with all human genealogy. He ignores, however, the claim that Christ came to save creation. Indeed, John's prologue can be understood as a rewriting of Genesis, reflecting the manner in which Christ recapitulates all history of the world in himself. Such a recapitulation far from signifying a turning away from the world is a turning toward the world as that which gives expression to the Father. Henry opposes Life to Creation and does so explicitly in a manner which owes much to a Gnostic inheritance. He claims the truth of Gnosticism to lie in the thesis that "the relation of man to God does not pass through the world."[110] We cannot understand the human in terms of creation because the human is uncreated, but rather generated.[111] But in that case the Incarnation loses its Christian significance. This significance relates directly to creation, and it is not by accident that out of Christological concerns there occurred a fundamental change in the notion of creation. It was first the early church fathers who developed the notion of *creatio ex nihilo*. Primarily, this notion—only firmly established at the Council of Nicea (325)—arose out of a rejection of the Platonic notion of an intermediary logos.[112] The identification of Christ with the logos of the *Timaeus* (which we can find, for example, in Origen) was finally rejected because it seemed to undermine the divinity of Christ. It was the Christological question as to what it could mean to say that the "word became flesh" which led to the formulation of a doctrine which, though hinted at in the Hebrew scriptures, was never fully formulated therein.[113] The 'out of nothing' refers to the condition of creation repeated in the Incarnation, namely complete self-giving love. A love without remainder, without reserve—it is that which is given expression in the term *ex nihilo*. This love is a kenotic love through which god lets himself be revealed as himself in creation. The love of kenotic giving allows for a participation of creature in creator, made possible by that which in worldly terms is weakness or powerlessness.[114]

That which is inescapable about creation is its materiality; that material being is from god—and the *creatio ex nihilo* means nothing less—amounts to a final break with the Platonic world of the demiurge and concurrently with any form of access to god through reminiscence. This is so because all that is, including material reality, comes from god, and only through what is can god be reached. The world leads to god, but because the world is created, nothing in the world is closer to god: there are no hierarchies, no royal roads.[115]

The Gnosticism of Henry's approach to Christian philosophy is reproduced in a different form by Jean-Luc Marion. Marion shares with Henry a project of 'Christian philosophy.' Such a philosophy he understands as heuristic. He rejects what he terms the hermeneutical understanding of Christian philosophy as—following Gilson—based on the claim that revelation was a necessary auxiliary of reason.[116] Such a view demotes Christianity to a secondary level below philosophy, makes it vulnerable to the charge of arbitrariness, and finally reduces revelation to the natural and hence loses the specificity of Christian phenomena.[117] It is this specificity which Marion wants to uphold: "With Christ, a newness lives in the world which is not of the world."[118] This newness Marion understands as the order of love (*charité*), and this order opened up a "realm of new phenomena to knowledge [*connaissance*], which remain invisible to natural reason alone."[119] In that sense, Christian philosophy mingles the supernatural (the domain of theology) and the natural (the domain of philosophy) and forms a "knowledge [*savoir*] which would discuss under natural light those givens introduced by supernatural light."[120] The crucial point here is that for Marion, Christianity introduces phenomena—such as the transcendence of love, the phenomenon of the face, and that of the other—which without revelation simply could not be seen.[121]

For Marion, these Christian phenomena all belong within a Barthian universe, which is one of distance from the divine in terms of a subject understood (though differently between Marion and Barth) in terms of this distance. Already in his early work *The Idol and Distance* he states that for god to become pertinent to us "it is first necessary that we experience his radical foreignness."[122] The distance to which the title refers is the condition of revelation—namely, the withdrawal of the divine from the world. It is that withdrawal which is effaced in the idol. This effacement Marion traces back to carnal love, which seeks to appropriate, to comprehend in its own terms. In the idol the divine comes to visibility and is as such made conditional on the human gaze. The icon, on the other hand, summons sight in letting the visible be saturated by the invisible: the "icon of the invisible God" (1 Corinthians 1:15). Marion's way of answering the question of how we can have access to that which is beyond being, beyond the world, is through the figure of the icon. He clearly draws here on Nicholas of Cusa, specifically in the emphasis on being seen by the icon, as being subject to the icon's gaze. But the issue of distinguishing the idol from the icon is not so straightforward.

As Marion makes clear, this distinction is not between types of entities, but rather ways of being.[123] There is no such thing as an icon or an idol in itself; only through the mode of their apprehension can they be distinguished. From the beginning Marion associates idol and icon with the Greek and Hebrew experience respectively.[124] The Greek experience is of the splendor of the visible; it is a cosmological experience, in which the gaze is anterior to its object. "The gaze is prior to the idol because an aim precedes and gives rise to that at which it aims."[125] The emphasis here is on the aim of the gaze, in other words, on the seeking out of its object. The idol is the object of seeking. The icon, on the other hand, "does not result from a vision but provokes one."[126] This discussion can be understood as a phenomenological commentary on the first chapter of 1 Corinthians: the Greek who seeks wisdom and the follower of Christ who is called. Indeed, it is this very opposition which underlies a crucial passage, where Marion attempts to show that the icon transcends the ontological difference. He does so explicitly by appeal to the notion of glory.[127]

Marion draws attention to the passage in St. Paul's letters to the Romans (4:17) where Paul speaks of god "calling non-beings as beings" (*kalountos ta me onta hos onta*).[128] This passage interests Marion because in it Paul uses the language of the philosophers—*onta*—but does so to surpass the distinction between being and non-being. For god there is an indifference between being and non-being. Such indifference to the ontic difference between being and non-being can only come from another place, beyond being. That place is the place of faith, the call, the as if.[129] This passage he reads in conjunction with 1 Corinthians 1:28, which states: "god chose the ignoble things of the world and the contemptible things and also the non-beings, in order to annul the beings [*kai ta me onta, hina ta onto katargese*]"—in order that no flesh should glorify itself before god. Here we are dealing not simply with an indifference to the ontic difference but to the ontological difference as well: here it is a question of the source of beingness itself. Marion sees precisely here the issue of glory as crucial in undermining the ontological difference. The world glorifies itself before god and in so doing undermines the ontological difference by reducing to nothing that on which it cannot found itself in this glorification. Only that *is* which can glorify itself before god.[130]

The point here is that being and non-being, Being and beings, can be divided by something other than the ontological difference—namely, according to glorification. Non-being is that which is of no importance, of no glory. What is of no glory does not appear, is not seen, is of no weight. This reduction to non-being is that which undermines the ontological difference by an inversion of the divine love: the world glorifies itself before god by viewing what is in terms of the world. As Marion puts it: "Before the difference between beings, before the conjunction of being to Being, before the fold of the ontological difference, the 'world' holds the discourse of the acquisition of funds—to glorify oneself before God."[131] In effect what is at issue here—as we have seen also with Henry—are two glorifications, that of god and that of the world.

Beyond the ontological difference is the glory of god, the gift of love which is without cosmic ground. In the course of this book that place of love will interest us greatly. But at this point I wish to again pose the question I have been posing to Levinas and Henry concerning the access to this glory.

The icon, Marion tells us, is "not seen, but appears."[132] Marion takes as his guide Paul's formula: "icon of the invisible God" (Colossians 1:15). Marion understands this to mean that the icon renders visible the invisible as such.[133] The invisible is the gaze, not of the one viewing the icon, but of the icon itself. The icon is a face that envisages "every face is given as an icon."[134] What the face offers us is nothing visible, but rather an access to the invisible, to that which is "not to be seen, but to be venerated."[135] That which is to be venerated is the invisible person, who gazes at me through the eyes of the icon. But how do we encounter this invisible person *in* the icon? How, in other words, does the visible lead us to the invisible? Again, as we saw in Henry, this occurs for Marion by means of a transformation in the viewer: "Contemplating the icon amounts to seeing the visible in the very manner by which the invisible that imparts itself therein envisages the visible—strictly, to exchanging our gaze for the gaze that iconoclastically envisages us."[136] Here the glory of the icon transforms us, such that we become the visible mirror for the invisible icon. But how does this glory shine? Does it not shine through the materiality of the icon itself? By understanding the icon as an inversion of the idol Marion is in danger of dematerializing the icon altogether. Yet if Christ is the icon of the invisible, he is so as an incarnate being, as a physical being in the world. God without being becomes in such an understanding an invisible god, whose visible manifestation—as Christ—remains unthought.

Marion's account of the icon widens into a general phenomenology of givenness, which attempts to find the condition of the phenomenon in phenomenality itself. Such a phenomenology amounts to an inversion of the idolatry of the concept which forms an anterior and limiting condition on the phenomenon. Indeed, this anteriority defines metaphysics, defines Greek thought: "In a metaphysical system, the possibility of appearing never belongs to what appears, nor phenomenality to the phenomenon."[137] In a manner which reproduces the movement from idol to icon, Marion moves from impoverished to "saturated" phenomena. This movement Marion sees already prefigured in Kant in the figure of the aesthetic idea, the representation of the imagination which gives more than any concept can expose. In such a case "intuition is no longer exposed within a concept, but saturates it and renders it overexposed—invisible, not by lack, but by excess of light."[138] To describe this experience of excess Marion talks of bedazzlement: "Bedazzlement characterizes what the gaze cannot bear."[139] But Marion immediately reminds us that to experience this incapacity "one must first perceive, if not see."[140] Playing on the meaning of kabod, Marion says that "the glory of the visible weighs, and weighs too much."[141] For this reason the saturated phenomenon is perceived only negatively in the mode of bedazzlement.

Marion is careful not to specify the objects of such bedazzlement. Indeed, in keeping with the difference between idol and icon, for Marion the difference lies not in the object as much as in its mode of being, or rather its mode of givenness. But in that case the gaze is decisive; the mode of apprehension decides the mode of phenomenon in question. If there is nothing in the object itself which makes it an icon or an idol, which makes it a saturated or an impoverished phenomenon, then where does the difference lie? This question becomes all the more pressing because in the case of the saturated phenomenon the gaze experiences the unbearable in the phenomenon. But *what* is experienced here as unbearable? It is the excess of phenomenality itself, which is generally hidden in a kind of natural attitude. This is confirmed by the reference to the myth of the cave in which the "eyes are filled with splendor."[142] This is not a case of the experience of an exceptional object, but rather is a mode of phenomenality by which objects are seen in the excessive light of the good.

What is striking here is that Marion is claiming a Greek philosophical form of universalizability for the saturated phenomenon. The classic account of the splendor of the visible is employed to illustrate the iconic, saturated phenomenon. This suggests that, as in Plato, the movement to the saturated phenomenon is a movement from the particular phenomenon toward the good. This is premised on a Platonic world of light in which all things are seen in the light of the world. Such an account is inherently horizontal; it understands phenomenon in terms of the horizon in which the phenomenon appears. That which saturates in this account is not the phenomenon, but the horizon of the phenomenon, the light in which it appears. The incapacity to perceive here is the incapacity to view the light in which the phenomenon appears.

But the phenomenon is saturated in another manner as well—namely, when it saturates the horizon. This is Marion's un-Platonic, indeed anti-Platonic account of saturation. It implies the appearance of an absolute in the world, whereas for Plato the absolute could only appear as world. A middle ground here is offered by the doctrine of transcendentals—Marion mentions four: *ens, verum, bonum,* and *pulchrum.*[143] The phenomenon can saturate its horizon but can do so relative to each of the transcendentals. In such a case the phenomenon saturates each horizon in turn, not being reducible to any one. The most extreme case, however, is that of Christ, which Marion gives without explicit acknowledgment. In such a case "a phenomenon saturated to the point that the world could not accept it."[144]

"The saturated phenomenon refuses to let itself be looked at as an object, precisely because it appears with a multiple and indescribable excess that suspends any effort at constitution."[145] The question, however, is how then the saturated phenomenon can be looked upon. It can be looked upon as an object, but when it appears as saturated it does so as a refusal of that gaze. Marion moves from speaking of the incapacity of seeing to the refusal to be seen. It is clear, however, that these are two sides of one process: the noetic and noematic, so to speak. The phenomenon refuses to be viewed as an object and as such cannot be looked at. But that which so appears can in fact be looked at as an object; however, to do so is to miss something. When Marion speaks of what the eye actually sees of the saturated phenomenon, we are thrown back on the viewer himself: the eye "clearly experiences its own impotence before the immeasurableness of the visible."[146] "Far from being able to constitute this phenomenon, the eye experiences itself as being constituted by it."[147] The 'I' becomes a "constituted witness."[148]

But the increasingly urgent question is, witness to what? The saturated phenomenon by virtue of its saturation becomes less and less that of which we can speak, less and less something in the world. Yet, it is precisely this which defines not a limit case, but phenomenality itself, as Marion states alluding to Heidegger's famous definition: "it alone truly appears as itself, of itself and starting from itself."[149] But this means—drawing a very un-Heideggerian conclusion—that the phenomenon taken in its fullest meaning is revelation; revelation, though, is of nothing which shows itself, but rather is of that which is experienced as one's own being before revelation in the figure of the gifted (*adonné*). But the incarnate presence of revelation becomes unspeakable here, as any speech of it falls back into idolatry.

World, Alterity, and Incarnation: Merleau-Ponty

The problem, the issue, which has emerged through the preceding analyses is of the place of contact of the invisible and the visible, of the divine and the human, of spirit and matter. This issue is central if we are to accomplish a coherent phenomenology of Christian life. If the Christian lives temporality as such (Heidegger), it is because she lives without dichotomy, without appeal to that which is above or beyond the event. But to think that is to think contamination, is to think the final overthrow of all sacral logic. That logic of immunity[150] is one which we find reproduced even in those thinkers who most clearly seek to avoid it. This is so because in attempting to escape the sacred they evacuate the world, evacuate material being, of all divine reference. But in doing so they understand Christianity as the inversion of the sacred, rather than its *sub*version. Because we cannot prepare a place for god does not mean that god has no place in the world; the difficulty is thinking that place without reification.[151] Only through a thinking of such contamination, of such profanation, can we think a *phenomenology* of Christianity, in other words, can we certify the access to the phenomenon which is the Christian phenomenon.

Merleau-Ponty may offer us some help here. Such a source of help seems at first unlikely. Merleau-Ponty himself distanced his thinking from Christian thought. Furthermore, Dominique Janicaud in his critique of the theological turn points back to Merleau-Ponty as a way of thinking the invisible which remains true to phenomenology. This 'remaining true' Janicaud understands as a faithfulness to the phenomenological reduction. As he puts it, "the suspension of the natural attitude ought not to lead to a flight to an other world . . . but to a deepening of the transcendental regard vis-à-vis experience and for it."[152] But if there are Christian phenomena, these phenomena require precisely a deepening of the transcendental regard to the point where the worldliness of that regard is ruptured and undone.

While from Levinas to Marion there is a constant concern to affirm that glory which opposes the glory of the world, Merleau-Ponty affirms the glory of the body. In *The Visible and the Invisible* he refers to 'a glorious body' and does so in the context of introducing 'horizon' as "a new type of being, a being of porosity."[153] The horizon is that in which world and earth meet and mingle. This is the being which makes the flesh of my body adhere to that of the world; it is an opaque zone where primary visibility does not come without secondary visibility, where the momentary body (*le corps momentané*) is not without a glorious body (*un corps glorieux*).[154] A glorious body Merleau-Ponty understands as the rarefied body (*chair subtile*), as the body which is in excess of what appears, which, however, incarnates the invisible. Yet the invisible is that which is manifest as a second visibility. There is, as Merleau-Ponty says, in perception a "paradox of

immanence and transcendence": the surface being of visible objects is itself constituted by invisible depths and dimensions.

In this sense the difference between the momentary and the glorious body
reflects that between spoken and speaking language (*langage parlé / langage
parlant*). Spoken language is conventional language, language already arranged
through sedimentation, sedimentation among other things of the creative acts
of language. The latter Merleau-Ponty refers to as speaking language. It is the
language which "creates itself in its expressive acts, which sweeps me on from
the signs toward meaning."[155] This expressive movement Merleau-Ponty shows
to be inherent in language insofar as it is signification before having signification.[156] The creative movement of expression happens in the midst of constituted
language and undoes it. Language points not alone beyond itself, but also before
itself, to a "mute world" prefiguring it, and becoming manifest in it. Silence forms
the horizon in which speech emerges, a horizon in which speech and the withdrawal from speech, spirit and matter, intertwine in both a promise of meaning
and a horror of inexpressibility. In the world, silence and speech intermingle,
and do so in the flesh. Merleau-Ponty stresses the intersection of tactility and visibility, of the glorious and the material: the glorious is not to be found through or
behind the material, nor to be found in the invisibility of the auto-affective flesh,
but rather is constitutive of the world as such. This is so because the world appears
to the flesh and more specifically to the desiring flesh. For Merleau-Ponty, sensation is dispossession, and desire is a function of this dispossession in the movement toward that which is other in the incarnate presence of another and the
finding of oneself as other in this movement.[157] The latter Merleau-Ponty refers
to as the "global and universal power of incorporation [*pouvoir global et universal d'incorporation*]."[158] Fundamental here is a primordial openness to the world
which Merleau-Ponty calls 'perceptual faith.' Such perceptual faith responds to
"a paradox of being,"[159] which is the paradox of visibility. This paradox lies at the
heart not simply of the human body but of the world as the domain in which visibility and tactility intersect. There is in such a view not a surface world and an
unworldy depth, or an invisibility beyond the visible, or an alterity above the horizon of the world. Rather, the world is the domain of intersecting glories (doxa)
which contradict one another. This para-dox is a contamination, seen from the
point of view of sacral anxiety.

The flesh for Merleau-Ponty is expression, and expression is paradoxical; it
is the locus of a conflict of glories, the glory of the world and the glory which
cannot come to the world, the glory of the silent and the invisible. This paradox
comes into appearance for us in the encounter with the other. In that encounter
we discover the inexhaustibility of the visible, that it is open to other, the visible
as a surface of inexhaustible depth. This depth I find in myself, too, and I find my
body as entwined with that of the other, indeed with the flesh of the world.[160] All

of this occurs in the patient and silent work of desire.[161] Desire for that which is not simply surface, but of which surface is expression.

This movement of desire toward that which shows itself as in excess of what it appears to be gives us the possibility of access to the glory of the incarnate god in the night beyond worldly perception.

It is this which Henry misses in his rather brusque critique of Merleau-Ponty.[162] The discourse on the flesh of the world does not arise out of a naïve realistic neglect of constitution, but rather is an understanding of constitution as desire. The object of desire is not constituted by the subject, nor is the subject by the object, but rather arises from an auto-constitution which first gives subject and object. The flesh of the world is that which first makes the flesh of the subject possible. Life comes from world, not the world of Galileo, but rather world as a "wild region" out of which expression emerges.

To think Christian phenomena is to think after Greece, but it is to think the mutual contamination of—in Greek terms—contradictories. The challenge is to think the contamination of flesh and the alterity of unworldly at once. It is this challenge which a phenomenology of glory and night aims to meet. It does so through a meditation on phenomena of Christianity which reveal an acosmic instance in the midst of the world. To think that is to pursue a phenomenology of world and a phenomenology of alterity together.

Plan of the Book

This book is divided into eight chapters. The first chapter introduces the key notions of existence, desire, and beauty. These are fundamental to an understanding of glory and aim toward a Christianity of the beautiful, hence of that which is first present in the world. The second chapter addresses the question of light and darkness as fundamental to any phenomenology and shows how the Judeo-Christian and Platonic accounts of light differ fundamentally. Only then can one make sense of a phenomenology of night. The third chapter introduces the question of glory in relation to being and shows how an ontology of glory breaks with the totalizing ontologies of the philosophical heritage, without withdrawing from ontology. The following chapter then discusses the issues which arise in the night: confusion, faith, death, and conscience. The central Christian doctrine is that of the Incarnation. Chapter 5 consists in an exploration of the notion of embodiment underlying this doctrine. The key to any Christian ontology is the nothing as that from which all things come: *creatio ex nihilo*. The sixth chapter tackles this question and attempts to draw implications from the Christian understanding of creation for ontology and truth. The final two chapters are attempts to develop an account of time and of thinking which is true to Christian phenomena, in both cases working out a temporality and understanding of the world which reveals that which is not of the world.

1   Desire and Phenomenon

Oɴʟʏ ᴡʜᴇʀᴇ ᴛʜᴇʀᴇ is desire for the phenomenon is existence a question. 'Existence' is the rupture of essence, where the nature of a being is a subsequent narration of its prior vocation and mission. Existence ruptures essence where phenomena seduce. Existence is vocational, is being led forth and led out by the call of the phenomenon. Existence is desire. Existence is not needy; an existent does not preserve itself but sacrifices itself through the vulnerability of its being in the face of the radiance of phenomena. Existence is being toward an other. No being fully exists, no being can fully be toward, can fully be as being called by the phenomenon. But, conversely, to be is to exist, to be at all is to be vulnerable toward the seductive power of phenomena.

Existence is threatened by degradation and tempted by dissolution. In its material being it is bound by endless drives to satiation which threaten to anaesthetize it in a limbo of self-forgetfulness; its spiritual being is tempted toward a Gnostic escape in angelic peacefulness. In both trajectories existence loses itself.[1] In its being-called, existence finds itself in worldly movement; the hierarchical structure of worldly being, however, depresses it. The worldly hierarchy is an order of attachments, which depresses existence by binding it in its needful valuations to possession.[2] Desire for the phenomenon discloses a place in the world beyond the hierarchies of the world: a being in the world, but not of the world. It is a place of mission, where the affirmation of self is subject to the acceptance of a sending (*missere*).

Phenomenon names the primordial attraction of entities for desire. Phenomenon is the happening of that entity for an existent. This primordial attractiveness is beauty fundamentally and pre-hierarchically.[3] Beauty draws out love and inspires praise. Love of beauty is fundamental to education; only through love can an existent be led out (*ex-ducere*) to things. Education begins there, begins with the beauty of the phenomenon. In appearing, the phenomenon appears as itself; as itself, in its self-revealing form, the phenomenon is beautiful.[4] Appearance as appearance is beauty. The appearance of a thing is that thing as it calls, as it allows itself to be called (named).[5] In appearing, the thing gives its name, not as a tool for signification, but rather as a word to be said in reverential praise. Desire is the response of praise. Appearing to existence, the phenomenon mutely utters a greeting and in such greeting calls its own name, and in invoking that name existence does not apply a general concept, but addresses it with words which are proper names. Desire speaks in proper names. In placing its tongue around the word it responds to the phenomenon in its beauty. Desire, love, and education all belong inseparably to the seduction of the phenomenon.

Phenomenon is singular, worldly, yet non-hierarchical. Phenomenology as the logos of phenomenon is a discourse unlike any other. It speaks not to describe, propose, command, or promise. It speaks rather to invoke the hidden source, the original epiphany, of appearance. That source is prior to language, as it expresses without concepts; it is prior to the self of the existent, as it calls that self forth, and this priority is temporal, is that of a time which is the source of chronological time. Phenomenology in order to speak this source requires therefore a *triple dispossession* of language, of self, and of time. This triple dispossession is phenomenology as desire. In desire it responds to the gift of phenomenon which is not outside language, time, and self, but outside each understood as possession. Phenomenology in that sense neither describes nor prescribes, it *prays*.

Phenomenology as prayer—is this not a contradiction, is this not to place phenomenology beyond logos? But prayer is logos under *epoché*—logos which is neither true nor false (Aristotle, *De Interpretatione*, 4.17a3–4). The language of phenomenology is neither affirming nor negating, because it lets that which appears appear in-itself. The in-itself is not subject to statements, but subjects them. The in-itself appears only in words of praise, and such praise is originary logos. With this logos science begins, i.e., with the desire to see things appear as they are—as they are in and of themselves; reason in its claim to self-sufficiency both hides and discloses this desire: in seeking grounds, it stops only before that which needs no grounds, the *causa sui*. The question, 'what is 'x'?,' is already derivative. Indeed, the question as interrogation is already a fall from existence as desire. Before the question, appearance is calling for question. But this calling is a calling to be questioned as it is. To be questioned as it *is* is to be questioned in no other terms than what this calling reveals itself to be. This is revelation in the full Judeo-Christian sense. Appearance as revelation is responded to by "let thy will be done" and more fundamentally by "hallowed be thy name."

This chapter will explore the inner relation of phenomenon and existence as desire. The first section will discuss existence and desire. The second section will explore beauty in relation to existence manifest as faith and mission. The third section will go on to show how existence understood as desire is conceived in a

Christian and non-Platonic sense. The final section will discuss the mode of discourse about phenomenon and existence and show that this discourse is beyond the dichotomy of philosophy and theology.

Existence and Desire

Existence is a Christian term,[6] because it expresses the irreducibility of a being to its essence. The existent—the being understood in respect of this irreducibility—stands forth in and of itself and is responsible for itself.

Existentia first translated *huparzis* and was defined in line with the etymology of the latter *prae-existens substantia,* pre-existing substance. But while such pre-existing substance may be present in god, to the extent to which there is existence outside of god such existence *is* only in relation to a source which it cannot make present. Existence is always belated; it refers to that which was never present to it and to which as such return is in principle impossible. However, this immemorial source is significant to it not through a nostalgic longing—as this source is not simply lost, but never possessed—but rather as a movement from the source which it discovers in itself. To exist is to have always already been moved; an existent is a being-affected. This being-affected is experienced in desire. To desire is to be moved prior to any decision or any choice. It is to experience the phenomenon as that toward which I am moved. Action is the taking up—or refusal to take up—this movement. Such a taking up (or its refusal) reveals a source which is prior to me, prior to any freedom, which, far from negating such freedom, first makes it possible. Understood not in abstraction as an absence of determination—an impossible concept—but rather as the movement of existence, freedom knows itself as a gift.[7] As a power to initiate which does not initiate itself, freedom is the experience of capacity in incapacity. Freedom discloses itself thus as the power of the *epoché,* the power of suspension in the movement of desire itself, of movement toward the world without being possessed by the world.[8] But such suspension is not primarily of belief in the being of the world, but rather suspension of my need for the world. If belief is in play here (and in the next section we will see to what extent it is), it is a belief in the being of the world as that which satisfies my needs. Such a belief, however, does not see the phenomenon, sees nothing beyond itself. In desire the existent experiences itself in relation to that which moves and affects it, but is always too late to capture the source of its being affected. That source shines through the phenomenon, but does so precisely by withdrawing from sight. In such a withdrawal the phenomenon places itself out of play and in the same moment places the needy self of the existent out of play. The epoché here effected is a mutual withdrawal of existent and phenomenon within the movement of desire. The reduced existent desires. But such a desire in responding to the phenomenon in its withdrawal sees not the world as its correlate, but rather an excess of world in the world. Nothing in the world can satisfy desire, not because it is insatiable, but because it is not hungry:[9] desire is not appropriative and as such moves beyond the proper of self and of world. Desire moves toward that which, in the self-giving of the phenomenon, gives itself by putting itself out of play in terms of the economy of the world.

What is not put out of play, though, is existence itself. In putting the economy of the world out of play existence reveals itself to itself as play. No longer taken up by the world, existence finds itself there for no worldly reason, but as a unique opening toward the world. This opening is given as being put in play.[10] In this sense, existence finds itself in a movement which it must accept. Existence is this acceptance, an acceptance of a free movement which it can neither initiate nor complete. But no existent can persevere in such constant acceptance (in the postlapsarian condition with the exception of the incarnate godman, that is at least the Christian claim), and must constantly lapse into refusal.[11]

As Heidegger tells us, existence is ecstatic,[12] is being toward: toward other people and other things. This movement is a movement in the world, but as a movement of desire it comes back to itself in the epoché, comes back to an interiority that turns away from the world. Such a turning is modesty. In modesty the existent turns its body from the world not out of disgust, but rather in a self-reflexive movement of desire. Modesty states, as Mounier puts it, "my body is more than my body."[13] My body turned toward the world, my body which can serve another's need, is less than my body; my body exceeds such need, my body desires and can be desired.[14] In this sense modesty must be clearly distinguished from shame. In shame existence discloses itself not in its excess, but in its nothingness, i.e., its being held captured by the gaze which sees the existent in its body as nothing more than a function of its need. Shame is a feeling of lack of worth in relation to an imperious gaze, which lays claim to the whole of the existent;[15] it is overcome not primarily through a reversal of the transcending act of the other's gaze (as for Sartre), but by a reassertion of modesty through the (literal or metaphorical) wrapping oneself in clothes. Such a clothing of oneself is not so much an attempt to hinder the other's gaze, but to excite the other's desire in place of the appropriative drive of his needs.[16] Immodesty too, which itself can be a self-clothing in response to shame,[17] as the throwing of the essentially hidden toward the light[18] hides itself in its very self-exhibition.

The intimacy of my being becomes shared with another, however, in love, where two turn together from the world into the interiority of their own privacy, their intimacy *à deux*. Here modesty gets slowly stripped away as the two strive to become one flesh. As one flesh they share a common turning from the world and show the world a common exteriority, hiding from the world their shared carnal being.[19]

An existent which experiences itself in modesty—or in its immodesty—is one for whom a turning away from the world is constitutive of its being. But such a turning is not from the world *tout court,* but from the superficial exteriority of beings in the world existing as mere beings of the world. This turning is a movement of wakefulness.[20]

Existence can be wakeful or slumbering. An existence which is only one of need slumbers. This is so because to exist in need alone is to exist toward the other in the homogeneity of the existent's own being. For such an existence the other is nothing except what serves its own 'interests.' But even those interests are not present to it because they are prescribed in the spontaneity of its own being. While other entities are nothing to it except as they satisfy its needs, it too is nothing to itself outside of the systems of relations in which it is inscribed. In that sense the slumber of existence does not equate with an absence of consciousness or self-consciousness.[21] A conscious existent lost in the satisfaction of its own need is slumbering though conscious. Wakefulness is attentive, attending—waiting (*attendre*)—on its 'object' such that it reveals itself to itself as being attentive. While consciousness loses itself in its object—is consciousness of its object—existence awakes in the experience of desire. Without desire the directedness of existence toward phenomena is one which informs phenomena. That which appears is 'informed' by the one grasping it. As such 'information' is never new, nor does it come from without; rather it is that with which slumbering existence impregnates phenomena in order in turn to appropriate them to itself. An existence which lives off information is one which can be found in the rocks in the riverbed, the trees in the forest, and in the Internet café. It is an existence for which appearance is two-dimensional, without depth. Depth is only in the self-appearance of that which appears, that is, an appearance in excess of the surface of its appearance. It is the resistance to any in-forming, which existence only encounters when its desire for that self-appearance is excited. When it is so excited it encounters the appearing in its appearance not at the surface of its being, but as a depth which cannot be informed, as that which hides itself from the world.

But for the most part existents relate to entities within relations of need. No being in the world is without need, that is, without relation to other entities for its being. 'Substantial difference' is generated out of such relations—this is what the revolution in science from Galileo to Darwin has taught us from physics to biology. The essence of a being is formed by that need, and in that sense every essence is itself relational, is itself a function of the relation of beings to one another. Need functions within systems of information. The properties of food (calories, fat content, carbohydrates, etc.), for example, are absorbed within an organism and pass information to that organism, which fulfill or fail to fulfill its needs. The more sophisticated the being the more relations of need it enters into. The apogee of this we find in the human being, for whom the earth and all upon it functions as information, as fulfillment of need. In that sense the human being is in essence—but not in existence, not in desire—all that is.

Desire is possible only in the relaxation of need: a being directed toward its needs is blind to the call of the phenomenon: its essence swallows up its existence. It is for this reason that ascetics attempt to limit their needs toward nil in order to feel desire completely.[22] Desire responds not to the apparent in the phenomenon, but to that which hides. In giving itself, a being precisely turns itself away, hides itself behind the apparent. To be a self is to be modest. Desire is for this self, for the self-revealing of its own hiddenness. Existence as desire responds to such modesty and in that response the only attitudes possible are prayerful reverence or blasphemous obscenity. Desire is reverential because it encounters that which appears in the excess of its appearance; its obscene, blasphemous violence is a fleeing from this reverence.[23]

In desire, existence is wakeful; it is attentive to the self-revelation of the other and in turn sees itself in its own reverential attitude as an existent. In desiring the other being in itself, the existent understands its existence as submission to the other. In its being sent toward the other and below the other, it experiences itself as subject to the other. Only through subjection can it be in the presence of the self-giving of the other, a self-giving which is complete precisely to the extent to which the self remains hidden. The wakefulness of existence is one which is attentive to an origin which can never be retrieved, to an origin which remains beyond its powers and which it cannot see, but for which it is seen.

If wakefulness is attention, is a reverential dispossession in the face of appearance, then the wakeful existence is ultimately that of the person. In Mounier's words: "Personal being is generosity."[24] Personal being opens itself up to the other. Generosity is the response of desire. The person is not the mask of the theatre, not the purely external disguise through which the voice speaks (*persona*), but rather the openness to the other being in its appearance. This openness is one of self-giving which sacrifices the self not in the sense of annihilating it, but rather in the sense of allowing the other being to come to speech through it. Generosity is speaking not to affirm or assert oneself, but to bring the other to appearance also for itself: to allow the other—and not alone the other 'person,' but anything—to reveal the articulation of its own being.

Desire is for the being in itself, in its self-revelation. Self-revelation is revelation of the self in its own manifestation of being. To be a self is to be in a singular way. It is then the being of the being, that which makes it what it is, which appears and which leads forth the desire of the existent: in each case singular, attracting desire. Clearly we cannot here be talking of generalizable properties. The curves of a woman's body may attract my desire, but so too the straight lines of a geometrical figure. What attracts desire in each case is different, and that which is generalizable—any woman with such and such curves or any geometrical figure with straight lines—is precisely not that which attracts my desire. In each case it is not the general quality which attracts my desire—at most that can excite my needs. I desire *this* appearing thing, *this* appearing person, which expresses itself or herself in and through such and such a quality. Something irreplaceable, at least now at this instance, *seduces* me in my existence and *educates* me not about general qualities, not about anything I can delimit in my experience, but rather about that which in my experience *transcends* that experience and any possible experience.

Desire is toward the transcendent and the singular at once. It is the singular being which attracts and excites desire, but it does so in transcending any particular quality it may have. Particular qualities, empirical objects of consciousness, are generalizable, but as such substitutable. Yet desire is not left without words in speaking of the object of its desire. But its words are not those which refer to generalizable properties, such as 'breasts,' 'softness,' 'precision,' 'harmonious,' etc.— or rather such words are secondary, understandable in the language of desire only on the basis of other words. Those other words include: being, truth, goodness, unity, and beauty: I desire her to be, I desire the universe's truth, I desire his goodness, I desire her 'warts and all' (in the unity of her being), I desire the beauty of that diamond. Traditionally these terms were understood as 'transcendentals.' In understanding the transcendental as it differs from the empirical, we can begin to understand not only the singularity of the phenomenon but also that attraction which calls existence into the 'mission' of its self-giving.

Beauty, Faith, and Mission

Beauty as Transcendental

The distinction between the transcendental and the empirical recurs consistently in thinking—philosophical, theological, religious, even scientific. This distinction arises when existence is awakened and aroused into its own movement. The movement of existence is a movement beyond the empirical, beyond the surface of appearance to the transcendent in appearance. This is a movement beyond the practical, beyond the instrumental, toward a being in relation to the other. It is a movement toward the singular and the universal, or rather toward the universal in the singular. On the empirical level universality is without sense or meaning. Empirically all we have to deal with are qualities which are generalizable and conceptualizable. Most of our language concerns such qualities, whether expressed propositionally or prescriptively, performatively or constatively. The process of generalization is one of substitution: what is generalizable can be substituted in respect of such a generalization by any other instance of that general concept.

The transcendental is that which is *not* contingent on a process of generalization. Nor is it contingent on actual experience. Rather, the transcendental is constitutive of any possible experience. In this sense it is universal. The universal is not empirical, in the sense that it cannot be instanced in empirical experience.

Rather, the universal is intuited in experience as essential to that experience—as transcending and making possible that experience. That which is essential to experience cannot be learned from experience, can only make such learning possible. To the extent to which experience concerns knowledge—and insofar as experience is of something which it is concerned to 'know'—then knowledge is possible only on the basis of the universal. Knowledge as that which is striven for is made possible by the universal, by that which constitutes experience, but must also be motivated therein. In transcending the empirical, knowledge is beyond all utility; that it can increase utility is a consequence but not a 'motivation' of knowledge. Correctly understood the difference between the transcendental and the empirical concerns the knowledge of knowledge. In other words, this difference goes to the inner motivation of knowledge within the movement of existence.

The passage from medieval to modern philosophy can be charted in terms of the distinction between the transcendental and the empirical. But this is also a history of loss, one which by losing sight of the movement of existence fails to account for the motivation of knowledge. While philosophy from the late medieval period to the beginnings of the last century was concerned to uncover the firm basis for knowledge, the *motivation* of knowledge was undercut. While the movement of knowledge has been affirmed as that from subject to object, the motivation for that movement has become opaque. Descartes's statement of that motivation—one which echoes that of Bacon, to be masters of nature—raises the question as to what motivates such mastery: either to enjoy the fruits of nature—which must in some way be attractive—or to manufacture an artificial world, the purpose of which needs to be articulated. But in neither case is the inner motivation of knowledge touched; it is rather presupposed. The movement of the subject toward the object is accepted as a given, and is then interpreted imperiously. But it is the motivation precisely of this movement of subject to object which must be understood. Husserl in his account of intentionality brought the history of forgetting surrounding this movement of subject to object to its culmination. But precisely in so doing he made this forgetting evident and, in his analysis of passive synthesis, discovered at the heart of knowledge the affective movement of being drawn to the object, the pull of the object which is not simply a matter of brute impressions, but an attraction through excess in the object. We shall return below to this account, but first we shall turn back to the medievals—more precisely, the theory of transcendentals in medieval philosophy.

The medievals, drawing on Plato's understanding of the ideas of goodness, justice, and beauty as belonging to all the forms, as being characteristic of forms as forms, developed an account of those qualities which transcend any particular genus or species.[25] There were many different accounts of these, but being, oneness, goodness, and truth are most often given. Beauty is cited also, but less often.

The transcendentals are the most abstract of qualities, belonging as they do in each thing which is, but at the same time they are also the most concrete. While general terms such as animal, tree, water, etc., are qualities abstracted from individual beings, the transcendentals are *manifest* each time differently in each being. To think the transcendentals is not to think of general properties, but to think that which manifests the being of the object: its oneness, its truth, its goodness. What the transcendentals make manifest—that which is not immediately obvious in the general concepts—is the attractiveness of every entity, an attractiveness which for the medievals is the being manifest of its creatureliness.

Before pursuing this account further an important objection must be addressed, namely, the relative infrequency of beauty—the transcendental most obviously a function of attractiveness—in the list of transcendentals. In the postmedieval period, especially under the influence of Protestant theology, Christian thinkers have been slow to grant a place for beauty, a tendency which some from Maritain to von Balthasar and more recently Chrétien have sought to reverse. A fundamental reason for beauty being treated with suspicion is the danger of idolatry. This danger can already be glimpsed in Plato's critique of the beautiful thing, precisely in the name of beauty. The danger is one of a bedazzlement of vision by the merely visible. The issue of such bedazzlement gave rise to a whole tradition of thought on the form of Jesus Christ in which his ugliness was postulated.[26] It was not the beauty of his form which attracted in such a view, but rather his words and actions: bodily beauty would distract from that. It is important to see here that it is not beauty or attractiveness as such which is being denied; indeed, the discourse centers around such beauty and attractiveness. The question rather is how such beauty is to be understood. One response to this is to transpose beauty into goodness (as Tertullian implicitly does). Indeed, the relation of beauty to goodness is a reliable measure to guide us in charting certain movements of thought from Aquinas to Husserl and beyond.

Any clear disjunction between beauty and goodness is un-Greek in a very specific sense, that is, as being acosmic. The word *cosmos* already contains the meaning of beauty. As Chrétien puts it: "a world without beauty would no longer be that which the Greeks would call κόσμος."[27] The cosmos is that which attracts thought, that which is attractive, beautiful. But if there is beauty beyond the world, then that beauty can darken the world in its shadow. Once the attractiveness of the cosmos is questioned, indeed once Paul identifies it with the flesh, with 'natural inclinations' as opposed to the spirit, then the severing of beauty and goodness is a constant issue.

But such a severing did not in any way follow automatically. For Pseudo-Dionysius "the beautiful and the good are one and the same."[28] And as it is beauty that brings all things into the same, and as it is through the erotic attraction to beauty that all things are ordered in relations of desire to one another, for Pseudo-

Dionysius to be is to desire and be desired. This erotic movement originating in the divine is the source of the ecstatic nature of existence: "Divine eros is ecstatic; it does not allow those that are touched thereby to be among themselves but bids them to be among their lovers."[29] The very hierarchy of beings is organized according to this principle. The initial movement of being and of knowledge is one of being attracted by the world. The influence of Pseudo-Dionysius on Aquinas and how the latter's commentary on the *Divine Names* is to be interpreted are a matter of controversy. It does seem clear, however, that Aquinas's teacher Albert the Great took from Dionysius the emphasis on *claritas* in relation to beauty and that Aquinas developed this further. In Dionysian fashion Aquinas speaks of beauty as claritas and the latter in terms of radiance and brightness. This radiance is that which makes something evident by making it manifest. It is in that sense that for Aquinas beauty is form, and the form of a thing is that which allows it to be manifest for the senses and the intellect.[30] What is evident here is an implicit metaphysics of beauty: for a being to be known, it must attract me. This attraction is not simply a contingent factor of my likes or dislikes, but rather that in the entity which shows itself to me as intelligible, as capable of being known. It shows itself to me at once both sensibly and intellectually. It is this mixing of the sensible and the intellectual which suggests that god the Son be understood as beauty. The Son, by bringing pure form and matter together, embodies the ambiguity of beauty as splendor which appeals from the entity to the incarnate being of the human intellect.[31]

The basis of such an understanding of attraction in things is undermined in modernity most clearly by Kant. Beauty and goodness in Kant—far from being one and the same—are radically distinct. They are distinct in terms of *telos–Zweck*, end. The good is related to an end and as such is related to interest. To have an interest is to seek a certain end and that end is to be found in a certain existent, even if in the case of the moral end that existent is the self. To transcend interest is to transcend all existents and, as such, beauty and existence are placed in utter opposition to each other. The Kantian thesis that being (*Sein*) is not a real predicate[32] goes hand in hand with his understanding of beauty in terms of disinterested pleasure. To deny the real predication of being is to deny that the standing outside of me of the thing is in any way constitutive of what it is. If that is denied, then the attraction of that thing, precisely as leading me from another place beyond myself, becomes opaque. In the *Critique of the Power of Judgment* the existence of the object is of no consequence in relation to taste, and it is the judgment of taste which has beauty as its object.[33] The pleasure at beauty is free because it is disinterested. Freed from any concern with the existence of its object, taste can contemplate in a state of pure epoché so to speak. Such a pure epoché is free because it is liberated from needs: only when needs are satisfied can the judgment of taste function.[34]

In the judgment of taste the full implications of Kant's critical philosophy are realized: pure contemplation does not concern being, because being is a matter of need. Pleasure is the determinate of the uniquely human capacity to be with an object in its pure attractiveness. But this attractiveness is not grounded in the object; it is a function purely of the taste of the observer. In this sense the difference between the charm (*Reiz*) of an object and the judgment of taste is crucial. The charm of the object relates solely to the sensibility of the subject; it is that which stimulates him. But such stimulation is only true of him; that charm or stimulation is simply the material effect on the body of the subject, the stimulation has no reference beyond that subject, does not disclose anything true of the stimulating object. The judgment of taste cannot relate to such a stimulation, but rather to a claim to common validity (*Gemeingültigkeit*). This claim is not based on any objective judgment, but rather on a judgment concerning the feeling of pleasure or displeasure which any subject would have.[35] The general agreement, which is claimed as a basis of such an aesthetic judgment, is not based on a concept—as it is not based on anything about the reality of the object—but rather on an idea: an idea shared—or claimed to be shared—by all observing subjects.[36] In this respect Nietzsche's polemic in which he accuses Kant of understanding art purely from the point of view of the spectator, rather than that of the creator, is well taken. But the issue is more fundamental: if beauty is a matter of pure disinterest, of pure subjectivity as it is without concept, then the knowledge of objects becomes ontologically ungrounded. Objects which come under concepts are objects of theoretical knowledge. But we relate to such objects with interest. Hence, theoretical knowledge remains tied to 'practical' (in the broadly instrumental, not in a Kantian, sense) concerns. Such concerns tie us to the world, which in itself remains hidden from us. This tragic state of being is alleviated only through an aesthetic liberation from—and a relaxation of—interest, which however understands beauty not as attractiveness, but as pleasure. The impoverishment of beauty and of world are here inextricably linked. Where the self of the thing remains foreign to consciousness, knowledge remains at the surface—no longer a response to being but a flight from boredom, as Pascal already saw.

This flight from boredom is experienced not in being drawn by entities, but by projecting toward them. Such projection reaches, however, not the entities themselves, but the entities in their being apparent. It is this being apparent that Kant attempts to capture in his discussion of *Erscheinung.* In an important footnote to the "Transcendental Aesthetic" Kant states that whereas Erscheinung is a predicate of the object, *Schein* is not.[37] Erscheinung is the appearance of the object to the subject which is inseparable from the representation of the object. It is that object understood in terms of that relation. Kant uses 'Schein' to refer to an overstepping of Erscheinung, such that the appearance of the object to me is understood to be a quality of the object in itself. Schein is the opposite of truth and is only understandable in relation to judgment: a Schein is the judgment of an appearance which crosses over the boundaries of possible experience and judges—to use Kant's example—that the rose is in itself red. While Schein is falsehood, for Kant the Erscheinung is the basis of all knowledge.

The thing as apparent in Erscheinung is the thing as it is experienced. As experienced the thing is a synthetic product of matter and form. The appearance to the sensible subject is of that which appears, but which appears only as imprinted with that subject's form—of sensibility and of understanding. It is for this reason that Kant can understand knowledge as transcendental "which concerns itself not so much with objects, but rather with the mode of cognition of objects, to the extent to which this is a priori possible."[38] The phenomenon as phenomenon is the object relative to our mode of cognition of the object. The transcendental conditions of the phenomenon are to be found not in the object of cognition, but in its mode. In this sense knowledge, a system of knowledge, is not founded in the nature of things, but rather in the understanding which through judgment lays the boundaries of the objects of knowledge. The nature of things is inexhaustible; judgment is limiting.[39] In this context the empirical is defined as all that which comes from experience. All a priori concepts then must find their birth certificates in the understanding, not in experience.

Why, however, does knowledge begin in experience? Why, in other words, does an experiencing being strive for knowledge? This is a question Kant can answer, if at all, only psychologically. In transcendental terms the phenomenon is one which cannot appear of itself, and as such cannot attract. In this sense the Kantian definition of beauty in terms of disinterested pleasure is a strict corollary of his understanding of appearance. In such disinterest the subject only experiences itself; beauty tranquilizes, and existence slumbers.

This tranquility and slumber is only superficially shaken by the sublime.[40] The notion of the sublime is already opened up in the *First Critique* by Kant's acknowledgment of the infinity—inexhaustibility—of the nature of thing. While the beautiful for Kant is directed—albeit indirectly—toward things, the sublime reaches beyond any such stimulus toward the formless, the infinite.[41] While the natural object may be the *occasion* of the mood (*Stimmung*) of the sublime, its true source must be found in the mind of the one making a judgment of the sublime: that the nature of things is inexhaustible is an idea in the mind, not an object of experience.[42] This is so because the experience of natural objects is an experience of purposefulness: the natural object is experienced as having a certain form, as being for a certain purpose.[43] While nature for Kant is the totality of appearances, these appearances are ordered teleologically. It is precisely when this teleological order is transcended by reason in the apprehension of violence and power in nature, that we experience the sublime. It is only here in such a situation that, for Kant, we can speak of the attraction of nature.[44] This attraction, though, is not real, is premised precisely on being placed as a spectator—rather in the manner of Aristotle's cathartic theatregoers. The experience of the sublime is one of attraction and repulsion, of joy and fear (*Frohsein und Furcht*) precisely when there is no real danger, when the overpowering force of nature is not really threatening.[45] Nature—in its power and violence—is here only an *occasion* of fear and joy. In the experience of the sublime that of which one is fearful and joyful is not nature, because the experience is precisely of a purposiveness, which is not of nature. This superiority over nature is that which characterizes the feeling of the sublime. As Kant puts it: "sublimity is nothing in nature, but only in our mind, insofar as we can become conscious of being superior to nature within us and thus also to nature outside of us (insofar as it influences us)."[46] This superiority in which reason transcends toward the infinite places the human again in a movement of transcending toward, but one which aims toward that of which the source is only found in itself.

The human interest is in the finite only; only when that interest is satisfied, when as Kant says hunger is satisfied and fear stayed, can beauty in its purposelessness and the sublime in its formlessness be the object of judgment. But as interest is in existence this can only mean a transcending of existence itself. If in that case we ask as to the motivation of such transcending, Kant can in the end only answer with a moral motivation: the relation to the infinite is precisely one of respect. But it is unclear what inspires this respect in the case of the sublime: there is no object, no source of this sublimity outside of the self. The movement toward the sublime, as Kant himself says, is a movement within.

Allure and Affection

Existence is only as a movement toward; yet to move toward is to move to that which shows itself in its appearance. The movement toward is a transcendence toward a transcendent. But this movement, if it arises solely in the subject itself, can never be anything other than a movement toward images of itself. Beauty in such a view is reduced to a narcissistic projection. In this sense all idealism fails to account for beauty. This is so because beauty can only be encountered when it confronts us with its own order. As von Balthasar points out,[47] if the totality of sense is projected onto the totality of being, then being becomes necessity-to-be, and no place is left for wonder. Without wonder, though, beauty becomes a mere phantasm.

Yet we can find a way beyond that lack, which equally is a way back to the transcendental in experience, starting with the later Husserl, in particular his analysis of passive synthesis.

The stimulus or charm (*Reiz*) of the object was for Kant connected with the judgment of beauty—this rose was the object of the judgment, which rose stimulated me in some sense—but the judgment of beauty did not concern this charm or stimulus. This term—Reiz—was in Kant's time gaining currency in the fields of medicine and physiology to refer to sensation. It came to be used to designate the causal action of physical agitation by the outside world on the central nervous system. Husserl quite self-consciously gave this term a "fundamentally new sense."[48] In Husserl's sense of the term—returning to its original, non-technical meaning—'Reiz' has the sense close to the English 'allure.'[49] Of central importance here is the manner in which Husserl understands the allure of the object as that which 'awakens' consciousness. This is rooted in his understanding of affection as the "allure given to consciousness [*bewusssteinsmässiger Reiz*]."[50] The pull of this allure functions in inverse relation to the attention of the subject: it is that which draws the subject's attention toward the object. The functioning of intentional consciousness is in direct relation to its being awakened by the pull of the object. That pull is rooted in the object's allure. The object draws me to it as something, as a unity.[51] But the object draws me toward it precisely by awakening my interest.[52] This awakening is twofold: an awakening and an arousing (*weckt . . . aufweckt*). The object raises an interest in the ego which is primary and foundational to the "active interest" and "positive tendency" toward the object. In the living present, in, that is, the life of consciousness as an already synthetic consciousness in its unthematic temporal constitution of objects, objects have for consciousness a certain potential to arouse interest and attention. This arousal starts with the object itself as having affective force, even if at any particular time that force is in actuality nil.[53] It is that affective force which awakens consciousness out of unconsciousness; passively the constitutions of consciousness are already pre-structured consciously. As Husserl puts it: "Awakening is possible because the constituted sense is actually implied in background consciousness, in the non-living form that is called here unconsciousness."[54]

The passive synthesis acts by motivation, by leading from one phenomenon to the next through a calling forth of the next from that which precedes. This calling forth is of phenomena but of phenomena as directed toward the ego. The ego experiences the object as that which calls for its attention, which draws it to itself. Primordially this calling and drawing are experienced in delight. Certainly what calls forth our attention can also be that which repels us. But even such repulsion must also fascinate and attract, and hence delight (*delectare*—to entice). Only a being which awaits attraction can be called on by a phenomenon and only for such a being can a phenomenon be 'motivated.' It is here in this initial allure of the object that the interest of the ego is excited. This interest is in the object as existent. Its interest in the object as existent is not primarily in the object as this or that, but rather in the object as delightful, as enticing, as pleasing. The object as delightful is that object as it surprises me, as it comes to me. This primordial transcendence is not that of the ego, but rather of the object which draws on my desires—desires which it first awakens within me. That to which desire responds is that in the object which, prior to its conscious apprehension, is attractive, delightful.[55] The delight in the object is not reducible to its 'objective' properties; these are only subsequently analyzable by consciousness. Rather, the object presents itself as delightful, as manifesting that which is its very transcendence toward the subject and from itself. This transcendental is beauty, which precisely captures the interest of the ego, because it manifests the object as an existent.[56]

For Maritain beauty is the radiance of all transcendentals united.[57] It is so because it makes clear the inner unity of the transcendentals, namely their attractive power on existence which makes knowledge first possible. This delight in the object of experience draws the ego beyond itself into being alongside others. To be an existent is in that sense to be in relation with that which attracts. To attract is to inspire trust. Such attraction, such trust, is not for or in anything in general, but for and in this thing, this singular appearance. But this singular appearance is a manifestation of that which transcends all experience, that radiance of the being of the object. Only in piety is such a radiance responded to, because only devotion allows radiance to be. Such piety requires faith.

Faith and Piety

The responsive movement of existence as desire is faith. A slumbering existence, totally immersed in things in their exteriority, has no faith. Faith responds to that which resists the imperious gaze, but calls to be taken on trust. That which is taken on trust is in excess of worldly appearance, is the appeal of the phenomenon. Faith alone hears this appeal, sees this excess. Merleau-Ponty speaks in this respect of "perceptual faith." Such faith comes before the reasons we have for it,[58] before, that is, any appeal is made to things in their exterior being. Such faith then is not primordially a resistance to doubt, not a negation of a negation, but a fundamentally positive openness to the world. It is not an openness though to a particular world, to the world of this and that, but to the world as such. In this sense perceptual faith is irreducible to specific beliefs, it has no direct object. Rather, it is a general state of being, which responds to that in entities which is irreducible to their generalizable qualities.[59] Faith is the acceptance of the invisible as "the invisible of this world, that which inhabits this world, sustains it, renders it visible, its own and interior possibility, the Being of this being."[60] This faith is both a confidence and a leap: it is a confidence in the world, one which comes before all reflection and all reasons and as such is—seen from the point of view of reflection—a leap: an acceptance without reason, one which cannot even subsequently find its sufficient reason.

Such perceptual faith is an openness to the world as that which is attractive. The openness of such faith is a primordial trust in the world, which allows the existent to be drawn to things, drawn to people. Beauty is the original 'without why.' To ask why of beauty is already to turn away from it, already to interrogate the original being-attracted. To the extent to which philosophy begins and ends with sufficient reason it evacuates all things of beauty and makes of beauty an epiphenomenon.

This primordial perceptual faith, Merleau-Ponty tells us, does not equate with faith "in the eminent sense" (Kierkegaard), which is characteristic of Christianity. He is right to see here the place of decision as central—faith in the eminent sense is decided for. But this fact alone does *not* mean that the latter is derivative from the more primordial perceptual faith. The decision is for Christ, the figure of Christ as the figure in which existence and desire, attraction and self-giving, are manifest and coincide. There is, in short, between the aesthetic and the religious a continuity and dependence which the Kierkegaardian emphasis on the leap of faith may obscure. The continuity here is stated quite starkly by von Balthasar: "We will not know the beauty of revelation until we have loved the beauty of the world."[61]

While philosophically there can be no direct justification for the exceptionality of Christ claimed by faith in the eminent sense, no such justification is here called for. At stake rather is how faith can extend to such a claim to exceptionality and what such a claim discloses in relation to the beauty of existence. The claim to exceptionality of Christ is a claim to the exceptionality of his mission: Christ is the "anointed one," the one "sent by god." This mission requires an understanding of being as existence, that is, as outside of itself, as responding to a call beyond itself, as missionary. Faith in Christ is a faith in an existent whose being is nothing other than his mission—whose being is his existence. As such it is a faith in that which breaks into the world but which cannot be understood in terms of the world. It is a faith ultimately in a beauty which is fully present in the world but whose presence refuses in an absolute sense the temptations of worldly hierarchies: of living by bread alone, of possessing power and splendor, of living in security and protection from suffering (see Matthew 4:1–11 and Luke 4:1–13). Such refusal is the converse of an absolute giving, a total existence as being toward and of personhood as generosity. The understanding of Jesus of Nazareth as the Christ and as god is rooted in the apprehension of his life as one of total existence.[62]

Such a total existence is a revelation of itself as itself. The figure of Christ, von Balthasar argues, is one in whom there is an identity between election, vocation, and mission.[63] Such an identity is possible only for a being without beginning or end. As such existence is most clearly manifest in a being without birth and death. The coming into and going out of the world are facts of human existence, which though point not to existence as such but to the finitude of human existents. Hence, understood in terms of the phenomenality of Christ, existence is infinite, not finite. The finitude of existence is a finitude of the movement of self-giving which is, however, ultimate only for entities for whom love is limited by need. Love is experienced as desire responding to a call which itself is a call experienced by each existent, a call which singles the latter out and calls her to that to which she is sent—her existence as her mission. Such existence is based in faith as we saw, but the faith in Christ is faith not in the world, but in an existent in the world which *exemplifies* existence in a unique and complete way.[64]

This example is complete because it is one of total giving, a giving with no residue. When Christ speaks of his divinity he does so in terms of his mission: he has been sent by god. More precisely he is the sending of god, he is god as sending. To receive this sending—to respond to that sending in faith—is to receive both the Son and the Father: "He who receives you receives me, and he who receives me receives him who sent me" (Matthew 10:40). In answer to the question, "who are you?," Jesus answers: "What I say is what the father has taught me; he who sent me is with me and has not left me to myself, for I always do what pleases him" (John 8:28–29). In speaking of himself he speaks of the Father who has sent him. This being sent is not an accidental occurrence of his life, but that which identifies him: "before Abraham was, I am" (John 8:58). Hence, the being of Christ is inseparable from the being of the Father. The task given him by the Father—the task of total sacrifice for creation—is a task which is both taken up freely and which had no beginning. Freedom here is not an arbitrary choosing of an indifferent mission, but rather the constantly renewed affirmation of his own being as mission, an affirmation of self, but of self as person, that is, as being toward others. In Christ the exercise of this freedom is perfect in the sense that he never ceases to affirm his own existence. But such a task is not given as a blueprint; it is given as a mission which can only be deciphered gradually and with great effort. "But as for the day and the hour, nobody knows it, not the angels of heaven, nor the Son, no one but the father alone" (Matthew 24:36). Christ neither knows nor wishes to know the time; he wishes only to be ready for it. In this sense it is impossible to understand Christ's being except in historical terms.[65] In fact this is radically the case: if Christ is "once and for all," the historical time of his being in the world is something unique, unrepeatable, both in reverse toward a past whose inner meaning is opened up and toward a future which is laden with eschatological promise. Christ lives time as time. His being from before time does not make his temporal existence impossible, but rather is the very possibility of that temporal existence. The key here is prayer: according to the Gospels, Christ always prayed concerning his mission. To undertake a mission is to be directed beyond one's own powers and to be so directed in obedience. Temporal existence for Christ is an existence in obedience. Such obedience expresses that the mission is both not his possession and not imposed from outside, but rather that which he lives in. To live temporally in obedience is to live time as time: precisely as that which points beyond its own finitude to a time beyond mortality, a time of pure existence, of pure giving without end. In this way humiliation and exaltation are combined. Ultimately this humiliation is that of the crucifixion, but it is constitutive of the mission itself. As von Balthasar puts it, Jesus Christ identifies with what is expected of him beyond his capacity to achieve it.[66] In this is expressed in its dramatic fullness the utter tension of the 'godman'—incapacity combined with infinite capacity.

Humiliation is fundamental to the example of Christ because it indicates in suffering the insufficiency of the self and the utter futility in worldly terms of desire and existence. But the worldliness of human life—its fallenness, to use theological terms—makes the way of Christ an example which such an existent is incapable of following. This is the case firstly because the acceptance of mission is always subsequent to election and vocation, never simultaneous with them. As von Balthasar puts it: "[man's mission] was not waiting for him, ready-made in some pre-existence: it was slumbering within him like a child in its mother's womb, pressing to be delivered out of the womb of his most personal freedom."[67] This most personal freedom is a choice to affirm an existence as yet slumbering; it is an awakening of desire. But this awakening of desire is finite both in its inconstancy and its finality in death. In Christ, on the other hand, his self-expression is that of a person and nothing else. But the example of Christ is not something which can be abstracted from the actual existence of Christ, because he is precisely the exemplary existent. What this means is that as Christ is only in the Father, so the finite existent is only in Christ. Such being in Christ is a being which is insufficient in itself. This insufficiency is not a defect, but rather the wound through which existence becomes possible. To be in Christ is to no longer be of the world. It is for an existent to take itself up in terms of a task which comes from elsewhere, from nowhere within the world's hierarchies, but from that place which cuts across such hierarchies.

The temporal existence of human beings, though always pulled back to self-hood, holds within itself the possibility of elevation to personhood. Such a possibility is won in and through freedom, but not freedom as autonomy. The claim to autonomy is based on an appeal to the authority of reason against that of societal convention. Reason, though, is in each case guided by its own pretension to self-sufficiency such that again we are left with abstraction: the clearly insufficient individual human being claims its very right to existence on a sufficiency it does not have and indeed if realized would make dormant its very existence. If, though, the claim to sufficiency undermines personhood, this very personhood need not necessarily find its limit in the 'rational being,' need not be confined alone to the human but potentially in all beings to the extent to which all beings exist, if only in slumber. This is not a mere anthropomorphism; to argue otherwise is to assume what would need to be shown, namely, that only human beings can be persons. But the vision of Isaiah—"The wolf will lie down with the lamb / the panther lie down with the kid" (Isaiah 11:6)—suggests precisely a personhood, at least in animals, where they seek out each other not out of need, but out of desire. That all things might be able to exist in desire, to exist in openness toward one another, is the opposite of anthropomorphism; it sees the possibility of other forms of personhood, other ways of being toward others. Neither is this animism, which is rather a view of things as informing one another as souls as well as bodies. Rather, it is the view that nothing is excluded from the message of peace that Christ brings.[68] Salvation then is not merely individual. As Mounier says, "Christianity is the religion of collective, even cosmic salvation."[69] It is universal and at the same time always singular—a response to an always singular manifestation of universal beauty.

The mode of actualization of personhood is already prefigured in the Gospel motif of gaining and losing life: "Anyone who wants to save his life will lose it, but anyone who loses his life for my sake, will save it" (Luke 9:24).[70] To be saved it is necessary to lose possession of life. It is to practice a form of reduction: in a similar manner, Husserl tells us that in losing the life of the natural attitude we gain an infinite life of transcendental experience.[71] Such a reduction leads us back from the world of our involvements to a structure of desire, where the movement of life finds expression in the being of the person. This leads not to a solipsistic realm but to a world of being toward that which is not an object of my practical or theoretical concerns but as that which is given to me in its own self-revelation.

It is in this sense that faith is beyond reason—beyond either practical or theoretical reason (understood in Aristotelian or in Kantian terms). Faith cannot rely on reason because it sees precisely what reason cannot see, namely self-revelation. It is for this reason that the 'glorified' Christ is said, according to the accounts of the Gospels, only to have appeared to his disciples. The objection raised already in the third century CE by Celsum that surely it would have been more convincing if he appeared to those who did not believe in him—the Chief Priests, etc.—assumes that such appearance is commensurate with worldly appearance. But, as Origen points out, revelation requires eyes not of the body or the intellect, but rather of faith.[72] This is as true of the crucified Christ as it is of the 'glorified Christ.' The eyes of faith do not turn away at the humiliated body of Christ on the cross, but rather allow themselves to be seduced by that humiliation as the expression of pure self-giving. The sight of this body cannot repel the eyes of faith. This does not mean that the eyes of faith transcend the aesthetic, but rather that they *transform* the aesthetic.[73] They see beauty in the broken and forlorn and offend the Greek aesthetic profoundly—something Nietzsche saw most clearly. But this beauty must attract, must seduce. Such seduction is not of that which can be unmasked "in its stupidity as an idol";[74] but neither is it the disembodied gaze of Marion's icon.[75] The seduction is precisely of a body which discloses itself in its acceptance of complete vulnerability, a body which discloses itself in piety. It is this piety, this obedience to its mission, which faith sees through its being carried out of itself,[76] through desire. In this way existence finds itself in faith before a source of itself of which it is incapable. The only response left to it is that of praise.

The gulf between beauty and the good from Kant through to Levinas is rooted in the breakdown of the Thomistic and Bonaventuran understanding of being. Fundamental to this is the breakdown of the Thomistic understanding of analogy and the resultant gulf separating Creator and creature. This gulf is made philosophically decisive in Kant, where god is finally banished from any onto-logical constitution and can only be retrieved as a moral god. But if that moral god is dead (Nietzsche), then only on the basis of beauty can god as creator and redeemer (the Christian god) be thought. Such thought is a thought giving praise. Giving praise is a movement of emptying, in which the existent is nothing other than its being-in that from which it is freed (ab-solute). Such an absolute being is creaturehood: to be created is to be absolved, to be radically set free, yet to be precisely in and through this being set free. That which is revealed in praise is the being-in of the creature, as the singular creative being, the singular manifesta-tion of the divine love, such that praise of the thing is at once praise for it and for the singular gift of god which is manifest in it—god is disclosed in every creature as nothing other than the creature itself in its absolute distance from god.

At this point two questions become pressing. Firstly, what is the nature of the desire which finds expression in such praise? And secondly, what philosophical value can a thinking which gives praise have?

Desire: Platonic and Christian

The beauty of the cosmos leads to the intuition of its goodness. The good, beyond being, is the order of the beautiful cosmos, where the beauty of the parts is in relation to the whole. As such nothing remains hidden in the world—the light of the good reaches every crevice. The desire for beauty is propaedeutic—the ulti-mate desire is to desire no longer. So is desire understood from the phenomenol-ogy of light.

For Bonaventure beauty has two elements, those of light and of darkness, of disclosure and of hiddenness. The desire for beauty is the desire for the hidden in the apparent, for the closed in appearances. As such no object can satisfy it, because it aims at no object, but rather at the self-revelation of the entity as phe-nomenon. Desire intuits in the light of appearance the hidden source of appear-ance, and in so doing it intuits the hidden depths of its own being, its own being as person. So is desire understood from a phenomenology of darkness.

Plato's statement, "the gods do not philosophize" (*Symposium,* 204a1), is never contradicted in Greek philosophy. The gods do not philosophize because the gods are already wise. Hence, they do not *love* wisdom. But as there is noth-ing higher that can be loved than wisdom, it follows that the gods do not love. For Plato to love is to desire what is lacking. This desire is for appropriation, for becoming oneself in gaining love's object. The lover wishes to become the object of his love. Ultimately the lover wishes to be wise. Love in this understanding is an ascent, one which motivates the ascent from the cave. It is a violent desire struggling against the materiality of existence, but itself prefigured in that very materiality. It is this that allows Plato to move from that love common to everyone (*pandemos*) to the heavenly love (180–181). But this heavenly love is as much a worldly love. The word Plato uses here, *ouranous* (translated generally as 'heavenly'), can just as easily be translated as 'worldly.' This is no contradiction: the love of which Plato speaks is a love for the worldliness of the world: light, sky, the divine domain as opposed to the dark materiality of the earth.[77] This is a love, which moves upward, not downward. There is then an imitation of the divine here, but not of divine love. Love, rather, is in service of the imitation, that which makes human beings strive to imitate the divine. This structure does not merely relate to the divine: at every level from the sensual to the highest intellectual there is a relation of love with that which corresponds to the nature of the soul. The sensual soul yearns for the things of the senses, the intellectual soul for the immaterial things, ultimately for the divine. This yearning is rooted in lack, but a lack which is prefiguring: the senses lack the things of the senses, the intellect the things of the intellect. Hence, the relation of love is that between the same: for such a love there can be no stranger. Furthermore, the love of wisdom is a love of that knowledge which characterizes wisdom, the knowledge of necessary and eternal truths. Divine knowledge is of such truths, which sees beyond the contingencies of the lower earthly world to their higher necessity. To see the world through divine eyes is to see it as a world in which nothing is lacking. The striving of eros leads to the disclosing of a world in which there is no lack and hence no love. Love evaporates in knowledge/wisdom.

Desire is a desiring *of* somebody or something *by* somebody. Desire, we have said, comes after the relaxation of need. Who desires wisdom? Not the one who is wise and not the one who thinks himself wise, but the one who knows himself not to be wise. Socrates is the prototypical philosopher because he begins in ignorance. The early Socratic dialogues do not so much end in positive understanding, but in an undermining of purported knowledge. This process of undermining arises out of a realization of lack. What is lacking is knowledge; knowledge, though, is that which molds the soul. To know, for Plato, is to know the forms. But to know the forms is not to know all the forms, but rather to know that which is form-like in the forms: beauty, justice, truth—in short, unity. To know unity is to be unified, to be one. To be one is to be one with oneself. But to be one with oneself is to be one with that which one is. That which one *is* is the being of the world in its material appearance and in its ideal form. As such the desire for wisdom is a desire to be one with the object of wisdom, to be absorbed into that 'object,' to be absorbed into being. Being an individual or being human even is merely a stage—and also in part a hindrance—in the journey toward a total non-differentiation with being. As such the very rationality of Platonic philosophy leads to a mysticism of the absorption of self in being.

It is for this reason that Platonic philosophy and Greek thought generally did not develop a robust concept of the person. The personal marks a resistance to such absorption of the self, an affirmation of the self as being irreducible to a mere lack. It is in the personal that an understanding of desire irreducible to the logic of lack is possible. It is precisely such a logic which becomes articulable in Christianity.[78]

If philosophy understood Platonically is the love of wisdom, Christianity embodies the wisdom of love. Pascal expressed this in his famous statement: "The heart has reasons, which reason does not know."[79] Those reasons are the reasons of love. That which is based on sound reason is ill founded as an estimate of wisdom. This is so because wisdom is that of the lover, not of the seeker of wisdom. It is a wisdom which does not know itself, because it is orientated not to wisdom but to love. While wisdom understood as an end and an attainment once attained—impossible before death—makes desire redundant, love's own wisdom is the ever-deepening realization of desire, of desire without end. While the end of Christian desire may lie in the beatific vision, this very vision is never ending, because of the ultimate hiddenness of god. Conversely the world for god is never complete: as fallen, it is in a constant turning away and turning back to god; as redeemed, it is still in the movement of redemption.

The person experiences herself in being called.[80] Her desire is excited not by any lack in herself, but rather by an abundance, an excess, which takes her by surprise and calls her to response. Such response comes from the person, requires a capacity to respond in the person, but this capacity is for that of which the person is incapable. This is the paradox of the personal, which is glimpsed in Jerusalem, not in Athens: that the person has the capacity to strive toward that which it is fundamentally incapable of reaching. Such a striving cannot have its source in lack, because lack is prefigured by its object: the existent lacks that which it already possesses as idea. That which I already possess as idea I am capable of at least conceiving. Desire for the excessive, desire as response, reaches for that of which I have no idea, that which I in no way possess and which I can receive only through *dis*possession.

The phenomenology of desire is split here, split in the self: split on the line of potentiality. The self has potential both for that of which it is capable and for that of which it is incapable. The self as capable expresses itself as 'I can.' Its capacities have worldly correlates, and its being is contained within the order of such correlations, which in different forms we find from Plato's divided line to Husserl's correlation of noesis and noema.[81] The ego in this sense, the ego which is split in the epoché, is one pole of a correlative order, which is identical, out of which identity the ego emerges as a moment. But as person the ego is called by that for which it has no capacity, to which it cannot correlate. Within this call is a rupture out of which no identity can emerge. In its existence, in its mission, the ego as person gives itself beyond its capacities, gives itself up as a *capable* being.[82] But in doing so it gains itself as a *responsible* being. It does so because it gains itself precisely in its being toward an other, with which it can identify neither in terms of correlation nor in terms of a joint project. The call of the other to a mission is the call to live existence in a singular fashion, in a singular being toward an excess which can never be exhausted. Such an ego exists in epoché in the sense that the world is lost to it as a taken-for-granted ground. But it gains through this not a world as correlate to the capacities of consciousness, but a world in which it exists as desiring. Such existence is life in and against the world.

The problem of desire is the problem of its insatiability—the problem of the overwhelming drive beyond the context of worldly appearance toward that which speaks through and in all appearance and which lies hidden, indeed buried, resistant at the core of the apparent. The truly ingenious in Christianity, the provocation which is phenomenologically and philosophically inescapable, is its insight into the inner unity of excess in appearance which the figure of Christ represents, and its insight into the reversal of desire at the origins of appearance in agapeic love, darkly and perversely reflected in the insatiability of human desire.

The perversity of the human—its transgressive orientation beyond the natural—is a common intuition of the Platonic and Christian discourses of desire. For Plato the human soul has a "beastly and savage part" (*Republic* 9, 571c) which threatens to overcome the rest of the soul. This inner beast is to be controlled through the rational desire for wisdom, a desire which corresponds with the order of the cosmos by aiming at that which is highest before that which is lower down. Ultimately this desire replaces the desire for pleasure with that opinion which aims at what is best (see *Phaedrus*, 237d). To aim at the best is to become best by allowing for an absorption in the best. Christianity following Judaism understands human perversity in terms of sin, in terms of a turning away not alone from god, but from the destiny ordained by god for the human. This turning away from both god and his own nature means that the human is incapable of overcoming his own perversity: to overcome it would mean to be human in the true sense, but that prelapsarian state is precisely what he has rejected. The mark of this rejected state can still be found in the human, precisely in his desire which both indicates his perversity and his ultimate redemption, one however which must concern all creation.[83] The perverse mode of expression of the human is that of existence coming to itself in releasing human desire and inspiring a self-giving in answering the call of Christ.

This call is encountered "in the least of these" (Matthew 25:45). That call is a call to be in the world in response to the excessive gift of the world. It is a call to respond to the world in love as a gift of love. This is not a fleeing from the world, but rather a way of being in the world. Such a way of being is driven, relates to objects in the world as objects of drives, which reveal themselves as more than what such drives can grasp. The anxiety of animality (subjective and objective genitive) is heightened in the human, and is so already in the senses: entities affect the human *in extremis* as incarnations of the divine or as purely exterior objects of lust—all sensual affection occurs in the human on a scale which ranges from the bestial to the divine. To speak the language of Augustine, in everything we sense the possibilities of *caritas* and *cupiditas,* two possibilities which tend respectively to elevate or dissipate human bodily nature.[84] This is the predicament of an animal called by divinity. In doxological terms, this is the place of perceiving and of giving glory.

Such doxological perception is perverse in the sense that it turns away from the immediate and finite impression of the object of perception toward an infinity of meaning hidden or reflected in its depths. These infinities draw out human desire in its quest for truth, its lust for pleasure, its playful (and musical) sense for harmonies.[85] From the bliss of the concert hall to the rapture of the brothel human desire is in the infinite. The human way of being animal—the way of awakened existence—is to be without natural limit. While slumbering animal existence lives in terms of its environment, awakened human existence lives in terms of an excess which is manifest through desire.[86] To think such excess is to question the Platonic hierarchy of desire through a recognition of the manner in which the elements of such a hierarchy—matter and form, idea and image, light and dark—interpenetrate, allowing for the unexpected and explosive appearance in the immediately apparent of the uncontainable, the opaque, the blinding indecision of light and dark. Only on such a basis is a phenomenology of revelation, which gives account for glory and night in terms of unworldly light and unearthly dark, possible.

Discourse on Phenomenon

Before examining further these two phenomenologies of light and dark, the second question raised earlier needs to be addressed. This question concerns the very form of the discourse of praise being proposed here.

There are many different forms of discourse on phenomenon. Indeed, arguably all possible discourses are ultimately discourses on phenomenon, if only phenomena of the imagination. We can distinguish between the literary and the non-literary, between the prosaic and the poetical, between the lyrical and the epic, and more distinctions could be added. Phenomenology claims to be a discourse on phenomenon which is distinguishable in at least two ways: it concerns not this or that kind of phenomena but phenomenality as such, that is, the phenomenon as phenomenon; and secondly it is a *scientific* discourse concerning such phenomenality. Questions arise, however, immediately as to the compatibility of these two claims: scientific discourse is concerned not with phenomenon as such but with particular forms of phenomena. Each such science has methods appropriate to a class of phenomena and not others. A discourse or method which claims to be appropriate for all phenomena runs the danger of being nebulous and vague.

Yet, the claim cannot be that phenomenology is true of all phenomena, but rather that it is true of phenomenon as such. In other words, the phenomena of physics or of history or of psychology are specific to those domains, to those discourses, yet in none of these domains can the question be posed, let alone addressed, as to what makes such phenomena phenomena. Thus, beyond the languages of particular disciplines is a domain of which those languages are necessarily inadequate and inappropriate. In other words, beyond disciplinary languages there is a language which is governed not by the disciplinary divisions of phenomena, but rather answers to the phenomena in their phenomenality. In this respect phenomenology intersects with a central theological concern—namely, that of the difference between human and divine language. For the phenomenon to come to language as and from itself is for it to come to language before human interest, but not before human desire as that radical openness to the self-revealing of entities.

Theological discourse concerns phenomenon as revelation, as apparent in and from itself. The content of revelation forms the manner of its appearance. Theology is in that sense, as Heidegger says, the science of faith.[87] But it is so only to the extent that faith is the apprehension of appearance as revelation. Theological and philosophical discourse intersect precisely on the question of the phenomonenality of the phenomenon. The discourse on the phenomenon remains therefore uncertain as to its status and its claims. If a phenomenology of Christian life is possible, however, its discourse must be pursued as a discourse of and on revelation, as a discourse between faith and reason.[88] A phenomenology of Christian life is a phenomenology of revelation; as phenomenology it is conducted under epoché.

The language of the epoché is itself 'set out of play'; it neither affirms nor denies. To speak descriptively in the epoché is to speak without *affirming* belief in the world. Such belief—such primordial faith—is the basis of all relations with the world. To speak without affirming belief is not a cynical exercise, is not a skeptical or a sophistic double speak,[89] but rather is a return to faith, but now as philosophical faith. Husserl's constant assurance that nothing is lost through the epoché needs to be taken seriously. The world remains the same, but now the affirmation of belief, constitutive of all constative statements in the natural attitude, is shown to hide the fragile call to faith implicit in normal experience: nothing is present for me without being hidden; the hiddenness of things is constitutive of them.

Their self-giving is a giving to a consciousness which has no *imperium* over them. Such a self-giving is of that which comes to consciousness, that which claims a selfhood beyond consciousness. It is a 'self' which can never be known to consciousness with clarity and distinctness, yet is constitutive of its knowledge. The question is how that self can be said. All that can be said of it is not that self itself, but aspects, profiles of it. The singular presence of an object to consciousness is a presence which can never be made present. Nor can it be accounted for in terms of givenness itself: the singular presence of the object—this not that—is its attraction, its pull of awareness and attention. It is this which awakens consciousness. The self-givenness of the object is its being-attractive. Attention, Husserl says, "is the tendency of the ego toward an intentional object."[90] Such attention arises out of affection. It is directed toward an object, but in itself, that attention having been attracted remains unsayable in any constative statement. It comes to appearance first only through the reduction or more precisely in the performance of the reduction. The language of that performance is a language of allowance, of letting be. To perform the reduction is to let the self-appearing of the object speak itself in the words of the ego. The ego must first dispossess itself of itself for this to happen. The reduction is essentially kenotic. In its *kenosis* it is an act of radical attention. Simone Weil describes such radical attention well when she states: "Attention consists in suspending our thought, leaving it detached, empty and ready to be penetrated by the object. . . . Our thought should be . . . empty, waiting, not seeking anything, but ready to receive in its naked truth the object which is to penetrate it."[91] The language of the reduction is a language of stripping away, so that the simple being of the object be disclosed in its simplicity. It is the language of humility, one which opens to that which comes from afar—epi-phany. It is a language which performs not in order to achieve anything worldly, to bring anything about in the world, but rather to let the very worldliness of things be disclosed.

"The key to a Christian conception of studies is the realization that prayer consists of attention,"[92] according to Weil. The converse is also true, that attention consists of prayer. Attention is essentially silent. Attention breaks with the chatter of talk and listens to the phenomenon in its appearance. Such silence is prayerful in listening not alone for the phenomenon but for the mission of the silent existent's existence, which it can hear only in silence.[93] Attention is a listening both for what the object says of itself and what it says to the existent. These are one and the same: the mission of being toward is existence as desire. Desire is as such silent; yet its silence is itself a song of praise.[94] Such praise performs the reduction by allowing the singular being of the object to disclose itself, but at the same time to show itself in relation to the world. The self-disclosure of the object is a disclosure of itself and of the world as it is from the point of view of that object. Praise is a letting be revealed for me of that being of the other in its being in and toward the world.

Attention is not expectation and is not anticipation. It is rather an openness to that which is beyond what can be expected or anticipated, beyond the existent's own projections. In that sense attention is not possible without hope.[95] The discourse on phenomenon is a discourse of hope, a discourse which understands the phenomenon as bearing witness to itself and to the world. Out of such hope it lets the other speak. But such hope is possible only if there is a place from which speech can come, but which is hidden from the existent. In its prayerful openness toward that of which it speaks, phenomenology faces the day and the night, the light and the darkness of self-revelation.

2 Light and Dark

DESIRE, BEYOND NEED, articulates itself in the intersection of light and dark. Such articulation expresses the self-understanding of existence. In vocation existence understands its being-called as personal or impersonal, as self-affirmation in transcendence or as self-annihilation in immanence—as ecstasis or depression. Here, metaphysical desire conflicts with transcendent desire—desire for world with desire for that which disrupts the world. The visible glory against the glory of the invisible.

Metaphysical desire journeys from a sensual light through a certain darkness to light as its own source, a journey expressed paradigmatically in Plato's allegory of the cave. Philosophies of enlightenment find their historical starting point and their abiding topology in this allegory. It structures the relation of humanity to divinity across theistic, deistic, and atheistic understandings: Darkness as the absence of light; light as the shining forth of a central radiance.[1] Hierarchies of being, teleologies of knowledge, desire of goodness and truth all radiate around a spiraling journey toward the light: light as the source of being and of knowledge. But behind such accounts stands the figure of fire, the source of light robbed from the gods of the sky by a god of the earth (Prometheus), all-consuming, ultimately blinding, destructive of being and knowledge. In this ambivalence of light lies the anxiety of metaphysics, driving toward that which is beyond human capacity in the name of the inhuman, divine animating principle of non-earthly knowledge. The ultimate struggle of metaphysics is not between body and soul, material and immaterial, but rather between the earthly and the celestial, the soil beneath and the sky above. The human is a being of the earth but directed toward the sky; hence the human fascination with birds and flight (from Icarus to space travel) indicates its ultimate ambitions and metaphysical goals.

This metaphysical understanding of light is challenged by another account, one found in Genesis and reiterated in the Christian scriptures. Here light is understood not in terms of a focal source, but as diffuse, not in terms of hierarchies, teleologies, and the seeking of a cosmic source of goodness and truth, but rather as the opening up of meaning, the original radiance of creation, the overflowing of goodness and truth in the "least of things." Light in such a conception enlightens through dazzling, radiates through darkening, possesses by fixating. This is the light of intimacy, of the gaze, of touch and of sound. While the Platonic sun melts all things into a play of light, here the singularity of each thing stands forth and claims from us the whole world.

Metaphysical desire is desire for light and dematerialization. It is driven by a disregard for the heaviness of dark materiality. It is, however, haunted by this darkness, by a source from which desire flees in its upward motion from ignorance to truth. This source of all sense escapes all understanding because all understanding is driven toward an end which denies its own pre-conditions. Gnosticism expresses Platonism pressed to extremes, however distorting that extreme may be of the original source.

Transcendent—acosmological—desire is a desire for that which withdraws from the light of the world. It refuses the upward deflection of light, tarries with the singular existent and attends to the latter's refusal of presence. In this refusal existence finds its own incapacity, its own being moved, its own "learned ignorance" (Cusa). It seeks its own origins in the dark night where, in the silencing of the capacities of its being in the world, existence experiences itself as nothing other than desire.

This chapter will be divided into three sections. The first will outline the metaphysics of light in a reading of Plato's allegories of the cave, sun, and divided line. Following from that a supra-cosmological understanding of light based on certain scriptural passages will be introduced. The final section of this chapter will explore a 'phenomenology of darkness' and show how it leads us beyond metaphysics toward a Christian phenomenology of Christian life.

Metaphysics of Light

Light is the essence of visibility and is itself invisible. It is the invisible possibility of visibility. Yet it can destroy vision—the essence of vision and of visibility, of the sense of sight and its accomplishment, blinds. At the heart of light is darkness, is that which annuls sight. The basic experience of the unbearable light at the source of light animates Plato's allegory of the sun; the image of the sun governs his other two allegories in books 6 and 7 of the *Republic:* those of the divided line and the cave. The naked eye cannot look at the sun. It can of course *see* the sun; it sees its light and its image at the periphery of its vision. But it cannot look directly upon it; it cannot allow the sun to be at the center of its vision. The eyes of the soul, however, can (according to Plato's account) look directly at the source of light—that origin from which light flows—and can bear this excess of visibility.

The eyes of the soul see not alone that which is in the light, but light itself in its invisible source. The invisibility of light that the eyes of the body can see only at the cost of being destroyed becomes visible for the eyes of the soul. As the source of light, the sun is—understood from the logos—at the center of vision. As such the sun *can* be looked upon but only by the eyes of the soul. The metaphysics of light carries over (*meta-phorein*) to another realm precisely to the extent to which it overcomes the destructive potential of light in substituting the eyes of the body with the eyes of the soul. This thought becomes clear in Aristotle for whom *nous* is that which illuminates things (see Aristotle, *De anima*, 430a15). As for Oedipus, true sight is gained not through the eyes of the body but precisely through their destruction. The paradox is that the organ of the body through which vision is initially possible cannot bear that visibility which it receives, because all it can see is that which is precisely not of light, but rather a darkness projected by light: the shadows on the wall of the cave. The cave dwellers with the unaided vision of the eyes of the body see not even images, but rather shadows: the eyes of the body do not for Plato see light at all or even lighted things, but rather the darkening of light, the slipping away of things into darkness.

While all that which can be looked upon is of the nature of darkness, of earth, of the absence of light, becoming,[2] the being of what can be seen is that which allows them to come into the light. What can be seen is that which shares only its form, its surface, with the light. The surface of things is that which is most sun-like, that which almost slips away into light. The metaphysics of light is, in this rather precise sense, superficial. Knowledge is not a matter of delving into the depths of things, but rather turning toward that to which they deflect vision, namely, the light in and through which they come to be there for us to know.

Plato's Allegories of Light

Fundamental to the metaphysics of light are Plato's three allegories of the sun, the divided line, and the cave, respectively. These allegories are crucial in summing up the middle Plato and in setting the context for much of the imagery and conception of the metaphysical journey, its goals and its desires, within Antiquity and within Christian (especially mystical) thought. These allegories form the topographical context for all philosophies of enlightenment—in the West, at least.

THE ALLEGORY OF THE CAVE

The allegory of the cave is an allegory of desire. It is not by accident that Plato chooses an allegory—a fanciful, imaginary tale—to express the movement of desire. Desire fails through its tendency to cling to particular entities; nothing in the realm of the senses alone can move it from this tendency. The sensual movement needs to be disrupted and is so only by departing from its order—the order of the literal, the obvious—to another order, which is not simply fictive but which claims to reveal the truth of the literal. This is achieved allegorically, by engaging in another discourse, producing another and strange agora (allegory: from *agore-uein*—*agora*) in which the order of sensory experience is uncovered.

On hearing the strange account of the cave, people fettered such that they could look only ahead of themselves, toward shadows thrown by a fire above them, Socrates' interlocutor can only exclaim—and in doing so speaks for us the readers, too—that this is a peculiar scene, literally, an image of no place—*atopos eikona* (*Republic*, 515a2). Socrates' response is crushing: The people in this scene are, he says, "like us" (515a3). Here very subtly we the readers of the story are being led to at once identify ourselves with the prisoners and to observe them as odd, unknown, fanciful entities. In listening to the story we are placed precisely where the prisoners cannot be—namely, that place from which the whole scene is apparent. But to the extent to which we identify with the prisoners we are understanding ourselves as being ignorant of the reality of our situation. If we resist the identification, Socrates is suggesting we merely prove all the more to be the prisoners he is depicting; if we accept the identification, then in that acceptance we distinguish ourselves from the prisoners in recognizing our situation as it is. Either way we are caught between identification and estrangement. This metaphysical tale introduces a bifurcation in the self. This tale does not simply illustrate an unseen aspect of our lives or invite us to draw analogies between our lives and an account of beings of a different kind (a fox or a lion, for example, in one of Aesop's tales). Rather, it introduces a break, indeed a rupture, between ourselves as readers of the story and ourselves as the story's protagonists. Its efficacy—one might even say its therapeutic efficacy—is based on that rupture and on the movements of identification, which take place across it.

Nevertheless, it is clear that even accepting this strategy of the story, the allegory is selective, not to say restrictive. No mention is made of the sense of touch, and while Plato does refer to sounds—the speaking of those carrying the images (*Republic*, 515b4)—this reference seems somewhat out of place: unless those people could throw their voice, presumably the prisoners would recognize that the sound came from above them, not in front of them. No such problems arise with the sense of sight, which indicates the cave allegory centers around the latter.

The contrast between touch and sight might indicate some of the issues here. Aristotle in *De Anima* states that the tactile sense is not moved *through* the medium, but rather *with* it.[3] In the case of the tactile senses the medium is moved *simultaneously* with the sense of touch. While in the sense of sight the movement of the medium—light—is first moved and through it the object becomes present to sight, in the case of touch its medium—flesh—is only affected when and for the duration that something is touched. The priority which light has over sight, the difference in causal order which is manifest here, is lacking in the case of touch.

The sense of sight operates through predication: I do not see qualities but rather things bearing qualities. My sense of sight is discrete; its knowledge of qualities is mediated. One consequence of this is that the sense of sight lends itself to likeness and representation in a manner in which the sense of touch does not. In touching a hard surface I sense the quality of hardness. That sensed hardness is like or unlike another sensed hardness, but is so on a scale of increasing and decreasing hardness. For the sense of touch there is no difference between real and a likeness of the real; there are gradations of qualities each as real as the next. Nor can one touched quality represent another. Because of the simultaneity of touch there is no room for images, which mediate a prior reality. The very basis of likeness and representation, the very basis for the allegory in the first place, is visual rather than tactile; and it is on the sense of sight divorced from touch that the difference of truth and illusion, real and non-real, is based and so too the hierarchies of being which derive from that difference.[4]

The prisoners are "like us" then apparently only in a restricted sense: they are like us insofar as we are *viewers* of the world and it is as viewers of the world that the question Socrates poses of these prisoners makes sense: "if they [the prisoners] were able to talk to each other, would they not suppose that the names they used applied to the things passing before them?" (*Republic*, 515b4). We can see here finally that this allegory is not supposed to be comprehensive, that Plato is singling out one particular activity for human beings, one particular way of experiencing entities as fundamental. That activity is the activity of naming; the way of experiencing is of seeing entities as such. Again a restriction is operative here. Language is mostly not about naming things at all, it is about commanding, pleading, asking, promising, etc. Naming, however, brings to linguistic expression the experience of the prisoners: uttering words not to act upon the world, not to act upon their colleagues, but simply to give articulation to pre-given realities. In using the word 'tree' the prisoners mean that a certain thing *is* a tree and the implication of this is brought out in the next line: "for the prisoners the shadows would be nothing other than the truth, the real (*alethes*)" (515b5). The name carries ontological weight: to name something a 'tree' is to state that thing *to be* a tree. If anyone wanted to know what a tree was, they would only have to have that thing pointed out to them. What appears to them as a tree, is, however—seen from the point of view of the one watching the whole scene—not a tree at all but rather the shadow of the manufactured image of a tree.

Socrates asks his interlocutor—and us for whom he stands—to imagine what it would be like for the prisoners to be released from their bonds and healed of their ignorance. Again the irony is that he is asking us to imagine what this would be like for those who are "like us." Again we are placed in the double position of being at once those in bonds and those placed outside this bondage. The relation of ignorance and bondage here is important: their bonds are their ignorance and they are ignorant of their bonds. Bondage is a matter of lack of knowledge, because bondage is delusion about their own reality. Release from this delusion, this bondage, is a form of liberation, but it is striking that Plato speaks of release and compulsion in the same breath: "When one was released from his fetters and compelled to stand up and turn his head" (515c4). The need for compulsion here is revealing: nothing in the shadows alone—nothing in the sensual world of shadows—will bring the prisoner to understand that they are shadows.[5] He needs to gain an insight into what a shadow is in the sense of the cave and that would only be possible if he transcended the world of shadows. There is nothing in the world of shadows alone which would motivate such a movement of transcending. Such transcending is a conversion, in the literal sense of a turning around toward that which is behind their backs. It is not that there are no good reasons for such a conversion, but the cave dweller is impervious to such reasons. He is impervious because he in engrossed in the shapes he sees, which amuse him.

The release is experienced as something acting upon the prisoner, disrupting his life and producing a rupture with his past. This rupture—correlating with that in the reader between her understanding of the allegory and her identification with the prisoner—does not happen gradually but rather all of a sudden, *exaiphnes*. In the famous discussion in the *Parmenides* Plato describes the *exaiphnes* as "this queer thing . . . situated between the motion and the rest, it occupies no time at all" (*Parmenides*, 156d6), an "instantaneous transition" (156e3). There is nothing in the past experience of the prisoner which can explain this transition of release. Something outside of his experience, something unprecedented, effects the break which is his release. He is compelled in the sense that something comes from outside him without waiting to be acknowledged by him, but rather with a force which would have appeared almost as the force of necessity (indeed the word translated as 'compulsion' is *anakazoito* in Greek, which comes from *anake* meaning 'necessity'). But this cannot be an alien force; otherwise its liberating potential would be unaccountable. On the contrary, it is a force which leads the prisoners back to themselves. In knowing only shadows they as knowers are only shadows of themselves. But to know themselves as shadows requires a form of knowing which only release from the land of shadows can effect.

The most immediate consequence of this release is pain. Release is something the prisoner suffers. This suffering makes him aware of seeing as never before. But he is aware of it not in its keenness—something which he could have tested on the shadows—but precisely in its blindness. He would be too dazzled to see the objects properly. The capacity to see varies in relation to the light; it is under the command of light. The sight of the prisoner is not a steady capacity, but rather has to adapt to the light and the object to be seen. Such adaptation can be painful and requires time. In his state of confusion, however, the prisoner is not given such time. Socrates asks, what would happen if the prisoner was told that all he had seen before was just nonsense and that he was now "nearer truth and reality" and "seeing more correctly" (*Republic,* 515d4), and replies that the prisoner would probably think that what he used to see was "far truer or more real" (515d8). Through this first attempt at liberation the prisoner now thinks in comparative terms between two levels of reality. He understands that there are degrees of closeness and distance from reality and truth. His belief about the relative degrees of truth and reality is false, but at least he thinks now in terms of *degrees* of truth and reality. To think in these terms is already to think in terms of light: things appear more or less strongly in the medium of light; the overpowering light of the fire makes them appear less strongly; the prisoner is yet to realize that this is because of an undeveloped capacity of sight in him.

While in describing the first attempt at liberation Plato speaks of compulsion, the prisoner's second attempted liberation is described in terms of him being dragged by force or violently (*bia*) (*Republic,* 515e6). This time he is taken out of the cave. While in the cave he is dazzled and fearful, far from being grateful for being taken out of the cave he is angry (*aganaktein*) (516a2). His anger is directed against the strange and the unknown, against that which is beyond the threshold of his knowledge as cave dweller. Slowly, he is being brought to realize himself as a cave dweller, as having been living in the *under*world, while believing himself to be in the world. If the first compelled release had been sudden, now he cannot at first see the things of the upper world (516a5). Such knowledge requires habituation, habituation to the upper world, that is to a world freed from the confines of the cave, a world of light not of shadows, which is to say a world which *is* a world, not a cave which is under the earth. What is true under the earth is relative to the conditions that apply there. To see the fire and the images would be to be nearer the truth and the real than to see only the shadows. But the prisoner does not actually see these, although he is directed toward them. His habituation to seeing occurs when he is released from the relative truths of the cave into the absolute truths of the upper world. In the upper world—the only real world, not the subterranean space of his former dwelling—he is absolved from the cave. In this world there is a clear hierarchy of truth in which reflections and the reality they represent are clearly distinguished and known. The movement here is from the reflections of things to the things themselves. He becomes habituated to looking upon human beings and other objects in their self-identity, as they are in themselves. The description becomes more and more disembodied. There is no more mention of the earthly pain. The ascent out of the cave is matched by an ascent of sight from the earth to the sky. Sight is directed increasingly at the heavens—*ouranos*: the opening in which things appear, the light which is penetrable without effort, the realm of sight, the opposite of the obscurity of the earth. What is occurs only because there is an opening in which it can appear. Similarly, what is known is only known because there is light to see. Being and knowing are tied to one another. This notion receives its ultimate confirmation in the figure of the sun.

Before the prisoner can gaze at the sun, however, he has to make his way up the hierarchy—a hierarchy of absolved reflection—of heavenly bodies understood on the basis of sky, the realm of light in which things come to be. These though are not the ultimate source of light. The last thing he would be able to do rising up this hierarchy is look directly at the sun itself, the self-identical sun, not any reflection of the sun. The sun is viewed through the medium of light, but the sun is the true source of light; hence seeing the sun through light is seeing it through itself.

Seeing the sun is not an end in itself. There is much debate as to why the liberated prisoner would return to the cave, but it is not always recognized that his return to the cave actually starts in his response to the sun. While at first he "gaze[s] at the sun" (*Republic*, 516b4), he soon begins to infer and conclude: what he has seen deepens his knowledge, correcting the mistaken notions of the cave dwellers (again this reflects the more schematic discussion in the allegory of the divided line). The sun, he concludes, is "responsible for everything that he and his fellow-prisoners used to see" (516c1). Almost immediately on looking directly at the sun, on seeing the sun as the first principle of all that is in the visible world, his thoughts return to the cave dwellers. In this he demonstrates that despite the severe ruptures, compulsion, and violence of his ascent from the cave, studied retrospectively a clear continuity can be seen between his concerns and those of his erstwhile colleagues. He has found wisdom and that wisdom reminds him (in a kind of reverse of the movement of anamnesis outlined in the *Phaedo* and the *Meno*) of the *apparent* wisdom of the cave. The journey from the cave only makes sense if the return is made; only that return confirms the relevance of the discoveries made in the upper world to the cave. Without that relevance the journey from the cave becomes a mere idiosyncrasy or a seeking after another world.

ALLEGORY OF THE SUN

The allegory of the cave concretizes the previous two allegories, those of the sun and the divided line. In each the metaphysical movement from the visible to the invisible is understood as a movement of light, a movement from darkness to light: a movement of enlightenment. But this movement is as much from light to light, from a light of the senses to a light of the intellect. This movement gives rise to difference, forges difference in its wake. Light distinguishes visible and invisible. The identity of light is the identity in this difference and as such governs the relation of resemblance fundamental to Plato's account. The allegories are governed by the relation of resemblance, and Plato makes this quite plain in introducing the allegory of the sun. He is attempting to explain the good and admits that any "direct" attempt would be beyond the "impulse that wings my flight today" (506e2). Instead he offers a resemblance of the good. The allegory is a resemblance of a resemblance, i.e., an image of a relation which is itself an image. The image of the sun resembles the relation of resemblance between the resemblance and that which it resembles.

The allegory of the sun begins with a reference back to a distinction worked out in book 5 of the *Republic* between beautiful things and beauty in itself. The centrality of light here—indeed of day and night—is made clear by Socrates when he states that the man who recognizes the existence of beautiful things but does not believe in beauty itself is dreaming (*Republic*, 476c3). To dream is to be confused between a resemblance and the reality which it resembles. Dreaming is nocturnal sight, the sight of one who does not see the sun, who sees without seeing distinctions. What such a man fails to see is the difference between the real thing and that which resembles it. It is not that he fails to see beauty: by the very fact that he recognizes beautiful things he must see beauty. But he fails to perceive the beautiful things as anything other than themselves. In the beautiful things there is an excess of what can be seen. Yet this excess is not immediately visible. Only thought can reach such an excess of sight. Dreams remain tied not alone to the senses but also to the desires tied to the senses (cf. 571e) and such desire hinders any transcending, any movement beyond the immediately perceivable beautiful things. The sight which characterizes such an immanent seeing is a darkened sight, the sight of dreams. Yet, of course, the sight so characterized is normal sight, the sight of normal perception. Metaphysics begins in showing that what we take for sight is not true sight. What we see is not an illusion, it simply consists of resemblances which we do not *understand* as resemblances. The task of thought is to follow the movement which leads from resemblance to that which resemblance represents.

This movement takes place within sight itself for Plato. In any seeing what we see is that of the thing which is facing us, its aspect, in Greek: *idea*. How then, on the basis of what shows itself to us, can we see something as it really is? How does reality appear to us? That there is such a reality is suggested by the words we use—the names referred to in the cave allegory. Aspects *of* a thing are ways of appearing of that *same* thing. What is the mode of appearance of that sameness, the aspect of the same? That aspect of the same is that which unifies, which gathers together the different aspects apparent to sight. One name—in Plato—for such unity is beauty. Beauty is the inner harmony gathering together and holding together the reality of the things in its appearance. This inner unity cannot be seen, it can only be thought. But sight is not indifferent to the thought of this unity. On the contrary, sight depends on it; only because this unity can be thought, can things be seen. Even the dream-state is one in which things come to sight; only the understanding of what such coming to sight consists in is lacking. It is for this reason that Socrates, having established that unity is a matter of thought and not sight, continues to discuss sight. The idea of the good, the idea of the idea, that aspect of anything in which that thing appears as it is, must be approached through that which resembles it and which is not indifferent to it, namely sight.

Necessary for sight is a third element between the seeing and seen. This third element, Socrates says, is "what *you call* light" (*Republic*, 507e3, emphasis mine). Calling the medium of sight light is to say more than one knows. It is to name that which appears as the binding of the sense of sight and the power of being visible (*horasthai dunamis*) of things. It binds two powers, two capacities of seeing and of being seen, capacities, however, which only become actual, only show themselves, in their true aspect (*idea*) in the light (507e5–508a2). Socrates asks, which of the gods of the heavens (*ourano theon*) is responsible for this? He seeks to localize the source of light in a supreme divinity, one which gives rise to something most precious (508a1). Light is to be understood in terms of its source, in terms of its origins. That source is the sun. Apollo the Sun god is the god of Delphi: the source of Socrates' mission. Here he returns to the source of his inspiration, the source of that impulse, which may or may not be in full flight. In locating the source of light in the sun Plato is locating the ordering principle of the cosmos in the movement of light. It is this movement of light in relation to its origin and source that Plato goes on to discuss.

This relation is one of cause (*aitios*). The sun is the cause of sight. Cause is being understood here in terms of resemblance: the eye is the most sun-like of all sense organs (*Republic*, 508b3). Its being resides in its resemblance to the sun. This is not a particular kind of resemblance, but rather all other relations of resemblance find their model here. The good "bears the same relation to sight and visible objects in the visible realm that the good bears to thought (*nous*) and the objects of thought" (508c1). Without the sun not only would there be no light in which to see, there would also be no power of sight in the eyes with which to see. The sun is the source of all three elements of seeing: sense of sight, visible objects, and light. It is that which holds all these together, which makes them possible. It is this place of the sun—this place of origin of being and knowledge—which shows its parentage: "the child of the good" (508b8).

As is illustrated in the cave allegory, Plato thinks the relations of light in terms of a hierarchy of being. Moonlight and starlight are lower realms of light; they illuminate only dimly (516b1). Sunlight, on the other hand, is that which gives clarity to vision. While the moon gives light which allows both the sense of sight and the object to be, the vision which results is a dim one. This is the world of night, a darkened world in which nothing can be seen distinctly. On the level of eyesight the difference between the bright illumination of the sun and the dim light of the moon, the difference between day and night, reflects a difference on the level of thought. Thought knows a similar difference and does so because its relations to things resemble that of the eye. So much so in fact that Plato understands thought in terms of sight, the directedness of thought in terms of an eye of the mind. "That which gives the objects of knowledge their truth and the knower's mind the power of knowing is the aspect (*idea*) of the good" (508e1–2). The good is that which gathers things together; the power of knowing is that which allows things to be in their self-disclosure to thought. The good is more beautiful than what it gathers together, because it is that which gives the vision of knowledge its inner unity. The good is the source of that reality, the source of that self-identity which is disclosed to the eye of the mind through the invisible light of the good. As such a source, it is itself beyond being and transcends being in power and dignity (509b10).

The good is not here understood as beyond the world, nor as other than the world of sight. On the contrary, Plato is claiming that the good is not an entity like any other in the world, but rather is that which allows all entities to be and to be known, that which provides the unity necessary for any entity to be what it is—to be identical with itself and hence to be knowable. The good is the ultimate principle of the world, the principle which lies at the basis of the world. Nothing could *be*, and nothing could be *known*, if it were not for the good. All knowledge is of entities in their goodness, and the goodness of entities is their place in the cosmos. The being of entities is their being as entities, which are in the world and are as such entities in a hierarchy of being. This becomes clear when Socrates is urged to complete the allegory of the sun (509c3) and he does so by outlining a new, supplementary allegory, that of the divided line. This allegory is introduced to make sense of the order of appearances in the world.[6]

ALLEGORY OF THE DIVIDED LINE

The relation of resemblance between the good and the sun is that between two triangular relations of correspondence between, on the one hand, the truth, the real object, and the knowing thought, and, on the other, light, the visible object, and sight. The allegory of the divided line now systematizes these relations in terms of two unequal rectangles, those of the realm of thought and those of the realm of sense. Both are understood in terms of visibility: the visible realm disclosing the invisible which it resembles. The invisible realm of thought resembles that of the visible realm of sense in the structure of relation between the enabling medium (truth, light) which discloses, the capacity for perception (intellectual, sensual), and the aspect of the object which is disclosed. These are not separate realms, but rather two inseparable sides of reality: that of sensible appearance and that of self-identity.

The intelligible, invisible reality of things is that which can be known— knowledge (*epistēme*); the visible realm is that of which there can only be opinions (*doxa*) (*Republic*, 509d4–510a1). That of which there can be knowledge cannot be otherwise: knowledge is of the necessary. Of that which is necessary there can be no opinions, there can only be knowledge or falsity. Opinion is of the contingent; it may hit the mark but only by being true to the way the object happens to appear to sensual vision at any particular time. The hierarchy between knowledge and opinion is one of degrees of reality. Both can be arrived at by two different forms of activity of the soul or mind, respectively (*psyche*): thought proper (*noeisis*) and mathematical reasoning (*dianoia*) on the one hand, and belief (*pistis*) and imagination (*eikasia*), on the other. Each form of activity corresponds in kind to the degree of reality with which it is dealing. Thinking is concerned with things as they show themselves in themselves—the forms (*eidos*). Things can be thought about in two distinct ways, either by reasoning from these forms, making assumptions (*hupethesesi*) regarding them (511b3), or in reverse, by moving toward a first principle (*arché anupothetos*) (511b4). The former manner of reasoning uses the form as an image, that is, as an object of belief, while the latter remains within the realm of the invisible and thinks from the form back to that from which it receives its being, the good. To think the forms as they are is to think them in terms of the first principle; to think the objects of sense as they are is to think them in terms of belief.

For Plato we are speaking here of four affections (*pathemata*) of the soul (*Republic*, 511d8): capacities of the soul to be *affected* by reality. All these activities of the soul are responses to being affected by different modes of reality, different degrees of being. In each case the soul must be attuned to that which affects it. Error occurs when the soul mistakes one mode of reality for another. Shadows and images are properly perceived by the act of imagining (*eikasia*); objects of sense are properly perceived by belief. The forms are perceived in their function as steps in a process of reasoning by the mathematical reasoning and in themselves by philosophical thought. To mix up these levels, to think, for example, of the objects of belief as the things themselves is to fail to correspond correctly to the mode of reality with which one is dealing. The education of the soul is an education in degrees of affectivity. But such affection is being directed toward that which can be named truthfully, that which appears in the light in such a way that it appears in varying degrees of clarity.

Light Allegories, Worldliness, and Babel

From Pseudo-Dionysius down until today the Platonic allegories of the cave and the sun have been employed by Christian thinkers. Revealingly, the allegory of the divided line has been less used. In purely Platonic terms there is here an incoherency: all three allegories hang together. In Christian terms, however, there are three fundamental reasons why the divided line allegory is not discussed. Most obviously, while for Plato belief (*pistis*) is a lower form of knowledge related to the senses, from Paul onward it names the way in which 'knowledge' of god in his truth is first possible.[7] Secondly, the structure of the divided line is one of correlation or correspondence between the nature of the object of knowledge/apprehension and the faculties of the soul. In Christian terms this denies the efficacy of infused grace, without which both faith and the very notion of revelation become incoherent. In other words, the Platonic schema assumes a correspondence between the nature of reality known and the unaided capacity of knowing self, and as such allows no place for divine agency in the Judeo-Christian sense. Lastly, implicit in the divided line is a hierarchical movement from body to mind, which is a movement ultimately away from embodiment. In Christian terms, not alone are the objects of the senses themselves creatures of god, but god himself became flesh, became an embodied, sensible being—in a Christian sense both sides of the line must relate to the corporeal.

It is nonetheless true that the motifs of journey, ascent, struggle, illusion, and enlightenment recommended the allegory of the cave to the Christian mystical tradition. Mysticism is not itself specific to Christianity, but rather takes up a certain oriental approach to the divine, which at the time of the rise of Christianity was growing in influence. The emphasis here is on a communication with the divine in which mysteries at the core of reality are revealed. As such the motif is one of journey from ignorance to enlightenment. Plato's allegory of the cave then is read in terms of the movement of liberation, from darkness to light. For Pseudo-Dionysius this movement was a movement up the hierarchy of being toward god. In this he takes up a neo-Platonic motif of a 'chain of being.'[8] The journey from the cave is a journey up a causal chain to god: a being is nearer to god and more divine the more closely it participates in the all giving—hence all causing—god. The epistemological and ontological issues are here closely connected: the object of knowledge is being; that which is closer to god has a higher degree of being. Hence, all knowledge ultimately is knowledge of god; the journey to god is a journey of knowing. Pseudo-Dionysius was faced, however, with a basic problem: the Christian notion of creation, which was at his time (fourth century CE) being formulated in Christological terms, denied any intermediary between god and creature, as every creature is related directly to the divine act of gratuitous creation.[9] He resolves this problem by saying that there is a hierarchy of beings from the point of view of creatures, but not from the point of view of god.[10] Hence, the cave allegory expresses the limited view of creatures and allows creatures to reach god by means of a ladder which in god's eyes does not exist. We cannot know god as he knows himself, but only in terms of the order of all being. But implicit here is a chasm between divine wisdom and human wisdom, in terms of which 'unaided' human wisdom remains a worldly wisdom, but one which recognizes its limits in reference to god, because god is transcendent of the world. The desire for god is manifest in the journey of knowing.

Following Pseudo-Dionysius there is a rich tradition of appropriation of the cave allegory. But fundamental difficulties in the very attempt at such an appropriation cannot be ignored. These difficulties come most strongly to light when one reads the cave allegory in the light of that of the divided line, as Plato intended. In a famous passage Paul states:

> Do you not see how God has shown up human wisdom as folly? Since in the wisdom of God the world was unable to recognize God through wisdom, it was God's pleasure to save believers through the folly of the gospel. While . . . the Greeks look for wisdom, we are preaching a crucified Christ: . . . to the Gentiles foolishness. (1 Corinthians 1:21–24)

The seeking after wisdom will never make sense of Paul's proclamation of the good news, "a crucified Christ," a savior who suffered shameful execution; philo-sophy will not aid, but rather hinder understanding. This is so because philosophy remains tied to the world, a world which did not recognize Christ. The allegory of the divided line—along with those of the sun and cave—is of the world. It is so because it produces in schematic form the terms of worldly relations: the correspondence of levels of reality of things of the world and the modes of apprehension of them by perceivers in the world. The underlying erotics of compulsion in the movement out of the cave is made problematic by the injunction not to seek wisdom, but to answer the call of god, a call that is without force or violence (1 Corinthians 1:26); but more fundamentally, the place of faith in Paul's account subverts the logic of the divided line.

What cannot be understood by human, worldly wisdom can only be accepted on faith (pistis), i.e., through a trust that god's promises will be fulfilled. In this vein, Abraham is the example of faith (cf. Romans 4:1–5). The faith Paul proclaims though is in Jesus Christ as the fulfillment of god's promise. Such faith is a response to revelation, that is, to the self-giving of god in a manner which could not be predicted nor fully understood, in an event which had no necessity but which sprung from divine love. Furthermore, it was an event in the world, the event of the bodily presence of god in human form. If Christ was necessary, if his coming could not have been otherwise, then his coming would not have had the sense of revelation. Nor on the basis of any assumption could his coming be deduced. His coming was a contingent event, one which could be denied, one to which unaided reason—reason without revelation—is blind. In this sense there are good Platonic reasons, in terms of the hierarchy of light, to conceive of that coming as a matter of belief. Yet, by placing this coming, this event, as the highest of things, the Platonic hierarchy is not simply inverted; the very basis of the allegories is undone. Not alone is pistis placed above noiesis, but by the same token doxa is placed above epistēme. The necessary unchanging reality which forms the object of knowledge, that reality which for Plato ultimately characterizes the cosmos—the beautiful order—is now a distraction from the highest reality and the highest knowledge, which appears in the world, but is not of the world. This dovetails very well with the transformation of the meaning of doxa already effected by the Septuagint translators of the Hebrew scriptures: doxa as glory. That will be the theme of the next chapter. For now what is important is that the divided line is disrupted not by a simple re-evaluation of knowledge, a placing of the knowledge of the contingent above that of the necessary—the practical above the theoretical—but rather by the recognition of an event which cannot be placed within the order of correlation fundamental to the divided line. That event calls for a response which transforms pistis from belief in objects of the sensible world to faith in unworldly events within the sensible world. The response of faith cannot be located upon the divided line, but undercuts its basic assumptions—assumptions operative in the other two allegories as well.[11]

Another allegory expresses such an event and opens the possibility of a turning away from the light of the world toward a certain form of a cavernous existence within the darkness of incomprehension and confusion: the story of the tower of Babel.[12] The story of Babel in Genesis is, like the cave allegory, a story of earth and sky, of desire and confusion, of darkness and light. But here the earthly desire for the sky is confronted with another desire, a desire from above, but one seeking an earthly response. The story comes in chapter 11 of Genesis where the Yahwist writer is attempting to explain the dispersal of humanity into various groups. While initially this dispersal is described in terms of a blessing by the Priestly writer (Genesis 9:1), the conflict between peoples calls for a more sinister account. Significantly, the dispersal of peoples is not for either writer to be explained by an immanent cause: "the whole world [left to itself] spoke the same language, with the same vocabulary" (11:1). Yet the fear of dispersal in the narrative is very real, and in response to that fear the people begin to build for themselves a city. Both spatial and temporal dispersion is in question here: by building a city they would remain together protected behind its ramparts; by making something great their trace would remain into the future—fame and glory (doxa): they would be spoken of as one, united in the name which their common work would bear. The tower would bind them not alone to the earth, but also to heaven. The world would revolve around their city which united not alone humanity, but also heaven and earth.

Already in the fear of dispersal is an anxiety of incapacity; the protection the people seek is a protection against transience, a protection against the ruin of time and space without trace. Their reaction to such incapacity is one of self-assertion, a self-assertion which is indissolvably tied to language, or more specifically to speech—to words spoken and words understood. The purpose of the tower was not so much to reach the sky;[13] rather, the people said to themselves: "Let us make a name for ourselves, so that we do not get scattered all over the earth" (11:4). 'Name' refers to character and reputation.[14] To make a name for themselves is to have their name spoken and in so doing maintain themselves in memory but as present, as a presence. The tower is that presence, made of the earth, but transformed by a strange alchemy—bricks from stone, mortar from bitumen—to be of the sky. In this the double aspect of language is reflected and brought to breaking point: of the earth, but free and sky-like. But language is here not manifest in the act of naming, the act of referential general terms, as it is for Plato. When they speak what issues is not truth in that sense, but rather, in speaking they command, plan, plot: "let us make," "let us build."[15] The inner secret of language here is speaking in such a way that understanding is possible not about the world as such, but as a project, an undertaking, which unites. This same language is the language of understanding, of making oneself understood, even when what one is saying is 'wicked.'

What is this wickedness, this offense which the tower represents? Certainly there is underlying this text a certain condemnation of urban civilization, a civilization seen to derive from Cain. But it is not the city as such which is at issue here, but the relation to language underlying the city: language as closed to the strange, as centered on the same: the same meaning which makes comprehension and unity possible. The tongue makes possible the oneness of humanity and excludes all which lies outside it. The tower uniting sky and earth was a tower which made world possible, a tower which articulated sky and earth under the oneness of the one sun.

This oneness is interrupted by a foreign desire and a foreign voice. Yahweh comes down to see the tower. He comes from elsewhere, he comes downward toward the city. He comes from beyond any horizon of the language of the earth in order to disrupt the earthly relation to language. "Now nothing they plan to do will be beyond them" (Genesis 11:6). They speak to plan; they speak to control. The response of god is not to stop their speech, not in fact to curb their tongue at all, but to make the sounds of their tongues incomprehensible to each other. God responds by acting to "confuse their language . . . , so that they cannot understand one another" (11:7). God does not destroy the tower itself, rather he dissolves their words and their project. The tower has no meaning without language which constitutes the common project. In Greek terms the people become barbarians to one another: their words are no longer meaningful articulations, but sound as inarticulate sounds—bar, bar. What is striking though is that the origin of languages, of diverse and meaningful languages is in this barbarism, this condemnation to barbarism. There is in this account no logos, no one and true language. The language prior to Babel is one which aims at wickedness; post-Babel are languages which must remain unfulfilled, whose movement toward each other is always thwarted. Without comprehension, the words of the other become opaque, but are not themselves meaningless. The diversity of peoples is a diversity of tongues and as such a diversity of meanings: what is meaningless babble to the other is meaningful to the native speaker. Through this confusion of meaning born not out of a lack of meaning, but precisely out of its excess, arose the diversity of peoples. This diversity Plato and the Greeks generally made little attempt to comprehend, relying on the lazy category of 'barbarian.' But once diversity is given account the issue of translation becomes unavoidable, the issue that is of the venture from the same into the strange. It is not by accident that only a few verses later the Yahwist gives account of the tongue of god and the response of Abram and that the command of god is one of translation from the familiar to the foreign: "Leave your country, your kindred and your father's house for a country I will show you" (12:1). That which disrupted worldly unity, the unity of command and plan, now calls for a renewed journey, but not this time one from earth to sky, but from familiar (the same)—county, kin, father—to the strange. This journey into the strange, not the closed discourse of the tower, will make Abram's name famous. Here the glory of Abram is not one of a name which binds the sky to the earth in a bound world, but rather one of obedience and response, both of which are based in faith. Such faith is an openness to the strange, to truth as the appearance from elsewhere—epi-phany—which precisely sounds in the mother-tongue as meaningless and inhuman sound, but which through a labor of translation becomes not more intelligible, but deepens its unintelligibility. In this way the relation to language is transformed into a relation not to that which is comprehensible, but that which I precisely cannot understand but which calls to me as a sense closer to me than all that is intelligible.

But this call is from a tongue which calls things by their own names. As Benjamin points out,[16] in the Genesis narrative of creation only the human is not named by god; the human names himself (as male, but as male only in naming the female first). In this sense the human is created in language not by language; the human essence is linguistic. But that very essence—so the message of the Babel story—is split, is divided, and is so due to the human denial of desire for the other, his degradation of language to a means of control and manipulation. The language of things is the appeal things make to us, an appeal which is responded to in the act of naming. But the act of naming is not propositional. It does not take the form, 'this is a tree,' but rather the form 'behold tree.' It names things with names proper to them. It names that which is as it manifests itself to be what it is. This self-manifestation is a making appear of the creative origins to which it owes its own existence. In its self-manifestation it gives itself not simply as brute presence, but as standing forth in the world, as that which gives itself to meaningful utterance.

The language of Babel is already a language of manipulation, a language which no longer attends to things. The Babel story suggests that the diversity of languages arises out of the failure of human language to attend to things, out of a turning away from things. In that turning away the world appears in its sad, mute silence.[17] This silence lies at the core of language in its diversity, where meaning arises not in the words but between them, as if the inner presence of things must remain always elusive. Yet, it is in this space of silence that expression is possible as the opening toward the other, as the addressee of my words.[18] But that movement toward the other is a movement from silence to silence: the content of my words fall short; only the gesture of my saying, the movement of estrangement expresses a desire to which the other can respond. After Babel the turning back to god occurs in the turning toward the other in the movement of translation, a movement which seeks its fulfillment not teleologically in its own products, but in its own absolute dispossession, in the speechlessness of ultimate untranslatability. This is a movement not as in the cave allegory—one from earth to sky and back again—nor one from dispersal of the shadows to the unity of the forms, but rather a movement of dispersal, a movement toward the dispersed as dispersed, that is, as coming from elsewhere, as dark and incomprehensible and yet as that which comes first in my own relation to myself as a being whose tongue articulates itself in existence as ecstases.

Existence experiences itself in its own ecstatic movement. As such in the articulations of its desire it gives expression to its own mute presence. In such articulations it hears the silence of its own being as movement toward articulation, a movement which is only glimpsed in the articulations themselves. To glimpse the movement of desire is to see language at the edge of its own articulability in a speaking language which is not yet spoken.[19] This, however, is seen precisely in the articulations themselves, which show silence insensibly in their own unmistakable clamor.

The question of translation—of understanding the dispersed as dispersed, of moving in faith toward the inexpressible and unworldly—finds no place in the allegories of light. This is *not* so because the cave and its shadows—the realm of doxa and of entities—have merely a negative value for Plato; in fact once they are seen in their true context by the light of the sun Plato affirms their being. Rather, the absence of translation arises from the understanding of entities in terms of their place in a hierarchy of being. However, as dispersed in the world, no people, no tongue, no language, is of the world; there is no world for which they are. Rather, at the core of the world an epoché occurs through which all light, all world, is bracketed, in the face of the untranslatable, inexpressible experience of the 'least of things.'

Light of Creation

The metaphysics of light articulates the experience of knowledge and being in terms of radical worldliness, that is, in terms of what shows itself in a medium of absolute transparency. It is a movement from darkness to light, from the depth of the earth to the surface of things turned toward the sky. This is the movement of understanding. Understanding cannot be anything other than lucent or obscure. The very lucidity of understanding is a matter of light for fundamental reasons. Understanding is of distance, of standing back, a viewing of its object in a mediated immediacy: through a medium which effaces itself, light as transparent. True, understanding is not solely visual; there is an understanding in the touch of the lover, the animal tamer, the craftsman, the surgeon. But tactility alone understands nothing; what is touchable is also and inescapably visible. The moment of vision in understanding is inescapable.[20] Vision is essentially comprehension: it requires a com-prehending action of light. That which light does not reach, does not touch, remains beyond vision. Hence, sight again depends on touch, but on a touch beyond the capacity of the seeing being. Understanding is a gift of light, a gift of capacity to the incapable; in the experience of light there is already a hint of grace. But that which is touched by light is that which resists light. Matter appears in this resistance to light. Yet, it is also how light itself appears in the interruption of its own transparency. In its visibility—as that which it is not—light invisibly appears. But this appearance 'after Babel' is of dispersed light, of movements of intelligibility which appear only as opaque to those toward whom they are addressed. Dispersed light is light as it comes to appearance in opaque darkness. Dispersal, the fate of human beings after Babel, calls for understanding. The event of Babel calls not alone for understanding in dispersal, but for understanding *as dispersed.*

Only such an understanding in dispersal and as dispersed can make sense of the call to faith experienced by Abram. Understood Platonically the call of faith is a call in the world and as such must find 'its place in the sun.' But the call of faith has no such place, indeed makes claims precisely to a non-place, a 'place' closed off to the light of the sun. Only in such a non-place can the figure of Christ be thought, and only in such a non-place is faith anything other than fallible belief. The light of faith is a light in and of dispersal. The account of such light is to be found *before* Babel in the creation narrative itself. This is not surprising: the account of creation was concerned not to make sense of a prelapsarian world, but precisely of a world living in the shadow of the fall, i.e., of understanding itself as fallen—as containing within itself the light which no worldly light can undo. It is not the account of the origins of the world as much as an account of the source of order and meaning in that world—a source, so the basic intuition of Genesis, which is to be found beyond and before the world.

The first chapter of Genesis supplies us with a rich account of such a light. This account is prior to any distinction between the figurative and the literal, because this very distinction assumes light.[21] Visibility and invisibility, sensible and non-sensible, inner and outer: these oppositions arise with light. And with these oppositions there is the possibility of language and intelligibility. Or rather, in the intersection where they coincide and come apart, a space is opened up out of a coincidence of opposites in which the voice, the mark, the thing shine forth as intelligible and meaningful. The question of light is not simply the question of one among other 'creations'; it is the question of the intelligibility of creation and the mode by which this intelligibility can be truly understood.

"In the beginning God created heaven and earth" (Genesis 1:1). The two principles of the universe—the worldly (ouranous) and the earthly—come into being in the beginning. At the origins of things is the difference between the worldly and the earthly. Nothing can stand forth to be seen, nothing can take on form, nothing can find any ground. There is no place for significance and hence no place for meaning—"the earth was a formless void" (1:2). Yet, there is a primary difference, that between heaven and earth, a condition of meaning which itself has no significance, which of itself gives no space for meaning. There is here literally and metaphorically only darkness. This is a primal darkness, a darkness without light; a darkness not said to be created by god—indeed the words used by the Septuagint translators to describe the earth, translating the Hebrew *tohu va-vohu*, are all privative terms: *aoratos* (invisible), *akataskeuastos* (unformed), *abussou* (without ground, abysmal). This is not surprising: a void prior to significance is without attribute. The only descriptions of it are retrospective ones which describe it as being deprived of those qualities of being seen, of form, and of grounds which the later days of creation will bring into being. The darkness of which the author speaks here is a common term for this privation of meaning. It is a darkness of which we cannot speak, because it is prior to all speech, even divine speech. Yet, it is *into* this darkness that speech and significance penetrates. Speech and significance begin in a setting up of distance in which meaning can emerge. More specifically this distance is one of vision and of sound. Indeed, sound and vision are intertwined, such that the very first articulate sounds are concerned with the possibility of vision.[22]

"God said, 'let there be light' and there was light. God saw that light was good, and God divided light from darkness. God called light 'day,' and darkness he called 'night'" (Genesis 1:3–5). Darkness precedes light. In the previous verse the reference is to "darkness over the deep." Darkness, which god names as night, is there between heaven and earth. Although god is not said to create darkness, it results from his creative act. The statement "let there be light" contains the first words of god recorded in Genesis. This act, this bringing into being of the place for light, seems at the same time to bring into being a place for language, for words. Yet, while light is created on the first day and hence day and night are divided, the sun and the stars are not created until the fourth day. Even then they are not mentioned by name, but rather as a "light to govern day" and a "light to govern night" (Genesis 1:16). Far from the sun being the source of light, it is one manifestation of light, a light which precedes it.

God's first words, "let there be light," form a command, structurally addressed to another. There was within Christianity a long tradition of understanding this in Trinitarian terms, that god the father is addressing his son and that the son brings about what the father commands. Whatever of such an interpretation (which finds little or no acceptance today), it is clear that these words assume—or even institute—a relation. These words cannot be understood monologically; the sentence and those which follow are not propositional. They do not describe a state of things, but rather bring about a state of being. They are speech acts, which do not depend on a context for their meaning, but bring about their own mean-ingful contexts. This is the fundamental sense of the light. Certainly the whole structure of days and nights, which frames the narrative of creation, depends on the creation of light (and its difference from dark), but more fundamentally the creation of light gives the possibility of distance and hence of a difference between that which is spoken and the context in which it is spoken. For this to be possible a speech act which brings its own context into being is required.

"Let there be lights in the vault of heaven to divide day from night" (Genesis 1:14). Only on the fourth day does god create the sun, the moon, and the stars. The source of light is not the sun; the sun exists due to light. A resistance is be-ing voiced here not simply to the worship of the sun, but more fundamentally to that which such worship can represent: the immanence of light, the hierarchical ordering of light within the levels of the world. Light in Genesis is that which god creates in order to allow for meaning not only in the world, but in the act of creation itself. In this sense the creation of light differs from the rest of the creative act: while the latter is structured in terms of days and hence in terms of a repeatable order of making manifest, the creation of light is that which makes such a meaningful order possible. Light in this sense is that which governs all of creation, and nothing lies outside of the order of light: light is that which "enve-lopes"[23] all that is, that which does not so much shine upon things as that which allows things to shine forth. Light, far from being that of the world, is of another source, not of the world but synonymous with the creative act of god.[24] In this sense light displays the creature character of things. Things are manifest not as surfaces seeping into light, but through the light which is the source of their being; not as entities within the hierarchy of the world, but as entities directly related to a light beyond the light of the world, the creative word of god. This thought reaches its ultimate extreme in the First Letter of John where he states: "God is Light" (1:5).

Understood in terms of Genesis, things appear not as basking in the radiance of the sun, but as drawing sight by means of light, by means of radiating presence, rather than through the medium of light. In Christian terms this is most manifest in the Incarnation. The kenotic presence of Christ is that of god who divests him-self of his glory, disguises then his ownmost radiance in order to appear in such a manner that he can be perceived by human beings. In this case, light as light is manifest in the world. Yet, as is also the insight of Platonic philosophy, light as light is not perceivable to the 'naked,' corporeal eye. In the case of the Incarnation, the incarnate form of Christ does not disguise his light—it precisely reveals it—rather his body shows itself under different aspects which could be perceived in distinct and indeed opposed ways. This distinction is not reducible to the faculties of the soul, but rather to the mode of openness to perceive. Such openness is understood by Paul and John in particular as faith and love.[25] The eyes of faith see not the spiritual reality beyond the material, but rather see the material, the bodily form of Christ, in terms not of the reflected light of the world but rather as the light itself. Such sight is a turning of sight, a turning away from the homogeneous to the heterogeneous, a sight for that which comes from elsewhere. But such sight is not *sui generis;* it is given by the object of that sight: seeing Jesus of Nazareth as the son of god is itself a gift of god. Nothing in the human being as a natural entity allows Jesus to be seen as light, rather as a refraction of light. In terms of the latter—in terms of the light of the world—Jesus is a man of little value or worth. In terms of the natural faculties of the soul, nothing more can be seen. There is nothing in the nature of Jesus which can be seen as anything but a man just as any other. To perceive him as other than that, indeed as divine, is to perceive a reality which is beyond nature, beyond essence, beyond all relations with entities in the world. It is to perceive in him as something which withdraws from the light of the world, withdraws indeed into darkness, while manifesting a light, which transforms both sensual and intellectual light. This light is that which comes without notice, which explodes in the world in a visibility invisible in the light of the world. This is the light of an event, of Christ as event, it is in that which eventuates itself in him that the 'glory of the Lord' appears.

The figure of Christ contradicts the Platonic metaphysics of light,[26] but is reconcilable with the account of light we find in Genesis. Christ is an event, the event which radiates in its own singularity, the singularity of a gift of love, which only love and faith can recognize. It has no place on the divided line because it calls for attention to itself as its own light, to its own body filled with light (cf. Luke 11:36). Only by being turned toward god can a being be filled with light, and Christ in his total devotion to his mission, to following the call of god, exemplifies such a being. But in that case in Christ there is no mediating light, rather in Christ is manifest the self-expression of divine love. As with the creation of light, Christ gives meaning to his own appearance. No other context can make sense of the appearance of Christ; the Hebrew scriptures can only retrospectively be interpreted as referring to him. But Christ by the radiance of his life places himself at a distance. No longer the medium of worldly light but rather leading beyond the horizontal space of worldly relations—not toward a vertical transcendence, but rather toward the strange illumination of things expressing themselves in the silence of their own impenetrable depth. It is in this sense that the light of Christ turns the light of the world to darkness. Here the light of the singular presence of Christ confronts the glory of the world. This is prefigured already in Isaiah: "Arise, shine out, for your light has come, and the glory of Yahweh has risen on you. Look! though night still covers the earth and darkness the peoples, on you Yahweh is rising and over you his glory can be seen" (Isaiah 60:1–3). And later in the same chapter: "No more will the sun give you daylight, nor moonlight shine on you, but Yahweh will be your everlasting light, your God will be your splendor" (Isaiah 60:19). The light of god makes the light of the earth appear as darkness, makes day appear as night; the fleeting light of the sun and moon will be replaced by the light which is their source, the everlasting light of god. We are speaking here not of a Manichean conflict: the light of the earth (worldly light) and that of god (heavenly light) relate to one another in terms of origins. But the self-assertion of the earthly and worldly effects a breaking off of all lines of origin of worldly light: light is the first and ultimate idol.

The figure of Christ binds together sky and earth in a way which repeats the tower of Babel by inverting, indeed perverting, it. Christ is announced as the "light to those who live in darkness" (Luke 1:79, echoing Isaiah). This light, however, is the light of a beacon "to guide our feet into the way of peace" (ibid.). The worldly polemos of earth and sky, the self-assertion of making a name, are abandoned in a way of peace in which one light allows another to shine. The way of peace is one in which the light of the sun in its light is seen to darken the light of entities, the light precisely of their existence, of their being toward, out of the depth of their earthly, material existence.

But it is only the eyes of faith which can see this. Faith is already in the midst of things, in the mode of trust. Trust is a response to the entity appearing—it appears to me [*dokei moi*] (to be trustworthy). Such an appearance is itself an appeal which is non-relative—it is not the entity as relative to this or that which claims trust, but rather the entity in and of itself as it forges relations from itself. As such the entity appears as it is to faith. Faith is the response to this appeal. Showing itself to faith the entity brackets out the world, refuses the world, that is, the world's glory. This refusal is in the name of another glory, a glory which it has of itself, not through itself, but through the one who named it, the one who sent it. The name for that glory is doxa. This is the *urdoxa:* appearance as it makes its own appearing appear.

Glory is the refusal of worldly light in the name of the irrelative, non-hier-archical light of the thing appearing in and of itself. A light which disturbs all order, all relations in its own name, its proper name. The name Jesus Christ ex-presses twice over this disruption: that of being sent by god. The being-sent of Christ is the expression of a sending which brings to words the essence of the light of creation itself: as the being of entities in their own origins. The urdoxa is the appearance of the thing as having within itself the mark of its own origin—a mark which brings to presence the creative act of god.

'After Babel' this appearance is an appearance which calls not for understanding within the pragmatics of a common project, but rather for the recognition of a voice as a singular light known only in its name, which has no meaning outside its own articulation. This appearance is the declaration of its proper
name, a sound which is meaningful only in and of itself. A sound which withdraws from the light of the world, to be heard only by a vision which penetrates
beyond the world, a vision of faith. The appearance of Christ is an invitation to
such a vision.

The phenomenology of Christ, the phenomenology of this god-man, lies at
the center of a Christian account of appearance. To recognize this meaning it is
not necessary to 'accept' the divinity of Jesus of Nazareth. Rather, it is impera-
tive to understand what it means to say that a man is in the light of the world,
but transcends that light. But it is also important not simply to universalize such
a meaning. Central to the Christian message is the uniqueness of Christ: Christ
came to save humanity and did so *once and for all*.[27] This is a stumbling block,
one which cannot be evaded. It privileges one time and one place; not as Greece
may be privileged, that is, as an eternal present, but rather as a pivot of history. But precisely this privileging allows a thinking of the body and of the event,
which is closed off in the eternal present of Greece. The phenomenology of Christ
in its very uniqueness allows us to think the body, the event, and in consequence
history, contingency, and time otherwise. Only through a rethinking of light and
dark is that possible. This rethinking is in terms of revelation, in terms of a light
which is beyond the light of the world, but appearing in the world. Such a light
can only appear as darkness. As such this understanding of light commits us at
the same time to a phenomenology of darkness.

A Phenomenology of Darkness

A 'phenomenology of darkness' seems an oxymoron. Phenomenology is the discourse on appearance; darkness, it would seem, is not appearance but the absence of appearance. Furthermore, 'phenomenology' as the logos of *phainom-
enon* (from the Greek *phos* meaning light) can be termed a discourse on light.
Nevertheless, phenomenology has been continually drawn back to darkness:
Heidegger, in an understanding of truth as un-forgetfulness leading in his later
work to a phenomenology of the inapparent; Merleau-Ponty, with his phenomenology of the invisible; Levinas, in his account of the horror of the *il y a*, all
engage in phenomenologies of darkness.[28] But all such phenomenologies have to
struggle with a fundamental Platonic and later Augustinian assumption, namely,
that darkness is a privation of light: darkness as non-being in the sense of being
a privation of being. Darkness, so understood, is ontologically speaking evil.[29]

Darkness is a withdrawal from the light of the world: on that Platonism
and Christianity can agree. But far from such a withdrawal being understood in

purely negative terms, it forms the core of the Christian understanding of truth, truth namely as revealed. Revelation is that appearance that exceeds the human capacity to receive it. It is in this sense a radical darkness, the showing of darkness as darkness. The figure of Christ does not indicate a way to understand the light of the world, but rather shows the exhaustion of the world and of worldly desire in that which lies beyond and before such a light.

The limits of light are expressed prayerfully—prayer expresses limits as limits. Such expressions are without fulfillment; are not expressions of lack of fulfillment, but rather of that which is beyond any movement toward fulfillment. Fulfillment is of form, of form reflecting light. Prayer is an openness beyond all form, beyond all order, but an openness which takes place in the world, takes place indeed at the worldly core of the world in the play of light. (As such prayer transcends intentionality.) The core of expressions of prayerful existence within Christianity have sought in the heart of the worldliness of the world to find the presence of that which is beyond the world, the creative origin of the world. At its best Christian art and ritual is in that sense worldly worldlessness.

Attending to the light of things is essentially an act of waiting. The 'act' of waiting is an act which subverts the conditions of action, namely light. Action is always in the light, but waiting is essentially without light. That which is in the light is no longer awaited—it is already there, already subject to me—but what is awaited remains hidden, remains enveloped in darkness. That which is in darkness is that which refuses the light of the world, which sends the light of the world back and by so doing both appears in the world and remains distant from the world. The darkness at the heart of all appearance is lost and missed in the onward rush of utility, where in the movement of worldly light each appearing thing immediately reflects in its surface back on something else. Only in the shock of revelation, where the thing appears in its irrelation, is this movement halted and disrupted. When in fatigue the rush of need is stilled, when in the sudden joyful allure of a thing attracting us unexpectedly in its beauty, when in despair an inner emptiness makes all appropriation senseless, we find ourselves seeing the sound and hearing the sight of things, being addressed by the language of things, as if for the first time. It is then that things appear in their inner darkness as calling toward a desiring existent. In such moments when the heart is given sway and the light of the world no longer acts as a guide, no clear hierarchies or transparent signposts direct the journey; not even the satisfaction of recognition remains. In darkness there is only infinity, unending night without form or shape. In darkness those senses for the infinite—hearing without end, touch without substance, smell and taste of pure elements—displace sight and dismiss understanding.[30] In darkness the secure distance of sight is lacking and presences are felt not as local, but as all-present, as everywhere and nowhere, felt in the crawling of skin[31] and in the heart filled with happiness or anxiety. Above all else, in darkness humility is learnt.[32] Not seeing, the self feels itself to be seen, feeling its darkness to be its alone—its words seem to echo back to it. Its desire is awakened not to anything prefigured in its will or understanding, but by that which affects it, surprises it, fills it with joy at that sweet presence, grief at that distance, fear at that unknowability, and hope in that promise.[33] Being in darkness is being in response to this hovering presence in fluctuating moods of compliance and resistance.

In the worldly light, the eyes see not light but something formed, a darkness reflecting light. That is the paradox of sight—only that can be seen which in showing itself withdraws from sight, which withdraws from the light into darkness. Platonism forecloses a critical examination of this phenomenon by flooding the world in light and recognizing in the intellect the faculty to see in that light.[34] But all the intellect sees in the end—in seeing the good—is light itself and that surface of things which reflects that light. The eyes of faith, the eyes for darkness, remain with the withdrawing depth of the thing, but instead of transcending it in the reflection of other things and the intellectual light, they see in that withdrawal a source of light without relation, a light of the singular reality of that which appears. The uniqueness of Christ is that in the darkness of his form he makes manifest a light which can be seen only through the eyes of faith. This sight is not a gradual becoming accustomed to light, but on the contrary a sight which is possible only by seeing in darkness.

The sight in darkness is a sight of faith. Faith responds to darkness and as such is a basic existential condition.[35] Its manner of sight is given monumental expression in the Gothic cathedrals of Chartres, Paris, Cologne, Milan. Such churches do not gather together the sky and earth around them, they do not gather the totality of entities in their unconcealment, they do not harmonize earthly solidity and celestial light,[36] rather they mingle earth and sky by an act of secretive alchemy. Darkness here is not a negative, but rather the darkening of the world and of the worldly eyes of body, and intellect is the only condition under which revelation can take place. The Gothic Cathedral embodies this movement beyond the earthly light toward another light, imaged in the saints whose representations the upper stained glass holds. The gloomy haze below does not so much signify a lack of light as it does the darkening effect of the divine light on the light of the world. The openness to divine light effects a transformation of earthiness through which the very stones of the building lose their weight and become celestial vessels. The verticality of the play of light intersects with the horizontality of corporeality and earthiness. Yet the light from the soaring heights places the embodied, earthy, and mortal being in the position not of viewer so much as of that which is viewed. From on high she is brought into the light, made subject and answerable to the light. As if alone in the vast surroundings, she is not engaged reciprocally with her fellows, but addressed by that which withdraws from her. In following the light she knows that the eyes which guided her in the world—be they of the body or of the intellect—will not aid her here. She is in the dark, is nowhere in the world (although in another sense—perhaps the only one the tourist knows—she is in Chartres or Cologne, Paris or Milan), has no orientation, no map, no visual model of action. She is in a dreamy world in which waking eyes can discern very little.

The Cathedral is not a cave in Plato's sense. There blindness is a temporary failure of sight, due not to any lack of facility in the perceiver, but rather to his lack of habituation to sunlight. The darkness experienced has only a negative value: it gives the prisoner a point of comparison and hence a sense of the degrees of sight and knowledge. When, on the other hand, mystical theologians such as Pseudo-Dionysius and John of the Cross speak of darkness—that darkness made manifest in the Gothic Cathedral—they understand it as a positive phenomenon. This is distinctive of Christian phenomenology: *understanding darkness as a phenomenon, not simply as the absence of phenomena.* This is inherent in the account of faith, which breaks fundamentally with the divided line. When John of the Cross speaks of faith as a dark night of the natural facilities of the understanding, will, senses, memory,[37] he is placing pistis not so much at the top of the divided line, but rather pointing to a lacuna between faith and the "natural facilities" of the mind. While for Plato a steady ascent is possible from imagination to intellect, for John of the Cross only through a turning away from the world, understood in its immanence, as a hierarchically structured order of appearance, is it possible to arrive at "divine wisdom." This turning away, however, is not itself a human capacity; John of the Cross stresses the powerlessness of the human being. It is only through being acted upon, and acted upon in secret, that is, away from the light of the world, that the soul finds itself in the dark night. This dark night is, through all the suffering inherent in it, a "happy night," because through it god is acting to prepare the soul for that which is beyond this world.[38] This dark night is an alienation from the world. This alienation is a relation to things in the world while withdrawing from the world. Nothing as such is an object of experience in the dark night, rather what is revealed is a radical passivity to which corresponds no capacity to act: this reveals the world as that in which there is hidden a deep alterity, which cannot be possessed and which cannot be known: that which reflects no light. Pseudo-Dionysius puts this in the form of a prayer: "that we may see the darkness beyond being which is hidden by all the light in beings."[39] This darkness is not a darkness of the world, but is rather hidden by the light in beings in the world. Worldly light in this sense hides as it illuminates. What it hides is that which only faith can see, namely, a darkness of senses and intellect through which appears nothing but the action of that which is beyond the world.[40]

The Cathedral is a place of liturgy, or rather the Cathedral is due to liturgy. Liturgy is not sacrifice; it rather expresses that in sacrifice which sacrifice itself cannot express: the limits of all worldly economy. As such liturgy expresses the sense of a limit of worldly action in its very performance. This paradoxical nature of liturgy is expressed by Lacoste as *"the expectation or desire for parousia in the certitude of the non-parousial presence of God."*[41] Liturgy breaks with the sacred ritual to the extent to which it seeks not the immanent sacred in the world—the gods in Heidegger's fourfold—but an opening in the world to a god transcending the world. Liturgy breaks with the exclusory mechanism in ritual, that of sacrifice, of making sacred through exclusion and death. For this reason there is no sacred place for liturgy; the symbolic, indeed allegorical, significance of all topological reference is made fully conscious. Hence, the turning toward the east in Christian churches is a turning not toward a sacred place but rather toward that place *symbolized* by the rising sun, namely, the coming of the kingdom. No identification is possible here though: no place requires of us an acknowledgment of its sacredness. As such liturgy is the rejection of divine violence, of the polarizations of victim and victor fundamental to the sacred logic (Girard)—rejection of violence in the name of peace. The Christian church is a place, as Lacoste puts it, of "fragile anticipation"; it obeys not the logic of place, but of non-place (*non-lieu*).[42]

Liturgical architecture, the architectural expression of liturgy, of openness to the unworldly at the heart of worldly order, is as such essentially anti-architectural architecture. While architecture classically aims to frame and symbolically represent the experience of being in the world spatially and temporally, Christian architecture—at least in its purest form, the Gothic—symbolically disrupts that experience. It is Christian liturgy in stone. The horizontal agons of human relations are disturbed by a vertical orientation which mediates communal togetherness. The mystery of the Eucharist is embodied in the very building itself which seems to transform earth into sky, dark into light. Worldly hierarchies are as nothing in this relation. Of course at the core of the Christian liturgy at the time such Cathedrals were built was a certain rather fixed hierarchy—that between priest and lay. The focus of the ritual was the altar; the altar and the choir were cut off from the nave by screens. But such screens had no architectural warrant and indeed spoiled much of the effect of the long lines intersecting between nave and transept. In this sense the demands of ritual, rather than liturgical demands, did not fit with the design of the church: its anti-architectural architecture subverted the ritualistic enactment of liturgical sense. As such the ritual introduced an element of violence.

Pushing beyond this horizontal violence, the lines of the stone drawing us toward the windows gathering light in a transcendent purity, the liturgical waiting is matched by a fragility in the very stones of the building: the Gothic cathedral weaves into harmony imposing presence and fragility, self-assertion and desire for transformation. The church proclaims the joyful experience of the inexperienceable. The inexperienceable is the non-relational relation to the absolute, peace itself: self-dispossession laying bare for that which transcends violence and agonistics. Liturgy is the place for such a happening in the world. To again quote Lacoste: "by giving itself from within the world a horizon not of the world, liturgy proves that the world is not intranscendable."[43]

That which silences theology, that "darkness beyond light of the hidden mystical silence,"[44] is the divine as the unreachable by means of the world. The silence which results is not simply a loss of words in the seeking after names, but rather a reversal of that very seeking. The darkness is not the appearance of something which cannot be expressed—as the *via eminentia* shows that expression, however inadequate, is available to theology—but rather the turning back of the desire for words as an inappropriate seeking after worldly correlates. The excessiveness of human desire comes to rest in the excess of divine revelation. What is revealed is nothing other than things in the world, which are revealed, however, as that which no horizon can contain.

3 Glory and Being

THE PLAY OF light and dark is a worldly play which, however, reveals itself as excessive in the appearance of entities to an existent in its existence as desire. The nothingness of such existents in their non-surrendering to play reveals itself as a lightness and a darkness of being not of this world. Ontology is not cosmology. Against the phenomenological tradition from Husserl and Heidegger to Marion it must be insisted that discourse about being is not confined to, is not limited to, discourse about world or the worldly. If it were, then there would be no sense in talking about singular existents. Existents in their singularity are not otherwise than being, but rather are being-hidden from the world, hidden in the depths of the world, a promise to let things shine forth of and in themselves at the 'end' (*eschaton*) of the world. The desire for truth, the desire to know things as and in themselves, is not a worldly desire, is not a desire for the thing as it is disclosed in the world, but rather as it would disclose itself not for anyone, not from any perspective or in any relation, but rather in its self-expression, that is, in the expression of its own worldless origin. Singular being is non-relational, and as such we are here beyond ethics in which being still reveals itself for me precisely as other (even though from a height). We are also beyond science in the sense that the being so revealed is not generalizable, or rather is lost in any generalization. But without this singular thing, no science and no ethics would be possible.[1]

The Christian narrative of Christ is a narrative of singularity, is a resistance to worldliness. It is, however, a resistance which does not simply flee from the world (although this remains always a possible modality of Christian response—the 'beautiful soul'). Rather, it resists the world within the world. It is a way of being-in-the-world, which is open to the light and darkness of things. Things in their singularity fail to exemplify general laws. They fail to correspond to the boundaries such laws lay down. Their radiance is not a reflected radiance, but rather a self-revelation, 'warts and all,' as we say. Singular beings are impure in terms of the world. They are mixtures of sky and earth, of matter and form, of sickness and health, of solids and fluids. They obey laws only in approximations, in strict terms they are outside the law, they defy the *sanctum*, they are contaminations of the sacred. The Christian narratives are narratives of such contaminations, of such impurities. In them the celestial divine is mixed with the earth, life is mixed with death, the sacred with the profane (curing the sick on the Sabbath [Luke 13:14–16]), the holy mix with the 'unclean' (prostitutes, tax-collectors, etc. [e.g., Luke 7:36–50]).[2] And all of this in the name of peace—peace not of the victorious, not of fear and submission, but peace 'which the world cannot give' (John 14:27), namely, a peace at the heart of things as desired and desiring, not the violent peace of the *polemos* of the world.[3] This is a peace beyond both politics and philosophy, a peace which can only be understood as glory, as the appearance of that which appears in the world as not of the world.

If ontology is not cosmology, then being-in-the-world cannot imply being-of-the-world. The distinction between being-in and being-of needs to be worked out. Such a distinction involves a dialogue with Heidegger, in particular the Heidegger of *Being and Time*. Going beyond Heidegger, the concept of glory as the appearance in the world of that which is not-of-the-world as it arises in the Judeo-Christian scriptures will be discussed. The intersection of being not-of-the-world and being-in-the-world within an existent is one which occurs in and through the impure. The question of impurity will be discussed with particular reference to the cross. On its own terms the impure is radiant. This radiance of things is non-relational and non-hierarchical—a singular radiance. At the heart of this radiance is an eschatological promise, namely the promise of a new heaven and a new earth. This promise is not, however, to be understood as a future state, but rather as the non-relational, non-worldly, transcendent way for things to relate in their own singularity.

Being-in and Being-of the World

In But Not Of: A Critique of Heidegger's Analysis of Worldliness

To be in the world does not imply being-of-the-world. This defines the Christian challenge to philosophy. It expresses in more ontological terms what the 'glory of the Lord' already proclaims: that what appears in the world is irreducible to the world. Sacred logic and pantheistic speculation are both refused by the simple Christian denial of an implication between in and of, an implication implicit in philosophy since Plato and inherent in philosophy's immanentist logic. It is an implication which grants plausibility to Heidegger's analyses of Dasein in *Being and Time* and which allows for his methodological atheism and his later renewal of sacred logic. It is an implication which the 'folly of the cross' resists.

In Old English 'of' had the meaning of 'away from' which is still retained in the word 'off.' This meaning of motion away from was superseded by the genitive only through the requirement to translate the French '*de.*' In other words, the genitive meaning was superimposed for external reasons on the word 'of.' But this superimposition was not without grounds: the genitive is a relation of source and belonging, a movement away in relation to its source. The movement away is a movement of becoming, a movement which is in constant relation to an origin to which it belongs. To 'be of' is to come from and belong to: to be 'of a certain family', 'of a certain town', 'of a certain species', and so on. Belonging here implies a relation of origin, irrespective of the contingency or otherwise of the relation: a member of a club is that because of the club, the origin of his being a member is in the club itself. As origin and possession being-of expresses dependence, as in 'they live of bread.' To 'live of bread' means to live by means of bread. Such dependence indicates a prior relation of belonging, a relation of belonging and dependence which makes appropriation—the appropriation of bread in eating, in this case—possible. To be of something, as in to be about something, indicates a relation of concern, a relation to that which is of issue for me. To 'be of' is to be concerned, to belong, to depend, to originate from. To be of the world is to be originate from, belong to, depend on, and be concerned with the world. A phenomenology of Christian life is of a life for which all such relations to the world are secondary, derivative, and indeed in the end sinful. Jesus of Nazareth states of his followers, "they belong to the world no more than I belong to the world" (Matthew 17:14). The relation of belonging to the world is a turning away from a more primordial belonging. The fundamental experience here is of origins, belonging, dependence, and it concerns the non-worldly not merely in the self of the person, nor simply in that of the other person, but in all things. This experience is of entities in their singular being. It is an experience of things which disrupts any implication of being-of from being-in, an implication which can be traced from Plato to Heidegger.[4] It is one which lies at the core of Heidegger's analysis of being-in-the-world.

The relation of being-in-the-world forms for Heidegger the basis of both theoretical knowledge and practical action (*Verhalten*).[5] The analysis should then be understood to be pre-theoretical and pre-practical, a laying out of the 'obvious' preconditions of all knowledge and action, a 'knowing the world' (*Welterkenntnis*) which is a pre-conditioning knowing, a knowing which allows for knowledge and action. Such knowledge is prior—a priori—because all knowledge and action relates to entities that are entities in the world. Already here before Heidegger engages in an analysis of innerworldly being the understanding of entities (*Seiende*) as innerworldly is operative.

Being-in is being-in-the-world. This is so not because Dasein happens to be in a container called world, but on the contrary because the relation of being-in is nothing like being contained. In other words, world is not here a contingent object of the preposition 'in,' but rather being-in is that which makes all positions possible, is constitutive of the being-of Dasein such that it makes all relations to entities possible. As Heidegger points out (drawing on Jakob Grimm's analysis),[6] the common spatial meaning of 'in'—spatial understood as being contained within—is derivative from the more original meaning of dwelling and being familiar. Crucial here for Heidegger are the semantic relations between '*in*,' '*bin*,' and '*bei*.' The entity which is in is that entity which we refer to as 'I am'—'*ich bin*.' '*Ich bin*' means "I dwell, stay near . . . the world as that which is familiar in such and such a way [*ich wohne, halte mich auf bei . . . der Welt, als dem so und so Vertrauten*]."[7] The word '*bei*' is difficult to translate—it means to 'be at' in the sense of being at home.[8] To be at is to be in relation, to be in relation to that place where I dwell, am familiar with, or indeed where I am a stranger, unfamiliar. Being at (*Sein bei*) is not a relation of two entities—Dasein and world—because a relation of two entities, a relation of containment or a relation of proximity, *is* only in terms of a prior relation of dwelling and non-dwelling, of familiarity and strangeness, which characterizes Dasein's being. As Heidegger puts it:

> An entity can only touch an objectively present [*vorhandenes*] entity within the world if it has the kind of being of being in—only if with its Da-sein something like world is already discovered in terms of which beings can reveal themselves through touch and thus become accessible in their objective presence [*Vorhandensein*]. Two entities which are objectively present with the world and are, moreover, worldless in themselves, can never touch each other, neither can '*be*' '*together with* [*bei*]' the other.[9]

Only an entity which is being-in can touch. Being-in is a relation of touching, a relation of being at. To touch is not simply to have no space between two entities, but rather to be toward another entity. To be toward an other entity is to be toward that which can reveal itself (*sich offenbar kann*). An entity can reveal itself, but can do so only through the relation of being-in. That relation is a worldly relation because the movement toward is that which allows entities to be in relation to Dasein and to one another. Being-in is a movement toward and is manifest in many ways of which Heidegger gives the following examples: "to have to do with something, to produce, order and take care of something, to use something, to give something up and let it get lost, to undertake, to accomplish, to find out, to ask about, to observe, to speak about, to determine. . . ."[10] All of these modes of being Heidegger understands as having concern (*Besorgen*) as their mode of being. To be in the world then is to be concerned with entities, concerned with them in respect to their relatedness to Dasein's concerns. To touch an entity is to relate to it as it relates to something else. Dasein finds itself in the world in the sense that it finds itself concerned with things, finds itself moving toward things in the course of its daily concerns. Entities reveal themselves to Dasein as that which can reveal itself, that is as possibility. Only if an entity reveals itself as possibility can Dasein concern itself with it. Such possibilities of entities in turn disclose Dasein to itself in the being possible of its own being.

Knowing of world is the knowing of entities in respect of possibility. Such knowing is expressed in the knowledge of entities as handy things (*zuhandenes*). In its concerns Dasein has "dealings [*Umgang*] *in* the world . . . *with* innerworldly entities."[11] An innerworldly entity is not a being-in-the-world, because such entities do not themselves relate to other entities as possibilities, i.e., do not deal with other entities in terms of a knowing of world. Such entities are neither being-in nor being-with. But to be in the world is to be with entities which are revealed only through the world; the world, though, is revealed only for Dasein. Such innerworldly entities Heidegger names *Zeug*, a useful thing. Zeug in German means everything and nothing: it is a something, which needs a qualifying adjective: *Schreibzeug, Nähzeug, Werkszeug, Fahrzeug, Messzeug*, etc. Heidegger believes this is what the Greek for thing—*pragmata*—was trying to capture: that which is only in its being useful. It is that with which Dasein has dealings. In understanding what it is which makes a useful thing a useful thing—what he calls 'equipmentality' (*Zeughaftigkeit*)—Heidegger begins with the following statement: "A useful thing 'is' strictly speaking never [*Ein Zeug 'ist' strenggenommen nie*]."[12] I translate this sentence word for word in the original German in order to show the emphasis of Heidegger's statement. A useful thing—that is, *one* useful thing—is a useful thing taken in isolation. This mug, for example, *is* in the sense that it is real, not imaginary. But the being-of the mug is abstract. Strictly speaking—that is, speaking with all phenomenological rigor—we can never speak of *a* mug or any useful thing, i.e., any innerworldly thing, in isolation. That is not just for the reasons which the unsatisfactory nature of my designation 'this mug' hints at (Which mug? Where? When?). More profoundly, to speak of a mug is already to speak of that on which it is placed, of that which it contains, of the factory worker or the potter who made or helped make it, and so on. In that sense, to the being-of the mug or any useful thing "there always belongs a totality of useful things in which this useful thing can be what it is."[13] This specifies the being-in of the useful thing, which is a condition of its very being: it can be what it is—a mug not a plate, a desk not a chair, a house not an office—only on condition of its belonging to a totality of useful things in which it has its place. This place is understood in terms of a relation of 'in order to' (*um zu*). An innerworldly entity is a useful thing. To be a useful thing is to be 'in order to. . . . ' But this relation of in-order-to makes a thing not alone a useful thing but a useful thing of a certain sort—e.g., a mug not a plate. Hence, in the structure of the 'in order to' there is the reference (*Verweisung*) of one thing to another. Such reference needs to be understood actively here: the thing is what it is through its inner reference, its inner connectedness to something else: such reference, such connectedness makes up its meaning. The meaning of the useful thing is contained in the totality of useful things to which it belongs; the relation here is one of priority: "Before the individual useful thing is always already discovered the totality of useful things."[14]

The being-of the useful thing is its being-in such a totality of useful things, that is, a totality of referential relations. Such relations, though, are discovered not in the thing itself, but through the dealings with the thing. In such dealings—hammering a hammer is Heidegger's favorite example—Dasein discovers the specific handiness (*Handlichkeit*) of the thing. In doing so it discovers the thing in its being as a useful thing. This being Heidegger names handiness (*Zuhandenheit*). The latter, Heidegger says, is the "being-in-itself" of the useful thing. In itself the useful thing has no being outside of the totality of useful things in which it is. It reveals itself, that is, its own being, to Dasein in the relations of dealings with it; in other words, its being is disclosed in the relation of dealing with. For this reason Heidegger can state: *"Handiness is the ontological-categorical definition of entities, as they are 'in themselves.'"*[15] This means that the being-of entities as they are in themselves is their readiness to hand; hence, all entities are only in their place in the world within the relations of dealings of Dasein in the world.

The world does not come directly to appearance here. The sight of dealings with things is not directed at the world. This is so because the world is not an innerworldly entity; rather the latter is only insofar as 'it gives' (*es gibt*) world. The world appears otherwise to innerworldly entities and in a sense appears despite them. Indeed, it is when sight is diverted from the 'in-order-to' relations of entities that the structure of reference becomes explicit. The totality of useful things Heidegger also terms the "context of useful things" (*Zeugzusammenhang*). This context appears in the destruction of reference which occurs when a useful thing breaks down. But it appears not as that which had been invisible, but rather as that which had already been seen in dealings with useful things: it is that which made them what they are. In the breakdown of reference, however, when the useful thing no longer directs (*weisen*) sight onward, then the totality of useful things shows itself as world. The rupture (*Bruch*) in the context of reference, which is discovered in circumspection (*Umsicht*) when a ready-to-hand thing is missing, Heidegger describes as the emptiness that circumspection crashes into (*stösst in*). This emptiness is inaccessible to circumspection—which is always concerned with entities—but is disclosed to it. Circumspection, in its concern with entities, is always concerned with them in terms of the open, the emptiness that is world. There is circumspection only in terms of that open, that open for possibility. This implies a relation of entities to world which is exhaustive of their being. Indeed, Heidegger states so much at the beginning of section 18:

The fact that the being of things at hand has the structure of reference means that they have in themselves the character of *being-referred*. Entities are discovered with regard to the fact that they are referred, as those entities which they are, to something. They are relevant and involved [*Bewenden*] together with something else. The character of being of handiness is relevance and involvement [*Bewändtnis*].¹⁶

'Bewenden' and 'Bewändtnis' are difficult words to translate, but the basic meaning is clear: the being-of entities as handiness is in their involvement in or the relevance to other entities. Heidegger understands these relations of involvement in terms of the prepositions 'with' (*mit*) and 'along' (*bei*). The basic experience here is one of being-in relation to entities as they refer beyond themselves to relations of involvement with and among other entities. These relations are only in Dasein's involvements with these entities, but these involvements reveal entities as they are. In revealing them as they are, Dasein reveals them in terms of that which is not itself an entity and which is experienced in the involvement of entities with one another as that for which they are already freed. This 'being given free' (*freigegeben sein*) comes 'before' the entity. This means that the totality—now understood as a totality of relevance and involvements (*Bewandtnisganzheit*)—is that which makes the individual useful thing possible, because only in that totality is the useful thing worldly and only thus can it be for Dasein. As Heidegger puts it:

> *Which* relevance things at hand have is prefigured in each case by the totality of relevance. The totality of relevance which, for example constitutes the things at hand in a workshop in their handiness is 'earlier' than any single useful thing, as is the farmstead with all its utensils and neighboring lands. The totality of relevance itself, however, ultimately leads back to a what-for [*Wozu*] which no longer has relevance, which itself is not a being of the kind of being of things at hand within a world, but is an entity whose being is defined as being-in-the-world, to whose constitution of being worldliness itself belongs.¹⁷

The useful thing is only within a totality of relevance and involvements. That totality itself depends for its being on Dasein. For Dasein the useful thing is only in relation to its own being-in-the-world, that is, its being-in relation to totalities of relevance such as workshops, farmsteads, but also cities, industries, holiday resorts, etc. Dasein's being-in-the-world is one of freedom; it is defined in terms of a letting be of entities as nexuses of possibilities through which Dasein both exists in the world and allows the world itself to appear to it. Innerworldly entities appear for Dasein primarily in terms of the nexus of being-in-the-world and concern about (*um*) the being-of-the-world, that is, the being-of Dasein itself. The key to understanding this is the account of worldliness Heidegger presents in terms of letting something be involved or relevant (*Bewendenlassen*).

The latter term in normal German means 'to leave it at that' (*es dabei bewenden lassen*). The letting here is a letting something be itself. The point of relating the useful thing back to Dasein is not to suggest that the thing only is because of the use Dasein has for it, but almost the opposite: only because of what the thing is can Dasein use it.[18] This letting something be involved is that which constitutes ontologically the being-of each useful thing, even if ontically it is neither involved nor relevant. The useful thing is only through this prior freeing and as such is only in relation to the being-in-the-world of Dasein. Heidegger goes on to say that "the previous disclosure of that for which the freeing of things encountered in the world ensues is none other than the understanding of world to which Dasein as an entity is always already related."[19] The disclosure of things to Dasein is only in an understanding of world: the encounter with things is possible only in terms of a prior—implicit—understanding of world. Only in these terms are things significant. Significance (*Bedeutsamkeit*) is what constitutes the structure of the world, of that in which Dasein as such always already is. "*In its familiarity with significance Dasein is the ontic condition of possibility of the disclosure of entities encountered in the mode of being of relevance (handiness) in a world that can thus make themselves known in their in-itself.*"[20] The claim here is not simply that Dasein discovers entities in their usefulness in relation to the totality of relevance, but rather that Dasein discovers entities in their being-in themselves as useful things. Only as such does Dasein discover entities in their significance.

Entities for Heidegger are discovered as objective presence (*vorhanden*) only in a deficient, secondary mode. This mug is objectively present; it is there and can be referred to in a sentence (such as 'this is a mug') which makes no—explicit—reference to the 'totality of involvement' in which it is. But such a sentence is an abstraction first of all from the "every manipulation and use"—indeed a refusal (*Sichenthalten*) of such relations.[21] It requires a "looking away from" (*absehen*) how things are discovered and encountered.[22] It involves a penetrating beyond (*dringt vor*) the things at hand.[23] Furthermore, when the useful thing fails in its usefulness and becomes conspicuous, obtrusive, or obstinate (in the sense of getting in the way), the thing shows itself in its objective presence. In this latter case the abstraction occurs not through an act of Dasein (refusal, looking away, or penetrating beyond) but through a failure of the thing itself.

It is striking that for Heidegger the thing draws attention to itself only by ceasing to be itself in the full sense. There is here a 'logic of failure,'[24] by which the thing only in failing draws attention to itself, but then discloses itself in its objective presence as that which is also constitutive of it as a useful thing. In itself the useful thing is in relation to the totality of useful things, the totality of reference, the totality of involvements. But in itself the thing does not attract Dasein, indeed it deflects Dasein's attention away to that for which it is useful

(*Wozu—Umzu*) and finally to the worldliness of Dasein's own being. The thing only attracts Dasein's gaze to itself when it is deficient. Only in that mode does it attract Dasein's gaze and does so then as an object of pure perception, an object of scientific knowledge. The thing is conspicuous only when it becomes unusable for its task: "In such discovery of its unusability the useful thing becomes conspicuous [*fällt auf*]."[25] What is discovered here is in the first instance the thing in its handiness; after all, it is the thing as not useful for such and such a task that is conspicuous, hence as a useful thing in a deficient mode. But alongside that something else is discovered, namely, that the useful thing also was and is constantly objective presence, objectively present (*vorhanden*). "Pure objective presence announces itself [*meldet sich*] in the useful thing."[26] The useful thing shows itself in terms of what was and continues to be, namely, being present as a thing. It does so because attention can no longer shift from the thing; it remains with the thing, and discovers in it an object which can be examined and which has certain qualities that can be predicated to it. Normally such attention is fleeting; the concern with the thing directs Dasein to seek to repair it and in such repairing the pure presence at hand withdraws. But of course it need not so withdraw and in that glimpse we discover a relation to the past, to constancy, and to the thing as bearer of qualities all of which are discovered as necessary to the thing as a useful thing. The further cases of obtrusiveness and obstinacy develop the same theme of the interruption of the movement of the things at hand, the movement from useful thing to useful thing in their interrelations of reference and involvement. In such interruptions the thing does not change, but rather attention is directed at it in the modes of repair, helplessness, and frustration. As such the things do not "disguise themselves as mere things,"[27] but they do show themselves as more than simply at hand—even if this 'more than' is related to their being as at hand.

This 'more than' is found both, so to speak, below and above the useful thing, in its objective presence and its worldliness. Strikingly, Heidegger uses the same phrase 'announces itself' (*meldet sich*) to refer to the appearance of world as he does to the appearance of the objectively present:

> But in a *disturbance of reference*—in the unusefulness for . . . reference becomes explicit. . . . The context of useful things shines forth not as that never seen before, but rather as a totality that has constantly been seen beforehand. With this totality, however, world announces itself.[28]

The objectively present and the world both appear in this disturbance of reference and do so as constantly having been before. Objective presence and world are closely related in their appearance; they come to appearance when the attention is no longer diverted from the thing. But in the rupture of the movement of reference a double movement occurs: on the one hand, the thing appears as being always already present; on the other hand, the movement of handiness discloses itself as always already worldly. The thing shows its worldliness and at the same time shows itself as capable of entworlding:

> That the world does not 'consist' of what is at hand can be seen from the fact (amongst others) that when the world appears in the modes of taking care . . . an entworldling [*Entweltlichung*] of what is at hand occurs so that it appears as something merely objectively present.[29]

The entworldling of the thing occurs in the shining forth of world because this shining forth is only possible once the movement of reference breaks down. The worldliness of the thing is always present and has constantly been seen, but it can announce itself, can become thematic, only in the breakdown of those dealings with things in which it first appears. The thing in this case appears not as that which makes up the world, but rather as simply there, objectively present, without meaning—or rather deprived of meaning—and whose being-in-itself remains unexplainable. In this way Heidegger shows why it is that philosophy has consistently forgotten the ready to hand: when world shines forth it is not the 'ready to hand' which is seen but rather the present at hand. The methodological necessity of Heidegger's analysis is to avoid this pitfall. Things are worldly or are deprived of their worldliness—the thing is not its mere presence at hand although it discloses itself in its constancy and its pastness. The question we need to pose here is whether such constancy and pastness can adequately be accounted for as objective presence.

Does the useful thing only draw our attention when it fails? The wider question here is how to account for this useful thing in its origins. That the world is not simply made up of useful things, but rather is the opening which allows them to be, does not imply that the useful thing is worldly in its origins. The issue here is that of the 'first word':[30] if all is worldly, how can anything come to be? To come to be is to come to be in the world. But such a coming to be in the world is a coming into the world, is a rupturing of the world to let that thing be. This rupturing comes to appearance not in using a useful thing and not in its failure, but rather in the moment when I tarry with that thing, not the mere looking (*Nur-hinsehen*) of theoretical behavior,[31] but a being *drawn in* by the thing, being 'attached' to it as *this* thing here. Things are in their appearance irreducible to their usefulness. This mug could function perfectly well as a mug, if it were somewhat wider in diameter, if was black instead of blue and white, if it tapered such to be narrower at the base than at the top. I notice these aspects of the mug not because the mug is broken, is in the way, or that the coffee is missing, but rather because it attracts me and I am inclined to tarry a moment with it. Such a being-drawn-in does not fail to see the mug in its usability, but sees in it an excess of that usability. That excess is suggested by the color or shape which attracts: but it is not that color or that shape which attracts, rather it is the manifestation of color and shape in this mug. What is manifest there is a certain irreplaceability: the place in the movement of reference—in this case of drinking, of coffee, of porcelain, etc.—can be taken by any mug, but when I pause and tarry with *this* mug, I have before me not any possible mug, but this one. It appears to me as this singular mug, and yet there is nothing in the experience which cannot be articulated in general terms.[32] Nevertheless, in the joints of this articulation, in the nothing of the non-articulating point of articulation, *that* is disclosed which cannot be expressed as such, namely, the radiance of this thing and its abysmal withdrawal. Its withdrawal is not into a simple presence at hand—as Heidegger makes clear, the objective presence is the realm of scientific knowledge, the realm of predication and general terms[33]—but rather a withdrawal from worldliness as such. What is pointed to here is not a constancy and pastness, but rather that which lies at the origins of such constancy, the immemorial past present that is not at hand in the thing. The wonder of this mug is its being there, its having come into being: this mug and none other than this mug. 'Before' handiness and objective presence, before worldliness and entworlding, is the coming into the world, the creative rupture of being-in in which 'this and not that' is possible.

To tarry in this way with an entity—to be drawn toward, seduced, and educated by it—is to experience it in its singular origin, belonging, dependency, and to be concerned with it in terms of these singularities manifest in it. No thing originates in, belongs to, or depends on the world; to be a thing is to come into the world—even *a* mug comes into the world through a process in which it becomes what it never was before. The time of the world gives no future and has no past; the time of things in the world is a time which comes from elsewhere, from an immemorial origin and an unknown destiny. The concern with entities in their singular being is a concern with them in their singular coming to be.

While nothing experienced or said of this mug has meaning outside contexts of reference in which this mug is, this mug by that very token escapes such contexts. It escapes *not* as an indefinable 'x' underlying such references, but rather as that which gathers these references together, as nothing in these references but as that without which such a web of references would have no basis, no anchor. It is that nothing at the core of the being of things, which requires elucidation. It is to that nothing that faith in the word of god refers. The faith in the word of god is a faith in that which speaks of things in the world as if they were not of the world. It is for this reason too that messianic discourse takes the form of 'x' as not 'x,' e.g., weeping as not weeping (1 Corinthians 7:29).[34] The negation here is a negation of the world, a negation of that thing in its worldly relations in order to reveal itself as it manifests an origin beyond itself. Here we are speaking no longer of innerworldly things, but of beings-in-the-world. In relation to others Dasein encounters a mode of being-in-the-world 'in' the world.[35] This entity—which is encountered within the world—is neither at hand nor objectively present. It is encountered not as itself, but rather as a way of being-in-the-world. Dasein experiences its own worldliness as a worldliness with others. But in that case the other never appears except in terms of its possible being-in-relation to worldly things. In the account in *Being and Time* Dasein does not face any other Dasein: it relates to other Dasein through solicitude, which in either of its modalities (leaping in or leaping ahead)[36] is directed not so much at the other Dasein as it is at Dasein in its being toward the world (it is in this respect that Levinas's critique of Heidegger seems indisputable). Face to face with Dasein is face to face with that which is neither present at hand nor ready to hand because it attracts me in the singularity of its being and points me to that which breaks with the finitude of the world. Face to face with Dasein, being-in appears as in excess of itself. To weep as not weeping for Paul makes sense only because he understands the human not simply as being-in-the-world but as being-in-Christ (*en Kristoi einai*) and Christ being-in-him. This motif of being-in-Christ is a central one for Paul. It does not simply refer to exceptional 'mystical' experiences (although some exegetes interpret it in this way), rather it refers to a fundamental understanding of being, namely the being specific to a certain event—the event of Christ. It is being-in-response to that event: this response transforms being-in-the-world, specifically in a liberation from sin and death (cf. Romans 8:1). This liberation is a liberation from the finitude of being: to be in Christ is to be in the infinite, to be in the one who was "from the beginning" and who has "defeated" death. In Christ is to be found joy and hope even when there is nothing in the world to justify them. This is a response to being "called in the Lord" (1 Corinthians 7:22). This call is a call to be outside the self and indeed it is in this being outside the self that the "folly of the cross" consists.[37] This 'ecstatic' being is existence which exceeds the ecstasis of which Heidegger speaks, because being outside the self means being outside the being-in-the-world which constitutes the self. This is made possible by living in Christ. To live in Christ is to understand the world from beyond any worldly sense: "I have been crucified with Christ; and now it is no longer I that lives, but Christ that lives in me" (Galatians 2:19–20). In this sense the self is no longer the subject of its being. The self experiences being not as its being, but rather as that being which was always and constantly remains. That being is hidden, because its expression in the world is confined to its referential and involvemental placement. It can only be made apparent in the moment, through a pure expression of being which is what the figure of Christ is. To live in Christ is to live the example of Christ, which is to live in devotion to a call and a sending, which is prior to the being of the self. Living in terms of the event of Christ a radical rupture of belonging is experienced. Such a rupture in belonging does not mean an end of worldly existence, but rather a being-in-the-world which is toward entities in the world as being prior to the world. This is the condition of being as neither Jew nor Gentile, free nor slave, neither man nor woman (Galatians 3:28). This is the way of being by faith, the way of being which lives in terms of the origin and the end of the world—in other words, in terms of a creative source which the self cannot contain and which hides itself from the world.

To be in Christ is to be in response to the infinite. It expresses a way of being-in-the-world and toward entities in the world that responds to that in them which exceeds them as useful things and as objects of perception and linguistic experience. Such experience of the infinite in the finite finds its exemplification in the incarnation. To weep as not weeping, is to appear not as the self which the world sees. In the same way the incarnate divine appears not as itself, but as a man. But appearing as a man is not appearing in disguise, as Zeus did in his seduction of Alcemene. Rather, as von Balthasar puts it: "Jesus the man, in his visibleness, is not a sign pointing beyond himself to an invisible 'Christ of faith'. . . . The image and expression of God, according to the Biblical assertion, is the indivisible God-man: man, in so far as God radiates from him; God, in so far as he appears in the man Jesus."[38]

Being-in-Christ is a being-in peace. To be in Christ is to live in the possibility of peace, not as a projection, but rather as a real possibility in the world. This is a messianic statement pointing to a possibility of peace beyond the agons of the world, a possibility which the Incarnation suggests is not to be deferred to a distant utopian time but intersects with the time of today.

Singularity and the Messianic

There is no place in the world for the messianic. The messianic is utopic: it is and has no place. It is a non-place in the world, or more precisely it reveals the aplatiality of all that is in the world, the inessentiality of its place to the being of an existent. The messianic is similarly achronic: it is and has no time. It is the non-temporal in the world, or, more precisely, it reveals the achronology of all that is in the world, the inessentiality of its time to the being of an existent. This is not to say that the messianic renders place and time meaningless, rather that it shows time and place in their determinate manifestations as encrustations of a becoming temporal and spatial which itself cannot be understood in terms of time and space already constituted. In the Christian understanding it is no longer possible to speak without qualification of the messianic as 'to come,' or as that which might come, nor is it possible again without qualification to speak as Derrida does of 'messianism without a messiah,' because the fundamental experience of Christianity is of the having come of the messiah.[39] As 'having come' the messiah is experienced as the one who has *already* transformed past, present, and future and transformed the place in which human beings live. In so doing the messiah allows things to appear as not being what they are (in the world), allows things to appear as of no place and no time, as beyond all reference and all involvement. It is important to insist on this: the event of Christ in having occurred draws all of time together in a moment, turns human and natural history as on a pivot, and declares an origin outside the play of difference. This is phenomenologically impossible, or rather is that which punctures the differential field of phenomena with that which such phenomena cannot hold.

The messianic appears in the call; the messianic is vocational. It is a call not of being or of the other, but rather a call which echoes in the 'least of things' and calls to existence as ecstasies. Such a call is to see things not in their worldliness but as they are at the 'end of the world.' But the 'end of the world' has already happened: things appear to an existence answering the messianic call as what they are not—for the world—namely as singular entities expressing their own unique origin. The messianic call is to see things in a state of liberation "from this present wicked world [*ek tou aionos tou evestotos*]" (Galatians 1:4). Such a liberation is from the world in the age (*aion*) of its ending, that is, in the age where existence in the world can be in the world as already ended. This is possible for Paul only through an event, the event of the coming of the messiah.

Paul and many of the early church fathers conceived the coming of the messiah in terms of a recapitulation of the past in the figure of Christ, a recapitulation which exceeds the life of Jesus of Nazareth and returns through to the Hebrew scriptures back to the very beginning of the world. It is in this sense that Christ was said to recapitulate the history of humanity and indeed of all creation. As Paul puts it: "he [the father] recapitulated [*anakephalaiokai*] everything in Christ" (Ephesians 1:10). Just as the head is the guiding principle of the body, so too the event of Christ is the guiding principle of all that is. This entails a re-reading of the past in terms of that event. The very uniqueness of the event of Christ means that the seeking of signs in the past requires a radical refiguration of that past, which is evident in the reinterpretation of passages in the Hebrew scriptures as prefiguring Christ. The uncritical and often forced readings which this entailed resulted from an understanding of the past as being transformed in its meaning by this event: the past is refigured in terms of the Christ event and takes on new and unprecedented meanings. This is captured in the designation of Christ as the 'new Adam.' The Incarnation repeats creation, but does so not through an agon of god and human, but rather through the intersection of divine and human in the figure of Christ. This intersection of divine and human means the irruption of the messianic in the 'present age' (aoin).

When in the present age the divine and human intersect—when the messianic intermingles with the temporal and spatial order of the world—then what is appears as if it were not. To appear as if it were not is to appear as the nothing out of which it comes. But this nothing appears in each case singularly because it is an appearance of aplatiality and achronology in the temporal and spatial thing itself. The thing shows itself *in its own nothingness,* which is to say, in its own absolute passivity toward its coming into being. Before all reference and all involvement the thing comes into being, comes into the world, and that coming into the world is the precondition of all its meaningfulness. The messianic allows that singular being of the entity to shine forth not as other than its 'at hand,' objectively present being, but as that attraction in the thing which hides itself as functionality and as objective presence. In so doing it does not give the thing a fixed identity, but rather brings out the tension in the thing between its self and its source which is its alone but cannot be regained in the self. The messianic displays a fundamental immemoriality in all things—its coming into being for which it was never present.

The messianic time is not the time of the future but of the now (*ho nun kairos*).[40] The present is a time of chronos *and* kairos, of temporal order and the disruption of that order. This disruption is experienced in the thing which shows itself in its abysmal origin and in the promise of its being: both amount to the same thing, namely, the showing itself as an entity whose being discloses the end of the world. What is disclosed here is origin and salvation, both of which express the relation to coming into being—creation. The messianic intensifies to breaking point the relation of creature to creator, entity to its abysmal origin in love. This relation is a non-relational one—a relation to an origin which is not present, which cannot be made present. To weep as not weeping is to weep in that non-relational relation, which is precisely no action in the world, but a non-action at the roots of the acting relation. The passing action of weeping is performed not in terms of itself, but in terms of that non-relational relation of the self to its origin which is expressed through weeping. That self-expression is a double relation of alterity to the immemorial origins of the self and to the eyes which see that self beyond the economy of the world. Those eyes are the eyes of faith.[41]

Faith, we have said, is the openness to the splendor of things. But in a messianic context it is more than that, or rather the splendor of things takes on a more profound significance. The double relation to alterity is seen only through faith, faith though understood as this eye for things beyond their surface exterior and their conceptual generality, an eye for the singularity of things which embodies generality and which appears externally, but which is never reducible to either. Faith is not opposed to the Law—to the realm of the general—but rather places the latter on its true footing (cf. Romans 3:31). Only in faith—only by the eyes which see things in relation not to the world but to the creator god—is each singular thing perceived; faith in Christ is the openness to Christ living in the believer and as such living in the world in terms of an origin and a promise beyond the world. Such a relation is a stepping beyond the self toward the other in faith. Such a step is done in peace.

Peace and Being

"War [*polemos*] is the father of all."[42] Worldly being is polemical. The world is only in the war of opposites, in erotic struggle for appropriation, possession, incorporation. Existence, however, is peaceful. Within the world existence is a movement of disappropriation, dispossession, disincorporation—a movement of privation in being-in-the-world. But such a movement is a movement of being as existence; understood otherwise it repeats the dynamic of struggle and strife, this time of strife against being-in-the-world. The (moral) "certitude of peace," of which Levinas speaks, cannot overcome the evidence of war because it has its source in a fundamental violence. This violence, the "good violence" of the other, is a violence of provocation rather than vocation, which calls the self not to its being but to the overthrow of its being (understood as being-in-the-world). It does this in the name of the "eschatology of messianic peace." But this peace is against history and against politics; it is an excess of totality which is 'otherwise than being,' beyond ontological categories. This assumes that ontological categories are totalizing and violent; on such an assumption the only peace possible is violent and interruptive of the being-of the existent. But in such a case peace becomes impossible, caught between the violence of being and the ethical violence of the other.

But cannot peace be thought ontologically? *Shalom* comes from *shalem*, to be whole, uninjured. It suggests harmony—not an opposition—of being and justice: the peaceful being is the one which is whole and not subject to injustice (injury). Indeed, in the Hebrew scriptures as an eschatological vision of peace was developed it was understood in terms of well-being and happiness. Peace in this understanding is the fulfillment of being, a fulfillment which, however, depends on the free gift of Yahweh.[43] That gift, it is increasingly understood in the prophetic writings, is to come through the messiah, the "prince of peace" (Isaiah 9:6). But what the messiah would bring is not the peace of empires, the peace won by war, but rather a peace which is not of the world—a peace which worldly concerns can never achieve. Such concerns are wicked if they are exhaustive of all concern and "'no peace,' says Yahweh, 'for the wicked'" (Isaiah 48:22, 57:21).

But the wicked is *not* the worldly as such. "Not because we are in the world do we turn away from God, but only if we meddle with the sins of the world," Tertullian states.[44] To meddle with the sins of the world is to understand entities in the world exclusively as being of the world. The point of faith is not belief in this or that doctrine,[45] but rather openness to things in the world in their unworldliness.[46] This principle is ultimately that of peace, the interruption of the erotic polemics of the world in which beyond the hierarchical order of 'thingly' relations that which is withdraws into its singular being.[47] Faith dispenses not so much with reason as with the ordering strategies—those of dominance and subordination—through which reason brings things in relation to each other according to an ultimate principle or principles. Reason does not work in peace. This is not to say that reason is violent or evil. Rather, reason in its necessary and often liberating operations can never allow things to be as they are in themselves, can never leave things in peace. To leave things in peace is to live with them peacefully.

It is to this peaceful living that Paul constantly returns. In Philippians he states: "Never worry about anything [*meden merimnate*]; but tell God all your desires of every kind in prayer and petition shot through with gratitude, and the peace of God which is beyond our understanding will guard your hearts and your thoughts in Christ Jesus" (4:6–7). Worry, that is, concern or care, about things is opposed here to desire. The passage parallels the exhortation not to worry about life, not to be concerned about things in their usefulness, in their involvement and relevance with respect to eating and clothing (Matthew 6:25; Luke 12:22). Life—*psyche*—Jesus goes on to say in those passages is more than food. This excess is an excess not alone of the worldly but of any power within the world: "Can any of you, however much you worry, add one single cubit to your span of life?" (Matthew 7:27). Such worldly concern is powerless over life; it cannot bring into being that which is not already in being. At the limits of worldly power is that which can only come from elsewhere: "Set your hearts on his [the Father's] kingdom first. . . . So do not worry about tomorrow; tomorrow will take care of itself" (7:33–34). Desire in the face of such powerlessness comes to appear as itself. It is in relation to god—in relation to the non-worldly—that desire appears and does so in its prayerfulness. Desire responds to the call of the phenomenon and does so in prayer and gratitude; desire brings nothing about but allows in its outward, ecstatic movement that which is godly to appear. That movement is a movement of mind and heart (*noemata* and *kardria*), of thoughts and feelings, which moves not in worldly concern, but in concern for things as they manifest themselves. In such concern—in such desire—people are guarded by the "peace of God." Such peace is a peace beyond worldly concern, beyond "our understanding."

Such peace is the non-relational relation to the absolute—peace itself. That which cannot be experienced is not another realm, not a transcendent realm beyond the world. On the basis of religious commitments it is of course possible to speak of such a realm. But even such accounts must begin somewhere, and they must begin in an intuition of a horizon not of the world. This is a messianic intuition, which finds its warrant in the limits of experience itself.

If Heraclitus is right to say that war (polemos) is the father of all, it is so only within the immanence of the world. Within the world, within the self-enclosure of a world in which nothing acts or is acted upon which is not affected by the world, there is nothing except agonistic conflict. War may (as Aristotle tells us) be for the sake of peace, but the more precious this peace, the more violence it legitimates. To strive for peace, to indeed fight for peace, is to increase war, increase the violent destruction of difference. Only that which has an effect beyond the interactions and interchanges of the world can offer peace. Not only can we not make peace, peace cannot be made. Rather peace comes if at all as a gift. The moment of being affected by a gift, by a love which seeks no return, is the moment of peace—a moment which escapes the time of the world.

Kabod, Doxa, Gloria

The messiah is the 'prince of peace' (Isaiah 9:6), who 'comes in glory.' 'Glory' translates *doxa*.[48] 'Doxa' we translate self-evidently as 'opinion.' An opinion is the statement of how things appear to someone. The Greek phrase *dokei moi* means, 'it appears so to me.' What appears in a certain way must come to appearance, must shine forth in some way, must show itself. In shining forth it brings light on itself. Hence, doxa has the meaning of fame. This has a wider political context: doxa has the connotation of one who states best how things appear, convincing his community that his viewpoint is true and hence warranting the good opinion of his community. He should be spoken of well and most importantly remain in our memories. Hence, doxa opens up a future. The one who can give the worthiest opinion is the one who corresponds best to those appearances and in so doing makes that which appears apparent, as if for the first time. Although doxa is subject to critique by Plato, for him too it has its proper place (as we have seen). In this respect he follows Parmenides, for whom the way of doxa is that which needs also to be learned.[49]

Now with the Septuagint translation of the Bible the difficulty arose of translating the Hebrew term *kabod*.[50] This term has the connotation of weightiness. It is that which gives any living being an external force or impetus and is in that sense close in meaning to the Latin *gravitas*.[51] The person with kabod has 'weight' in his community. The weightiness of the person is that which makes him stand out, be apparent in an emphatic sense. In that sense it can be a word for riches: the man with riches stands out, has a standing. In fact in this original sense kabod approaches the pre-philosophical meaning of *ousia:* it refers to the property owned by the person. Jacob's whole wealth is referred to as his kabod (Genesis 31:1). When used in reference to god kabod refers to that which makes god apparent. While the difficulty is to think an invisible god, when he does reveal himself the appearance is referred to as kabod. The weightiness of god, however, is such that it cannot be seen. God can only show himself by *not* appearing in person. For this reason throughout the Hebrew scriptures (and this can also be seen in the New Testament account of the Ascension) the appearance of god is cloaked in a cloud. God shines too brightly for human eyes to see (cf. Exodus 24:13). There can be no correspondence to his appearance. His appearance is hidden because it breaks with the possibility of appearance in this world. That which is beyond the measure of this world reveals itself only as that which cannot be made apparent. As Karl Rahner puts it: "[I]n communicating himself as *deus relevetus* he becomes radically open to man as *deus absconditus.*"⁵² To capture this meaning in Greek the translators of the Hebrew scriptures used the word 'doxa.' The appearance of that which appears—doxa—in the case of that which is invisible comes to mean the manifestation of that which does not show itself. It refers to the invisibility of god, invisible in the sense of being blinding to human vision, an excess of light.⁵³ The glory of the Lord lies precisely in the fact that no eye can see him as he is. Doxa comes to mean that which shows itself only by blinding, that of which there can be no opinion, because there can be no correspondence. Knowledge is not ruled out here, but rather transformed into a knowing which cannot claim mastery over its object. The proper response to this glory is not thinking in the sense of seeking after wisdom. Glory calls not for opinion, not for discussion and argument, but rather for praise (*doxazo*). The praise of god is a *giving* of glory.

Between the Classical and biblical senses doxa means appearance and non-appearance, opinion and praise, worldly fame and that 'which is not of this world.' While the specific meaning of 'glory' is not Classical, that meaning indicates the transformation the word underwent in the encounter between the Greek and Judeo-Christian worlds. It also indicates the core of the conflict at the heart of the cross which "to the gentiles [is] foolishness" (1 Corinthians 1:24). That which is insignificant, indeed "less than nothing," for the world, brings god to appearance in the world. The appearance of things is no longer simply that which arises in the opening of the world, but that which bears the trace of that which is not of this world, but which calls from beyond it (cf. 1 Corinthians 1:26). Encapsulated in this word 'doxa' is fundamental phenomenological difference, which concerns the place of epistēme, knowledge, in relation to the world. As we have seen, the Pauline account of pistis, faith, subverts the divided line in terms of forms of understanding, so too here at the more fundamental level of the division between epistēme and doxa relations become subverted. 'Epistēme' takes on a negative meaning in Paul. Epistēme distracts from the divine. Knowledge of things in the world, as they appear and as they indicate their invisible forms, leads not to god, but away from god.

All knowledge in the political world is opinion, and in that world opinion as the showing of the world as it is for me brings with it relations of glorification and praise. In that world the opinions of the most powerful and the opinions which convince and garner power call not alone for agreement but for praise. Such praise and glorification is not simply for individuals or parties, but for the political world as such: the political world is one in which power is never without glory and glory is never without power. To the extent to which epistēme is permitted within a body politic it is so as inglorious, as not partaking in the glory of the world. Both Socrates and Christ function as fundamental challenges to such political glory, but in diametrically opposed ways. In the case of Socrates

glorification as such is called into question. In the anti-political stance to which
he gave at least some inspiration, philosophy attempts to block glory and glorification through a critique of political doxa. In this sense it could be said that the
philosophical critique of doxa glimpses the issue of glory as an underlying aspect
of doxa, but responds to it by conceiving the polis in terms of the wider cosmos—
indeed in Stoicism this reaches a logical end in the notion of the cosmo-polis.

In John's Gospel, however, but more emphatically in Paul's letters, there is
a shift in the meaning of cosmos, from the world—in a cosmological sense, in
which case the heavenly bodies and not the mere affairs of men are of central
importance—to an 'anthropological' sense in which the world refers to the affairs
of men, what we might call the worldly.[54] In this sense, Christianity launches a
critique of the political as does Greek philosophy but from different perspectives:
while philosophy subordinates doxa to epistēme, Christianity exploits the element of glory implicit in political doxa in order to invert and subvert it.

In Paul his addressees are admonished that faith in Christ demands that the
believer live in the world as if not being-of-the-world (1 Corinthians 7:29–31). The
justification for this is the 'glory of the cross,' that which in the eyes of the world
is as nothing becomes the manifestation of god's love. Epistēme is undermined
not in relation to the world, but rather is understood as confined to the world,
confined to a world understood now as the human, political world. Doxa is not of
the world and as such escapes the boundaries of epistēme. Implicit in Paul is so
to speak a squeezing out of any space for philosophy: things in the world are distractions because they concern the human only as human; what is to be glimpsed
is that which is not of the world in the world. The object of philosophy is then
either the world, which is merely human, or the divine, which no philosophical
speculation can reach because it is from beyond the world and as such cannot be
sought, but appeals and can only be awaited (1 Corinthians 1:26).

Such waiting is prayerful and liturgical. Both prayer and liturgy are given
an important place in the later Plato; in the *Laws* he speaks explicitly of praising
and praying to the gods (*Laws* 7, 801e). He does so, however, in a manner that in-
tegrates such praise and prayer into the proper functioning of the body politic.[55]
In Paul, on the contrary, praise and prayer interrupts, disrupts the world in the
name of that which is not of the world.

Prayer to a king and prayer to god are different—if related—acts. To pray
to god is to acknowledge not alone one's own impotence, but the impotence of
any worldly relation. Prayer is care at the limits of its power. Whether prayers of
petition, lament, thanksgiving, all prayer is implicitly or explicitly an acknowledgment of weakness, impotency, and an act of praise not of the one with more
worldly power (the king, the sovereign) but of the one outside the economy of
such power. In that sense the Christian god is radically apolitical.[56] Praise and
glorification of this god is an acknowledgment of the contingency of the worldly

as such. While the Greek and Roman pre-Christian gods were higher potencies in the worldly polemos, the Christian god marks a radical refusal of the political, indeed a flight from religion as a political expression.[57] It is of course the case that this flight has through the history of Christianity been curbed and reversed by an integration into the political, a move from worldlessness to worldliness, from a religion of the end of the world to a world religion under Constantine. This is betrayal certainly, but one which expresses the ambivalent place of the Christian in the world *as if* not of the world. This ambivalence forms the context of the Christian account of glorification and praise.

To pray in the Christian sense is to be placed between world and worldlessness. The present is understood eschatologically as already manifesting, but doing so secretly, secreted from the world, the kingdom to come—and at the same time appealing for that kingdom. This appeal is an affirmation of openness toward that in the present which does not depend for its meaning on a system of signs, but rather acts to indicate an approach, an address of the 'to come' (*à venir*), incarnated in the present. The direction of signification changes: instead of a sign pointing to its signified, the sign bears the mark of the singular movement of address. The sign does not in this sense make the divine present, nor does it substitute for the divine, but rather indicates an infinity in the present which the present cannot hold. This infinity is suggested by language itself which both aims to capture things in their finitude through a clarity of reference and at the same time always expands beyond that finitude toward an infinity indicated by the lack of ends in linguistic expression. This infinity of language—its polysemy, ambiguity, non-referentiality—is affirmed and made explicit in the event of revelation where the propriety over language is finally disclosed as illusory and the fundamental openness of words toward the infinite origin in things is revealed.[58]

It is thus that Christ can be understood as a sign: precisely as broken, Christ testifies to the infinite distance to god.[59] The sign is revelatory to the extent to which it opens up such an infinity in itself, which ruptures any system of signs in which it has its place. It is to such a revelation that prayer responds. It responds, however, not to any constative content in the said, not even to a saying without the said, but rather to a silence, constitutive of revelation.[60] Revelation is constitutively silent in that revelation reveals nothing. The words of the scriptures do not together make up revelation. Those words can be reworked into the propositions of moral philosophy, such that as with Kant we can say that revelation as such is inessential.[61] Any attempt to understand Christianity as a "message" ends in emptying revelation of all meaning. What is missed is that which can only be understood in and as silence, namely the coming into the world of that which is not of the world, the being addressed by someone in the world who is not of the world.[62] Such silence is not simply a void, an emptiness: the silence happens between the words, between the works and acts. It is responded to in prayer, that is, by turning away from the normal commerce of words, a "taking of attention to the highest degree," as Simone Weil says.[63] But this does not mean attending more closely to what concerns the self anyway, but rather attending to that in things which goes beyond its powers to perceive or to act upon.

In praising god the Christian does not simply put god on the highest pedestal—that is as Nietzsche has shown the route to nihilism—but rather lets all worldly hierarchies dissolve. Hier-archy is the initiatory power of the holy. To see things in the world hierarchically is to see them in terms of this initiation of the holy. To see things in that way is—paradoxically—to see them in an unworldly equality. It is not by accident that the term 'hierarchy' is of Christian coinage: it both affirms and destabilizes the ancient order of being. As understood by Pseudo-Dionysius who coined the term, 'hierarchy' is the ordered ranking of beings in relation to god, but this order is to be understood dynamically as a way in which understanding and activity approximate to the divine, to his creatures, and back again. It is an order not of institutional power, but of access to the divine through imitation by means of purification, illumination, and perfection.[64] Hence, the function of hierarchy is to bring creatures toward unity with god. Indeed, as Pseudo-Dionysius affirms, from the point of view of god there is no hierarchy of beings, there is rather only double ranking order of holy initiation and of beings-in-the-world which equally share in that initiatory power for their being.[65] The praise of god is hierarchical in principle in the sense that it affirms the relation to a holy beginning, a beginning before and beyond the self and its power; but such praise does not assert a hierarchical place.[66] Prayer is rather a making room for grace, a making room for god's self-sanctification and self-glorification in the world.[67] This self-glorification is not subject to any pre-given hierarchy, but rather names the recognition of a light and darkness before which one stands as before an abysmal origin and which appears both immediately and mediately, both as unworldly and as worldly.

The crossing of worldly and unworldly is symbolized in the cross, the crucifixion of Jesus Christ.

Glory and the Cross

The ancient gods—Greek and Semitic alike—abhorred death. In Homer the hero knew his death was imminent when he sensed the god or goddess who championed him fleeing from his presence. The destiny of death was that which not even Zeus, the father of the gods, could stop—nor could any god be present to it. Death separated the immortals from the mortals as that which the immortals could not know—neither of themselves nor of others. Knowledge of death separated the human from all other beings, including the gods.

In this respect the death of god, the crucifixion of Jesus of Nazareth, was a monumental event, a seismic shift. Despite its clear articulation by Paul, the nature of this event was difficult to comprehend, to integrate. For many amongst the early church fathers only the death of the man Jesus of Nazareth was comprehensible—the divine did not die.[68] Since then the notion of the death of god is a controversial one theologically. But if Christ is to be understood as 'true god and true man,' then this should extend to death as well; otherwise the 'victory' of the resurrection seems a hollow one. With this death not alone did a god enter the presence of death (as in the case of the 'raising of Lazarus'), but had known death, had died. Not just death, but a humiliating death. The humiliation of death is made manifest in the crucifixion. No greater testament could there be to the earthly corporeality of the incarnate god.[69]

The crucifixion makes manifest god as powerless: powerless against his enemies, against suffering, against mortality. This powerlessness gives ultimate expression to desire: it is the powerlessness beyond appropriation, the powerlessness namely of love—*agápe*. John Caputo hints at this when he says: "suppose that God's power over human beings is limited by love."[70] Except this is not a limiting of power as much as an expression of the limits of power. No power in the world can withstand the crucifixion because it testifies to a love beyond all worldly erotics. It testifies to this not by any action, but by an extreme passivity. This passivity is in the name of the kingdom, which is not of this world: the kingdom to come.

It is in this sense vital neither to rush past Good Friday nor to elevate it to the speculative heights of a moment of absolute spirit (Hegel). The death of Jesus Christ either has a meaning as such, or the resurrection far from giving it that meaning becomes a rather comic and demeaning sequel. The suffering of Good Friday is the suffering of a man/god. In other words, these sufferings cannot be sublimated. Glory is the appearance of suffering as love, that is, as without reward. There is no account which dissolves such suffering, which makes them good again (*wieder gut machen*, as the German expression puts it). Rather, the description we give needs to take into account what that suffering itself means. If there is a glory, if what appears in the world can point to something which is not of the world, it does so by unsettling worldly relations. A body appears in glory by appearing not alone as that which is in excess of its worldly appearance, but as that which puts the worldly relations in which it plays 'out of play.' This requires that the body appear so to 'eyes that can see, and ears that can hear.' Jesus of Nazareth suffers without appearing as anything more than an object of fun, less than a dog, to the Roman soldiers who whipped and mocked him. Yet Mark relates the Centurion as saying, "truly this man was son of God" (Mark 15:39). The account of suffering which we find in the Synoptic Gospels speaks of the humiliation and anguish of suffering. Death is suffered as that which expresses the ultimate passivity of the human being—death as not simply an end, but as an end*ing*, something suffered in pain, fear, and humiliation. The possibility of embodying light and sky as glimpsed in the transfiguration is slowly undone in the body feeling itself in the heaviness of its own immobile earthiness. Yet, as John in his account makes clear, this suffering is also a glory and a glorification. (In this John is not contradicting, but rather complementing the synoptics.) In the acceptance of suffering, i.e., in the openness to both the agent of suffering and the self's own vulnerability to that suffering, the cross signifies being as a giving, which exceeds the polemos of the world. The glory of the cross lies in that condescension of divinity to the final earthiness of the flesh in showing the unworldly destiny of earth and flesh.

The glory of Christ is expressed in the suffering cry of "*Eloi, eloi, lama sabachthani*" (Mark 15:34); this is the dark night of Good Friday, which Easter Sunday cannot wipe out.[71] The death of Christ goes to the heart of his revelation: nothing which Christ said required a revelation; there are no esoteric truths there, no hidden mysteries.[72] The mystery lies in the life and death itself, in the revealing of the light as suffering and death. It is not the outward movement of the message (the "good news") which gives meaning to the withdrawing motion of suffering and death, but rather the reverse. In the night of this death, in the attraction and the rejection, the hope and the despair, death appears as a mode of being-in-the-world which is an assertion of not being-of-the-world. Death suffered in this way is martyrdom, a bearing witness to the insufficiency of the world. Death as martyrdom is witness to a claim which nothing in the world, considered only as of the world, can make. In terms of the world, death is nothing other than for the individual an end of existence and for the world the end of one point of view on the world. But that point of view is in terms of the world infinitely substitutable. Just as the heavenly constellations return finally to the same place (the "great year"), so too one existence can finally be repeated, down to the last detail. Cosmologically—for a discourse which does not go beyond the world—the eternal return of the same is an ultimate and unavoidable truth affirmed in different ways by Heraclitus, Plato, the Stoics, and Nietzsche. The affirmation of the uniqueness of Christ, the affirmation that is of a historically significant moment—unrepeatable, unprecedented, refiguring of past and present—is the denial of return, the affirmation of a being irreducible to the world. This affirmation implies a fundamental change in the understanding of death.

"Dying he destroyed our death . . ." Those words of the Catholic liturgy depend for their resonance not on a belief in the afterlife—such a belief was not (and is not) peculiar to Christianity. Rather, they mean a bringing of death into the realm of the living, a living with death in an unprecedented manner. Death, which in the ancient world was kept beyond the walls of the city and far away from sacred space, is now placed at the center of the holy. The dead and the divine were reconciled in one and brought within the city. Christian churches are tombs: built around altars which contain relics, bodies between life and death—dead and yet making present the principle of life, the example of Christ. The Christian worships among the dead, walks the way of death and crucifixion in the church, and goes through death in entering the church.[73] Death is no longer unclean, no longer accursed. Rather, death as a leaving of life becomes a way of living: no longer a preparation for death but to live now as if after death, as if death were destroyed.[74]

The glory of the cross is the 'victory' over death. This victory does not lie in the resurrection as if the latter rescued meaning in the wake of a meaningless death, but rather in the free acceptance of death out of agapeic love. As Stanislaus Breton points out,[75] this victory is only meaningful if there is something in human beings which does not flow from the world. In that sense the cross returns us to that nothingness which is not of the world, the nothingness of an origin which has no reason, the origin of our singular being. But such a return is a return to things in the world as expressions of that origin in a love without ground.

Radiance of Things

The return to things as expressions of an origin without ground is to return to things in their own radiance. Things have a "splendor of their own" (1 Corinthians 15:40): both earthly and heavenly bodies have doxa—glory, splendor. Splendor, glory is of the thing itself, or the thing as earthly or as heavenly. If for Paul the invisible is to be understood by means of visible things, this is not to be understood Platonically in terms of imitation or resemblance: the invisible is that promise of a spiritual destiny in the visible. While the life of *psyche* is in the world and of the world, the *pneuma* is the being-of that thing in its own singular being, as that which is not simply of the world. The promise of a spiritual destiny is earthly and heavenly things facing not the other entities in the world and not themselves; they are seen not in the light of the world but as light.[76] As von Balthasar puts it: "We see form as splendor, as the glory of Being."[77] Such an appearance is not of that which is present as an object in its superficial, i.e., surface appearance, but of that which shows itself only as an absence in the appearance and which in such ambiguous presence appeals in and through the singular thing as perceived to the heart as that organ guided by faith, hope, and love.

The theological virtues of faith, hope, and love capture a way of being with things which understands them in their promise. It is a way of being toward things in their splendor. Each is directed toward the 'to come'—a future present in the thing itself, a *parousia*, which is already a presence of the coming in the present.[78] Each is implicated in resurrection, in a future beyond the death of the now. Each now is a death, in which even the inanimate by its participation in time dies in the sense of being lost forever. But every moment proclaims both death and life everlasting: the gift of a future beyond the death of the moment, a gift the promise of which is to be found in all things. This is the profound truth of Leibniz's *Monadology*: nothing *in the world* goes into or out of being.[79] This truth is supplemented by Kierkegaard: things go into and out of existence only through god.[80] But this promise is never fully confirmed; being of the everlasting can never find rational or sufficient confirmation. The existence of things is an existence which, without faith, hope, and love, ends in despair.

Things appear as that which cannot be fully captured in constative sentences. The tree I see out my window is an ash tree, it towers above me, its branches reach skyward, its leaves go back and forth in the wind. I can make these statements more precise. I can say that it is a 'common ash.' I can give the Latin term for ash tree—*fraxinus excelsior.* I can give the exact measurement of the height of the tree, and I can give also the measurement of the angle of the branches, the speed of movement of the leaves. These sentences do not merely miss the thisness of the tree; they also freeze the movement of time. In formulating these sentences I am already speaking of the past and in speaking of the past as if it were present I am passing over the difference of past and present, the difference namely of the promise of the future which allows time to pass, allows a becoming past. No constative sentence can capture this difference, no sentence which refers albeit indirectly to a belief *that* I see such and such. The promise of resurrection in things, their inner splendor, points rather to an attitude directed toward the future, of which I can only believe *in*.[81] This belief in the promise of things is a faith which goes beyond the seen to that which cannot be seen, which is never fully present, which no evidence can fully justify, and yet makes all perception and all knowledge possible. In Luke's account of the incident on the road to Emmaus the disciples, in recalling their discussions with the man whom "their eyes were prevented from recognizing" (Luke 24:13), said, "did not our hearts burn within us as he talked to us on the road and explained the scriptures to us" (Luke 24:32). While their eyes failed to recognize him, their hearts were touched. It is the heart which is the locus of faith—faith is not merely a cognitive act, but an act of self-giving, which expresses existence in openness toward the being-of the other in its singularity.

Such faith is an openness toward things in the promise of their being. While faith recognizes things as broken signs, as signs which indicate a rupture in the system of signs, the affirmation of the ultimate goodness of things is an affirmation of hope. Hope is an excess in faith, a faith that things can be beyond the possibilities of human doing or conception. While in faith the self recognizes things in their self-giving and in the gift of their future, hope is in the transformative power of that gift: hope is not simply a belief in things, but is also a readiness for the presence of the whole splendor of things, a readiness for things to reveal themselves in their splendor and glory.

Being toward things in the promise of their being is not pre-structured by expectation or anticipation. Such a being toward is an openness to the thing as that which cannot be comprehended, hence cannot be given to worldly experience. As with faith, hope is a theological virtue because it arises in the being called back from an experience of existence of man (*vir*) as power (*vis*)—hence it is understood by Aquinas as an infused virtue, infused into existence by god. Open toward things, hope is an emptying of the self not in the form of self-annihilation, but rather as an assertion of the self as empty for an initiative from the holy—*hier-arché*—that is, for that which has no origin in the world. In that sense hope is only possible in humility. The humiliation of suffering, of ending, only defeats hope misunderstood as expectation. Understood correctly hope is the condition which allows for conditionless openness to things in the promise of their future.

The moments of faith and hope are bound together in love: "the greatest of them is love" (1 Corinthians 13:13). To see things in their splendor is to let them be. To let them be is to let them be in the singularity of their beings. Such a love is not an erotic love, or if it is, is so at that point where the erotic drive falls back in the face of its goal. The avoidance in the Christian scriptures of 'eros' was not guided by misogynist motives nor did this express a disgust of the body, but rather aimed to avoid the almost inescapable appropriative aim of eros.[82] Love as understood by the Evangelists is the opposite of this: not appropriative but self-giving, self-giving to the point of death and beyond. Love is measured not by reciprocity, but by non-reciprocity, by a giving with no expectation of return: 'love your enemies and do good to them, and lend without any hope of return' (Luke 6:35). Understood in this way, there is nothing higher than love: love is not a servant of knowledge. It is not so because knowledge remains on the level of the constative, while love is a prayerful openness to things. Hence the exemplariness of the self-less love of Christ, of a sacrifice, to which any response is uncertain. This giving of oneself is a giving which is open to the promise in things of that which is beyond the polemical erotics of things in the worldly agon.[83]

Such a perception of things sees a peace beyond violence, a peace which the world cannot give but which emerges in the world. As a loving perception it—like violence—abolishes differences.[84] Love is not indifferent, but rather is the seeing of things beyond difference, without relation to others. This is a seeing not of the thing in the horizon of other things, but in its own deep horizon of its singular being. Violence—by contrast—abolishes differences by imposing a sameness either of conformity or of dismembered bodies. Yet, the singularity of things resists such sameness and such dismembering by retaining its own stamp on being, which both provokes violence and in its very provocation remains beyond its reach. In that sense the radiance of things is both present and eschatological, is the presence of an eschatological promise at the heart of things.

"A New Heaven and the New Earth"

Essential to the eschatological is its presence. The *eschaton* is not merely the myth of a time after time, not simply a promise of some ill-defined afterlife, but rather the intuition in the present of the possibility in things of radical transformation. Such a possibility is not to be confused with an Aristotelian notion of potentiality. The possibility in question is not one which can be expressed in the form 'I can': it is not a potentiality to act or not, not a potentiality for non-potential, and hence not to be understood from freedom as a faculty of the human being.[85] There is nothing in the present which is capable of such transformation, which has any faculty to allow for such a transformation. This is so because the present is a present to . . . , is a being present as related to another, indeed to a system of involvements which define being-in-the-world. The possibility in question is rather one which arises in the ab-solving of all such relations, that is, through the encounter of existence with its own origins encountered in the beauty of the existent in its singular self-manifestation. It is a possibility which occurs but is not present. This appeal to an eschatological possibility is one which neither seeks after a lost paradise nor dreams of a future world, but rather hears and sees in the things of the world that which resists and withdraws from the polemical agons of the world, revealing existents in their singularity.

Such a withdrawal is variously understood as praise or as suffering: "Then I heard all the living things in creation—everything that lives in heaven, and on the earth, and under the earth, and in the sea, crying: 'To the one seated on the throne and to the Lamb, be all praise, honor, glory and power, for ever and ever'" (Revelations 4:13) and "We are all well aware that the whole creation, until this time, has been groaning in labor pains" (Romans 8:22). Both these images are equally fantastical: the thought of any non-human creature or object either groaning in expectation of the second coming or as singing praise to god is to go beyond any anticipatable experience. And yet, the first case account is claimed to be a revelation; the second is prefaced with "we are well aware." Before dismissing each as rhetorical maneuvers it may be useful to pause and examine in more detail first the Pauline text. The line quoted is to be found in the following passage:

> In my estimation, all that we suffer in the present time [*tou nun kairou*] is nothing in comparison with the glory which is destined to be disclosed for us, for the whole of creation is waiting with eagerness for the children of God to be revealed. It is not for its own purposes that creation had frustration imposed on it, but for the purpose of him who imposed it with the intention that the whole creation itself might be freed from slavery to corruption and brought into the same glorious freedom as the children of God. We are all well aware that the whole creation, until this time [*achri tou nun*], has been groaning in labor pains. (Romans 8:19–22)

This is a passage in which every word calls for commentary. It concerns the history of salvation—creation, fall, and redemption—and understands the second coming as relevant not alone to humanity but to all of creation. For all creation time is not a neutral, indifferent measure, but rather one of loss and hope.

The mention of this time is an abbreviation of what went before in verse 18: *tou nun kairou:* in this present *kairos*. All of creation is included in the kairological event of the Incarnation and the eschatological promise of the second coming. The place of humankind is a key one, of course. Its sin brought about frustration and corruption; through a human being salvation is gained. But here it is the commonality of human and non-human that is being emphasized right down to the promise of the same glorious freedom for both. According to Saint Bonaventure, salvation came through a human being because a human being brought together the lower and higher in nature.[86] The latter is a basically Greek thought, but one which is being employed in a non-Greek context: the *historical destiny* of the world centers on humankind. The event of the Incarnation reveals a divine desire as the meaning of that history, a meaning which displaces human beings in relation to creation by reference to an event within the world, which is not of the world. In such a view creatures in the world are understood in terms of such a divine desire. This desire is not for the appropriation of things, but rather for their fulfillment, their teleological expression not as instruments or means for something else, but rather as themselves. This desire for the full *self*-expression of things is eschatological in the sense that it points beyond the world, beyond the present economy of heaven and earth, toward a "new heaven and a new earth," but does so with reference to the present being-of things now, in the world, as what they are. As such, as we see in the passage from Revelations, the things in the world are both subjects and objects of praise. They are seen to praise god in the sense that their self-expression is an expression not of their worldly needs and relations, but rather of their indebtedness to an origin which lies at their basis and toward which alone they are fully themselves.

The becoming truly oneself of things is novel, because things in the world exist only by not being themselves. In the prophetic texts god's holiness is the antithesis of the laws of nature.[87] This is so because holiness is not in the laws of nature, not in the necessities of worldly relations, but rather in the possibility of transformation of all things into the singularity of their own being. The new heaven and the new earth represent the covenant of god and humankind in the conjunction of heaven and earth as finally fulfilled. Again this does not mean imagining a world beyond the laws of nature (although clearly in purely religious terms such an imagining is operative). Rather, such imaginings reflect a perception of the world in which the possibility of holiness, the possibility in each entity as a singularity of being in excess of the laws of nature, is manifest. Such a perception is of beauty and majesty, of tremendous and awful power, of things in the world. Such a perception is of things neither—to use Heidegger's terminology—as at hand (*zuhanden*) nor as objectively present (*vorhanden*), because things are neither instruments nor objects of knowledge, but rather expressive plenitude, with a depth of self beyond all relations and relatedness.

Being-in-the-world is not being-of-the-world. Being-in-the-world and of the world is to be as a superficial, that is surface, being. Being-not-of-the-world is a being toward the depths of being, a doxological being of praise. It is one which gives glory and which plunges into the dark night at the heart of the world and of all that is in the world.

4 Night, Faith, and Evil

> Every aesthetic which simply seeks to ignore . . . [the] nocturnal sides of
> existence, can itself from the outset be ignored as a sort of aestheticism.
> —Hans Urs Von Balthasar, *The Glory of the Lord,* vol. 1

IN PRAISE, IN giving glory, things are understood in their singularity, in their
unwordliness. The light of the world can no longer dull that singularity; the entity shines forth and fixes vision on the singular alterity of its being. Yet in John,
Christ talks of himself as the "light of the world" (John 8:12), and Matthew and
Paul talk of Christians as lights for the world. This discourse of light, the discourse of a light of and for the world, is one which nonetheless denies the worldliness of that light, refuses the Platonic, metaphysical account of light. Such a
denial and refusal implies a reinterpretation of night as not the time of readjust-
ment from light (cavernous) to light (worldly), but as revelatory. It is revelatory
not just of Christ but of the "least of these," the singularity of the creature saved
from its relativization in the world, saved for its own absolute being. Nothing in
that being—not its dark materiality—is foreign to that light. Yet, the singularity
of being of the entity places it before the light as its own origin from which it
may turn. This turning is now not from the things of the intellect to those of the
senses, not then a turning from one aspect of one's being to another, but a turning
away from the very source of one's being. Judeo-Christianity opens up that radical possibility, that possibility of sin, i.e., of evil as a turning away (per-version)
not from the world, but from the radiant shining forth of the origin of being in
the self and in others.

The radiance of self and others is not apparent to the eyes of sense or of
intellect, but only to the eyes of faith, and faith is not easy. The difficulties and
hardships of faith consist in the passing from the light of the world to the singular unworldly light of god in self and others. That passing is a passing through
the nocturnal, the dark, secret, enticing but foreboding darkness which is at one
with glory. The nocturnal is a time of confusion, silence, prayer, and death. The
intuition of the incomprehensibility of god is an insight into the insufficiency of
the world, that the world cannot sufficiently answer the questions which arise

within it. Within the world reason remains insufficient to itself; the limits of reason are the limits of the world.[1] At the limits of reason an action is encountered which cannot be sufficiently reconstituted, which remains irreducibly an action for which I cannot be the cause, either in fact or in thought. This ultimate passivity marks the final limit of idealism. In contrast to Feuerbach's claim—"Deny idealism and you also deny God"[2]—it is in fact at the edges of idealism, if anywhere, that the question of god arises first *to question* philosophy.

Night, darkness is ambiguous, however. The eyes of faith in looking toward the source of being are subject to illusion and deceit. The turning away from the worldliness of the world is a turning toward an unknown land, without guide, without signs. Satan—the adversary—is the name for the false god, the one who claims to be the true source, the one who holds out the true destiny for human beings and for creation generally (Genesis 3:1–5). Beyond all mythological representations, this figure marks the source of evil as the giving glory to a false god. Hence the first commandment is: "You shall have no other gods to rival me" (Exodus 20:3). Only in the context of a supra-cosmic phenomenology, that is, of an account of appearance taking its cue from that which no horizon can hold, has such a concept of evil any sense. 'Evil' as sinfulness begins and in a sense ends with the first commandment.

This chapter is divided into four sections. The ambiguity of night and the relation of night to light will be discussed in the first section. Carrying on this theme the next section will discuss the confusion inherent in night and its relation to truth. Such confusion is a confusion of the understanding expressed in faith. The relation to night is a relation to the darkness of origin and end which is disclosed in the voice of conscience, a voice which is not of this world. The voice of conscience expresses death.

Night and Light

Night is ambiguous. Faith is in the night, but in night there is no safety, there are no guarantees, only confusion and danger. The relation to night is expressed in the following passages:

> "His [Yahweh's] covering he made the darkness / his pavilion dark waters and dense cloud." (Psalms 18:11)

> "Night is the time for sleepers to sleep and night is the time for drunkards to be drunk, but we belong to the day and we should be sober." (Paul: 1 Thessalonians 5:7–8)

> "Your Father who sees all that is done in secret will reward you." (Matthew 6:4)

Darkness, secrecy, and clouds seem to be the elements of this god. He hides himself from view and seeks that those who glorify him do so in secret. If the account of glory indicates a god of radiance, this is at the same time a god of the night. And yet Paul speaks of the followers of Christ as belonging to the day. To 'belong to the day' (*hemera*) is not to belong to the ephemeral, the passing days of the world, but rather to belong to the day in the sense of Genesis: the day as light of god, not light of the sun. Paul speaks of the "day of our Lord" (1 Corinthians 1:9), the day as *eschaton*, as ending of the world. Belonging to the day, then, is belonging to divine radiance of glory, which breaks with day as the time of the sun, the time of clarity and of what can be grasped in a glance. The day of the Lord "is coming like a thief in the night" (1 Thessalonians 5:2). It is a day which is as night. It is for this reason that being of the day requires an instruction not so much in terms of activities of the day, but of the night. To belong to the day is to live as not belonging to the day, but rather as belonging to the night. Belonging to the night means not to live in the night as that which is secreted from the day—by sleeping or by drunkenness. In terms of those belonging to the world it is right to sleep and wrong to be drunk in the night. But for Paul these activities are equally to be avoided because the night is not a respite from the day, but rather the time when the true day appears. The true day appears as night, because it appears in the darkening of the intellect and the senses—both of which perceive only through the light of the sun. As such the 'glory of the Lord' is a glory of the night:[3] In the Elohistic tradition in particular the divine is hidden in darkness. The very core of the divine appearance is a deep and sometimes oppressive and threatening darkness (cf. Exodus 20:16, 19:21).[4]

Night, then, is not the opposite of day. The god of night is also the god of day; darkness itself is not god's creation. But the light of day accepted without question leads away from god, because it leads to distraction in the finite surfaces of things, rather than in their infinite recesses. Such distraction is not a concern with things in the world as such, rather it is a concern with things in the mode of the noon-day sun, in the mode of bright illumination, where the eye is dazzled by what the thing or person lets the world see. What the world sees is the thing or person in its relatedness to and involvements with other things or persons, ultimately in relation to the sun as that which gives sight. But each such thing or person can be substituted by another in the chain of relations within the world. Distraction is dispersal, that is, the being with things as they indicate other things, as they indicate the world and their own worldliness. Such dispersal is a dissipation of desire, a giving of oneself as surface to the surface of things, a pursuance of need which satiated and exhausted gives way to sleep, before erupting again in the light of morning.[5] This is the life of sin in the strict sense of a turning away from god; turning away from god is a turning away from the secret and the hidden toward the open and surface. But things and people, in letting the world see them, hide from the world. Every person as a person in the world comes forth clothed, hiding their nakedness. Even and most especially the dancer who offers to show her nakedness dresses herself in her dance and forbids each approach.[6] The faces we meet disguise themselves for us. They appear to and for me in their worldly being, for me as customer, passerby, colleague, friend, lover, father. But in responding through my own disguise I recognize their appearance as disguised, an appearance which hides in its appearing, as darkness beyond the world hidden by the light of the world. This recognition is not simply cognitive; in fact it is through desire that I recognize the hidden depths in others: I desire more than what I am given, because I desire what refuses my voyeuristic gaze—be it the gaze of my body or that of my intellect. I desire that which sees me behind veils,[7] that which cannot satisfy me in giving itself, because its self-giving is at once a self-veiling. This very desire is a desire for beauty. As von Balthasar puts it:

> form as it appears to us is beautiful only because the delight that it arouses in us is founded upon the fact that, in it, the truth and goodness of the depths of reality itself are manifested and bestowed, and this manifestation and bestowal reveal themselves to us as being something infinitely and inexhaustibly valuable and fascinating.[8]

Worldly vision must give way to another vision, a vision which does not see, which 'sees' in darkness, which is never satisfied, and seeks no substitution of that on which it looks. It is such a vision of which Gregory of Nyssa speaks when he says, "the vision of God is to be never satisfied in the desire to see Him."[9] But this vision of god is not a turning away from the world—god is nothing of the world, but is in everything in the world. Hence, this turning is a turning toward things in the world through an overcoming of the light of the world by what Cusa calls an "absolute sight," which is the "limiting of limitations."[10]

Things are limited by their boundaries, by that which draws their borders from other things. But such boundaries are never fully seen. The boundary of a thing, its *finis* or its *limes,* cannot be fixed in the vision of the body, only in that of the intellect (geometry). In our bodily being we know how to deal with the limits of things or persons. In touch we feel the surface of things and their hidden depth. The limit is the outer reach, the outer movement toward others, and also the last boundary and defense against others. The depth of the thing is its presence in the world and its resistance to the world: it is present in the world as resisting the world. In resisting the world it resists me too, it resists in asserting its limits. Such assertion provokes.[11] It provokes violence, the attempt to destroy those limits, the attempt to break down that resistance, the attempt to annihilate that singular view of the world. But it can also, it does also, provoke love. Love cannot rest with the indifference of worldly disguises, but rather seeks to understand the limits of the other in its limits, to limit the limitations of those limits by seeing them in the finite expression of infinite depth. While relative sight sees only the finitude of the other—its limits relational to other others—absolute sight sees the limits of the other as expressions of its unique being, as manifestations of the thing in its infinity, as that which discloses the limits of my own faculties, in showing itself to me as it is. Beyond knowledge and imagination in the darkness at the depth of things Cusa states, "I find a power most stupendous." Using the example of a tree, he goes on to say that while the eye of the intellect can perceive a tree potentially in its seed, in this darkness 'I' see the seed as a certain explication of almighty power.[12]

In retiring to a hidden and secret place the other calls me to parry with it, to lose myself in it. It seduces me beyond what the eyes of my body and of my intellect can see; the eyes of faith are my only guide. God is in those secret places, because in seeing the other in secret I am seeing the other in relation to god, that is, in relation to that in it which is not of the world. My desire to see the other is my desire to see in it that which no articulation of limits could see; which rather comes from letting the thing be singularly, hidden, its own limits. But this is to see it not in the light where its limits appear against other others but rather to see its veiled self as veiled, that is, as dark.[13]

Confusion, Silence, and Response

Night brings confusion—the mixing together of what the light of day keeps apart. The limits of entities are neither clear nor distinct, nor are my own limits. My own place in the world is no longer secure; from all sides encroachments press upon me. Such confusion is beyond language—words lose their currency, they fail to denote or connote, fail to name or effect. Hence, silence reigns, but a pregnant silence of new but impossible articulations. This confused silence calls for response, a response which has no precedent, a response for which I have no orientation, the response, namely, of prayer.

The light of day has no place for prayer. When things are clear, predictable, and unambiguous, prayer has no role. Only where no oversight is possible, where insight has no mastery and foresight can guide no action, is it meaningful to pray. Prayer, then, is of the night. The night is a negative time in terms of the world—it is a time which is not counted as time, a time of the non-necessities of sleep, drink, and debauchery. Freed from the pressures of the day, the pressures of achieving the necessities of life, night offers respite. It is a non-time[14] when things can appear beyond necessity—beyond their place in the relations of being. In the night things appear as enticing, as 'objects' of desire, when matters of the morning can be forgotten. This forgetfulness is a possibility for existence distanced from the day. In that distance existence finds itself outside the movement of worldly concerns and driven beyond the level of its own power, but as such placed at the limits of the ethical. At the limits of its power, existing nocturnally, things appear beyond expectation and anticipation, where differences of good and bad are no longer discernible. In the night the movement of existence as desire exposes itself in its vulnerability. Faced with such exposure existence can retreat into dormancy and find its relief in sleep. It can also make night into day by giving full reign to its erotic drives for appropriation, which the moral conventions of the world hinder. But in facing desire as desire, in facing its own powerlessness before the attractive force of existents, existence responds to the nocturnal in giving to the absolute the time it might otherwise give to sleep.[15] In giving attention to that which escapes its attention in the bright light of day, existence discloses itself as desire in its sleeplessness. In this time of non-necessity existence is disclosed as being with things in the world, attending to them as distanced from the world. That attention is a prayerful heedfulness to things as they disclose themselves not in their distinct identities, not as objects of perception or intellect, not given as themselves in their own self-identity, but rather as disclosing in themselves a being there, a unique originating presence, absolved from the world, calling for a response in a place without conditions.

Sleepless response to such a call is keeping vigil. Keeping vigil is a way of existence in which existence comes to itself in its lack of grounds. Keeping vigil is a decision for sleeplessness, a decision in the sense of a turning toward rather than away from existence in its self-expression. It is, as Lacoste says, "the purest form of the self positing itself, . . . the epitome of an affirmation of our freedom."[16] Keeping vigil is not only expressed in prayer. As Lacoste makes clear, it can take the form of doing philosophy, writing poetry, and so many other activities.[17] But all of these are prayerful in their attention beyond the day, in their nocturnal non-experience.[18] In the night, in the absolution of light, existence is prayerful in its attention to things beyond all use and knowing. In this attention things appear as unusable and unknowable. They appear as demanding patience, as they show existence as waiting without the conditions to receive. The patience of vigil is such a patience, a patience out of powerlessness, out of the incapacity to receive what is given in its originating givenness. This patience is a primordial patience, because it subverts our being-in-the-world by opening up an origin prior to the initial being-in. This patience is liturgical because it is an awaiting of that which does not belong to, depend upon, originate from, or concern the world.

Such awaiting is a readiness for unworldly appearance. Its mode of appearance is that of the sudden, the place of articulation of being and non-being.[19] The sudden arises out of dark silence, unexpected like the first word, and heightens the confusion of night. Pseudo-Dionysius talks of Christ's mode of appearance as the sudden (*exaiphnes*).[20] Nothing prepares for the manifestation of god as human; on the contrary, such a manifestation is an epiphany of absolute transcendence in immanent form. Such transcendence does not shine forth in the day, but rather hides itself, appears not to the worthy, but rather to those who have eyes for the dark. Such eyes are not those which see in the dark as if it were day—not lamps which make night day—but rather eyes in which the "proud spirit of

Reason" has been vanquished.[21] The proud spirit of wisdom seeks to know and to master, to see in the light of day; it is the self-satisfied preening of oneself in the mirror of the superficial reality of things. Eyes for the dark are those which have learned humility, have learned, namely, that what the day has to offer cannot be equal to itself.

The humility of the night allows of the faculties of sense, imagination, and intellect to sleep, to fall into a state of deep passivity. There is a love which is passive in this sense, a love which seeks only to be imprinted by the other, to experience the other in the fullness of its being. Such a love is expressed as admiration, which is a true humility before that which appears as wondrous. As Marcel makes clear, such a state can only appear as a *humiliation* to the extent to which the subject treats itself "as a power existing for itself and taking itself as a center."[22] Humility without humiliation is not objectively determinable, but rather is a function of openness to the appearing of things in the radiance of their own being, that is, as true. Such openness is not without desire; to the contrary it is driven by the highest desire, that "through not seeing and not knowing, to see and to know that beyond sight and knowledge."[23] That which is beyond all sight and knowledge is that which is turned away from the world, that which in the thing and the person turns toward that which no worldly being can know or see. Hence, the desire to see and know here is a desire to be open to the singular being of the entity as it presents itself in its own self-expression. This is a desire for night, for—again quoting this line from Pseudo-Dionysius—the "darkness beyond light of the hidden mystical silence."[24] This then is a desire for understanding, but understanding in the form of a secret enlightenment, not of any esoteric doctrines, but rather of the singular being of things as manifestations of divine love.

Evil originates in the perversion of such love; in this sense evil is a Judeo-Christian concept. Irreducible to a moral concept of bad it concerns the turning away from god which is at the heart of sinful life. This opens up a radical possibility of human life, that is, life in and of the night. Once the possibility of being not of the world is opened up then the scope of evil extends to infinity. It does so because the question of evil—the questioning of existence in terms of evil—is a question concerning that in existence which exceeds the eyes of the world. Evil can be lived without appearing to the world, because it concerns *not* the rightness or wrongness of acts committed, but their inner source. It is for this reason that evil finds its ultimate, if negative, expression in the first commandment, and that sin can be characterized as alienation from god.[25] The consequences of Adam's sin, according to Genesis, are loss of vision of god and physical death. I shall return (in the final part of this chapter) to death, but here the issue of vision is significant. The loss of vision for god involves a decoupling of vision and desire. The tendency to harmonize these through an effort at self-possession recurs frequently in the history of philosophy. Implicit in such an effort is the assumption of a self-autonomy and a source of the self in itself. Such a view is atheistic in its basic tendency because it sees the good as rooted in a free choice of the self, which once achieved may correspond to the divine. But such correspondence is a secondary concern: the good here is that which the self possesses of itself; the good in such terms is alienation from god: sin for Christian life.

But such alienation is only possible in the awareness of a god who transcends the world. Only such a god can call for a goodness which is beyond the morality of the world. Yet without revelation this god cannot be recognized. He can be recognized precisely in things understood in terms of their divine origin: "the invisible existence of God and his everlasting power have been clearly seen by the mind's understanding of created things" (Romans 1:20). In created things, yet distinct from them, the creator can be seen. The intellect in seeing created things sees them in this distinction—the failure to do so ends in idolatry (Romans 1:23, 25). The failure here is a failure to see created things in their difference from the creator and more positively to see them in relation to their creator.[26] To see, thus, is a possibility which did not require the event of Christ; it precedes such an event. This passage from Romans (1:18–32) has often been used to defend a natural theology; but it speaks not of any logical reasoning from nature to god, but of a manner of perception in which the creator is seen in the beauty of creatures. In this it reflects the lines from the Wisdom of Solomon: "If, satisfied [*terpomenoi*] by them [the 'good things seen' (13:1)], they [those 'who are unaware of God'] have taken these for gods, let them know how much the Master of these excels them, since it was the very source of beauty that created them" (Wisdom 13:3). This perception of the source of beauty is missed not by an attraction to beauty, but by a being satisfied by beauty, in other words, by an erotic appropriation of beauty in the satisfaction of needs. Treating beauty thus is perverse in its consequences—in relations (especially sexual) with one another and relations (of covetousness, of envy, etc.) with things—and is so due to a deeper perversion, namely, the turning away from god as the source of the beauty of things. That turning away is idolatry—the turning toward the divine in things as the satisfaction of need. Idolatry has its source in perception, but a perception which expresses a relation to things as objects of satisfaction not objects of desire. Hence, the first (and second) commandment is directed toward perception and dealing with things; evil has its source in the perversion of such perception and such dealings.

The first two commandments concern god, or more specifically the relation of god and world. The gods which are denied are the gods of craven images, worldly gods. The prohibition on images is a prohibition of placing worldly constraints on that which transcends the world. The justification for this prohibition in Deuteronomy is that god is *heard* not seen (Deuteronomy 4:15). What is heard is a voice, a call, which is a calling to a mission of existence. That call comes from elsewhere, places existence in relation to it, does not allow itself to be confined to light, to the horizon of visibility. Listening to this call, existence is open to the divine epiphany in things aware that this epiphany is a call manifest in things revealing a hidden creative origin. Evil is deaf to this call. But evil is also a response, a response to a call. Evil is a deafening to the call manifest in things, but is itself a submission, a passivity to being in its original privation. Concealment, secrecy, disguise is constitutive of all revelation; being revealed is being concealed. That being concealed, that darkness of being, lets things appear as evil. Evil is ontological before it is ethical; it is a privation of being at its very origins. Freed of the constraints of the world, in the night beyond all worldly light, is a freedom unfettered, demonic. Provoked by the origin beyond all appropriation, shown the contingency of the worldly, a principle beyond all worldly calculation is opened up, a principle of a time beyond all worldly time, a time to end time, a vision of apocalyptic destruction.[27] Evil mimics good ("Evil be thee my Good," Milton); it is a submission, a passivity but one which acts out of that passivity to channel all power and truth in itself. Evil does not take responsibility for itself, but answers a call beyond itself, at the origins of itself. In the name of that which no eye can see nor ear can hear, 'I' can decide the fate of humanity and the world. 'I' give glory to a hand which is not of this world, which works in me and through me, and as reward for this homage 'I' receive great power. In one form or another this evil is destiny, that belief in a fate which nothing in the world can undo. Filled with this dark sense Macbeth can say:

> Till Birnam wood remove to Dunsinane I cannot taint with fear. What's the boy Malcolm? Was he not born of woman? The spirits that know all moral consequence have pronounced me thus: 'Fear not, Macbeth, no man that's born of woman shall e'er have power upon thee.' . . . The mind I sway by and the heart I bear shall never sag with doubt nor shake with fear. (5.3.1–10)

These same sentiments can in different terms be expressed by the martyr. The privation of being can appear as the fullness of being. The danger here is great and has profound moral and political consequences. To give higher instance to that which is outside the world removes all political and conventional constraints. These are the consequences of a supra-cosmological ontology, an ontology which places the source of being beyond the world. If glory is dark, and if we give glory in the night, then evil and good cannot be distinguished on any scale of comprehension, but only by developing a way of seeing in the dark, a nocturnal understanding.

Night, Understanding, and Faith

It is a recurring thought in Western Christianity that to approach god it is necessary to be aware of not knowing him. Nicholas of Cusa puts it simply: god can only be approached by someone who knows himself to be ignorant of him.[28] There is no ladder of ascent to god in this view; no knowledge of any created being is closer to knowledge of god than any other. Indeed, Pseudo-Dionysius goes so far as to say that divine transcendence is the transcendence even of the difference between god and creation.[29] At one stroke the luminous order of the understanding is undone and in each thing the nocturnal possibilities overwhelm the understanding as a capacity of apprehension. The eyes for the night are thus not so much eyes turned away from things in the world, but eyes turned toward them in the mode of glorification: of giving praise for them as the gifts of god.[30]

Understanding is always understanding-from before being understanding-of. 'As I (we) understand it' is implicit in every act of understanding. Understanding is situated; every act of understanding begins as *having been* situated. As having been placed, understanding can never justify itself. Although directed at its object, understanding is always related back to a basis which cannot itself be understood. Every attempt to understand the situation of understanding begins with its own being-situated. Ultimately this being-situated is in relation to that which understanding cannot comprehend, cannot seize, but at most can touch. Indeed, it does touch it; it is contingent with it, because this being situated gives understanding its basis. The luminous order of understanding, its projection on that which reflects it to itself, distracts from its dark source. This ultimately passive relation of understanding to its own possibility is a relation of faith.

When with understanding existence is brought back to such being situated, the power and capacities of the existent—be they sensual or intellectual—are disclosed as powerless to make sense of its position. It is for this reason that, as John of the Cross tells us, what the soul can do of its own accord serves to hinder inner peace.[31] Inner peace, the state of passive receptivity, is one in which the soul awaits what it cannot do of its own accord, that is, what it cannot do with the resources at its disposal, resources of sight and knowledge in the light of the world. To be in such a night requires humility and readiness. It also requires a detachment from possessiveness of and to things in the world. But these are means to knowledge: knowledge of god and knowledge of itself.[32] Both are intimately connected, because the knowledge of itself is the knowledge of the being-situated of its understanding, the knowledge of an original passivity. Such knowledge is a knowledge in which the understanding knows itself; such knowledge cannot be itself the achievement of an act of understanding, but rather can only be received as a gift. Such knowledge is precisely a knowledge beyond the capacity of an existent to know; it is beyond this capacity not because of the contingent limits of knowledge, but because the very act of knowing distracts from it. Only through a "darkening of the understanding" and a "dark night for those natural faculties of understanding, will and memory" can such an understanding be reached "no longer . . . by means of its natural light, but by means of the divine wisdom."[33] Furthermore, divine wisdom transcends the talent of the soul and hence is darkness to it.[34] Inasmuch as the understanding by natural light is natural, the darkness it suffers is profound, insofar as this darkness makes the world become strange for the soul.[35] This sense of strangeness, indeed of alienation, is something positive in relation to things in the world themselves. The soul now marvels at the things it sees and hears, which seem to it very strange and rare, although in strictly empirical terms they are unchanged and mundane.[36] This is a seeing of things in relation to god, as seen in divine wisdom, that is, as creatures not as worldly relata. Such a state is not divine, because it comes not through acts but through receptivity: for all the faculties to receive divine infusion they must remain passive.[37] The purging of the faculties, capacities, of the existent, then, is not their destruction but the return to their original being, namely, as passive rather than active. The understanding, the senses, memory, the will are all returned to their original state of readiness for that of which they are incapable.[38] To be with things in a state of passivity is to understand them in terms of themselves, is to understand them as they work on the soul, not as they appear to sight and knowledge. This is the knowledge of faith—*pistis* as *gnosis*—a knowledge which is wise and divinely wise, because it assumes no human wisdom, but reduces that wisdom to the event of its origins.[39]

The dark night of the soul is a night of waiting, a waiting in faith. The natural light of the eyes no longer guides but leads astray.[40] "The sun . . . instead of affording vision to the eyes it overwhelms, blinds and deprives them of vision. . . . Similarly the light of faith in its abundance suppresses and overwhelms that of the intellect."[41] Disguise is the "white garment of faith": "Faith darkens and empties the intellect of all its natural understanding and thereby prepares it for union with the divine wisdom."[42] Faith blinds understanding, which John of the Cross likens to midnight as the darkest moment of night. Faith guides only a soul which is in darkness, and it guides by hearing not by sight.[43] In darkness the soul seeks the guidance of a voice, a voice which speaks to it from nowhere and everywhere. In the night such a voice is taken on trust.

Faith is not a rejection of the understanding, not a mere retreat into the irrational, but rather a blinding of the understanding in its worldly motion. That worldly motion has an origin which the world does not know, an origin known only from within. This origin is the dark source of an existent's being as being-situated, but as being-situated amongst entities. That being affected of the existent's own being is responded to in an outward movement toward things as expressions of unique ways of being affected. My being with things is a being attracted by them. Before all intention is attraction. The primal surrender to this attraction, a surrender which in Christianity is radicalized in the self-surrender of Christ, is a surrender of faith: a surrender to him who first surrendered himself to each human being.[44] Such self-surrender is manifest in things as created; this manifestation is the primordial beauty in things, a beauty which glorifies and engenders trust. Such trust is a seeing in the dark, without a guide. The singular presence of the thing blocks the world, blocks the diversion to the world, and draws us into the darkness of a truth without light. In that very movement, however, an unease, a dread of the ugliness of things emerges. The very dark singular being of the thing which draws and attracts, motivating the first movements of perception, fills us with dread at the ugliness that lurks in the hidden depths. This dread can in turn give way to horror, a horror not directed at any particular quality or event, but at the very darkness in which we find ourselves. The singular being of the entity which we face in perceptual faith, a singular being not yet diluted into generalities and generalizations, brings us in the midst of things—*in medias res*—and leaves us no room for distance.

Faith is essential in the Christian account not because the objects of faith are irrational—in the main, Christian writers have argued for the compatibility between faith and reason—but because they are sudden, surprising, without precedent, without clear grounds. If the event of revelation could to some extent be rationally reconstructed, it would still lack any rational necessity; it would remain an event which is suffered, which is only possible in openness toward the world, an intuition of primordial beauty and dread at the darkness of things. The 'fear and trembling' of Christian faith discloses the fundamental modality of perceptual faith: an openness prior to and supporting understanding in its 'natural light,' prior to the drive toward rational reconstruction and rationalization.

The sight of this faith gives itself to that which it cannot see. This 'blind' act of trust is a trust in the world, which nothing of the world can justify. Heidegger, in his account of interpretation (*Auslegung*), accounts for the latter as a making explicit of a prior understanding of the world. This prior understanding is grounded in a fore-having, fore-sight, and fore-conception.[45] This fore-structure cannot itself be brought to interpretation, but rather is pre-given in every interpretation. What is pre-given is prior to the act of interpretation itself. That which for Heidegger is always in play in interpretation, namely, fore-having, fore-sight, and fore-conception, is taken up implicitly by the understanding, but finds no justification therein. The 'justification' rather is written into the ontological constitution of Dasein, hence of existence itself.[46] That justification is nothing which can be articulated by the understanding, but rather a prior trust constitutive of the movement of existence itself. That movement—as making possible all justifications and reasons—has the characteristic of a leap.[47]

Such a leap cannot be given rational reconstruction. It can only be related in stories, where it is glimpsed in terms of the logic of the story itself. Two stories in particular can be illustrative here: those of Abraham and of Thomas the twin. In both the dark night of faith gives rise to understanding.

Abraham, whom Paul terms "our father in faith," is the exemplary figure of an openness to the epiphany of the unworldly in the world. This openness is so great that Kierkegaard can only say of him: "Abraham I cannot understand, in a way all I can learn from him is to be amazed."[48] In the place of understanding there is amazement. Abraham cannot be understood, because every act of understanding him situates him, places him by means of projection. Abraham, however, cannot be situated because his sacrifice of Isaac is not a project at all but an act of pure receptivity. Abraham hopes that god will not take Isaac, but awaits god's actions in a state of pure receptivity. Such a pure receptivity is singular, is not pre-figured in any way. As such faith places the singular above the universal. Opposing the singular individual to the universal Kierkegaard puts it as follows: "faith is just this paradox, that the single individual is higher than the universal."[49] Implicit in the Abraham story is this superiority over the universal. This is a superiority over the ethical, in Kierkegaard's terms, that is, the claims of universal laws, based on what Kierkegaard calls "an absolute relation to the absolute."[50] This relation remains inaccessible to reason, as reason remains on the level of the universal. Faith challenges Greek philosophy here by reaching below the understanding, by finding that movement which subverts the understanding.

Abraham's action is personal; it has no relation to the universal except by violating it. No ethical law can be derived from Abraham's actions; there is no reason that can give grounds for them. Abraham did what he did, Kierkegaard says, for "God's sake and, what is exactly the same, for his own."[51] He did it for god's sake because god required proof of his faith and for his own sake in order that he might provide that proof. Kierkegaard speaks of this trial as a temptation. Temptation in this case is itself the ethical. The temptation is to act ethically and in consequence self-possessively. This is the temptation to seek goodness on one's own power. The "knight of faith" gives up this temptation and in so doing acts with no certainty of success. He transgresses the universal and does so only for the glory of god.

"Abraham cannot be mediated, which can also be put by saying that he cannot speak. The moment I speak I express the universal, and when I do not no one can understand me."[52] Not alone can Abraham not speak but no one can speak about Abraham. Abraham's story is impossible in the sense that it cannot be told. This is so because Abraham "gives up the universal."[53] This giving up of the universal is prompted by the voice of god. It is the hearing of that voice which leads into the dark night. In this dark night the world becomes strange; this strangeness is beauty. In renouncing things I have no strength to get them back, Kierkegaard tells us.[54] Faith is a passion, is a being affected by things and as such is hard to separate from the aesthetic. Kierkegaard in separating the aesthetic and the religious assumes a faith which calls away from the beautiful. Yet, it seems that the very attitude of pure receptivity allows things to be seen in their beauty, namely, as that in which god as their origin appears. While Kierkegaard understands god in terms of voice and hearing, the incarnate god is a god of sight also. In fact a god at the intersection of hearing, sight (and touch). We are not yet in a position to explore these issues in the detail necessary (the next two chapters on creation and incarnation will do so). For now, however, it is crucial to explore further the relation of faith and understanding with respect to another story, that of Thomas the twin.

While Abraham's faith is aural, in John's account of the appearance of the risen Christ to Thomas the senses of sight and touch are brought in intricate relation to that of hearing. The receptivity of Thomas is one which permeates the senses while indicating the interruptive and temporary way in which the invisible becomes visible, tactile, and aural. The story of Thomas is one of a movement from incomprehension to belief. This is what the figure of Thomas represents in John's Gospel.[55] He is always faithful, but without understanding, trusting not because he comprehends, but because of his belief in Jesus of Nazareth. The question, which the story of Thomas raises, however, is how such fidelity is possible when the physical presence of Jesus, this entity in the world which can be seen, touched, heard, is gone. The story of Thomas is "recorded so that you may believe" (John 20:31); it aims to show the movement of faith in an exemplary fashion.

The story itself is one of the most familiar of the Gospels. While the disciples were together in a locked room on the first day of the week (the Sunday), the risen Christ appears to them. Thomas was not with the others. When the disciples relate the story to him, he responds angrily saying that he would not believe unless he could satisfy his own senses (sight and touch) with the evidence of Christ's resurrected body. Christ appears again and offers Thomas the evidence he seeks. Thomas responds by saying "my Lord and my God." Thomas is here a pivotal figure. He both disbelieves the witness of others and is himself a witness. He straddles the place of witness and that of those who come after. Although we know him as 'doubting Thomas,' this term has little scriptural basis, and indeed doubt is hardly the correct term here: his initial reaction was not so much one of skeptical doubt as of simple refusal—Jesus' word describing his state is *apistos,* unbelieving—his final statement one of faithful affirmation, indeed the strongest Christological statement in the Gospels. This movement of negation to affirmation is not a movement from doubt to certainty as much as a movement of perceptual faith beyond the capacity—power—of the senses. There has been much debate as to whether Thomas in fact touched the wounds of Christ. He is invited to touch, but we are not told if he does so. A careful reading of the text would suggest that John does not simply neglect to narrate the actual touch.[56] What he tells us is that Thomas replied to the Christ's invitation to touch with the words "my Lord and my God." This was his immediate response, not to actually touch. Earlier Christ had told Mary of Magdala not to touch him (John 20:17). But this prohibition and his later invitation are not to be understood in terms of a sacred taboo. If it were so, then Christ's invitation to touch would have been disingenuous and Thomas's fate would have paralleled that of Uzzah in touching the Ark of the Covenant (2 Samuel 6:8). Nor is John suggesting that the risen Christ is immaterial, something the Synoptics stress is not the case. Rather, what is significant is that in response to Mary he says not to touch him in the sense of holding on to his worldly presence; in the case of Thomas all tactile testing is redundant because Jesus has touched him by recognizing him, by giving witness to him. What he saw was that which gives itself to be touched, that which in touching is itself touched. In this sense the many representations of Thomas touching the wounds of Christ are not without grounds. Jesus gives himself to be touched, but the revelation is that giving not the actual touching. In addressing him with the words, "do not be unbelieving but believe," Jesus is not asking Thomas to believe the evidence of his senses alone, but rather to believe in him as the Christ. He is asking him to believe in his example—the example of his life and death—as that which comes from god. In other words, he is asking him to transcend that which is offered to touch and sight toward that invisible movement of gift and self-surrender manifest in that body which is touchable and visible.

The revelation given to Thomas is of an embodied voice, a voice which comes from an incarnate entity, and a voice which addresses him. It is to this voice that Thomas responds. But he responds to this voice as a voice speaking to him of that which he can see and touch. The voice is one which invites a dwelling with that which appears in bodily form in the world. The invitation is also an admonition—not, however, of the senses, but rather of a certain manner of being sensual. Thomas's refusal to believe is based on his need to act, his need to perform acts of perception, to gather evidence and consider it: "Unless I can see the holes that the nails made in his hands and can put my finger into the holes that they made, and unless I can put my hand into his side, I refuse to believe" (John 20:25). Thomas is here not simply wanting to see the holes, or even to touch the surface of the skin, but to put his fingers in the holes, to delve into the holes. The Greek word here is *balo* (from *ballo*) which contains an undercurrent of violence: to move into, but with the sense of wounding or at least of subjecting. Thomas's words hint at an image of rape: his touch is the touch of anger, of a fidelity betrayed. It is this anger, this violence, which Jesus confronts with the words "peace be with you." That peace is a peace of receptivity beyond the violent agons of the world. The body which he presents is a body to be seen and touched, but one which can no longer be violated. It is in the presence of a body beyond violation that Thomas responds. His response is not just to the figure in front of him, but to the possibility of god in things, the possibility that is of a peace beyond all violation, of a final end to the violent impulse of appropriation which had just driven him.

In response to Thomas, Jesus says, "You believe because you have seen me. Blessed are those who have not seen and yet believe" (John 20:29). Thomas believed *because* he had seen. Sight, though, itself requires belief, requires perceptual faith. To see is to believe, to trust. But this trust as a movement of understanding seeks on the basis of that initial trust evidence for what is and what has occurred. Here that movement is being reversed: not to seek more and more evidence, but to receive that which is beyond the evidential. This reversal requires a dispossession, a divestment. For this reason belief is contingent not on sight as such, but on having 'seen *me*,' that is, Jesus as the resurrected Christ. As such the 'because' here implies no necessity. The appearance of Jesus before the crucifixion was a public one. These appearances are, however, in private, are to those who were faithful. Such faithfulness is not a substitute for faith, but pre-figures faith. Faith, though, is in that which requires an interruption of the world, a coming to appearance in a manner which sets aside the worldly order of appearance. Such a coming to appearance is in the world, but breaks with the world; is in material form, but disrupts the laws of normal materiality; appears to the eyes of the body, but calls on a seeing which is beyond all worldly sight. The witness of which John speaks is a witness to that movement, to a moment in which material reality points not to a higher reality, but rather to its own destiny, "a new heaven and a new earth," as that of which no eye has seen and no ear has heard.

Thomas then is predisposed by a faithfulness to the person of Christ, that is, a faithfulness to the mission of existence manifest in him, to see beyond that offered to sight, the surface, to a significance manifest in that entity but pointing toward a sending which cannot appear because it overwhelms the horizon of the world and the capacity of worldly perception in the senses. Those who have not seen are those who are no longer contemporaneous with the events of the life of Jesus. These are the disciples at second hand of which Kierkegaard speaks. They believe without seeing. This does not mean that their belief is without sight—they believe, after all, in the once visible Christ. Their blessedness arises from their situation: they cannot see him and believe on the basis of the testimony of those who have. This brings into stark relief the relation of understanding to its own historicity: that which is past cannot be made present, but the belief in that past event is a belief precisely in it as past, as inappropriable and as always hidden. The testimony of others is a veil which cannot be drawn back but rather which can be experienced as a veil, as revealing the hidden as hidden.[57]

Thomas's words are an act of testimony. It is testimony to an event which was surprising and contingent, one which overcame him and to which all he can do is respond. In this sense, too, Thomas is pivotal: his testimony refers to an event which has occurred, and acknowledges a coming to understanding which is belated. The belatedness of this coming to understanding leads to a refiguration of the past—a rebirth. Yet, that refiguration does not result in an understanding of the world in terms of natural reason. The very uniqueness of the event of Christ means that the seeking of signs in the past cannot generate reasons. Rather, the past is refigured in terms of the Christ event and takes on a new and unprecedented meaning. This very character of the Christ event reflects itself back to creation itself, which first in the light of Christological insights becomes understood as *creatio ex nihilo*. But what is seen in the event of Christ is a nothingness at the source of things—namely, a mission, a sending, a vocation which answers a call which breaks asunder the economy of past and present, of effort and reward, of striving and success. What is thus revealed is a love without grounds at the origins of what is. As such the faith of Thomas is a recognition of love to which he is inadequate: his recognition of Christ responds, but cannot be adequate to Christ's recognition of him.[58]

The faith of Abraham and the faith of Thomas end in nothing. There is nothing that can justify them. Yet it is a faith which calls for understanding, but an understanding which reversing its natural direction finds at its source the limits of its own light. Faith 'in the eminent sense' reverses the movement of the senses, a movement which parallels that of the understanding in its concern with things in the world. Faith responds to an address, a voice, which tells existence of nothing in the world, but rather of its own withdrawal from the world in its movement toward things in the world. This voice speaks of knowledge which the world cannot have, because it is originary to the world. It is the voice of conscience.

Conscience is fundamentally misunderstood as a voice of social conformity. It is rather that voice which calls existence to a place beyond worldly light, to a place of listening to a voice in which existence is called back to its own origins. It is the forum in which the self encounters itself in its relation to its unworldly source.

If conscience is the encounter of the self with itself in the movement toward its immemorial source, death is the encounter with the other in the limitation of its limits, in the dark of its inner light. For Homer *skotos* is the darkness that overcomes human beings at the moment of their death and only humans are capable of experiencing it.[59] In death the worldly relations with another are no longer actual; so long as the occasions of those worldly relations are avoided it is possible to live as if that death had not occurred. In encountering such occasions, however, the absence of the deceased and their non-substitutable being becomes manifest: it is not anyone but this singular one who is absent. In death the deceased can be more not less present: no ceremony, no ritual, is so focused on one person as the funeral rites are on the corpse of the deceased and this is so because the funeral marks the end of a future. In death and the call of conscience the unworldliness of self and other reveal themselves in their nocturnal being.

Death and Conscience

Death and sin are intertwined in the Judeo-Christian account: according to Genesis death came into the world due to sin. The corollary of this is that freedom from sin is freedom from death. As Paul puts it: "The life-giving law of the Spirit in Christ Jesus has set you free from the law of sin and death" (Romans 8:2). Conscience for Paul does not depend on revelation, but is irreducible to convention: it is the "Law engraved on their hearts" (2:15). This inner law, this law in the secrecy of the heart, is a law of a being aware of itself (*con-scientia*) in its own withdrawal from the world. For conscience, acts in the world are meaningful not in their worldly appearance, but in relation to the heart which the world never sees. Conscience is in that sense personal. The person is the only reality that we know and that we shape from within, as Mounier says.[60] Such knowledge and action 'from within' is the knowledge of being turned away from the world in being toward the world. The secrecy of the heart, the being with myself in my worldly being and my being with others—animate and inanimate—in their being with themselves (a dormant being in the case of the inanimate) is a turning away from the world in the admiration of that in myself and others which the world cannot contain. That is the inner movement of conscience. It is a movement of sincerity. This movement is best exemplified in the Sermon on the Mount.

"Do not imitate the hypocrites" (Matthew 6:5). To imitate the hypocrites is to imitate an imitation: the hypocrite acts like a good person, but is not one. To imitate here is already to do falsely, because it is done to show the world. From the Greek *hypokrites* meaning actor, performer, the one who wears a persona, a mask, hypocrite refers to a performance without inner affirmation, a splitting of the self between inner and outer. The hypocrite is the one who is scrupulous in following the law and does so in a public way so that all might see. It is the fact that they do this in public which Jesus criticizes most, and he instructs his followers instead to act in secret, because "your Father who knows everything which is done in secret will reward you" (6:4). The accusation has to do with the importance placed on how one's acts appear to others. What appears to others differs from what appears to god; the latter appearance is in secret, because it goes on in the inner heart of the person: "your Father who sees everything which is done in secret" (6:18). What is done in secret is that which is done in the innermost soul, where no one else can see except god. Hence, the person in acting from within is seen by god; only the external appearance can be seen by others.

If the hypocrite is concerned with the outer manifestation, the sincere person is not: she is ultimately unworldly, in the sense of being unconcerned with appearance. But of course to be unconcerned with appearance is itself to appear so. It is striking that in the passage from Matthew's Gospel the deception of the hypocrite, who gives the appearance of holiness without having it in his heart, is contrasted to another form of deception, this time of the sincere person. In his case the "left hand must not know what the right is doing." In other words, he should hide his acts from all sight, except the sight of god: when he is fasting he should "put oil on . . . [his] face, so that [his] fasting may not be seen by others" (Matthew 6:17–18) because "what is highly esteemed in human eyes is loathsome in the eyes of God" (Luke 16:15). Hence the importance of secrecy. In this view, sincerity is not so much a matter of a true appearance of the inner self, as a rejection of outer appearance altogether: sincerity is the state of the human heart seen by god. What is for the eyes of god must be kept away from the eyes of people. Action in the world involves an inner withdrawal of the heart from the world.

Christian conscience is a movement of freedom from the world, which finds its corollary in a freedom from death. The voice of conscience calls for a free acceptance of death as the ultimate withdrawal from the world eventuated in the world. The issue here is not the fact of death. If Genesis does imply that death as a fact came into the world through sin, this needs to be understood less literally. Crucially, the fall is characterized by shame (Luke 3:7) and fear (3:10). The voice of conscience is heard in shame, a shame based on self-assertion, hence on the affirmation of the self and world, which fears death as the ultimate limit to the power of such self-assertion. Death in this sense is not a punishment for sin, but rather in turning away from god it is feared as that disintegration which mocks all self-assertion, all worldly ambition, which affirms its dependence on the world in its very declaration of independence. It is for this reason that the voice of conscience, the voice of the heart in the pre-Greek scriptures,[61] speaks not of independence, but of a fundamental dependence. For Paul to follow the call of conscience is to act "for the glory of God" (1 Corinthians 10:31). While only in the secrecy of the heart is such glorification apparent, the vulnerability of the other's conscience to the example of one's own actions is voiced by conscience also: "Sinning against your brother and wounding their vulnerable consciences, you would be sinning against Christ" (8:12). Nor is a good conscience a cause of self-certainty: "It is true that my conscience does not reproach me, but that is not enough to justify me" (4:4). Conscience then is that which ties the self to others and to god and does so beyond all convention and worldly wisdom. The call of conscience is a call to live in terms of those secret bounds. To do so is to live in acceptance of a fundamental dependence, that is, to live in Christ, to live in that origin which the world cannot contain. Mortality best expresses such fundamental dependence. The call of conscience is to live such mortality as mortality, to live death not as an external fate at best to be accepted with indifference, but as something which has already been overcome.

Death is not an event in the world: it is in worldly terms impossible. Leibniz saw this most clearly. If being were to be understood immanently as world and hence purely in terms of a system of signs—as a *mathesis universalis*—death would have no meaning: "there is never complete death . . . what we call deaths are enfoldings and diminutions."[62] Death is impossible. It is impossible in itself and it is impossible for me. But despite this impossibility, its reality is undoubted. We know nothing more certain than that we will die. But death is a darkness in which no worldly light can shine. We express this when we say that with death 'a world goes out of existence,' i.e., a way of being in the world, the uniqueness of which the world itself cannot contain, ceases to be in its movement toward things in the world. The extinguishing of light is an extinguishing of the light of the world. The Christian does not await this as a fate over which he has no control, but accepts it as a gift of transcendence. Christian life is a life of conversion, a life which understands itself as having already died, in the sense of having already passed beyond mere being-in-the-world (and hence beyond being-toward-death). Paul states this most forcefully: "when we were baptized into Christ Jesus, [we] were baptized into his death. So by our baptism into his death we were buried with him" (Romans 6:3–4). In another place he states: "you have died, and now the life you have is hidden with Christ in God. But when Christ is revealed you too will be revealed with him in glory" (Colossians 3:3–4). This death Paul defines as "being dead to sin," in other words, living toward god not toward the world. To be revealed in glory is to be revealed as being not of the world, that is, being revealed as being of an immemorial origin.

The philosopher prepares for death (*Phaedo* 64 a 3) because death is the "release of the soul from the body" (64 c 3). Death makes possible the acquisition of "pure knowledge" (66 e 4). The philosopher then must be half dead or "live in a state as close as possible to death" (67 e 1). Death is a stage in the chain of being, a stage of reaching pure spiritual existence, but also of de-individualization. Death in this view is not to be feared because it is nothing; death rather is a deliverance, a liberation. This view of death finds further development in the Stoics, in particular in the Stoic doctrine on suicide. Death in the Christian life, on the other hand, is not to come but rather is already past. All that is left is a death as the end of being in the world. But this death can be only properly endured if the Christian lives not as close as possible to death, but as if already dead. As if already dead is not to live without a body, but rather to live in the body as an expression of an origin which was never present.[63] Before my birth is an origin which is my non-being in the world. The finitude of existence, the temporary nature of human life, is that into which I come. I find myself within that finitude and in living my death I experience that finitude as alienating—not as something alien, but as something which makes me alien from myself. Living death as impossibility is to turn to the dark origins of the light of one's own life. It is a movement of de-alienation in the sense of an awareness of myself as given from beyond myself. That awareness of an inner 'mineness' which is not mine, but something beyond me and before me, is that which Descartes points to in the *Third Mediation*.[64] The self in the depths of its own being finds not a source of life in the procreative act of its parents, but a sending into a state of finite existence, into a being in the world, which nothing in the world can cause. In discovering its self (*autos*), the human being discovers its own being-given, its own being as radically in relation to an origin which it is not. In this sense to be mortal, to live death, is to be authentic as a heterogeneous being.

To live death is to live a 'secret life,' a life in the eyes of god. This is a life lived in conscience, lived, that is, as if seen by god. But to live such a life is to live in darkness: to live where neither the senses nor the intellect can act as guides.

Life 'after death' is a manner of living in this world. Death in Christian life is not, as for Plato, something to prepare for, because death has already been destroyed—there is literally nothing to prepare for. Belief in the destruction of death is to live after death. Such a life is one which distinguishes between life and survival, such that life is an expression of living, of that relation to its source in the withdrawal from the world, in its own darkening. Such a living does not fear death, as death is merely an end of survival understood in terms of a finite length of time. Life is lived not as a struggle with necessity, but rather as an expression of freedom. To live is still to survive, but survival serves life, and life is lived in the singular. Such a life faces the darkening of the world without the consolation of the world to die in recognition of the finitude of the things of the world in their worldliness and their infinite potential. To live the singular, unique event of one's own dying—no one can die in my place, no one can take my dying from me—is to live the singularity of one's own being. This is not solipsism, rather it is a living of my own being toward others in the expressing of my inner relation to them. That effort of expression is always partial, always undermined, always being emptied of depth and exposed as superficial. But to live 'after death' is to be in the mode of such expression, what may be termed authenticity.

Night is not the opposite of glory but its inner essence. To experience glory, to give glory, is to be in the night. It is to sense, imagine, will, and think in the dark, in excess of what gives itself as life. In this silent night the human being encounters the origins of its own self-expression, the origins of language which are the origins of its very being and the being of all creatures which appear to it. To speak here of creatures is neither accidental nor arbitrary. Glory and night name the appearing of things in themselves as beings which are singular manifestations of entities in the world but not of the world. This means nothing other than being created. Creation, however, in Christian terms can only be truly known through the second creation, the Incarnation.

5   Incarnation and Asceticism

[Christ] is written on our flesh.
—Aquinas, "Sermon on the Apostles' Creed"

THE "WORD BECAME flesh," because flesh is word: flesh manifests itself as it-self, as something which comes to word. The fundamental insight of Christianity, namely the divine becoming flesh, only if flesh already is more than it gives itself to be. The word can become flesh only if flesh is not foreign to the word, only if flesh is already a manifestation of the word. Such a manifestation is a pushing forth toward fulfillment, a striving toward that which already contained *in nuce* in the flesh continually articulates itself therein. The Incarnation is, then, in a fundamental sense the manifestation of flesh as flesh, its ultimate self-articula-tion. The word in becoming flesh does not impose itself on flesh, but allows flesh to appear as an articulation of itself and of being as created, as manifesting the word which was in the beginning. The Christian understands being as created, as not only coming from, but making manifest the word, which is one with god. In her own incarnate being, in her own relation to her flesh, she has the most in-timate experience of that creation, the self-relation of which she has in common with not just other persons, but all animate life (albeit in a slumbering state in many).

The experience in question here is of the body as more than, in excess of, itself. Only a being which experiences an excess in its embodied being can say of itself, 'I am a body' or 'this is my body.' The self-reflective act of self-designation is constituted by a movement beyond the body in its very identification with the body. This self-relation can be understood dualistically, or at least in terms of a relation of mind and body, of the immaterial and the material. But such an un-derstanding in the end destroys the person, either by dissolving her in the uni-versal (Plato) or imprisoning her in an angelic self-mirroring (Descartes). The incarnate Christ indicates the excess of embodiment not as in excess of embodi-ment (immaterial spirit, soul, mind, etc.), but rather as an *excessive embodiment*. An excessive embodiment means a dynamic being toward itself as an embodied being, a continual making manifest of itself as an expression of its being. The body in this sense is never simply itself, but is a constant articulation of being, of its relation to other existents and to the source of its own existence.

This excessive embodiment forms the phenomenological basis of the Resurrection. With the latter event the thought of a non-bodily destiny, of a stripping itself of all action and passion, is made incoherent. All human—and all creaturely—destiny is irrevocably tied to the body. The higher world, the world of "a new heaven and a new earth," can only be understood, then, as a transformation of embodied being—not its destruction or domination. In such a view the human body has written into it a higher human destiny, a destiny which answers the way of being of human embodiment. While in the *Phaedo* Plato conceives of human destiny in terms of a postmortem existence in fulfillment of the yearning of the soul for knowledge and indeed for identity with the universal, an identity only to be gained with the loss of the temporal and corruptible body, indeed a loss of the personal in the eternal,[1] Paul ties human destiny in the face of death to that of the body. He distinguishes between the besouled body (*soma pyschichon*) and the bespirited body (*soma pneumatikon*) (2 Corinthians 4:7–12; 5:1–10). The besouled body is that body which is vulnerable to disease, temptation, need, death. It is the animated, living body. Soul though owes its origins beyond itself, beyond either earth or heaven, but in a unity of heaven and earth, made manifest in Christ. It is to this pneumatic source that through faith in Christ the body can return so as like a seed it will through death regain its origins in spirit (1 Corinthians 15:43–44). This destiny is not in the power of the body in its natural, i.e., animate (besouled) state; it is rather a gift, grace. But grace does not act alone; grace empowers, brings new powers—powers not in the nature of the body—to bear on the body. The response to this empowerment is a way of living in self-relation to the body, which we might call asceticism: in Paul's terms an asceticism whose aim is not to subject the body, but to 'spiritualize' it.

In the body's relation to itself, the existent experiences itself as a depth which can never be made transparent to itself. In the body it experiences the heavy earthiness out of which arises, almost miraculously, an impulse of sky and air which is manifest as life. The surprise of this admixture of sky and earth as the mystery of life makes any reduction of life to earth (be that in biological, chemical, or philosophical terms) impossible. As earth the body shares with the material world around it an opacity and darkness, a night-like withdrawal, which seems to resist all intelligibility; yet in its movement, its form and self-formation, its gesture and expression, its aspect is toward the sky, is sky-like in the manner in which it shows itself eschewing all modesty. The earthiness of the body becomes sky-like in the gestures of its self-articulation. This mixture of sky and earth is the first desecration, the first impurity. The consciousness of this impurity and desecration characterizes human consciousness; sacred logic and ritual attempts to undo the desecration and re-establish in a manner which remains always provisional the exclusion of earth from sky.[2] The play of ritual strives through the logic of sacrifice to reform a balance and harmony. This harmony is generally a hierarchical one in which either the earth or the sky claims dominance. Philosophy arose historically at a time when in cultic terms the (Olympian) gods of the sky were dominant and this dominance is reaffirmed in the hierarchy of soul and body, of spirit over matter.[3] Philosophy—as Platonism, Stoicism, even Aristotelianism—affirms the logic of the sacred by striving to purify the soul of the body and the body of the soul in an order which guards as much as possible their mutual exclusion. It is with Christianity that this logic is taken to its conclusion and exploded. The incarnation gives divine sanction to desecration, to impurity.[4] It denies the sacred logic of the world and explodes all hierarchies of sky and earth, affirming life by denying the ultimacy of death.

This chapter is divided into three sections. The first titled "Athletes, Philosophers, the Called" traces asceticism from the Greek Olympian athletes to St. Paul. The next section examines the 'example of Christ' as a model of ascetic practice especially amongst the 'desert fathers.' The final section explores the 'glorious body.'

Athletes, Philosophers, the Called

The incarnate self experiences itself and is experienced as irreducibly expressive. But its self-expression is an articulation of itself within the boundaries of worldly relations of gender, class, ethnicity, ability/disability, sexual orientation, amongst others. The embodied self is itself only in relation to these relations and the laws, customs, and institutions which embody them. These form necessary mediations in the self-relation of a being, which is always in excess of itself. Its excessive being is a self-transcendence which in identifying itself runs a continual risk of exclusion, where conformity to existing modes of self-identity involves a refusal of its own being. This ambiguous situation is inherent in the self-relation of an incarnate being; it is one which is accentuated to breaking point by the Incarnation. The Incarnation above all else manifests the mediation of human and divine, of world and alterity. This mediation remains irresolvable, it remains at once human and divine, worldly existent and other than world, visible and invisible. As a mediation the Incarnation is an entwining of opposites, which resists all dialectical sublation.[5] This is the paradoxical in the Incarnation, that which is both glorious and hidden in its glory, an appearance of the non-apparent, the invisible in the visible. The Incarnation cannot be understood dualistically, because the oppositions which I have listed cannot be separated in it, even conceptually: once such a separation (analysis) is made, the Incarnation is lost. To give phenomenological rigor to such a phenomenon it is necessary to think it from the experience of incarnate being, the experience of such being primarily in its self-relation, in its realization of its own incarnate being.

Self-relation prior to all self-reflection is manifest in the animate body in its very kinetic—self-moving—being. A self-moving being is one which, if only in a dormant fashion, relates to itself. This embodied self-relation forms the phenomenological basis for any understanding of the Incarnation: the Incarnation concerns not just the becoming human, but at the same time the *becoming animal* of the divine. The divine becomes a being with those characteristically animal needs, inclinations, and bodily processes, which for the human can lead to unease, even disgust.[6] Here the boundaries of sacred logic and its attendant rituals are undone; the Christ-figure manifests a divine acceptance of the most animal and 'earthy' of bodily processes. Yet at the same time it indicates that such an acceptance is dynamic rather than static, that incarnate life has within itself a destiny which exceeds its present state. What that might be is suggested in Paul's designation of Christ as the second Adam and his death a new creation.

In the Incarnation the figures of god as creator and savior are united. Christ as the second Adam brings the prelapsarian human being to appearance in a fallen world.[7] The question, then, is what this means regarding embodied existence. According to the Genesis account, the bodily effects of the fall were firstly a recognition of nakedness, then mortality, and lastly relations of hostility and domination between men and women, human beings, and their natural environment: humanity and animality (Genesis 3:16–19). Christ is a figure of peace because he exemplifies the possibility of going beyond this state, of reaching beyond relations of mutual hiddeness and struggle. Such a figure would suggest *both* a clarity of self-relation and other-relation, in which the worldly boundaries and structures of mediation are no longer necessary, *and* a state in which the body is no longer vulnerable to those forces of disease and injury and those relations of material exclusion and inclusion which characterize our world. But, while making apparent the prelapsarian state, Christ lived within the boundaries of the postlapsarian world. Nakedness, death, and conflict then become modes of bodily existence, which are contingent upon worldly relations; the laws, customs, and institutions which all in varying degrees reflect the bodily state of a naked, mortal, and vulnerable being are both necessary for incarnate self-relation and ultimately inessential to the human being in its 'true' (i.e., Christ-like) state. The paradox of the Incarnation is thus understood as manifesting the paradoxical state of a being which both experiences the glory of the world and perceives in its own incarnate being a glory that darkens the world in opening up an existence impossible to it, yet essential to its being. In short, the glory of the Incarnation for the existents that follow it—re-enact it—is their own glory, which they are incapable of manifesting. The contradiction and paradox— the glory beyond and outside the world, the claim which nothing in the world can satisfy—makes necessary, but ultimately impossible, the ascetic practice of Christian life.

"Ascetics" comes from the Greek *askeo*, which means exercise, particularly physical exercise, and was used in particular to refer to the exercise required of athletes preparing for the Olympic games. Through working on itself the athlete's body comes to relate to itself both as a power to act and as a heaviness manifest in its initial awkwardness as well as its tendency to fatigue. The athlete's life is an ascetic life dedicated to disciplining the body in order to optimize its speed, strength, and grace. The athlete's discipline of the body is not an action toward some natural optimal state of the body—the animal body has no such optimal state; it is subject to the ascetic will, to the infinite—though not of course un-limited—optimalization. The speed and power of the body is limited, but those limits are not prescribed, and are never definitively reached (next time I can jump a little higher, run a little faster, throw a little farther . . .). Exercise is the relation of the body to its own weight and to the weightlessness of its surroundings. Ani-mal beings struggle toward the light, strive for the weightlessness of light, breathe the air which is the invisible, unearthly source of their life. But they are weighted down by the earth, which never quite succumbs to worldliness: by the fatigue of their legs, the phlegm which fills their air passages, the waste of their defecations.

Such athletic discipline is foreign neither to philosophy nor to Christianity: Plato put much stress on the athleticism of the guardians, even while criticizing excessive physical exercise (*Republic*, 410d4); Paul used the metaphor of athletics for the ascetics of faith (cf. 1 Corinthians 9:24–27); and the 'desert fathers'—the great ascetics of early Christianity—were described as "*athletae Dei* [athletes of God]."[8] Athletics discloses the body in its ambiguity: of earth, living in and by air, aiming to defy its earthiness, but being a body only in its earthiness. The light-ness and grace of the athletic body could—we might suppose—be achieved by separating sky from earth: enacting the feats of the athlete through the mind—soaring high, shooting accurately, reaching the finishing line.[9] Such achievement required its own ascetics, in the interests of intellectual not bodily prowess: the overcoming of the weaknesses and limitations of the body not through a perfect-ing of its strengths, but through the subordination of the body to that capacity for intellectual work, namely the mind (*nous*). Aristotle explicitly speaks of a par-ticular ascetics of philosophy, without which knowledge of good and bad cannot be taught (*Nicomachean Ethics*, 1179b20–30. For the Stoics asceticism becomes a matter of controlling, indeed dominating, the body: the wise man actualizes the proper cosmic hierarchy of mind and body.

Ascetics, whether making sky-like the earthiness of the body or subduing the body to the mind, involves of necessity an action of the embodied being on itself in its incarnate self-relation. Such a self-relation is one of a living incarnate being in an ascetic exercise on itself.[10]

For athletics, for philosophy, or for Christian life, some form of self-deni-al is necessary. This implies the presence of drives and passions, which need to be curbed or refined. The body in its activity and its passivity is subject to that which—such is the common assumption of these diverse ascetics—will enslave it, if allowed to continue unchecked. A key motivation for ascetics then is liberation: either from earthiness (philosophical ascetics is a turning away from the earthiness of the body for the sake of the sky-like things of the mind) or from worldliness (Christian ascetics is a turning away from the of-the-worldness of things in the world). What philosophical and Christian ascetics share is a striving for independence, which Nietzsche rightly saw as lying at the roots of ascetics. But again the independence in question is distinct: philosophical independence is that of self-sufficiency; Christian independence is independence from the world to disclose the person's absolute dependence on god as creator *and* savior and on her neighbor.

Independence for the sake of dependence is a preparation to listen to the call. The call is the always-already-present call of creation. Christian ascetics listens to the call of origins. That call is from elsewhere, a call to oneself as an existent whose origin is before and beyond itself. Ascetics in the Christian sense is self-denial of its own self-love as agent and initiator of action and meaning. As such it is a free act of limiting its own powers. That limitation of freedom is obedience. Obedience manifests the body's ascetic relation to itself as that which contains the origin of itself as a strange, unworldly presence. This presence is that of the word, the word which can only seem a distant and inscrutable source unless it, too, is found in the flesh, in the self-reflexivity of the self's own self-relation. The figure of Christ manifests this for the Christian, and his is an example that can be followed.[11]

The Example of Christ

If ascetics is motivated by a striving for independence, its central concern is the relation of activity and passivity in the body. A fundamental question here concerns the genuineness of the body's activity, specifically, the sources or origins of activity. Does the body initiate its own activity, is it the source of its own actions, or is the body rather like a wild horse (Plato, Descartes) that acts on impulse in reaction to signals from things in the world? If the latter is the case, no liberation can be found in the body: the body takes its lead from elsewhere. Despite its apparent actions, the body is, according to this understanding, essentially reactive. The analogy of a horse is not accidental: the body as reactive/passive is understood as animal. The problem of the body, of ascetic practice, then, becomes one of dealing with such passive animality. The issue here is one of dynamics: how to become and remain human while being animal, while having an animate body. There is no such place, no clear ontological location for the human. While experience presents so many aspects of difference between human and non-human animals, none of those differences has ontological fixity. They rather seem like anomalies concerning not categories of being, but dynamisms of self and world (trans)formations. The question of how to become (and remain) human does not allow for purely theoretical answers; it is a question which has to be answered in a way of life. Hence, the philosophical way of life aims at, or more precisely beyond, the human. Here the figure of the sage is instructive: the sage is not the prototype of the human—indeed it is doubtful if the true (Stoic, Skeptic, or Platonic) sage ever existed. Rather, the sage is the one who transcends the merely human—toward the divine—through ascetic practices that aim to give space to that humanity—that active, free, initiating being—by controlling animality.

These two dualities, those of activity/passivity and of humanity/animality, do not just form the context of ascetic practice, but are transformed by the event of the Incarnation, death, and resurrection of Christ. This event is not simply of significance for the history of asceticism, but philosophically speaking opens up a second way of being embodied, living the body beyond hedonism, but, far from repressing, exalting the body.

Christian ascetics is the act of following the example of the death and resurrection of Christ. As we have seen[12] the Christian lives with death, lives with death not as the end of life, but rather as that which may be overcome in every moment of life through living like Christ. Ascetic discipline seeks to detach the body from all its attachments to the world, all those attachments which make death fearful. But it does so not in the interests of *apátheia,* but rather to open itself up to its ultimate pathos toward its own origins. Attachments to the world Paul refers to as flesh (*sarx*).[13] The goal of asceticism is to expel the flesh (*sarx*) so as to acquire the body (*soma*).[14] Acquiring the body is the goal of asceticism, ultimately acquiring the 'glorified body' of the resurrected Christ.[15] Sarx is sometimes translated as the 'natural man,' but what is at issue here is a difference in the nature of human corporeality, which separates it from the rest of animal life. This is revealed already in Genesis with reference to nakedness. Only the human feels shame in nakedness, only the human dresses—places between himself and (his) nature a veil.[16] This in a sense is the first self-denial, the denial of the self before the other, the hiding of the self in its corporeal nature. Such modesty is a being with things in withdrawing from them. In its dress the human being conceals itself in showing itself: conceals its corporeal self in its fullness from the world in the very act of expressing itself—in its dress as much as its actions—to the world. But it is only through the fall that the human feels itself naked, because it is only then that the difference between sarx and soma arises. The corporeal relation to things becomes one of appropriation. It is for this reason that Paul, in a passage in Colossians after listing such earthly things as sexual vice, impurity, uncontrolled passion, and evil desires, adds "and especially greed [*pleonethian*], which is the same thing as worshipping an idol [*eidololatria*]" (Colossians 3:5). Literally 'pleonethia' means to want to have more. That wanting to have more is a will to self-sufficiency, which in effect is a self-worship and idolatry. Such a will is based not on bodily integrity because it aims to increase the range of the body, to incorporate as many things as possible: *ousia* not *parousia*—being as substance not being as before the presence of the coming.

Flesh is not simply the external being of the human, but also that of human institutions. The Law itself is fleshy—appropriate only for the flesh. Its holiness resides in being a gift for the flesh, but one which "while we were still living by the flesh the sinful passions aroused by the Law were working in all parts of our bodies to make us live lives which were fruitful only for death" (Romans 7:5). To follow the example of Christ is to follow the priest whose authority lies not in terms of descent through the flesh (Hebrews 7:16), but who released those who listen to his call from the Law "having died to what was binding us" (Romans 7:6). The flesh of the world is that which binds existents to the world. It is the outward expression of human, animal corporeality, which governs—enables and restrains—the corporeality of individual human beings. This is understood by Paul in terms of sin. The Law as the expression of the corporeal being gives expression—if only negatively—to the most destructive of corporeal tendencies. No human institution can overcome such tendencies, only at best control them. This control is, however, always unstable and subject to death. At best it can uphold a balance of worldly interests, which is a form of justice. If, however, the flesh is to be overcome, so too must the institutions of the world; the otherness of the body is to find expression not in its obedience to laws, but in its obedience to an origin it finds in itself. Institutions have a tendency toward evil particularly as they institute differences and conflict. The Christian ascetic's death to the world is one which nullifies such conflicts in the name of the body. The becoming one with the body is a stripping off of "your old behavior with your old self . . . [a putting on of] a new self which will progress toward true knowledge the more it is renewed in the image of its Creator; and in that image there is no room for distinction between Greek and Jew, circumcised and uncircumcised, or between barbarian and Scythian, slave and free" (Colossians 3:10–11). In a corresponding passage in Galatians Paul speaks of Jew/Greek, free/slave, and male/female (cf. Galatians 3:28). It is not that differences disappear: the Christian continues to live in the world, as Jew or Greek, male or female, free or enslaved, but these differences are understood as exterior, as not penetrating into the material body of the self, which is exemplified in Christ.[17] Again, this ascetics is an exercise in messianic difference: being Greek but not as Greek, being a slave but not as a slave, being a woman but not as a woman: being in the flesh of the world, but not as being in the flesh of the world, being oneself in one's bodily being (soma).

The stripping off of the old self is not a suppression of the self's being as Greek, enslaved, or woman, but rather living as an expression of the self in its singular being. The old self is a Greek or enslaved or female or any other form or combination of forms of being as defined by the agonal relations of worldly being;

the new self lives its being Greek, enslaved, female as necessarily finite modes of its own being in Christ. To live these modes of being is not as instituted in the laws of the flesh, but as ways of living as Christ lived. Living in peace in this sense does not mean quietism: on the contrary, living as a bodily being (soma) means living a destiny beyond any fleshy prescriptions as to how it is to be female or Greek or enslaved. Nonetheless, the Christian still lives in the world, and already in the later Pauline letters the implications of this—that, namely, the second coming is still to be awaited, that worldly existence will continue, and that institutions, laws, and church as a worldly institution with hierarchical organization are necessary to the preserving and maintaining of the message—become evident. The Christian as a being in the world does not live as soma, but rather in the difference between sarx and soma. But living in the difference between psyche and pneuma, the "benevolent dualism"[18] of Stoic and middle Platonic thought is impossible for Christians. Such benevolent dualism assumes a relation between body and soul as based in that of master and slave, while the Incarnation and Resurrection express a dynamics of transformation and identification: to reach the stage of a 'sage' is not to master the body as a slave, but rather to transform it.[19] Clement of Alexandria states the difference starkly: Ancient philosophers resisted desire; Christians should feel no desire at all.[20] While for the Stoics apātheia was the state of the rational self not being affected by desire, here the self is identified with its bodily state and is required to "make himself a eunuch for the sake of the kingdom of heaven" (Matthew 19:12).

In the context of the Incarnation the body cannot be understood as simply passive. The Incarnation defines revelation: it is the visible manifestation of the invisible. The body of Christ, then, is passive and active, both subject to external temptations and a manifestation of the inner self. God is invisible, yet is—as Christ—visible. Through a self-emptying—*kenosis*—the Son divests himself of his glory, so as to appear not as he is, but like any other man, indeed as Paul puts it, as a slave. Hence, his body appeared both as it was and as it was not: as the body of a man, and as nothing more. In the body itself a difference was drawn, between what can be seen and what cannot be seen. What can be seen appears to others, or more precisely to the bodily senses of others; what cannot be seen appears to the eyes of faith as that which inscribes the thing of sight with a sense which has no visible correlate, but rather finds resonance in the inner relation to itself—conscience—and toward god "who sees all that is done in secret." This distinction between inner and outer is not an external difference, however. What is at issue here is a dynamics of transformation: the exteriority of the body is its vulnerability to that which is outside itself and outside its capacities—temptation, delight, death. The interiority of the body is that which expresses the self of the person in its relation to its vulnerability. Ascetics is the transformative mediation of that difference.

Once the human, and even the divine, is understood as being incarnate, two different and apparently opposed consequences follow. On the one hand, the possibility of transformation of the human into the glorified body is opened up. It is not by accident that following his description of the kenosis of Christ, Paul states that Christ "will transfigure the wretched body of ours" (Philippians 3:20). On the other hand, if the human is identified as flesh then the difference between animal and human has to be within the flesh or nowhere else. The example of Christ does not so much lead to higher spiritual reaches as it does bring the one responding to that example to the limits of the self-relation of the body.

The identification of the self-relation of the body with the divine in its parousial promise takes as its point of reference the prelapsarian state of pre-social human life. The stripping away of sarx leads not to a hierarchical being in the world of Platonism/Stoicism, but rather the being adrift in the world—not cosmopolitanism but exile in the world. This promise of a prelapsarian existence is of course one which remains unfulfilled. In the light of this promise, however, those fundamental bodily realities—pain, vulnerability to injury and disease, mortality—are lived as contingent on an event (the fall), not on the nature of the body itself. A postlapsarian living toward a prelapsarian state can mean a withdrawal from the world, or an immersion in it as that which remains, however fallen, from creation. In what follows, I will chart these two possible responses, which though not exhaustive, indicate two ways of bodily self-relation in the face of the Incarnation.

Glorious Body

Early Christian asceticism is exemplified in one of its most extreme forms by the Desert Fathers. A critique of public life which we find most forcefully expressed in the sermons of John Chrysostom in fourth-century Antioch sought to turn Christians away from the public space toward the household, toward privacy, and more specifically an identification with the body as the locus of the exercises of self-denial and purification called for from a Christian.[21] Once the identification with the body is made, the human concern shifts to private matters of life: food, sleep, sex, and death. Indeed, the body becomes no longer a neutral, indeterminate extension of the natural world, whose use and very right to exist was subject to civic considerations of status and utility. Furthermore, such a concern with the body has a strong egalitarian aspect: from the emperor to the beggar the same issues arise. But at the core of this egalitarianism is the startling fact that that which concerns the ascetic, that which are the concern of all—food, sleep, sex, death—are themselves the concerns of animal being. It is for that reason not surprising that the greatest fear of the Desert Fathers was that of *adiaphoria:* indistinction between human and animal.[22] The conscious attempt by early Christian ascetics to reach a state comparable to Adam before the fall, a condition prior to culture, prior to all excess possessiveness, struggled with the possibility of a fall into animality. The way of reaching a prelapsarian condition was meant also to mark the difference between human and animal—that way was through food. There was a prevailing view amongst the Desert Fathers that the source of sin and desire was to be found in excess nourishment—indeed the view was current that the fall was not due to a sexual sin, but to greed. These two realms were nonetheless closely related: excess of food led to sexual desire.[23] The possibility of slippage between human and animal opened up by sexual activity and consumption of food made an ascetic discipline essential in such areas.[24] Furthermore, there was a strong Encratite tradition in the East according to which the eating of meat brought human beings down to the wild, carnivorous nature of animals.[25] Through ascetic discipline the body, instead of falling into such indistinctness with the animal, would become master of itself and would be autonomous in the sense of tending toward independence of the outside world even for nourishment. The body in such a view was an autarkic system and should function like an idling engine.[26] Defecation was a sign of excess: the body is and should become integral and whole. The body, then, is active to such an extent to reduce its dependence on its environment to as close to nil as possible, in order to turn it toward god. The dependence on the environment becomes formalized and stylized. The example of Christ, not the demands of the flesh, becomes the guiding instance. The turn here is from time to eternity, which, however, was to be wrought through the body, not in rejection of it.[27]

The working of the body on itself gives the human an opening beyond the worldly, the lack of which for Heidegger defines the non-human animal.[28] The latter is destined to dependency on its environment, to respond to its environment without glimpsing the possibility of any other instance.[29] The working of the animal body on itself is governed by that need to respond, governed by habits of response built up precisely by its own working on itself. This way of being Christian, this incarnate self-relation, is one which experiences its own embodiment as shameful, as a sign of its fallenness. Its shame before its own embodiment is an experience of its own sinfulness, as its embodied being draws it toward things in the world in relations of absorption. The autarkic aim is one of turning the body away from that which excites and satisfies it as flesh, toward Christ as the embodied overcoming of flesh. In the flesh the Christian experiences a darkening of itself, but its overcoming of that darkness is through a glorification of the body, one which makes it invulnerable to the world. In Christ, in such a view, is to be found the exemplar of a body that works on itself in the interests not of optimizing its relations to its environment or of removing distractions from the mind, but of exemplifying a bodily existence without bodily needs, i.e., the existence of the resurrected body. The distinction then becomes one not so much of mind and body as between the body in its dependency on its environment and the body as a pure expression of spirit, that which St. Paul calls the "spiritual body."

The ascetic aims to transform its embodied self into a "spiritual body." As is the case with any body, the spiritual body is in space and time, in the space of the world, and the time of its own life and the generational life which it makes manifest: a mortal but also generational time. The living being is characterized by its tendency to generate. It is precisely this temporal horizon which that fundamental aspect of the incarnational ascetic body—namely, sexual renunciation—seems to foreclose. Furthermore, it does so in opposition to the corruptibility of the present world to time and the contingencies of place. With Christianity the world ending is central: eschatology displaces cosmology. Crucial here is not just the perceived imminence of the end of the world (among the early Christians), but the understanding of the world as ending. With Paul, messianic time is opened up, the time of the end of time.[30] Neither the body nor sexuality can then be considered in terms of the world alone, but of an eschatological destiny. Within the Jewish tradition sexuality is ambiguous from the beginning of the Torah: sexual desire is linked directly to the fall and yet mankind is commanded to procreate (be fruitful and multiply; Genesis 1:28). In St. Paul's eyes, due to the imminence of the end of the world, this Gordian knot can be cut: there is now no need to procreate because the world is coming to an end. Clearly here asceticism is directly related to an affirmation of the world's finitude. But this does not amount to a simple rejection of the body, since the end of the world does not lead to the end of the body, but rather to the end of a particular form of embodied existence: flesh. Fleshy embodiment will give way to a spiritual body and this will be brought about through a second incursion, so to speak, into the world, a cutting asunder from without of the ways of the world. The ways of the world are by their nature things of the flesh. By "flesh" Paul often means sexual drives. In terms of the divine commandment, the flesh was no longer relevant to salvation. Those generational bonds both to the past and the future which the Law instituted were now no longer binding. But the power of the flesh remains. Furthermore, the sexual drives are connected with the other bodily needs which tie the human body to its environment, and of these Paul states clearly that nobody hates his flesh (Ephesians 5:29). Hence, Paul rejects any advocacy of total celibacy as an undermining of those social bonds which keep the flesh in check.

Nonetheless, the more radical voices which came to be heard from Origen onward proclaimed total chastity as an ideal for all Christians, an ideal which amounted to the privileging of the continent body which manifested a principle of reversibility: the generational flow of life could be halted and the end of the world could, so to speak, be foreshadowed. Understood in the context of contemporary medicine the vitality of the body far from being manifest in frequent sexual activity was dissipated by that activity. Coitus amounted to a draining of vital spirit from a man; hence frequent sexual activity, it was claimed, would lead to effeminacy and infertility.[31] The total abstinence from sexual activity far from being a rejection of the body can be seen in that context as an attempt to heighten the vitality of the body. Hence the post-pubertal eunuch was an ambiguous figure as he kept his vital spirits intact.[32] In the light of this we can read strongly Cassian's rallying call for a "departure from the flesh for one who is dwelling in the body."[33] Taking leave of the vulnerabilities of the flesh makes possible a body which expresses fully (or near to fully) the living spirit of the person.

But the path to such self-expression is a painful one. Indeed, it is in pain that the flesh comes to be thematic for itself. Returning to the model of the athlete: the pain of exercise, of training, is the descent of the body in fatigue. The body is made vulnerable to itself through the exercise of self-discipline—and ascetic discipline, no matter how it is carried out under the authority of others, remains essentially a self-reflexive movement. In its own vulnerability to itself the body's own drive to self-preservation and appropriation comes to appear as itself but also as not identical with the self. This is paradoxical: the body appears in its own *self*-preservation as less than itself. It appears to itself in pain—in the self-inflicted pain of privation, denial, even direct hurt—as not ultimately interested in its own survival. Furthermore, it recognizes in suffering that which is not simply to be endured but as something meaningful. It is in this very suffering that the difference of sarx and soma implicit in play comes to appear in its full significance.

'Soma' refers not just to the material reality of the body but to the person expressed in and through that materiality. Through the disciplining of the body the person is raised to a new height. For the Desert Fathers the real progress of the ascetic was to be measured in terms of his imagination, or his heart, or will.[34] To not engage in sexual activity was only an external practice: the real battle was against sexual imaginings.[35] It was in the inner recesses of his heart that the Christian encountered god, and the ascetic practice was aimed at making the body subject to the heart. This subjection was not simply confined to the waking, conscious self, but to the sleeping, dreaming self as well. As Nietzsche points out, moral sentiment does not prevent a man from being deceived every night by his dreams;[36] ascetic practice was finally successful if even the dreams did not betray the purity of heart of the person. That purity was at once a purity of flesh in the sense of ritual purity and a bodily purity in the sense of an inner purity of dream-states, which habitual practice could achieve to the extent possible. The absence of sexual dreams and the absence or near absence of nightly emissions was for the Desert Fathers, as detailed by Cassian, a final test of the purity of heart of the monk which held nothing back either from god or his fellow monks.[37] The monk must be willing to disclose all his thoughts to his Superior; those of which he is ashamed to so disclose are for Cassian clearly from the devil.[38] The ebb and flow of sexual desire marked a gap between body and spirit—a gap which, through the ascetic transformation of the body, could be overcome.

While the transformation of the body aims at the example of the glorified body of the resurrected Christ, one no longer vulnerable to temptation, hunger, and death, the working on the body takes place precisely in the context of such vulnerabilities. It is by exploring these vulnerabilities, precisely in resisting them, that the activity and passivity, earthiness and celestiality, of the body become manifest. The self-reflexive moment in which the existent experiences itself as being affected arises out of the body's relationship to itself. To place the vulnerability of the body at the center of the ascetic life makes sense only in the context of a strong sense of the body's integrity, i.e., of the body's limits as clearly delineated and guarded by moral prescriptions. Integrity indeed was a key term for St. Ambrose for whom there existed an invisible frontier between the virgin body and the polluting admixture of the outside world.[39]

The point of bodily integrity is not, however, to make the body invulnerable or self-sufficient. The drive to independence from things in the world is the opposite of autonomous solipsism. Rather, it seeks to relate to the world in its inappropriability. Dependence on the world arises out of greed for appropriation. Invulnerability to the temptations of greed is the becoming vulnerable in the presence of what is. Asceticism is the preparation through the example of Christ to be open to the sending of an immemorial origin of creation.

Embodiment as Play

The Desert Fathers have a central place in the history of the Christian account of the body and the ascetic because they crystallize two traditions in ancient thought on the body: that of the Stoic and that of the Judeo-Christian. These traditions share a concern for the protection of the (male) self from animality and femininity. Furthermore, although the aim of the Desert Fathers' ascetic practice is not apātheia but rather openness to the Other (god), both traditions share the goal of invulnerability with respect to sensual pathos. The central motif governing the ascetic of this Christian type is the glorified body of the resurrected Christ—self-relation taking that glorified body as its model. But it is possible also to think the Incarnation in the glory of its pre-resurrected state; to think Christ not in his triumph over death, but also and first in his suffering of death. Furthermore, such a thinking and such an ascetic practice leads not to the autarkic and invulnerable state, but rather to a being attentive to that which binds and connects the self to animal and material being. To think this we can think the ascetic being again, once more taking our clue from the athlete, but beginning with play.

Play is, as Eugen Fink tells us, a symbol of world:[40] in play the worldly relations of appearance and concealment are manifest. But it is also a symbol, a secret sign, in which existents recognize each other in their singular relation to that which sets play out of play. The Incarnation in rupturing the world does so by mixing that which according to the logic of the sacred should be kept separate.

In that way it affirms life, and specifically created life, as the mixing of sky and earth. This mixing is possible—and not simply monstrous—because it sets the play of the world out of play, but does so by propelling that play toward and beyond its own limits. In so doing it discloses play as a receptivity to its own epoché, a receptivity rooted in the playful encounter of the body with itself.

Play is of nature. Play comes to the fore in animal nature, in the animal's dynamic relation of its own materiality and its disclosure of the transformative possibility of matter working on itself. At play human and non-human animals can for fleeting moments become equals.[41] No longer relating as master and servant, predator and prey, caregiver and patient, in the fun of the game both lose themselves in a primal exercise of movement and energy: chasing, wrestling, competing, playacting—all accompanied by vocalizations of excitement, yelping, shouting, grunting, laughing. At this level beyond or before all functionality the human and animal relate to each other through fun. Such relations have implicit rules, which all aim to keep the game at the level of pretense, and these rules apply to human and animal alike: they are to be observed in the play of animals without any human involvement and extend so far as spontaneous self-handicapping on the part of an older or stronger animal playing with a younger or weaker opponent. All this points to a difference between pretense and the real and a pre-reflective level of awareness of that difference in playing animals. With this awareness comes a difference in mood: a lightness of mood, what we call playfulness.

The significance of play is rooted in this difference between pretense and reality as expressed within the relation of the body to itself. In play the body expresses itself to itself beyond the limits of biological or physical necessity.[42] By responding to a pretended situation the body manifests its activity to itself and to others. As being without extrinsic purpose play allows the body to be manifest beyond all functional relations and to show itself as its own self-expression. In play the animal is freed from the force of the real, the seriousness of purpose, and is free to give expression to its own embodied being. Again such self-expression does not imply an apperceptive self-relation, but it does mean an intrinsically motivated being active of the body.[43]

As pretense, play is also imitative. The mimetic quality of play allows young animals to act out hunting, fighting, and other serious actions, without actually being involved in those situations. In other words, play is—as its etymology suggests—also exercise or more precisely exercising *oneself*.[44] Play is an exercising on oneself, a pretending, an imitation. Exercise is playful, and as such play is a (preconscious) preparation for the real. The body in manifesting itself also works on itself; play in its effects is such a self-working of the animal body on itself.

The desire to play is not to appropriate and consume but to move between rival self-expressions, to be in an agonistic movement without end, i.e., without decidability. Whatever the details of his account, Huzinga correctly shows play to be fundamental to human culture. But the roots of this are to be found in the animal—specifically mammalian—free space of play. Play is not ontologically poorer than the real, but rather the way of expression of incarnate self-relation as performance. Performance, Victor Turner states succinctly, "is always doubled, the doubleness of acting . . . it cannot escape reflection and reflexivity."[45] In this performance the world's temporal and spatial dimensions intersect within play as rhythm. In the experience of rhythm the movement of play is manifest. This suggests that the repeated emphasis by certain theorists on spontaneity in play—of free choice to play—is misplaced. Play is as much something which *happens to* the players. Hence, the centrality of ritual and ritualization in play. The ritual theorist Ronald Grimes puts it this way: "we cannot escape ritualization without escaping our own bodies and psyches, the rhythm and structures of which arise on their own. They flow with or without our conscious assent; they are exclamations of nature and our bodies."[46] In ritual the body does not just have its place, but it reflects the cosmic order: hence the emphasis on the wholeness of the body and the allergy to porosity which is generally found in ritual cultures. The wholeness of the body reflects the cosmic order and defines holiness.[47] In line with its theatricality the actions of the body are transformed in ritual into gestures.

Play is both fundamental to human existence and an expression of human animality: even the element of ritual is evident in animal play, indeed can be said to be inherent in the very mode of pretense in which it is expressed. Pretense here does not mean untruth, but rather an engagement which enjoys action for its own sake, enjoys, that is, itself in the act of its own self-expression. That self-expression is primeval in the sense of bringing forth an original way of being—a way of being which precedes the self—into the space of appearance. The self-relation in play is one which allows the self to appear to others and itself as its own embodied being, but one which expresses its embodiment in giving itself over to a playfulness, a rhythm, and a ritualistic habit which both transcends it and which comes to expression in it. The Incarnation as the becoming flesh of the Word, the becoming (human) animal of god, can be understood as pretense in the playful sense. In performing the human god becomes an actor, takes on a role in the worldly drama, but precisely as being not of that drama, but its source—from before the world was—the incarnate god discloses the world as performance, and as such shows the limits of worldly glory as no more than the glory of an actor playing a part. Such performance does not negate the real, but rather 'reduces' the real to the event of its appearance, to the coming forth of the real as world, and indicates that it is in the incarnate self-relation, one which delves to the depths of the body's own materiality, that likeness to the source of all being is to be found. The Incarnation makes manifest the invisible glory of god, but does so in the least of things. This materiality and consequent emplacement of the self-relation in re-enacting the Incarnation is most manifest in liturgy.

Liturgy is playful in its breaking from the necessities of the world, but radicalizes that playfulness by bringing the crisis of being and non-being to breaking point.[48] It does so by opening up to that which is beyond the world as coming to presence in the play of ritual action. While ritual play suspends the necessities of the world precisely in the mode of 'as if,' liturgy opens a space for the non-necessary as such. In doing so it opens up a space in the world in which the contingency of the world as created comes to appearance. Such an appearance is of the world as appearing in relation to god. There is nothing in the immediacy of experience which justifies liturgy: liturgical action is an action in the form of an 'as if,' but in this case not simply the 'as if' of imitation, but also the 'as if' of the new, the 'as if' of the 'to come,' the parousia.[49] Furthermore, in opening up the contingency of the world, liturgy breaks or has the possibility of breaking with ritual's allergy regarding porosity. The Incarnation is a mixing, a contamination, and this is reflected in the Christ's rejection of ritual purity. "Nothing that goes into someone from outside can make that person unclean" (Mark 7:15).[50] It is rather the porosity of things which is made manifest in the Incarnation, that things appear in their singular being not monadically, but rather as openings beyond themselves, as receptacles of a sending and a fundamental affectivity by the beauty of things. This porosity concerns also the animality of the human. The movement of liturgy is one of openness and reception, rather than wholeness and placing boundaries.

In the very movement of liturgy is manifest the specifically human in play, namely the moment of dispossession and disappropriation. As Lacoste states: "[the human] is the only animal capable of challenging his participation in the play of appropriation."[51] In play the appropriative movement is suspended in the pretence of performance. But while the animal never moves beyond the appropriative performance itself, the human is capable of a self-impoverishment. The Incarnation serves as an exemplar of such self-impoverishment by the kenotic movement of its self-manifestation. That kenotic movement, that emptying itself of its glory, manifests the world as itself night, the dark space from which alone however the light of the divine performance can be seen. Such a sight, the sight of faith, is the sight which desires the invisible presence. In such desire the existent separates herself from human society in order to find beyond that society the flesh of god. Such desire is both an inner and an outer movement, in its inner and outer interchange.[52] In that desire the existent in its visible self is implicated as a seeing being, as a being with inexhaustible depth. This depth is hidden to the existent; in its very exercise vision ignores and forgets itself. It is out of this self-forgetting that liturgical action emerges.

Both modes of re-enacting the Incarnation in ascetic practice share a movement beyond the Law, beyond the institutional, the instituted, as it prescribes a formation of bodily being, all in the light of the promise of a prelapsarian world. Both as such give scope to a certain violence, a certain disruption of the publically ordained modes of bodily being in the world. As such they both reflect the shock of the Incarnation: an existent being in the world, claimed to have meaning and significance beyond all worldly relations. But the two modes of living this embodied relation show the ambiguity of the situation which the Incarnation inaugurates. The self-relation of an embodied being, working on itself, taking as a model of its self-relation an existent manifesting both materiality and divinity. The invisible divinity of Christ is not beyond or separate from the visible, but rather is in the visible itself. It is in this way that the revelatory presence of god can take external form. The meaning of the divine is held in its sensible, material articulations, existing *Ineinander*, intertwined chiasmically. Such existence is as much in the world as being not of the world, and in living toward the world ending, can either be lived in a withdrawal from the world or in an entering into the earthy reality which the world likes to hide. The ambiguity of living the life in the example of Christ reflects the ambiguity of a fallen creation—both turned toward and turned away from its true, but hidden, origins.

6 Creation

Created things are darkness in so far as they proceed from nothing.
—Aquinas, *The Disputed Questions on Truth*

CHRISTIAN LIFE LIVES the world as created, aims toward god as creator: lives the world, that is, supra-cosmologically. Christian life is not governed by cosmology and as such does not live creation as a cosmological doctrine. The doctrine of creation expresses things as things in the world in relation to that which is not of the world. As such it expresses things in relation not to necessity (hence not to cause), nor to actuality (hence not to presence), nor to possibility (hence not to any capacity of things), but rather to freedom as the origin of ontological modalities.[1] Freedom understood as original is love—*agápe*. The basic Christian insight into things is that they are only truly understood in relation to a free love out of which they emerge. The life of faith as preached and practiced by Christians is a way of being with things as creatures, that is, a way of being with them as expressions of love. This is faith as the insight into the insufficiency of all reason. Creation means the insufficiency of reason in its immanence. Being with things in faith is being with things in excess of their worldly appearance: being with things in desire. This desire finds its fullest expression as a self-giving, which *needs* no response to fulfill it, but which itself is a response to things in their beauty through a creative expression of truth as self-dispossession.

This chapter is divided into four sections. The first examines the paradoxical formula, *creatio ex nihilo*. It is crucial here to understand what leads to such an account of creation and what it means. The next section explores the concept of 'nothing' operative here and contrasts it with other notions of nothingness. The third section takes up the underlying notion of creation, namely, that of divine love, and shows how this concept is incompatible with an ontology in terms of a chain of being. The final section of the chapter examines the implications of the notion of creation for knowledge and shows that it undermines the account of knowledge as adequation.

Creatio ex nihilo

The creation story in Genesis is a story of a master craftsman.[2] The divine gives the measure for all making; through the repetition of creation in the Incarnation the divine becomes the measure of all action.[3] Creation, both as the creation of the world and as the incarnation of Christ, manifests a significance for all making and all action beyond that which appears in worldly terms; visible effects and products signify the invisible movement of expression, that is, the bringing into being. Art, the artwork, is for the sake of this bringing into being. Through the creativity of the artist such bringing into being is aimed at. It is so not out of indifference: the thing brought into being is not just anything, but is that which most fully *is* for the artist. This being 'most fully' is that which is meant by the term 'expression.' What is 'most fully' is that which is most significant. Significance is meant here not in the sense of indication—that which indicates, the sign, is indifferent in its own being—but in the sense that it calls attention to itself, expresses nothing but itself, such that the artist can no longer understand when the critic looks elsewhere for its meaning. The meaning is in the work and nowhere else—otherwise the work is not 'most fully.' The artist works on material to make such an expression. The self-expression of the artist is not to be understood as a stamp, an imprint marked in pliable material: then the work again becomes a sign, a sign of the inner self of the artist. Rather, the artist finds in the material that meaning which she does not know until she finds it. The work is a coming together of the hands of the artist and the given material of the earth. In the successful work the artist fuses herself with the work, mixing or rather confusing inner and outer, meaning and matter, to create a singular, significant work.[4]

In speaking of this process we, inheritors of Plato and of Aristotle, think almost irresistibly in terms of matter and form. The artist in this understanding forms matter into that which expresses an idea. Such a conception is of course never fully true even on its own terms: matter is always formed for us; it would otherwise be ineffable, unknowable, unperceivable. Prime or formless matter is, so to speak, a limit idea, an idea of that making at the origins of the world: demiurgic making. Within the world as we can know and perceive it, making remains within the limits of the demiurgic, is a *trans*forming of matter, and as such depends on a pre-formed and hence pre-structured matter. But this making, understood in terms of the demiurgic, is governed by the irreducible terms of matter and form, such that the singular origin of things remains hidden. All things have a dual origin; their singular being is derivative of a contingent bringing together of matter and form. The contingency of this bringing together is a contingency in the world, is a temporal moment of an eternal world. All bringing together of matter and form imitates temporally the eternal harmony of form and matter which is the world.[5]

Creation as it is spoken of in Genesis shares something in common with the Platonic account of the demiurge. Only with Christianity does the basic assumption of that account—the assumption that matter falls outside the divine creation—become questioned and eventually rejected. With that rejection goes also a rejection of the eternity of the world. The thing within the world now has a singular existence which is stated as an existence *out of nothing.*

Creatio ex nihilo is a particular Christian interpretation of Genesis, one which has no unambiguous precedent in Judaism.[6] The radicalization of the latter account of creation is not motivated by the figure of the creator god. The utter transcendence of god (and hence the transcendence of his will), as understood in Judaism, is compromised in the doctrine of the Incarnation. Hence, although the doctrine of creatio ex nihilo was defended in terms of the unconditionality of divine will, the latter is unlikely to be its chief motivation. Contingent motivations were clearly those posed by the growth of Gnostic doctrines in the early centuries of Christianity, which in certain instances denied the goodness of all creation and hence of the creator god.[7] But these accounts were particularly anathema to Christians because they compromised the place of Christ. The chief motivation for the new doctrine of creation arose rather from Christological concerns as to how to understand the person of Jesus of Nazareth as "true God and true man."[8] The intricacies of this debate cannot detain us here; the crucial point, however, is that if this man were god he can only be understood as a repetition of creation, a recapitulation of the act of creation and everything which followed thereupon. Creation is god's expression and representation of himself, is a giving of himself for the sake of the product of that creation. By becoming a creature, he re-enacts that self-giving, re-enacts it in the kenotic act of emptying himself of his divinity. John expresses this act succinctly: "The word became flesh and lived amongst us" (John 1:14). In becoming flesh he is at once creator and creature, at once Lord and slave (Philippians 2:7). What Christ reveals, then, is that the transcendent understood in terms of creation is to be found not beyond the material, but within it. A new sight and a new hearing is called for to see and hear creation. Christ is the second Adam because through him the words of god are once again to be heard—as they were by Adam—in the things of creation.[9]

Although understood by Paul as the second Adam, as god amongst humankind, the difficulty of such a conception is well illustrated in the early Christian churches. Some denied the humanity, some the divinity of Christ. Some—like Justin Martyr and Origen—while accepting the divinity of Christ saw him as a lesser divinity, understood him as the intermediary of god in explicit analogy to the role of the logos in the *Timaeus*.[10] Some Gnostic writers—notably Marcion— guided by an understanding of material creation as corrupt, understood the god of creation either as evil or as a failure and posited a higher god, a purely spiritual god, of whom Christ was the messenger and whose mysteries would lead to union with this god beyond all material reality.[11] In response to these various understandings, the 'orthodox' Christian position became articulated in the third century, and formulated doctrinally at the Council of Nicea (325), namely that Christ was equal in being (*homoousia*) to the father. This meant a rejection of Origen's Platonic understanding of the place of Christ, but also a rejection of Gnostic dualism: Christ was one with the creator of the world, not simply an intermediary. That god took on material form, that material form manifests—to the eyes of faith—god as the second person of the Trinity, makes a Gnostic denial of the world impossible. Taken seriously, the Incarnation affirms that all of creation came from god. This means that matter, too, was created by god: outside of god's creation there is nothing. Christ repeats and renews creation by taking on material limitations. In so doing he places matter on a level with divinity. The Christian account of creation arises not from an understanding of god as limitless, but rather from an understanding of him as taking on limits; it arises not out of a voluntaristic denigration of matter, but rather out of an acknowledgment of matter as containing the power of divine creation.

Nonetheless, it is clear that central to this account is an understanding of creation as unconditioned, as standing outside the world and bringing the world and all it contains into being. This can only be understood in terms of a freedom which sets conditions and is not conditioned. It is in this freedom that the human being is understood as created in the "image and likeness" of god (Genesis 1:26).[12] Paradoxically, freedom becomes the source of evil: a free being is one who can choose evil. The world is contingent on divine freedom, and evil comes into the world through human freedom. At the origins of things, at the origins of the world—but not as that which pre-exists worldly order—is evil. Only when divine and human freedom are brought into identity—in the freedom of Christ—is the possibility of a world without evil revealed (but by the same token the unheard-of depths of possible evil are also revealed). Such a world is an impossibility in pre-Christian thought, or rather it is a possibility only if all men become wise in the apathetic Stoic model, something which it was doubted any individual had ever achieved. In Christian terms this was possible only through obedience to the example of Christ, as Christ had been obedient to the father.[13] Such obedience though is not a matter of following the law. If Christ is the fulfillment of the law, obedience to him is not the obedience to anything which can be formulated propositionally, but rather to the *example* of a life. Such obedience is only possible as self-expression, as creation.

Christian freedom is the paradox, indeed apparent contradiction, of situated unconditional freedom. Taking its example from Christ, it is a freedom which lives its situation as a situation, that is, as historical, as historically given, and as potentially historically transforming. But it seeks in that historical situation an eternal significance. This is not the boon of "living immortally in the minds of men" (Cicero), but rather of giving glory—*ad majorem gloriam deo.* Such a glorification of god is not for the sake of another person as a being-in-the-world—not for the sake of the 'public,' nor for the sake of 'family,' or 'friends'. It is directed toward god as the origin of the world, but also as god who was on the earth. Thus, the directedness toward god is at one and the same time a directedness toward others and toward oneself. Glorification is praise, but also proclamation, a showing of glory—not my glory, but that glory which is other to me. Such a giving of glory is directed toward an other who sees the existent's act of expression in terms of the freedom from which it comes. This other who takes the act up in this way need not exist, may indeed never exist, but is as a witness to the work of freedom as it enters into an eternal communion with the one who has found expression in that act. This is not an ahistorical eternity, but rather the being in a situation as an absolute givenness of the grounds of being. It is a being in a situation through an expression of creation, expressing being in relation to grounds.

Understood in these terms, the attempt of the artist (as the exemplary case of free, creative acts) is to discover anew, beneath the taken for granted of culture—the already constituted reason, through which things are 'understood'— the things themselves in their self-expression. Such an attempt seeks to come before all culturally transmitted memories in order to find at its source that which gives life to such memories. That immemorial source is divine freedom; such divine freedom is experienced in desire. In desire the excess of things over their worldly appearance is made manifest. Such a manifestation is what the Christian means by truth, that is, the manifestation of things not in relation to their worldly being, but in their singular relation to an origin of their singular being. Such a singular relation to singular origins is at once obscured in its very expression. The free act of expression shows itself in the movement of its execution, and loses itself in the products of that movement. As truthful, such a movement allows the thing to appear from itself and in itself, and this can occur only through a self-dispossession, which marks a break in the economy of the world. But this does not amount to a mere receptivity: the pure receptivity of which we spoke in the last chapter is itself an act, an act of prayer. Artistic creation is prayerful to the extent to which it brings something into being which is not in the artist's control, which rather stands forth as a product of her freedom in the service of the thing whose truth it embodies. Such creation of an object allows the thing to emerge as created, as it is in relation to its own grounds. The freedom of the human being to create allows the thing to appear in relation to its grounds in enacting the human relation to its grounds.

Implicit in this notion is an interrelation of human expression and the world as created. Expression in its desire for truth is a movement of self-dispossession, a movement of self-giving in response to the self-giving of things. But such expression always loses itself in the particularity of its products. The Judeo-Christian story of the fall gives account of such failure of expression; salvation is the opening up of its possibility. What is at stake here is not simply the salvation of a particular species—humanity—but rather of creation itself as a self-expression of its creative origins. This is formulated eschatologically by Paul in a text we are quoting here for the second time:

> the whole of creation is waiting with eagerness for the children of God to be revealed. It is not for its own purposes that creation had frustration imposed on it, but for the purpose of him who imposed it with the intention that the whole creation itself might be freed from slavery to corruption and brought into the same glorious freedom as the children of God. We are all well aware that the whole creation, until this time [*achri tou nun*], has been groaning in labor pains. (Romans 8:19–22)

The history of sin, the fall, salvation, redemption, final glory are not confined here to humanity but concern all creation. For all creation time is not a neutral, indifferent measure, but rather one of loss and hope. The mention of this time is an abbreviation of what went before in verse 18: *tou nun kairou,* in this present *kairos.* All of creation is included in the kairological event of the Incarnation and the eschatological promise of the second coming.[14] Creation concerns humanity and humanity's other in equal but distinct measure: it concerns them in terms of the grounds of their being and of their history. But humanity is distinct to the extent to which it is concerned with the truth of creation. That concern is a concern with peace, with the singular self-giving of creatures. That concern with truth is a fallen one in the sense that it aims at an immemorial peace, but its very aim at that peace undermines it. The Christian answer to that fallenness is humility: the humility of waiting, the patience of letting appear.

Fallenness is misinterpreted as humiliation, whereas it is in fact a call to humility. It is crucial to read it as part of the creation story. The creation story is an impossible one: it attempts to put in narrative form those origins which are only traced in the present. This marks not simply the limits of myth, but the finitude of human speculation: interpretation from a present and that which can be made present to a past prior to any present, a past without presence. That present is one of death and suffering of a being which can transcend both, and the world of which they are a reality. The creation story attempts to make sense of that tension through an account of the origins of humanity. The centrality of that concern is evident throughout, beginning with the understanding of the human as in the image and likeness of god. To be with things as in the image of god is to be toward them in the way of their creator. Adam by naming the animals completed the act of creation, by giving each of them something by which they would be known and recognized. The human being in this account shares in the freedom of the creator, and this freedom sets the human apart. But unlike the freedom of the creator, this is not an originary freedom (an-archic freedom), but an originated freedom (*arché*). It is the freedom to initiate relations with things, which pre-exist the human being. This is a freedom to know things in terms of their good-ness, in terms of their purpose as expressions of themselves. But that knowledge allows things to be in their singular being. The "tree of knowledge" represents a self-initiating knowledge, the knowledge of the thing in terms of the possibilities of its good, and the perversion of that knowledge as an appropriation of the thing against its being, its use as drawing out and exhausting its singular being.

The fall is the pretension of finite reason to autonomy. It is a turning away from the relation of absolute dependency (Schleiermacher) in which finite reason is directed toward an infinite freedom which posits it.[15] This fallen state is for-ever rediscovered and reaffirmed in the act of creative expression. In this act of expression a silence in the world is rediscovered, a pregnant silence of meaning not yet articulated, a world at the crest of beginning. In reaching for this archaic expression the human in the person of the artist (but in this respect the artist ex-presses the human situation most authentically) discovers herself as already situ-ated with things which have their own relations to beginning. That beginning, that free love, is, however, itself silent. That silence, that darkness from which all things come, haunts creation and all efforts at its expression.

The Nothing

Creation out of nothing. What is this nothing out of which creation comes? *Ex nihilo nihil fit* (nothing comes out of nothing), states another pithy saying, which seems to disallow any notion of *creatio ex nihilo*. Together they would state: cre-ation out of nothing from which nothing comes. Creation out of nothing would create nothing.[16] Furthermore, being as created is being on the brink of noth-ingness, being which could also not be. The fundamental Christian insight into being is its precariousness: to be is to come into being out of nothing; in being there is no final ground for anything to be.[17] If the ground for being is not within being, then every existent *is* not ultimately in terms of being as such, as a whole, as a totality, but rather in terms of that which is outside being, nothing. Being created is being in relation to nothing, that is, being not in and through other existents in the world, but in and through a nothingness which emerges anew with every existent.

Creation out of nothing creates nothing—not in the sense that there is no thing created, but rather that with every created existent the nothingness of its being is retrospectively revealed. Here we must think Bergson against himself:[18] the retrospective movement discloses not being but nothingness in the sense of a seeing of all things in their full totality (as matter and form) as being only in respect of what they are not, namely, in respect of an origin which transcends them radically. The existent as a singular existent is neither matter nor form, but rather that which shows its own origin as nothing in or of it. That showing is of what has been, what remains, but remains nowhere. The existent shows itself in its presence, but the infinity of that showing (what Husserl calls the inner horizon) indicates not only a finitude of perspective, but also beyond the finitude of the existent an infinitude of the existent which is nothing in being. That nothing is retrospective in the sense that the existent recapitulates its having-been always in relation to an origin which it is not. The existent seen in its singular being is seen as the existent in the retrospection of its being.

The singular relation to a singular origin is perceived in the tarrying-with the existent. *This* existent, this rose for example, cannot be reached by 'rose' as category or word. Yet, the word and category are fulfilled only in the 'this.' That fulfillment is the affirmation of this existent in its anteriority to material and formal nature. In that sense the existent as singular being gives praise to its creator, or rather to the original nothingness out of which it arises.

The claim of creation out of nothing is that creation does not depend on anything outside of the creator. This can be understood as divine self-expression (Hegel) or conversely as divine abdication (Weil). These two understandings capture two distinct interpretations of the relation of being to a source which is nothing of being, beyond being. Yet, that nothing is traced in creation itself. That tracing in creation is a making present of nothingness and its radical absence, is expression and abdication at once: expression insofar as it is a pure being from the creator; abdication as it is only in its setting free from the creator that the existent comes to be. It is this tension, which is in a state of contradiction only in respect to the totality of being that, however, creation transcends, which characterizes Christian being with existents in the world. As such, a radical dichotomy is opened up that Christianity detects and elaborates in existents between their being and nothingness. Employing Augustinian terms in non-Augustinian fashion, creatures are both used and enjoyed: used in respect to their worldliness, enjoyed with respect to their origins. Out of this tension it was possible for diverse and opposed relations to existents to develop consistently with a Christian understanding of creation: that of care and love for existents (e.g., St. Francis of Assisi), and that of technological exploitation. Created existents are both in relation to the world and in relation to god. It is the tension of this 'both/and' which lies at the core of being with creatures.

Creatio ex nihilo is an interpretation of Genesis in *terms of the Incarnation*. This is to say that the beginning of the world is understood in terms of its redemption. Understood in that way, beginning and end interpret each other, not in the sense of a return and completion, but in the sense of a retrospective penetration of nothingness, of dark night at the beginning of, and throughout, things. The Christian account of Christ as the second Adam, as repeating the first creation, imbues that first creation with a kenotic significance.[19] Just as the kenosis of the Incarnation is an act of self-giving for the sake of another, the kenosis of creation is god's emptying of himself in setting forth that which is other and which stands over against its creator. In that relation nothingness is opened up: the 'not' dividing creator and creation, in which god is revealed as nothing in the world, the creation of the world as coming from that nothing which is god.[20] The kenotic act of creation is beyond reason and cause, is the origin of all reason. As such, as the principle of sufficient reason states: 'nothing is without reason.' Nothing escapes the range of reason, lies before and beyond reason. Leibniz's dictum speaks against itself and does so once the Leibnizian understanding of god as *causa sui* is left behind.[21] This is so because understood as creator god is nothing (in or of the world) and as such relates to the world and himself beyond the relations of reason or cause. Experienced as singular beings, entities in the world reveal not the world, but a relation to an invisible source, god as nothingness. As such, they share with Leibniz's monads the fact that "they can begin only by creation and go out of being only by annihilation"[22]—in other words, the power of beginning lies not with things in the world, but rather is that of the creation of the world itself.

It is not by accident that Leibniz, in speaking of creation, refers to annihilation and hence violence. Creation brings into being singular and unique viewpoints on the world,[23] which provoke desire both as love and as hate. Nothing in the existent is without reason, and reason ultimately is inadequate to respond to that existent. Freed from reason, freed from any understanding of existents in terms of totality, desire explodes as joy but also as rage. Singular entities have "no windows" and are the "sources of their own internal actions,"[24] a source which teaches me, but which refuses me and in so doing reveals my own powerlessness. Beyond totality violence has no limit; its limitlessness is in direct proportion to its failure. Provoked to violence against the singular being, the world of that existent remains closed to me. Faced with the entity in its singularity is to be faced with the entity as it resists all utility, all appropriation, all commerce. The desire for that entity is a desire for its own nothingness, a nothingness which remains inappropriable and indestructible not alone for me but for that existent itself. All existents remain foreign to me, and that foreignness, that final rejection which remains beyond all acceptance, is a denial of any net of reasons in which I try to ensnare it.

Sin, in that understanding, is at once a turning away from god and from the nothingness of existents as creatures. Sin is the annihilating response to the nothingness of creatures, a response which attempts to annihilate that nothingness. The commandment to love can be considered the first commandment, because in the light of it the Ten Commandments are not so much rules of moral behavior as they are exemplifications of ways of being with existents in relation to their origins.

As created, existents exist from a silent darkness. Tarrying-with existents as creatures is to be toward them as nothing of being, to be *ad nihilum*. Out of nothing, nothing; there is nothing out of which nothing does not come. Nothingness clings to creatures as the source of creation in the kenotic act of god.

Nothing is without reason: god is without reason, but so too are entities in their singular being. Nothingness is the silence out of which all things emerge. The gap between creator and creature is not an absolute one, rather the gap is manifest in creatures themselves between their worldly appearance and their own unworldly origins, between the existent in the generality of its being and the singularity of its manifestation. The existent in its origins and its singularity is a creature in that it reveals its own nothingness and the nothingness of its creator. The nothing out of which god creates is the self-transcending movement of divine kenosis poured out not for the world taken in abstraction, but for every being in the world—for this woman, this man, and, yes, for this butterfly, this snail, this flea. In the desire for the singular existent is disclosed the insufficiency of all ground or reason. In this sense desire transcends reason. If nothing is without reason, desire is for that nothing—that groundless ground. Christianity allows for the affirmation of this groundless ground, because it thinks it as nothing: the world as creation is a being given to itself, being which cannot contain its origins within itself, an-archic being in that sense. To think the arché of that anarchy is to think being as that which appears only in its nothingness, that is, in the excess of being. What appears in this way are entities as beings not of this world, that is, as being in excess of the economy of this world. That is the beauty of things as singular entities, as entities without ground. Christianity names the affirmation of this groundlessness love, *agápe*. Love interrupts the discourse of being as the nothing which each entity reveals as that source of its being. The love of creative origin is disclosed in desire for that entity in its singular being.

Love and Created Being

"God is love [*theos est agápe*]" (1 John 4:8). Not that love is an attribute predicated of god, but god is the origin of love. Or more profoundly, at the origins of all things is love. As all measures are worldly measures, measures of that which is in the world, then it follows from this that the origin of things is immeasurable. All things as originating in love are in their being beyond measure; all calculation, all economy of things, is provisional and partial. This is the ontological sense of the experience of god as love. The experience of god as love is the experience of existents as creatures and creatureliness as traced in the singular being of the existent in experience. Such an experience is one in which understanding that singular existent in its contingent beauty, one experiences the givenness of that existent as gift.

All existents appear within a worldly economy. The experience of gift is one which is always already brought into economy. Derrida has shown the economy of the gift, the irreducible worldliness of exchange,[25] but less attention has been paid to the gift in economy. In every economic exchange there is at least the possibility of a moment, which is more than mere politeness, when after an exchange has been made, we (vendor and purchaser) thank one another. Such an interaction reflects the thanksgiving which finds expression in prayer. It is striking that in the ancient Greek and Hebrew languages there was no word which corresponds to our expression 'thank you.' Where we would express thanks, in these languages it was necessary to praise. Such praise recognizes that which is not reducible to money in the act of the other and the goods exchanged. I do not simply take what I need, but I give praise to the giver and praise that which is given, the purchased thing.[26] In this sense the anonymity of the exchange, the substitutable nature of the participants, is itself an abstraction from the personal relation of seller and buyer—a relationship built on trust. The expression of praise states *inter alia* that this person is trustworthy. To the same extent to which there is no pure gift, there is also no pure economy: what I purchase is no exchangeable thing, but rather this thing—*this* apple, *this* bottle of wine, *this* piece of meat—and is more than I need, more than that which will satisfy me: it is a taste, a look, a smell, a texture, which takes me beyond the satisfaction of my needs to the plenitude of creation. In praising I praise the one who gives and that which is given in the singularity of their respective being.[27]

Such praise gives articulation to the being of the entity as created, as in excess of worldly economy. The entity is articulated in the gift of its singular being; to praise it is to desire as created. To do so is to perceive the entity as having its being out of love. Such being out of love is that which is expressed in the Christian doctrine of the Incarnation as the repetition and recapitulation of creation as expression of love. This love is paradoxical to the extent to which it appears to attribute to god an inordinate love of unworthy objects.[28] This paradox is in fact stretched to breaking point: the love of god is such that it does not depend at all on the worthiness of its objects. The injunction to "love your enemies" expresses the core of the Christian understanding of divine love; as such this injunction expresses the Christian understanding of the relation to existents as created beings.

In Luke's version, the injunction to "love your enemies" arises in the context of his account of the beatitudes. In his account of the "Sermon on the Plain" the four beatitudes and four curses are structured in terms of a series of reversals.[29] The reversals are not to be understood as referring to this present world and the next future world, but rather to the immanence of this world and the transcendence of god. In this world that which is not of this world appears, that which transcends it. The kingdom of god belongs to the poor understood as those whose desire transcends the mere worldliness of things. The beatitudes and curses chart a series of reversals in terms of oppositions between rich and poor, hungry and well-fed, laughing and weeping. The final beatitude sums up the previous three: "Blessed are you when people hate you" (Luke 6:22). The curses conclude with:

"Alas for you when everyone speaks well of you" (6:26). Desire should not be for the love of people in the world any more than for satisfaction from things of the world. In effect Christ is calling those "who are listening" (6:27) to be prepared to be hated.

The oppositions which structure the beatitudes and curses suggest conflict (polemos). But the logic of reversal extends to conflict itself: instead of responding to hate with hate, the relationship is reversed by responding to it with love: "Love your enemies, do good to those who hate you . . ." (6:27). Hate is to be responded to with love. The command to love is itself paradoxical, all the more so a command to love one's enemies. To love is to do good (*kalos*). Kalos means beautiful or noble; used as an adverb it means right or appropriate (*en kalo:* in the appropriate place). To love my enemy is to act toward him in an appropriate way. Appropriate to what? Not to the enemy as such, but rather to the one called (Jesus is speaking directly to his disciples, unlike in Matthew where on the mountain he addresses the crowds).[30] The command to love can best be understood as an *expression* of love.[31] In other words, the command, "love your enemies," expresses the love Jesus has for those to whom he is speaking. This is not so much a commandment in the sense of the Law, but rather a *declaration* of love. Christ is described by Paul as having died for those who were his enemies: those who were turned away from god—"while we were enemies, we were reconciled to God through the death of His son" (Romans 5:10). From the mouth of Christ, to love your enemies amounts to saying, 'love as I love you.'

Further on in the passage it states: "if you love those who love you what credit [*charis*] can you expect?" (Luke 6:33). Such 'love'—so the logic of this passage suggests—is actually no love at all. Love is measured not by reciprocity, but by non-reciprocity, by a giving with no expectation of return: "love your enemies and do good to them, and lend *without any hope of return*" (6:35). In respect to enemies, love is without hope of return, your enemy remains your enemy, the gift of love is without recipient.[32] There is no appeal here to a common humanity grounding the love of an enemy, nor, pace Aquinas, can we say that we should love the enemy for the sake of the one who is truly worthy of love, namely, god in whose image he is.[33] The love of enemies is direct, not indirect (as Aquinas's solution would have it), directed at those who are other than me. I am not the same as the object of my love; there is no notion of becoming one in love. In love not only does the other remain other, but the other remains beyond the reach of my love. This is so because the other, as enemy, is the one turned away from me in my singular relation to my own origins. In that way we are all enemies to one another. When the question is posed to Christ, "who is my neighbor?" (Luke 10:29), he responds with the story of the Good Samaritan: my enemy is my neighbor.[34] In effect my neighbor is commensurate with my enemy: the world is not divided up into friends and enemies; the enemies referred to in the command are not an identifiable group of people.[35] The imitation of Christ is the imitation of one who is in the world, but rejected by the world. As god's love is for all in the world, which turns away from him, the love of enemies is for all that which turns away from me, i.e., which sees me only in my worldly aspects, sees me only as an entity amongst others. Love of enemies is a turning away from the worldliness of the other to an open submission to her as a unique view of the world.

'Love of enemies' expresses in most radical form the response to the nothingness of creatures. It is senseless in worldly terms, indeed absurdly self-sacrificial in a world where friends and enemies exist. It can have sense only if there is no difference between friends and enemies or rather that the difference between friends and enemies has been rendered as nothing.

For Christian life there is nothing higher than love: love is not a servant of knowledge, as it is for the Greeks. Nor can love take its model from knowledge in the sense of an appropriation of its object. Rather, love is practiced in relation to other existents and is enacted through an 'imitation of Christ.' God's love of sinners is manifest both in creation and in the Incarnation; to listen to Christ is to follow his example in loving one's own enemies. If it is only through Christ that one can know god, it is only through following his example that one can know Christ. In that case the practice of following Christ is itself the highest knowledge. Such knowledge, however, cannot be expressed in predicative terms. The love of an enemy is not the love of any quality; there is indeed nothing in the enemy which gives good reason for the love being shown him. Love is not given on the basis of a correspondence between lover and beloved, rather it is given precisely in the lack of such correspondence. For this reason the desire, which characterizes this relation of love, is not one of fulfilling a lack; if it were this account of love would lead to despair not to blessedness. Rather, this is a love manifest in acts in which the self gives of itself beyond any demands of justice.

Such a love is beyond the economy of the world. In 1 Corinthians when Paul introduces his hymn to love, he calls the way of love *eti kath' hyperbolen hodon.* *Hyperbole* means exaggeration beyond measure. One could translate it here as 'beyond excess.' This is a way which is not simply excessive, but is beyond all relation to anything within the economy of human life. Hence, this is not a comparative statement, but rather says that the way of love is beyond all measure within the worldly economy. The way of love, that love expressed in the command to love one's enemies, is a way beyond the worldly economy.

The creative love of god is not other than the love of Christ. The imitation of Christ is the imitation of the incarnational love of god. If that love is the creative love of god, the love that creates what it does not lack and which thus makes possible enemies, then it is a love for all creation. The place of humankind is a key one, of course. But as we saw in the passage from Romans it is the commonality of human and non-human which is being emphasized. According to Saint Bonaven-

ture, salvation came through a human being because a human being brought together the lower and higher in nature. This is of course a basically Greek thought,
but one which is being employed in a non-Greek context: the *historical destiny* of
the world centers on humankind. The event of the Incarnation reveals agāpe, a
divine love and a divine desire as the meaning of that history, a meaning which
displaces human beings in relation to creation by reference to an event within the
world, which is not of the world. This event, as a repetition of creation, understood as love, does not just historicize being: the nature of that event undermines
all hierarchies of glory.

Echoing a distinction of Scholastic thought between material and formal
glory, Leibniz states: "God derives infinitely more glory from minds than from
other beings, or rather that other beings only provide the material for minds to
glorify him."[36] This view reflects again the divided line: the mind alone acts with
knowledge. The mind alone can ascend the steps of being from the lesser to the
greater, all of which it can contain as knowledge. Understood as created, however,
the 'least' of things is an expression of divine love: to be as creature is to be an
expression of god. But no expression of god can be known to be greater than any
other. To claim to know that would be to claim to know god independently of his
self-expression. The Incarnation denies this possibility, precisely by revealing the
divine as hidden in the 'least of things.'[37]

Implicit here is a fundamental challenge to the erotics of worldly being. This
challenge is affirmed in the desire for truth, which goes beyond any desire for
knowledge in the narrow sense. This desire for truth is one which is possible
only through a reduction of the chain of being, a reduction of things from their
enmeshment in relations to their singular being as expressions of love. The desire
for knowledge in the philosophical sense is inseparable from, while not being
reducible to, an erotic drive for appropriation: a drive to appropriate things as
ideas, as concepts, which find meaning and sense in their systemic interrelations.
This drive is operative not just in the sciences, but in every aspect of human life.
Human society and culture operate through such systems, in which things are
only in relations of desire. The underlying desire is one for appropriation, for becoming oneself (*propre*) in gaining love's object, ending in narcissism: the lover
becomes the object of his own love. Such love begins in lack, but a lack which is
pre-figuring: the senses lack the things of the senses, the intellect the things of the
intellect. Hence, the relation of love is that between the same: for such a love there
can be no stranger. This love lies at the origins of philosophy. The love of wisdom
is a love of that knowledge which characterizes wisdom. That is the knowledge
of necessary and eternal truths, a striving beyond the contingencies of things to
their higher necessity. To see the world thus is to see it as a world in which nothing is lacking. The striving of eros leads to the disclosing of a world in which there
is no lack and hence no love. Love evaporates in knowledge/wisdom.

Intentional consciousness is structured erotically: it is conscious of itself precisely in its lack or failure. As empty consciousness, intention strives for fulfillment in the givenness of the object. Indeed, there is a striving already there in an implicit and unacknowledged way before the conscious ego is activated at all. The tendency of the object coming toward the subject is responded to by a turning toward the object, which is pre-predicative, pre-conscious. In this context Husserl speaks of the attractiveness of the object and the ego yielding to its stimulus even at this pre-conscious level.[38] For Husserl, the cogito's interest is in its intentional objects; this is in the end a cognitive interest striving to *know* its object, whether in a theoretical, practical, or carnal sense. For Husserl fulfillment of such intentional consciousness is in principle possible, albeit constituted temporally and intersubjectively. What Husserl calls the internal horizon of the object can be brought to intentional consciousness. Yet Husserl recognizes the excessiveness of the object to intentional consciousness. One of the key insights of Husserl's early phenomenology is that the object is perceivable in itself only in and through its adumbrations: it manifests itself in its adumbrations. Hence, the object 'in person' is never present in anything but a finite mode. The presence of the object is never one of pure transparency in accordance with the cognitive model (despite the fact that Husserl, in his own interpretations of his analyses, tended toward such a model), but rather the presence of an object never fully satisfies the intentional consciousness; instead it intensifies it, in a manner which suggests the movement of desire toward an object.[39]

This movement is an erotic one, which seeks fulfillment in the object. But what Husserl's analyses show us is that this erotic drive is both inspired and refused by the object in its ambiguity. The object shows itself and withdraws in its self-showing. The withdrawal is the appearance of the excess of the object, the excess of its givenness over that which is given to intuition.[40] Such excess points to the primacy of desire: desire as opposed to need is not fulfilled in its object, but hollowed out by it.[41] What this shows is that the drive of eros finds its limit in the excess of the givenness of the object. That excess is not accountable in erotic terms and yet it is precisely the object in its excess which provokes that drive. Desire begins in affectivity, in the passivity of being acted upon by the object. This being acted upon is itself a gift, a gratuitous giving of the object. The object, however, as acting upon me is not the object of erotic drive but the 'subject' of agapeic gift. As that which is in excess of any correlation to consciousness the object reveals itself as in excess of its worldliness. In its discovery of the object as given, as irreducible in its appearance to the horizons of the world, the thing is uncovered as in the world but not of the world, i.e., as created.

Fulfillment in terms of intentional consciousness means that the object is disclosed as corresponding to an intention: fulfillment is in terms of an object, an entity of which certain aspects remain hidden and absent. This hiddenness and absence of the object is not something lacking in the object in the sense of that which cannot satisfy the desire for the object. Rather, it is an excess of the object perceived. Hence, the givenness of the object remains insurmountable; the subject cannot be adequate to that givenness. Understood in terms of the erotic tradition of philosophy this would mark philosophy as tragic. But such an understanding is not true to the object in its givenness. As given, the object exceeds the intentional gaze and must do so.

Understood as created in terms of the intersection of eros and agāpe the perception of things and of persons, in line with Romans 8:19–23, constitutes no fundamental difference: in both cases what is disclosed is the limit posed by created things not in terms of their lack of satisfying potential, but precisely as being in excess of all possible satisfaction, as being double: objects of erotic drive and 'subjects' of excessive gift.

Understood thus *creatio ex nihilo* can be reformulated as *creatio ex caritate*.[42] Love is nothing in the sense of being without sufficient reason.[43] In terms of such love all things are equally groundless as they have their source in the love of god (subjective and objective genitive), which is without reason. Leibniz understands *creatio ex nihilo* in terms of that "substance which carries with it the reason for its existence,"[44] but that is to understand creation in terms of sufficiency. *Creatio ex nihilo,* understood as *creatio ex caritate,* is absolutely contingent; it is a contingent act which opens up the history of creation. But if that love is without measure—and its manifestation in the world knows no worldly measure, although its glory can appear to me only in the world and hence in being—then it is bestowed as much on one being as on an other. The hierarchy of beings, as Leibniz shows,[45] is based on the principle of sufficient reason; in relation to love it loses its basis.

Phenomenologically speaking, there is no priority among appearances: this tree on a hillside, this deer in the snow, or this girl in a hospital bed are all equal in terms of appearance. Understood as created, no existent in the world is privileged; only events enacting that creation can give place to that which breaks with the economy of the world. In its openness to the singularity of appearance phenomenology tends toward an overcoming of erotic striving in its acknowledgment of that in the world that is not of the light of the world. In this sense phenomenology sees things, all things, in relation to an instance in terms of which all things are equal, all things are frustrated, all things are fallen into the ambiguity of their worldly appearance. But this fallenness is that which all things have in common not as a shared property, but rather as an *event* to which all things are related and can be understood in terms of such a relation.

Truth, Justice, Adequation

"To call is to create, while to share is to be created."[46] Creation is a calling, a calling into being. That calling is repeated in the act of expression, whereby—most clearly, but not exclusively, in the case of art—desire holds out for a word which has no precedent, no model. In the failure of that desire, in the limits to which that desire brings us, we find not lack and frustration, but rather a shared state of being as creatures. The desire for truth is the desire to be true to that shared being, to give articulation to the being of each thing as it is. This is a desire to let the other be in the silence of its own being. Such a silence can be heard in the movement of expression which each word articulates. That movement of expression comes from the other itself as an existent, as a coming to being out of the nothingness of its own being. Such existence is a response to a call which cries out of nothingness, which addresses no particular thing, but which rather lets a standing forth occur in the call itself. Understood as created, existents are in their very existence responsive. In other words, Christian life is a being with existents which do not initiate themselves, do not create themselves, but are singular responses to a loving call. The singularity of that call resides in the being of the existent itself; singular being does not reside in essential difference, but rather in the event of coming into being.

Desire responds to the responsive being of the existent and in so doing recognizes the shared creaturely being with the existent. The being of the existent is its self-expression, understood as an expression of its common insufficient being. That self-expression, which is the very being of the existent, provokes a response. That response is an approaching, a being held under sway by the seductive power of the existent, drawing desire, while that very self-expression in its being given shows me a self which I cannot have, but which I can be with. Such a being with, such a tarrying-with, is not a turning away from the other, as Levinas claims, but rather a silent acknowledgment of a shared being called in the agapeic being of creation, a being that subverts all erotic appropriation.

This tarrying-with is a movement of truth. To be true to the existent in its being created is to be true to it beyond any adequation, beyond any equality (*adaequare*). The traditional account of truth in terms of a relation of adequation between intellect and reality is blind—and necessarily so—to created being. Truth in such an understanding is a matter of predication: to state a truth about something is to state something true about it, to state a certain quality as being true of that thing. To say the dog has white spots is to state a quality of that dog. The truth is a matter of the qualities predicated, not that of which they are predicated. To convince ourselves of this we need only ask: what is this dog of which we make these predications? That question can be answered only with more predications. An infinite number of these predications would not move us one step closer to the being of which they are being predicated. That being is necessary *to* the predication, but is nothing *of* the predication. That being remains ineffable. The subject is that of which qualities are predicated, but is itself not predicated of anything else. But if truth is a matter of predicative sentences, this means that the subject remains both necessary to truth and yet nothing true can be said of it. True statements can be used to describe all the qualities which inhere in the subject; the subject itself remains ineffable. Considerations of this sort reduce the subject to a mere empty placeholder, an X. In such a case, however, truth is literally nihilistic: there is nothing of which truth is.

The subject is nothing, yet this nothing grounds all truth. Of that nothing, nothing true can be said. But in everything which is said—true and false—of this subject, it is being addressed. Every truth statement addresses that of which it speaks, and such address is irreducible to the truth said. There is in every truth statement a direction (in German *Richtung*), which—if the aim is true—is correct (German *richtig*). The address is the straight directedness (Latin *addirectiare*, 'to make straight') of the truth statement, a directedness, however, which is always anterior to the statement itself. Such an address reaches or does not reach a subject and it is that reach which is fundamental and necessary for truth. Such an address repeats the creative call insofar as it is directed to nothing in the world, but to that origin of the existent which remains invisible to the world.

In addressing the existent I am beyond all worldly truth. The being of the existent is its being a subject; only where substance is understood as anterior to individuality can such a subject be understood in worldly terms. What Christianity opens up is the desire for the subject in its individual, singular being. But such a desire for the being-created of the subject ungrounds truth, sets it free from any holistic mooring, and allows it to float on the sea of shared addressability—a being-addressed which is shared amongst all singular, created existents.

In the self-giving of the existent is its self-withdrawal, a secreting of that self: hence, seduction. But while that seduction calls on my desire for truth, it also wounds me by calling me, calling me as that which is created, which comes too late. These wounds are ambiguous. Origen (alluding to the figure of Cupid) talks of god's love as wounds.[47] They can be responded to in a self-giving and disappropriation, allowing the prior being of the existent to come to expression in my own words. But this remains a provocation which can easily be responded to in violence. Truth turns to violation, to destruction: that which calls to be named as it is demands of me humility, but such humility can turn to anger. The love of enemies is made difficult precisely because of the sometimes unbearable provocation of the enemy. The violence of my response is that of my anger. In anger I respond to the provocation of the existent. Such anger is an affliction.[48]

The Christian intuition of the agapeic origins of existents robs us of the serenity of an Aristotelian approach to anger. For Aristotle "the man who gets angry at the right things and with the right people, and also in the right way and at the right time and for the right length of time, is commended" (*Nichomachean Ethics*, 1125b32–33); the good man is one who responds to provocation according to the Aristotelian mean: neither irascible nor lacking in spirit, but patient

(1108a4–8). This view, however, makes sense only on the assumption of underlying justice. Anger responds correctly to an unjust provocation. But if truth responds to the nothing of the existent, it responds also to that which is beyond justice.

Truth and justice both lay claim to adequation, yet in the case of both the claim to adequation is ungrounded, set loose, by the intuition of creatureliness. All response is measured by the injunction to 'do justice.' But to do justice to something is to fulfill the being of that thing in the response itself. But as such the injunction always comes too late. To do justice, to be true, is to give expression to the existent. This giving expression fails and fails for the same reason in the case of truth and justice. Both are undermined by agāpe—in the sense of showing an original truth and justice which is excessive of the world and must remain beyond worldly appearance.[49]

The feeling of injustice is manifest in anger, which is itself retrospective. Anger retrospectively perceives injustice, perceives an origin as a past which was never present. That injustice cries beyond all worldly measure to heaven. It cries beyond all worldly hearing to a love which knows the injury to be singular, redeemable only through transformation. Transformation, though, is a relation not to worldly action but to creaturehood. In this way forgiveness is in excess of all reparation; it is an excessive giving because it responds to a shared relation to the creator.

But if agāpe is beyond justice, then the agapeic response must be excessive. There is no adequate response because the thing itself does not adequately respond to its own origins. Christian love in its very excess threatens to give way to a violence which is not limited by any appeals to justice, because the appeal to love itself transcends any such appeal. The appeal to love beyond knowledge and hence beyond justice opens up the possibility of unlimited violence. The excess of the appeal to love is responded to by a violence which aims to destroy the source of that appeal. In breaking with the economy of the world, the laws of that world, the laws of balance and reciprocity are set aside in the name of a supra-cosmic call.

7 Aion, Chronos, Kairos

THE CHRISTIAN WORLD, the world without worldly measure, is a world of in-adequation, a world which in its openness to peace beyond agon and economy releases also a profound violence. Truth and justice appear in this world as that which the world cannot contain. This mode of incarnate appearance is being in the world as that into which existents come and out of which they go. This coming and going, this not having been and will not be, are events in the world, but are not reducible to the world. Temporal being is that being which comes into and out of existence: these are not simply external facts, but are the becoming temporal as such. Temporal being is that being which lives in relation to its coming into and going out of existence. This existent being is an anomaly, an anomaly which lies at the source of both philosophy and Christianity. At the heart of this anomaly is the insistence of a singular being to be in a manner which places it against the world. This being against the world finds different echoes—the tragic acceptance of Greek drama, the preparation for death of Greek philosophy, and the living in salvation of Christianity. Each of these modes of being against the world are modes of being temporal in relation to that which transcends finite existence.[1]

The name common to Greek philosophy and Christianity for this tran-scendence of finite existence is 'eternity', in Greek, 'aion'. Aion, however, can be translated in many ways: 'life time,' 'ages,' 'world-time,' 'for ever,' 'everlasting' are just some.[2] This diversity of meanings points us to the problem, the question of eternity as it arises in the experience of time. The experience of time is the experi-ence of the tension, the mortal struggle between existence and world. Like every tension this can be experienced as either harmony or diremption. The (philo-sophical) Greek and Christian tend in opposite directions, toward harmony and diremption, respectively. Again in broad terms these are tendencies to subject time to world and world to time, respectively. Experienced as subject to world the intuition of anteriority in time is experienced non- or pre-temporally as anteriority in thought, in logos. The most radical thought of flux in Greek thought, that of Heraclitus, is still a thought of worldly flux, a flux which confirms the world and the time of the world; the Heraclitean logos is a logos which gives place to time—gives world in which there can be time. In contrast, the Johannine logos— the logos which becomes flesh—gives time to place, in other words, gives time in which the space of the world becomes displaced by that through whom the world "had come into being," but who "the world did not recognize" (John 1:10). In giv- ing time to place the logos allows space to be place, to be the 'where' of events, which give names to places, names which make those places, as we say, 'places apart.' Such places—such time-spaces—are not identified as part of a sacred hi- erarchy. In their apartness they are neither vertically nor horizontally orientated; instead, they materialize time, materialize a moment not of time without space or space without time, but rather an unrepeatable interpenetration of space and time, where those two terms are themselves transformed. No map exists for such places, no schedule for such times, rather they are anterior to such confines and themselves give rise to that very anteriority.

All thought and life in all its expressions relates to a past which is not its own, a source which no act of thought, no living of life can master. All thought and life in its expression remains vulnerable to what is still to come, to that end- ing, which it can never know. This experience of time is an experience of lack, of threat, potentially of humiliation. This humiliation of time is not simply an external, foreign force, but pervades the inner being of all creatures, of all those that live and think. It is a humiliation which is felt as past and as future, and as present only as it is darkened by the shadows of future and past. The present is the time where fullness, safety, and glorification are glimpsed as possibilities, but as possibilities which to be real must endure, hence must again be subject to the has-been and the to-come. The glimpsing of such a possibility, however, is a glimpsing of the possibility of happiness in the sense of *eudaimonia*. What is thus glimpsed is the possibility to be happy in time, but in time which is not time, time as ever-present, a tenseless time, eternal time. Greek and Christian thought have both found themselves directed beyond time, toward such a present which will never end, as it has never begun—has no source beyond or outside itself. Yet, Christian—unlike Greek—life and thought is lived precisely in the shadow of an ending, the shadow of the end of the world. The eternity it saw and strove for was one beyond the world, beyond all worldly things. This eternity of god was pre- cisely not an eternity of the world, and as such became an increasingly negative, apophatic notion. The Christian account of eternity emerges from a rethinking of the humiliating action of time, in which in thinking time thought finds itself inadequate to time. This is not to say that time cannot be thought, but rather that in thinking time thought finds in itself the inadequation of thinking to that thought and thinks and lives itself as such inadequation.

Time subject to world is time in harmony and adequation, a cyclical time reflecting, and reflected in, eternity. This account of the eternal can be traced from Heraclitus to Plotinus. The specifically Christian experience of time is that of the kairos, as the interruption of time by the eternal. Such an interruption subjects the world to the time of the singular life. This time, this Christian time is a time in the world, a time which falls back constantly into the time of the world, but which challenges that time in its emphasis on the mortal time of the singular existent, whose time is the possible time of god, the time of love and of utter contingency.

Time of Adequation

The history of the word 'aion' from Heraclitus to Aristotle charts a certain course of thought on the experience of time.[3] This course could be characterized as one of a forgetting of life. This forgetting involves a gradual lessening of the tension between the experience of existence and world in Greek thought. In case these terms seem anachronistic, it should be clear that what is at issue here is the experience of change and flux in its harmonious tension with the intuition of permanence. This tension, which is at the heart of the Greek experience of being, is not one between Heraclitus and Parmenides, as a textbook account of this history would suggest, but rather one to be found in every Greek thinker. With Aristotle the shock of this tension is no longer apparent; it has been domesticated in an account of time as measure.

In the history of philosophy the first mention of aion is to be found in Heraclitus. The fragment is well known. It goes as follows: "*Aion pais esti paizon pesseuon. Paidos he basileie.*" Diels and Kranz translate as follows: "*Die Lebenszeit ist eine Knabe, der spielt, hin und her die Brettsteine setzts: Kabenregiment*" (Diels/Kranz [henceforth D/K], B52). I suggest the following translation into English: "Liveliness is a child in play, placing pieces here and there on the board. To the child, kingship." The play of the child gives expression to something of ontological priority, namely, the giving over to play, which contains a moment of pure liveliness.[4]

By translating aion as 'liveliness' no denial is being made that the word has a temporal meaning, which Diels and Kranz capture with *Lebenszeit*, 'lifetime.' But the question is how this time is to be understood. This is only possible from the phenomenon of liveliness. The intensity of play can be seen in the earnestness with which the child gives herself over to the game. Gadamer has rightly remarked that a player who does not take the game seriously is a spoilsport.[5] The earnestness of a child's play is to be seen in the fact that she plays as if the world were not there. Initially in such play, in this intensity, nothing comes to light, rather there occurs a darkening. The apparent innocence of play should not blind us to the element of madness inherent in the giving oneself over to the game and the concurrent shutting out of the world. In understanding the Heraclitus fragment the crucial question is how we are to understand what the child in play can tell us of liveliness. In playing there is a temporal element which we have encountered in chapter 5 with the play of the animal, namely, the giving over in the present. Aion then is a child that loses itself in the present. This would seem to indicate that the chronological followability of time disappears. We must, however, allow ourselves to be guided by the phenomenon of play. Play has the character of imitation; the playing child imitates the aion. But this means that in the strict predicative sense, the child is not aion: the child plays it rather, and in this play there occurs an excess of life. In this excess of life, aion is played out. The temporality of aion appears in the play of the child, which, however, itself happens as imitation. For this reason aion cannot mean 'time' in the sense of temporal phases which follow one another. While in Orphic mysticism aion is said to be the child of chronos, for Heraclitus the situation is the reverse. The child in play is not aion, but is rather—as I will attempt to show—chronos.

How then does the child imitate aion? It plays with pieces of a board game (*pesseuon*). There is in the secondary literature a discussion about whether what is at issue here is a game which requires skill and strategy or simply a game of chance.[6] But the question must first be raised: What is the aionic character of the playing of such a game? As every game, it consists in motion, in this case locomotion. The motion comes from the child. The pieces with which he plays receive their motion through the child and the happening of the playing. In the motion of the pieces through the child from here to there, earlier and later arise. This 'earlier' and 'later' exist simply in the motion itself; only while the pieces are in motion is there an earlier and later. What is important to notice here is that there is no teleology in the game: the game does not serve some end outside of itself. The play does not have the goal, for example, that once there is a winner the pieces which were in movement come to rest, to a state lacking in motion. This can be seen by the fact that there is only one player: not victory but play for its own sake is here at issue. Play has no reason outside of itself.[7] The board game happens in the motion of the child; it has its origin not so much in the pieces which make up the game, as in the playing child, in the intensity of its play.[8] Hence, it has its origins in the child that acts—like the animal—as if the world were not there.

It may appear as if this expression, which I have now used a number of times, 'as if the world were not there,' is hard to reconcile with the meaning of aion which was also common in Heraclitus's time, namely, as 'world-time.' But, while play is characterized by its intensity, this in-tensity changes over into ex-tensity, explosivity. This can be seen in Heraclitus to the extent that he speaks of playing with board game pieces. To the extent that these pieces are placed in motion and in this way a relationship of earlier and later arises, the intensity of play with its self-losing in the present is broken through. It is in this moment no longer the case that the present is shrunk practically to a zero point; rather the present opens itself up and breaks asunder. It is with this opening that time (chronos)—which can be read from motion and which plays out the aion—happens.

It is with this happening that a space-time, a world, opens itself. According to Heraclitus, the child receives the kingship of this world. This does not mean that the child created a world in which he can then be a king, rather that in his play a world arises, which comes over the child in such a way that he finds himself in that situation. The child becomes king because he finds himself in a kingdom, in a world, in which he is playing out liveliness, and which is constitutive of this liveliness. In contradiction to that which one would expect from the play of a child there arises suddenly a world and its time. In this state of finding himself as king another aspect of play, which has as yet remained in the background, shows itself, namely, the 'sudden.' The world is not an object of an intention or of a plan, but rather it happens of a sudden, and in happening overcomes the playing child. The child plays as if there were no world, but through the liveliness of the play, which means the change-over (*metapesovta*) from in-tensity into ex-tensity, he finds himself in the world which arises through the child, that is, his playing as an imitation of aion.

In this fragment aion is not defined. It is not stated that it is identical with a child, but rather that it is *like* a child. In the motion of the playing something else announces itself, namely, liveliness, which, however, cannot itself come to appearance, because it lies at the basis of the world.

It is true that both play and childhood are used by Heraclitus as examples of insignificance and that in this he was very much in line with Greek thinking.[9] Given these facts it would appear that, contrary to what I have been arguing, this fragment is a critical, indeed polemical, commentary on the insignificance of human life-time (aion).[10] The attempt could be made to challenge the claims regarding play and childhood on the basis of which such an interpretation is made.[11] But the present interpretation is confirmed rather than refuted by the insignificance of child-play for Heraclitus. It is precisely its insignificance that makes play an appropriate phenomenon to represent aion. Aion does not appear in and as itself. It is not the playing child; rather it comes to appearance *in* the play of the child. In isolation from play aion is not something which can be examined in terms of its nature, but rather is the happening of time in which something appears. Heraclitus's concern in this fragment, as in many others, is with the possibility of appearance. What is decisive is not so much what comes to appearance, but rather *how* it does so. What appears is the living entity: the happening character of its coming to appearance is liveliness. If this is the case, then Heraclitus must seek a sign rather than an account (logos) (cf. B 93). This sign is not to be sought in that which is of significance, because there the aspect of happening is veiled by the very meaning of that which appears. One could say that Heraclitus's whole endeavor in thought is to avoid the question of *what* something is, in order to reveal the *happening* of its appearance. He is not concerned about understanding what night or day are, as supposedly Hesiod was (cf. D/K B 57), but rather with the happening of over-turning without which there would be no day, in the same way as without such over-turning there would be no justice (see D/K B 23). This over-turning is without ground, because it is not to be traced back to an appearance, or rather the sign of it is to be found between two appearances. Play forms precisely this between-space. The seriousness of everyday life is set aside. The difference between the way uphill and downhill is for our everyday interests of real significance (see D/K B 60), but is founded on the identity of the way, which comes to appearance in the over-turning of the uphill into the downhill and vice versa.[12] It is beyond the seriousness of our lives, beyond the significant, that the coming to appearance of things reveals itself. For Heraclitus this coming to appearance occurs there, where it is least expected. The unexpected must however be expected (cf. D/K B 18). In other words, one must be in readiness for the happening of appearance in a place in which it is least expected: perhaps even in the play of a child.

In time—chronos—as the expression of liveliness, the time of the world appears. In this sense, the harmony of time and world, of change and permanence, is secured in unity which is one of unending war. War (polemos) is the father of all things (D/K B 53), and the order of things—the cosmos—is a unity in motion, is ever-living fire (*pur aeiloon*) [D/K B 30]. This unity in motion is the world for Heraclitus, a world which is heard in the logos, in which all is one (*estin hen panta*) [D/K B 50]. The logos gathers together the explosive liveliness into a musical unity, the unity which is found in the lyre and the bow, Heraclitus's favorite images (D/K B 51, B 48). In such a unity life and death are interchangeable; the time of existence is subsumed in the time of the world (D/K B 26).

The relation of aion and chronos is reinterpreted again in Plato's *Timaeus*. As it appears in that famous passage, aion has been translated as '*aeternitas*,' '*Ewigkeit*,' '*eternité*,' 'eternity.'[13] Plato's 'definition' of time in this passage is that time (chronos) is the moving image of aion (*Timaeus* 37d4). If one were to translate this back into the language of Heraclitus's fragment, it would read: time plays out in its motion liveliness—aion. This motion is not to be seen as a decline, as a lack, but rather as that which gives time similarity with aion. According to Plato, the Demiurge gave the cosmos time in order to make it as similar to the original (*paradeigma*) as possible (37c9). For Plato the cosmos is a living being—with a soul, the world-soul—and for this reason self-moving. The heavenly bodies owe their motion to their principle of life, their soul. The concept of the "world-soul" corresponds to Plato's fundamental assumption that being means liveliness. It is for this reason that Plato, when he wishes to express the temporality and movement of the original, of that, in other words, which comes to appearance in the visible cosmos, uses a word which can characterize both liveliness and the essence of time. This word is available to him from Heraclitus: aion.[14]

It is an Aristotelian prejudice to conceive aion qua eternity as unmoved and to assume that chronos is distinguishable from aion through its motion. A careful reading of Plato's text shows that motion cannot come into question as that which marks the fundamental distinction between time and eternity; it is rather the case that the difference is to be found *in* motion. As its moving copy chronos plays out the aion. In contrast, chronos does *not* correspond to the aion insofar as its being is characterized by dispersion. Time exists in a disrupted manner in the sense that it lacks containedness, which shows itself in the sense that one can say of that which is in time that it was or will be (*Timaeus*, 37e7). Because the motion of the heavenly bodies gives rise to an earlier and a later, it tends to fall into the unmoved. This is manifest for example in the 'it was': what was is no longer—it no longer lives and is thus unmoved. The unchangeableness of the aion consists precisely in its motion, which never changes. It is hence the unpassing in time which allows it to stand in the relation of copy to the aion.

These considerations lead to the conclusion that seen from the point of view of time, aion is to be understood as such an intensification of motion, which excludes decay or destruction. Aion in that sense means pure motion and in this sense pure time. What this means, however, is that 'eternity' is not timeless but rather temporal in a pure sense. That is the case when it is thought on the basis of liveliness.

The pure temporality of aion is reflected in the unpassing of time as chronos. The unpassing does not consist in an ever-unchanging constancy, but in intensity and explosivity, in the turning over of one into the other, hence in play, in which the inner connection of time and eternity appears. This connection is very close. Time for Plato is not—to use Aristotelian terms—the measure of motion, but rather is itself the motion of the cosmos.[15] Time cannot essentially be a measure, because it is the copy of the liveliness of the original, of liveliness as the being of the cosmos, and this liveliness is with Heraclitus to be understood as time, namely as lifetime. Time participates in the life-force of the original, otherwise the talk of world-soul would have no sense. Pure motion is motion without change, a motion which excludes becoming younger or older, a motion without 'it was' and 'it will be.' How such a motion can be phenomenologically understood can be grasped with reference to the Platonic discussion of *exaiphnes*, the sudden, the moment, in the *Parmenides* (*Parmenides* 155e–157b).

It is significant how Plato interprets the distinction between the sudden and the inner-temporal in the *Parmenides*. The sudden transition (*metabole*) does not occur in time, because in time there are only continuous changes from one state to another. But although the transition does not occur in time, it is not timeless. It is rather time itself. Between movement and rest there is motion itself. What is in rest is not free from motion, without motion, because only what is mobile can rest. Only the living being can rest and move itself. Hence, the transition from rest to motion is not a change from a motionless to a mobile state, but rather an intensification of motion itself, which motion encounters without external ground. In Heraclitean terms one would say that this intensification is play.

The sudden is the unexpected, hence that which finds no grounding in the past, because on the basis of the past one can expect only continual change. The sudden is the arising of, and losing in, the present. This means that the self-losing in the arising of the present is played out in the sudden. In play it is a matter of overcoming the linearity of inner-temporality, in order to bring the sudden to appearance. When the child plays out the aion, it plays the sudden, the pure moment, which is at play both in rest and in motion. The transition from the first to the second is no change, which can be understood as loss, but rather the happening in which the difference between rest and motion is maintained in its common belonging. This common belonging lies at the heart of liveliness. In the moment this common belonging is brought to appearance through being imitated.

The difference within motion, which is the difference between time and eternity, is a difference experienced not in a removal from the world, but rather in an intensification of that which binds all living entities together, namely, that intangible element of liveliness. Such liveliness is that which binds the time of every existent to the world, that which holds together world and mortal existence, such that in the experience of liveliness the fullness of time appears as that sudden transformation which holds being together in its worldly orderliness through binding change to permanence. This intensification can only be experienced anew—for every game is new, has never been played before. It is only possible through the element of surprise, which is constitutive of the sudden.

It is characteristic of Aristotle that he defines the *exaiphnes* in the *Physics*—without mentioning Plato—as follows: "what has departed from its condition in a time imperceptible because of its smallness" (*Physics*, 222b15). In opposition to Plato, for Aristotle the sudden is *in time*. This cannot be otherwise for Aristotle, because for him time is the measure of motion; the sudden is that which, though imperceptible, can be measured at least in its effects: "it is the nature of all change to alter things from their former condition" (222b16). Furthermore, it is significant that in the context of this definition of the sudden moment Aristotle refers to change as decay, destruction, and forgetting. In the *Physics* he attests to time as being the cause of decay, because it is the number, i.e, the measure, of motion (*kinesis*). It causes forgetting and destruction and only accidentally the coming into being of things (cf. 222b19–22 and 221b1–2). This is a fundamental philosophical decision which introduces the now (*nun*) as a definition of time, hence making time into an abstract measure. It is significant in this regard how Aristotle reduces in two different ways the word 'aion.' Firstly, he attempts to explain, or explain away, aion as a compositum of two words: *aei* and *on,* "always existing" (*On the Heavens,* 279a26). This etymology is, however, disputed.[16] Whether the etymology is correct or not is not the main question, but rather what is decisive is the fact that with this explanation, the sense of liveliness disappears. Secondly, Aristotle often reaches back to a meaning of aion which is pre-Heraclitean, and pre-Platonic, namely, as the time of a single life, hence not as a principle of time, but as a particular unit of time (see 279a22–24). In this way Aristotle undercuts the connection between life and time in aion.[17] In tandem with this he understands time as the agent of destruction alone. Given this view, it is consistent to look beyond motion and change for that which is stable and eternal. This, however, is the first step in the denial of life with which, following Nietzsche, we too hastily charge Plato. Life is thought differently by Aristotle as by Plato. It is thought precisely not as that on the basis of which time and the intensity of time can be understood, but rather as a form of existence among others, which can be outlined in accord with its essential nature. There is no trace here of an experience of life or of liveliness which cannot be grasped in a concept or set apart from other forms of existence. Such an experience is no longer to be found in Aristotle and he does not seem to notice its absence. The forgetfulness of life is radical in Aristotle precisely because 'life' has not been forgotten, but rather is being researched. Precisely because life is still being spoken of, it need not be remembered. Forgetfulness does not arise out of indifference, but precisely when that of which one becomes forgetful stands as an object of scientific concern. The forgetfulness of life is a forgetfulness of an explosivity in life itself. This explosivity is an expression of the world, an expression which perhaps returns in the Stoic notion of recurring conflagrations. This explosivity comes to expression in language, but a language of motion and poetry, a language most clearly articulated in Plato's dialogues. The liveliness of being can be found in the logos which holds together this explosivity in a correspondence that allows liveliness to find articulation in the cosmos as such.

The motion of the aion is reflected not just in time—chronos—but in the many 'times,' the times of peoples, which in dispersed form imitate the perfect movement of the world-soul. It is for this reason that the *Timaeus* begins with an account of history—the history of Athens—precisely as a history of cycles of growth and destruction (*Timaeus,* 23b–25d). These motions of intensity and explosivity integrate existence and world and do so in ways which can hardly be remembered, but can be thought, thought by a logos which most excellently imitates the pure movement of the aion and does not fall too far into the dispersed movement of time.

Time beyond Adequation

In the New Testament[18] aion is used in the sense of ages, a sense which harks back to a pre-Heraclitean, pre-philosophic sense: aion as world-time, in the sense of ages of a people and a city. Aion is sometimes used in the plural to indicate all the ages (e.g., 1 Corinthians 2:7; Colossians 1:26). Implied here is a prolonged but not unending time, the time of the world, which however had a beginning and will end. But now the aion is not one age which leads to another, but rather the age of the world understood as the world of all of human history and as the time of that world, the time which comes to an end. Aion in some places takes on the meaning of world (cosmos) (cf. Mark 4:19; Matthew 13:22). Time now is that which ends, that which is finite. In such an understanding existence enacts a time which has the possibility of being beyond world-time, a time which is not beyond the horizon of the present, but inscribed therein. It is this, eschatological time, which is inscribed in the present, undermining any experience of sovereignty in the present. Thus the Christian attempt to think the eternity of god breaks radically with Greek thought by denying the premise of its account of eternity, namely that the subject of that eternity is the world. Before any thought of change and the passible in god, the crucial turn is to think the eternal as other than the world. Such a thinking immediately requires a thought of the presence of the eternal which is not that of the life of the world, but of something beyond the world. As such it is an account of the relation of time and eternity, which is not one of imitation, not one in terms of relations of image and paradigm. Such a thought requires a new term outside of the interplay of time and eternity. That new term is supplied by St. Paul: kairos.

Kairos is time as life, as living, but not the explosivity of young life reflecting the full liveliness of the cosmos, but rather the rendering asunder of a life, of the life of an existent, such that past and future become radically open to rethinking, reliving, and revision. Christianity is the thought of *re*demption and *re*pentance, of *re*thinking and *re*living: not the coming to articulation of past and future, but the disarticulation of natural time. With Christianity the alternative opened up by Aristotle's forgetting of life—the alternative, namely, of practical reason thinking with the flow of time and theoretical reason thinking time from the standpoint of eternity—is replaced by a practice in the light of the eternal. This eternity, however, stands not so much outside time, but happens in a moment and radiates through past and future, transforming time into history, natural cycles into the linearity of salvation. The linearity of the latter is not that of an arrow going ever forward, but rather of a light shining outward in all directions. The past is not done, but is seen as if for the first time, from the kairos.[19]

We encountered the kairos previously in the discussion of creation in the last chapter, specifically in the discussion of Romans 8:18: *tou nun kairou,* in this present kairos. This present kairos is a time orientated toward a certain event—namely, that of the death of Christ, which recapitulates all previous time. This moment is a world historical moment, but is such only because it has its source outside the world: within the world there are only sectional conflicts, events which bring good news for some and inversely—and necessarily—bad news for others. The claim is that this moment has universal relevance not because the differences between human societies are superseded in a capacity shared by all human beings, but rather because the 'all who can hear' can follow the message of this event without losing their distinctiveness, their individually distinct appropriations of ways of life. The importance of conversion here is not to reject the past life, but rather to transform it. That transformation takes the form of repentance and forgiveness: the rethinking and remembering the past, which memorizes it for the future. Time is renewed—time, no longer the measure of decay, is now the materialization of change.

The kairos is the time of interruption of chronological continuity—the kairos lived and thought from chronos, from the mundane time of everyday events. Christianity begins and ends in the kairos because it begins and ends with the Incarnation—the event in chronological time but signifying nothing of the chronological. That the Christological event can be measured chronologically, has a certain duration, a certain worldly date, is not without consequence: for the kairos to occur it had to intervene, disrupt the temporal, chronological continuity of time. But the moment of the kairos is not measurable in chronological terms: it refers to the time of revelation, in which the horizon of possibility of chronological time was said to be radically torn asunder, but was so in such a manner that those who were contemporary to this disruption could utterly fail to recognize it. The knowledge involved here, then, is not one which tries to comprehend and possess, but one of dispossession, a knowledge which perceives time as no object, as no thing indeed, hence as that which allows for no possession. St. Paul refers to such knowledge when he states, "Of times and moments [kairos] you know that the day of the lord is going to come like a thief in the night" (1 Thessalonians 5:1–2). But such knowledge is one of faith. This is not a knowledge of what can be predicted or can be predicated; it is not a knowledge of law, that which can be written out, but is that which grounds all knowledge (cf. Romans 3:31) and as such has no object. The moment demands faith, demands an understanding based not on the past or the future, but on an openness to the transformative possibility of the moment. It is an openness not to a determinate possibility, but rather to the impossible, to that which negates the horizon of the present. Neither the 'space of experience' nor the 'horizon of expectations'—to use the categories of the historian Reinhart Koselleck[20]—can contain the event itself. In the moment of the kairos time is lived not as merely the backdrop of events, but as a power of difference: the moment ruptures experience in a manner which allows for no return. The kairos in opening up a new time allows for those with faith no return to their past lives, but rather opens up a new time.

In living the new time the Christian lives "temporality as temporality," living and thinking the parousia not as presence, but as precisely that which does not appear in the present. The non-appearance of the parousia is not its simple absence, but rather the manner in which it darkens the present with the promise of the 'to come.' This is a darkening, because it heralds a coming which has been prefigured in the event of the coming of the Messiah. The present of the kairos is a present in relation to a transforming, but obscure event, and the promise of a repetition of that event, not as obscure but as blinding. The past here—that of the event of the Incarnation—offers no positive guide in relation to the present, as it finds itself darkened by the promise of overwhelming light. It can only offer a negative guide, which is to avoid complacency, to not follow the lead of those who say: "how peaceful and quiet it is" (1 Thessalonians 5:3). Living under such guidance is living in a constant readiness for the sudden. This is a paradoxical manner of life: the sudden is precisely that for which there can be no readiness. The extent of readiness for the sudden makes the sudden less sudden, more expected. To live in relation to the sudden is then to live in readiness not for the positive, the known, the object of understanding, but rather for that which is no object and refuses understanding. Such living cannot be learned, can only arise from a feeling, a sensitivity to an event experienced in faith, and a desire for that event to come again, but a desire which in turning toward god allows for the inadequacy of all preconceptions of this coming.

The sudden (exaiphnes) is no longer the fulcrum of worldly being, holding together permanence and change, being and becoming, but rather characterizes the manner in which the eternal is made manifest in the world.[21] In Luke's account of the message of the angel to the shepherds of the birth of a savior, Luke states: "And all at once [kai exaiphnes] with the angel there was a great throng of the hosts of heaven praising God" (Luke 2:13). The voices of praise, of glorification, arise suddenly and do so after the angel has given the most unlikely of signs of the savior: that there is in a manger a baby wrapped in swaddling clothes. The sign is inadequate, the sudden songs of praise incongruous. Yet the praise is to god in the highest heaven, not to the baby, or rather to the baby as sent by god. It is this sending into time which defeats all chronology—Matthew's patriarchal genealogy of fathering breaks off before Jesus and speaks instead of Mary ("of her was born Jesus" [Matthew 1:16])—of which Paul (whose conversion is similarly referred to as happening suddenly [Acts 9:5]) speaks often in his letters. Yet Paul's concern is not so much the kairos as having been, but the living with the kairos, living with the sudden as that which is to come. It is true that with this suddenness of the 'to come' an eschatological time is opened up, a time of the ending of time. This time is lived in the shadow of the end, the end as the eternal. The ages of the world (aion) are coming to an end, not in order to be repeated again in the wake of a great conflagration (as for the Stoics), but rather to be finally set aside. The kairos opens up the possibility of an end to world-time, which does not mean the end of existence, but rather the living of existence in terms of the anteriority of time, the time not before all time, but the time in which the world came to be, in which time as chronos was possible. To conceive of the time of existence as other than world-time is necessary when the eternal is experienced as that which breaks into world-time and opens it up in the kairological moment. Such a time of existence in the darkness of the parousia is still, and is necessarily, a time in the world. Time now becomes ambiguous—that in which the eternal occurs, but that which binds existence to the world, the world which cannot contain the eternal.

It is precisely time in this sense which St. Augustine attempts to conceptualize. His analyses of time and memory account for the Christian experience of time by an inner movement. This inner movement does not so much refuse the natural time of Greek ontology (as it rests parasitically upon it), but opens up time in a non-natural or rather proto-natural dimension. The paradox of time from which Augustine begins is classically Aristotelian, namely, that "we cannot rightly say that time is, except for its impending state of non-being" (*Confessions*, 11:14). Again, in keeping with the Aristotelian analysis, Augustine understands time as the measure of passing. For time to be, something must be passing. But this passing is reducible to nothing: "if what can be known of time is that which cannot be divided into even more minute parts, then that is the only thing which should be called 'present'" (11:15). There is no such thing as the present, because the present is only the indivisible moment, and all moments can be further divided. Of things in the world we cannot speak of their presence. 'Thingly' reality then exists on its own terms without ontological support: "when it is present it has no duration" (11:15). Augustine's attempt is to understand the power and nature of time (*vim naturamque temporis*) (11:23). It is clear that time is, that it has being and indeed power. Yet, when we look in the world—that domain which it seems is most clearly subject to the power of time—we cannot find it. Faced with this conundrum Augustine resists any attempt to identify time and world, as would be the case if time were the movements of the planets. He reasons that this identification cannot be, because time is a measure and that measure is independent of the movement of any particular thing. Furthermore, measure requires mind—*animus*. The Platonic solution here would be to understand mind in terms of the world-soul. But Augustine's question concerns the power and nature of time as experienced by a being who lives in relation to the eternal, as that which took incarnational reality in the figure of Christ. This happening of the eternal in time cannot find its measure in the world-soul, in terms of which the new time it heralds is a chimera. Hence, Augustine turns away from the things in the world toward the impressions (*affectiones*) these things make on his mind: "It is the impression that I measure, since it is still present, not the thing itself" (11:27). In perceiving time—Augustine uses the verb *sentire*, to sense—we are in relation to that which is not in the world. The temporality which begins to be discovered here is an ecstatic temporality, but its ecstases are directed inward and upward, are directed not toward the world, but precisely to that in our experience which we cannot find in the world: present, past, and future. Time is characterized by persistence in change, because only that which persists allows measurement. That persistence is to be found in the mind: "Yet the mind's attention persists, and through it that which is to be passes toward the state in which it is to be no more" (11:28). Through this inner movement things take on a permanence not as inner-worldly things, but rather as those things as they affect the mind. In this sense the ontological problem of the non-being of time is resolved by Augustine by internalizing it, by distending the present in the mind through the capacities of memory and expectation (11:23). These capacities correspond to modes of appearance of time, as past and future, apprehended through memory and expectation. These modes of apprehension of the appearance of past and future are modes in which past and future appear. For them to appear something must be—not, however, the past and future themselves, but signs of past and future, signs which are real and are apprehended in the present (11:20).

Things of the world are in this way transcribed as images and signs interpretable by the mind. Nothing is as it is, but rather is only as present, that is, as taken up. Interpreted through memory and expectation, things are temporal, are aspects of existence. Things are beings in time, as persisting in time, only in relation to the mind. In this sense the human mind reflects the mind of the creator god. What this relation to mind means, however, is that past events do not have a fixed significance, but have significance with respect to the images which are retained of them in the mind. In a remarkable passage Augustine extends this outward to include all human history:

> What is true of the whole psalm is also true of all its parts and of each syllable. It is true of any longer action in which I may be engaged and of which the recitation of the psalm may only be a small part. It is true of a man's whole life, of which all his actions are parts. It is true of the whole history of mankind, of which each man's life is a part. (11:28)

Clearly here the relation of attention is being extended beyond that of Augustine's—or any other finite person's—attention. The attention which holds together past and present and reads them in terms of images and signs is the same attention which holds together the whole of human history. The only mind that can hold the whole of human history together is the mind of god, and in the next paragraph Augustine turns to the Father as eternal. This seamless move from the recitation of a psalm to the history of mankind does not indicate a proximity between temporality and eternity, but rather that attention in its unifying tendency gives an interpretation of significance which resembles that in the mind of god. Such resemblance, however, can only be partial; because of the changefulness of human existence it is continually in flux. But precisely this flux, this changefulness of human time, is that to which Augustine owes his own conversion: to convert is not simply to act in the present but rather to refigure one's whole life—and to do so in the light of the refiguring of human history in total. For Augustine the possibility of conversion, of redemption, and of forgiveness lies in this mutability of past time. This mutability did not simply amount to a retrospective movement of meaning in which the end result of an action gives meaning to its beginning (although such retrospective movement is given greater sense by Augustine's understanding of time as flowing from future to past). Rather, the mutability here is fundamental, owing to that which is beyond and before being in time, namely, the eternal.

The kairological transformation evoked by Paul and found throughout the New Testament is given systematic sense by Augustine's understanding of time as the movement of significance through memory and expectation. The kairos disrupts memory and expectation, but it is precisely in understanding time in these terms that the full import of that disruption can be grasped. In explicit opposition to Plotinus (and Plato), Augustine understands time not as an image of eternity, but as precisely that which is not eternal and hence *is* not. The temporal movements of memory, intuition, and expectation are distentions of the soul that allow an existent to be in the world, but can never reach the eternal, are indeed turned away from the eternal. The closing paragraphs of Book 11 in introducing the figure of Christ make clear the fallen, provisional nature of temporality itself for Augustine: Christ points not to an intensification of time, but to the possibility of liberation from it—a liberation only possible after death. The dispersion of time, the dispersion between past, present, and future, even in the unity of the sung hymn, can be overcome only through a forgetting of the past (11:29). Such forgetting is achieved in hope: not the expectation of a future which passes away, but an outstretching (*non distentus, sed extentus*), which attains the simple, atemporal unity of a saved self (11:29).

Temporality as understood by Augustine allows no way toward the eternal. The eternal comes rather *to the temporal* through grace: through the revelation of Christ (with respect to divine truths) and through divine illumination (with respect to universal, worldly truths). This forms the first and most basic break with the Platonic inheritance. Time in Augustine's terms is the chronology of human affairs. Once disrupted by the eternal, by the incarnational presence of Christ, this chronology undergoes a transformation which is fundamental to Christian temporal experience. In freeing the experience of time in human existence from natural time, from the cosmological time of Aristotle, Augustine shows how the action of the eternal allows for the past and future to be transformed through a rethinking of the meaning of the signs of both traced in that existence. The eternal is absolute alterity, that which confounds memory, intuition, and expectation.[22] Temporal experience on its own cannot account for this intrusion, indeed remains blind to it, seeing only things in the world as signs and images. The capacity to see the kairos is a capacity beyond temporal existence, but the kairos can affect such an existent by provoking the movement toward the unseen in faith.

By understanding eternity as other than time Augustine gives a context in which the full philosophical import of the kairos as the entry of the eternal into the temporal can be understood. This is the key to the paradox of the moment, as Kierkegaard describes it. Only if the eternal enters into the temporal is there Christian temporality. Otherwise if the temporal and the eternal remain external to one another, then "the historical is merely an occasion" for learning about the eternal, and the Socratic situation, with its attendant chronological relation, remains.[23] When the eternal enters into time, temporal experience is transformed. Past loses all necessity. This is so because what the kairos indicates most clearly is the 'coming into existence' of the event. Kierkegaard saw here the symmetry of past and future which the kairos brings to light—against Aristotle, for whom the past had relative necessity and the future defied the law of the excluded middle. Once the kairos occurs in the faith of those who believe in it, the coming from elsewhere of both past and future, the coming from elsewhere of time, as a coming into existence, is revealed. Nothing of the past is then necessary, but rather is the coming into existence of what was not.[24] The very distance of eternity and time means that time has no immunity to eternity, nor eternity to time: when they intersect they do so by a process of mutual contamination. This contamination is one in which the temporal flow is interrupted, the time of the event and the natural flow of time appear in conflict. This conflict is all the more pressing because it requires that it be responded to with a fundamental commitment, a commitment which concerns the whole of a life. That commitment of a life, the life-time which it encompasses, claims a priority over the world-time, which it interrupts. This interruption, however, is only accidentally public; it happens in secret, in the heart of the one who perceives the eternal in time.

This is the happening of the Messiah—a messianism *with* a messiah, a messiah already come, as being already in the world, as imposing a determinate way of being on those who have faith in him—a religion, a messianism, and a *fidelity* to the Messiah who has come once and for all. What is at issue here is an "advent of justice," but one which does occur (pace Derrida) within a specific "horizon of expectation and . . . prophetic prefiguration."[25] While Derrida understands the messianic as radically indeterminate and undecidable (and does so explicitly as that which is not confined to the Abrahamic tradition[26]), once we are talking about an event for which messianic significance is claimed, then the 'without' becomes 'within.' Being with the impossible defines faith in the messianic event. Such a faith does not see and yet believes, because it perceives the event as that which is unseen, which the light of the world refuses.[27] Derrida, in the context of a "nocturnal night," speaks of such a "faith without dogmas which makes its way through the risks of absolute night."[28] Dogma, however, is inseparable from the event as it is retold, retained, and instituted through time. 'Dogma' has the same root as glory, namely *dokein*—'it seems.' Dogmas are articulations of how the event seems, articulations which fail to capture that event not because they are false, but because of the messianicity of the event itself. Such dogma is not a refusal to take the risk of absolute night—although the relations to such dogma may amount to such a refusal (dogmatism)—but rather always inadequate articulations of it: illuminated accounts of nocturnal events. Faith here is a form of knowledge,[29] but one which knows the appearance of the eternal in the temporal, a knowledge inadequate to its object. The privileging of this one event as the once and for all is philosophically significant in that it presses to its extreme the contamination of the absolute and the contingent in Christian thought. It is this which Augustine's time analysis prepares us for: the moment of incarnation transforms past and future and does so in the light of an event, understood as messianic, but as one which refigures prophetic announcement, and which can be perceived only within a horizon of expectation. The event is strictly impossible, because contradictory. That the eternal can appear in the world is contradictory, if the eternal is the world itself. And this contradiction is precisely what is meant by the unworldliness of the event.[30] The event cannot be, cannot happen, yet in affirming its happening and affirming this happening in ontological terms—"the word becomes flesh"—Christianity bases itself on the claim that world-time can be thought in terms that contradict it, because it has a source anterior to itself. Messianism with a messiah is a claim to anteriority, which is the anteriority of the other to time as occurring in time.

When John has Jesus say, "Now, Father, glorify me with that glory I had with you before ever the world existed" (John 17:5), this anteriority is being expressed. The glory of the cross, the glory of the total self-giving of god as human, is an event which through its absolute intervention in chronological time, in its refusal of the splendor of that time, brings a glory into the time of the world which is the presence of that origin in creation—the contingent act of love. The anteriority here is not an anteriority of thought; it is a coming to presence of the beginning of time itself. That absolute moment is one in which the economy of world-time, the cyclical movements of the planets and of historical epochs, is disrupted by a beginning which is before all such cycles, a beginning which was never present, which cannot be remembered, which remains dismembered, scattered in the entities of creation, in which—if at all—the event of such glorification will resonate.

Such a way of being with the Messiah is one which radiates throughout time. In this sense the response to the Messiah is a forgetting of the past (the life lived before the event), through a recalling of that past. Such recalling does not find already given truths, but rather re-reads the past in such a manner that it reflects the glory of the event through retrospective revealing of the past as it was never present. In other words, remembering in the light of the kairos is not parasitic toward perception, not an image of a past perception, but rather a discovery of signs in the past of that which could not be perceived or known in that past. In this way the alterity of the eternal in breaking through into the temporal does not so much change the way the past was understood, as it changes the manner of experiencing pastness as such: the past now is that which hides what can only be revealed kairologically. In other words, the past becomes historical. The interpretation of scriptures changes radically from a forward-looking expectation of the Messiah, which will fulfill the expectations of the past, to a reading from a future foreign to that past, through which the signs are understood only in light of that of which they are perceived to be signs. This is a perception of faith in a singular person, Jesus Christ, whose life transforms time by radiating to the origins of time and pointing to its end.[31]

This is a temporalization of time, a making temporary of time: as temporary, time is itself 'measured' by another time. This other time is the promise of salvation which the kairos opens up, the promise of a time beyond worldly economy, of a time beyond all sacrifice, a time of peace. But that time is not a time before or after time, it is not a supposed time before time, but a time of the end of time which is the kairological aspect in every moment. The end of time is the end of measurement, the excess of measurement in all time, the moment through and in which world-time opens to its other. Can this time be called justice? Can this time be termed a "structural messianism, a messianism without religion, even a messianic without messianism"?[32] Certainly the time in question is a time of alterity, which is the time of the eternal for Christianity. But this alterity has a definite form, a definite time and place. The event of this time and place is a singular one: both determinate and ineffable in its determinations. It is the time of this messiah, who has come, in whom and in no other the martyr, the witness, gives faith. The purity of the impossible, the undeconstructible, inverts the figure of the scapegoat, but does not escape it. It remains tied to a sacred logic by retaining this one place, unscathed and safe, for justice. The genius of Christianity is to embody justice in a time and place, as the materialization of time, in a figure who in claiming to speak on the authority of a non-worldly mission, by incarnating that mission, contaminates all things with an unworldly destiny and in so doing *doubles experience:* as reason and faith. This doubling of experience is an intermingling, in which all time is at once banal and exceptional, worldly and eschatological. Justice in this context is only in the movement beyond the world, which is always also a movement toward the world.

The Possible Time of God—Love, Contingency

Christian temporality allows no priority to future, present, or past. The kairos in transforming past and future does so equally in terms of endings—the ending of the world, the ending of time, the world as created and ending. The finitude of human time here is understood in terms of the finitude of the world. The world—cosmos—is understood as the public space of human relations, because the transitoriness of the latter reflects the constant ending of the former. The human can no longer be understood simply as an entity in the world, because the world is that which ends. This is not hubris on the part of Christian thought: that experience of the darkening of the world, of the extinguishing of the light of the world, was the experience of a message of salvation. Participation in the eternal could no longer mean participation in the liveliness of the world, of the world-soul, but rather participation in that which lay at the origins of that world, which was anterior to that world. Living temporally meant to live the kairos as the way to the anterior of things, a way not through thought alone, but through living the darkness of the world, the darkness of the ending time.

I refer here to this time as an ending time rather than an eschatological time only to emphasize the darkening of time which is at issue here. Time is experienced as coming to an end not at a certain point in the future, nor as beginning at a certain point in the past, but rather as beginning and ending in the present moment. Each moment is lived in imitation of the kairos, that is, in relation to the glory of the anterior of the world.

Because the event of the kairos is unseen, and cannot be seen, in the time of light, the time of the world, the light of the world darkens for the eyes of faith. This darkening is an illumination, an illumination in which all time—from the beginning to the end of creation—is compressed into the moment, the time in which the Christian lives and in which she acts in relation to the end. This is the profound significance of Augustine's reflections on time: life is not lived as a continuous stretching from birth to death, as a 'holding together' of a life (*Zusammenhang des Lebens* [Dilthey]), but rather as moments, each containing the totality of human history and destiny. Such moments are not of the world, as they are lived in imitation of Christ—of the creation, fall, redemption, and salvation—lived, that is, as moments which express the anterior, original time of divine relation to the world.

Being in the world and not of the world is being in time as a measure which bears the eternal within, and being of time as differential, as the breaking in of the eternal in the moment. No Christian life is lived exclusively in either, although the saintly living of a life is judged in terms of the latter. Comparing saintliness to heroism and wisdom, Louis Lavelle states the following:

> while heroism belongs to the instant and wisdom to the duration of time, holiness belongs to eternity—but to eternity which is incarnate in time. . . . in its undivided unity it [holiness] fills the whole of existence and cannot be reduced to one particular instant or even to the totality of all the instants of time. In an instant it opens a way into eternity—into an eternity that lasts and gives its continuum to all duration.[33]

The saint is neither the hero nor the sage because the latter are concerned only with nature.[34] The saint, on the other hand, is concerned with 'second nature.'[35] The saint is not concerned directly or primarily with things of the world; his concern with things in the world is in terms of their origin beyond the world. This entails that his concern is not with natural necessity, and that he does not rely on himself, but rather that he "transforms life for us into a perpetual miracle which, without disturbing in any way the natural order of things, shines through that order and reveals itself to us."[36] Lavelle speaks of memory as the means of spiritualization of life, one which in the case of the saint operates both in his own recollection of himself and in our memory of him. But in fact the spiritualization of life in time is one which operates both through memory and hope. The saintly life is miraculous in the sense that it brings together memory and hope in transforming the moment into a time lived in relation to a beginning and an end beyond and before the world. This saintly life is a life of time as ending. That which holds together this living of ending life is love. The saintly life is a loving life because it sees the world as an expression of love, an expression which is manifest temporally.

Such a life in relation to the beyond and before of the world is a life lived in desire of god.[37] As such the Christian living of temporality can only ultimately be understood as an expression of desire for the anterior of time inscribed in time: a movement of love in and beyond time. This movement of love is that which responds to a prior love and for which sin becomes first visible. Sin, as a turning away from god, is a turning away out of a striving for needlessness, for being sufficient unto itself. The story of the fall is characterized by a specific form of temporal relation. "You will not die! God knows in fact that the day you eat it [the fruit] your eyes will be opened and you will be like gods" (Genesis 3:5). The erotic structure of temporal existence, the striving to possess what is lacking, begins with the temptation itself. The serpent introduces a relation to the future in terms of lack: the present is one of blindness and fear (of death); overcoming this present involves taking possession, refusing the relation to god and taking the position of god. Thus, as Augustine makes clear, the sin of the fall was not corporeal in the Stoic sense of the corrupting desires of the body, but rather happened in the soul, by a turning to time. This turning to time is a turning away from the anteriority of the divine relation, the relation of creation, toward a future as escape from that relation in the erotic temporality of appropriation. Out of this erotic dynamic no passage to the eternal is possible; it rather increases the distance to the eternal. There is here no possibility of a sublimation of eros in the way we find it in Plato's *Symposium*. The call of god is experienced therefore as a call *from* erotic temporality *to* the agapeic gift of time, the gift namely of the time of creaturehood. Such a call is to the time to which the self remains insufficient, the time of self as creature as relating to a time before time, time as anteriority.

198 | *A Phenomenology of Christian Life*

The relation to time as anteriority is a relation to the world as ending, the world as inscribed with the contingency of its own origins. This contingency is lived in relation to death as a prefiguration of the world ending. Experienced as such death is an interruption of world-time not as some future event, but as now, as already being. 'Now' death is the absolute passivity of the existent. It is the ever-present entry of the eternal. Christian death is not the gateway to immortality (that idea is found elsewhere, not least in Socrates' arguments for the immortality of the soul in the *Phaedo*), rather it is the acceptance of the eternal, an acceptance already effected in the 'second birth' of becoming Christian. Pascal in his posing of the wager gives expression to this passivity: reason cannot give any proof as to the nature of death; only faith is possible in the face of death. In the end for Pascal this amounts to listening to the reasons of the heart, through which alone god is perceived. Such a listening is a listening to that god who reveals himself in the event of the Incarnation, listening to love as pure gift—agāpe. This is a gift of life, which in breaking into time transforms temporal life into a lived openness to the eternal as that which has already come.

To live and think such time is to live and think inadequation and insufficiency, but not to live or think them as humiliation. This is a life of humility. The life of humility, the incarnate, ascetic life, is a living of time in relation to an eternal which disrupts it. As Barth states, only pride perceives such humility as humiliation. Without hierarchy there is for Christianity no place for pride; pride is without place in the agapeic givenness of time from temporal anteriority. Living in respect of such anteriority is always passionate. As von Balthasar states, the relation of distance between divine and human is a relation of rapture. But as an experience of relation to a past, an anteriority, which remains always immemorial to it in its very living and thinking time in memory and anticipation, it is also true to quote Hölderlin: "*Schwer verlässt Was nahe dem Ursprung wohnt, den Ort* [That which dwells near to its origin is reluctant to leave the place]."[38]

8 Thinking Night and Glory

THIS BOOK IS offered, as stated in the Preface, as an experiment. The experiment is to think philosophically in a Christian manner. This attempt does not simply mean a dismissal of the Greek: indeed it relies on such thinkers as Pseudo-Dionysius, Augustine, Aquinas, Kierkegaard, von Balthasar, Marion, and others, who to varying degrees attempt to integrate Christian phenomena with Greek philosophy. But nonetheless, as each of these thinkers acknowledge, Greek thinking—philosophy as Greek—breaks down eventually in its attempt to think the Christian. The phenomena of Christian life are fundamentally contradictory, and again we can find traced from St. Paul through Augustine to Nicholas of Cusa to Pascal and beyond what Cusa called the 'coincidence of contradictories.' Contradiction without synthesis, movement of thought without dialectic, reason faced with the paradox of the singular which cannot be contained within the whole: in short the singular as epiphanic—appearing from elsewhere.

Thinking in response to the epiphanic encounter in the embodied, temporal, indebted situation of the existent expresses itself as praise. Praise is not a leave-taking of the body, of the situation, of time, but rather a dispossessing of them, whereby the body, situation, and time are lived and thought within the eternal. Thinking takes place in the body, in a situation, and in time and finds the eternal in them. Such thinking is faithful and logical: faith, not as belief, not as opinion, but rather as the movement of response to the unseen in the phenomena—a faithful logic before any division between reason and faith, responding to the appearance of transcendence in immanence. That appearance is rupturing, disturbing, but this disturbance, in order to be thought and to be lived, requires eyes that see in the dark, that are neither blinded by the light nor defeated by the dark. Such eyes are embodied, living, and yet anticipate and recall an origin which is inscribed in the present as an enduring but ending past.

Christian churches are not houses of god, but rather tombs, as Nietzsche rightly said. Christian thought happens within such necropoli, amongst the bones of the dead, the very altars containing the bones—'relics'—of the saints. Here living and dead intermingle. This indifference of life and death manifests Christian love, a love which knows no favorites, nor comparisons, but is a singular, creative loving movement toward existents in their singular being. This love delights in contamination; contamination is the event of revelation as the incarnation of glory. Kenosis is an emptying not of glory itself, but rather of distance. Glory comes close, comes to presence, and all that comes into its presence lives through being contaminated by it, thus overturning the sacred logic of exclusion.

In this final chapter the nature of this paradoxical, non-dialectical thinking— thinking the eternal in the corporeal, the dead in the living, night in glory—will be explored and articulated in relation to its ultimate point of orientation, namely, love as agāpe. Such an orientation is beyond all hierarchy, requiring a thinking and living which is non-hierarchical. In more positive terms, such a thinking is one which is responsive, which understands itself as being initiated from elsewhere, but at the same time understands itself as taking ontological root in the world, as asserting its place in the world in asserting responsively the being of the world.

Thinking Love, Thinking Lovingly

The thought of love is a thought of a gift whose source is not given. Agāpe does not appear in the world, but rather shows itself in all appearance. That which appears in the world shows in its appearance the shock of its own contingency. This shock, the way of appearing of this singular entity, is its own unjustified assertion of itself, the assertion of its being here, now, and present. That assertion which characterizes perception—this perceived object is, and demands acknowledgment—is not a matter of consciousness, nor of deliberation, nor of intention. That assertion (*ad-serere*) is simply the being of the entity toward that to which it is joined (*serere*), namely, the world. This being joined to the world neither owes itself to the entity itself nor to the world, which in its coherency can account for the entity only in its positionality, not its singularity. To be this singular being is to be in relation to its source. In perception the assertion of the being of the entity is thought as the gift of that entity here and now. Such a thought betrays itself continually through articulating the entity in the joints of its worldly being. Yet, it is in this very betrayal that thought rediscovers the singular being, precisely in re-penting (*re-penser*) its turning away from the entity. Thinking the singular being in this sense is a continual re-thinking, a continual attempt to retrieve what has been glimpsed, namely, the agapeic source of the entity.

Nothing is brought to light here. Rather, a darkness is sensed at the core of the entity itself. That darkness is sensed, always too late, in the feeling of having betrayed. Such betrayal is a giving onward (*tradare*), rather than a giving back, a moving on and away rather than a tarrying-with. Such a moving away is living time as a now-sequence, where every moment is superseded by the next and each singular entity retains interest only to the extent to which it can show new aspects. Repentance begins in the moment, when all of a sudden the entity in its beauty calls the perceiving self. In that calling the entity is seen no longer as it reflects the light of the world, but as a movement toward the world, from its own depth. Furthermore, the movement of language, the movement based in the satisfaction of the entity in words, is ruptured by the silent witness of the entity to itself as being in excess of all attempts to articulate it, as never reaching satisfaction in language. The luminous being of the entity in its existence traces a movement from, which can only be glimpsed too late and which cannot be said. But what is glimpsed there is a darkness, which is more revealing than the light of day. Against the hierarchical movement of Plato's cave, Christian thinking insists on tarrying-with this darkness, as the eternal origin of the singular being of the entity.

Such a tarrying is silent and in its silence recognizes the limit of knowledge in the face of the singular; but this limit is not itself a limit of experience. Rather, tarrying is a way of experience, which allows itself to be led—seduced—by the entity, in the darkness of its being. This is a being-with the entity as creature, as that which is from nothing. To be with an entity in this way is to be with it in its own being nothing, that is, in its own creaturely being. The way toward an entity is a way of dispossession and self-denial, a way, namely, of allowing oneself be drawn in by the entity. Such self-denial is a denial of knowledge, utility, and language, which shows the common roots of all three in an intuition of the entity revealing itself. Such a revelation is only glimpsed, but in returning to the site of that glimpsing, in a repentance of all turning away, the space is left to be touched by the entity. Such a being-touched is always happening, is a condition of all knowledge, but in moving on it is always being surpassed. Thinking the singular being of the entity is thinking being-affected, is thinking sensibility.

To think sensibility and affection as such, that is, as they appear to be, is to repent, to be reduced—led back—to reverse the normal movement of thought. This repentance is a reflection of sensibility on itself, a making intelligible of sensibility, which is always already intelligible but always hides its intelligibility. The entity which appears does so to a sensing being. The sensing being allows itself to be turned away from itself and the world, or rather from itself as a worldly being and denies itself the light of worldly experience, humbles itself before the entity as a singular assertion of being in the world. The sensing being is powerless before this entity because its powers all lead it away; its powers are treacherous. To be true to the entity, to think it in its singular being, is to renounce all power and to succumb to the entity in its beauty. That beauty is its singular form, which gives itself as a coming to form, as a coming to itself. To be affected by an entity is to be affected by that entity in its own self. Its own self, however, is a movement of coming to be itself, of taking on its own form; whether this movement is a conscious one or not makes no difference here. That movement is a movement from beyond itself, a movement from beyond all visibility and all appearance, a movement which is sudden, momentary, an appearance from elsewhere, which comes from the inapparent (ex-aiphnes).[1] A tarrying-with seeing, hearing, touching of the entity is in each case to perceive that which indicates the singular being-here of the entity, which in its assertion of being, at the joint of that juncture, holds on to that source neither contained by, nor appearing in, the world.

In being affected by the entity the sensing being is being affected by that coming to itself of the entity. Its being drawn into the entity as sensed is at the same time a living in its own sensing. Such living in its own sensing is not simply a matter of self-awareness, but also of self-responsibility. Sensing itself as being drawn into the coming to itself of another entity, the affected entity recognizes its own coming to be, its own originating anterior to anything in the world, as before and beyond all worldly horizons. It senses itself as not alone sensing, but as being called to be true to its own origins beyond yet in itself. The taking up of that call is the self's original act of responsibility on an ontological level. We can thus say that only what is not of the world can sense in the world, whereby it asserts itself in the world. But sensing is initiated through the world: only through the worldly relation with the entity can sensation happen at all. To sense is to be affected, to be touched from outside. It is a being-passive. Passivity is a manner of being toward entities in the world; it is a manner of existence. Only an existing being can be passive. The passivity of this relation is one of entrance and orifice toward the world: of letting in and being drawn toward. This passivity is a primordial being wounded, an opening up of the body as a mouth (os), which takes the entity (as one takes a warning, or an insult, or a beating) before expressing it. This wounded being-toward is a being which neither initiates nor projects itself, but rather finds itself in medias res: in the middle of things and in the midst of itself. The wounded being finds itself as already wounded, as already opened up by entities in the world, and in sensing those entities finds itself as a penetrated being, as a doorway from, and a window on, the world. The kairotic moment of tarrying-with is a moment in which the vulnerable place in the sensing being is opened up—kairos in Homer is not a temporal term, but refers to a place in the armor of the warrior where a spear could pierce, a place of physical vulnerability for him but of opportunity for his enemies.[2] But such a place of opportunity is the aim also of Cupid, whose arrows wound the lover. The love of god—the love for enemies—can be compared to Cupid's arrows.[3] That place of opportunity is sensibility itself, the place, namely, where there is the opportunity for an entity to pierce the onward movement of chronos and bring the sensing being to a standstill, a nunc stans.

In this standstill the erotic impulse, the forward movement of possession, penetration, and incorporation is stilled, and in that stilling the object of such erotic movement is allowed to be present in its givenness. What is received in this stilling is not simply the entity in its worldly being—that is also given erotically—but the movement toward the world, toward its own form, of the entity. In short, what is received is the entity as an agapeic gift. Only in the heart of the sensing being can this be given, because only in the night of the soul of such a being, where worldly light has been extinguished, can the apapeic gift be manifest. Such a contemplative attitude is a turning away from the worldliness of entities not from entities in the world. It is a turning toward such entities, a turning toward which, however, finds itself in its being toward, and as such in its being from.

Thinking the World without Hierarchies

To think the singularity of singular being is to think the existent outside all structure. Thinking origins, thinking originating being, is thinking the entity as it comes to language. Such thinking is necessarily retrospective. Christian thinking is characterized by a backward movement: repenting, it finds redemption in forgiveness. Such movement recognizes outward difference as positional. Such positionality is being on the surface, indicated by signs which point always from themselves, imitating the light of the sun. But the existent's 'place in the sun' is its place as represented in signs. The existent itself, however, is a sign which manifests itself. It is a sign in the sense that it indicates itself in its difference from itself; this difference is a difference of self and origin. The existent manifests itself as coming from beyond itself, and this difference explodes its emplacement in the difference of signs. The name, calling the existent, does not capture or contain the existent, but rather responds to the withdrawal of the existent which echoes in the words themselves. Hearing this echo is hearing the word not in its difference, but rather in the coming to sound, the coming to meaning which the word expresses but also betrays.

Without worldly difference there is no hierarchy, just as with it hierarchy is inevitable. Difference in the world implies before and after, that which is closest to the arché and that which is furthest away. No matter how unstable, no matter how contingent, how provisional or hypothetical, difference assumes a system of difference, and each system is ruled by the law of origin and derivation. In the singular relation of creature to creator this rule is undone due to the very distance from the creator. This distance from the source, the origin, the arché, reduces all measures to nothing, or rather makes nothing the measure of all. From nothing as measure, affirmation and negation are both equally inadequate to express the being of the existent, which is, rather, a relation to that which is not (of the world) and hence cannot be affirmed or negated by sentences structured in terms of the world. In that sense Nietzsche's famous declaration that "we are not rid of God because we believe in grammar"[4] is incomplete: the belief in grammar is overcome through a recognition of the nothing underlying the subject, the rupture in being at the core of the sentence, which reveals a divinity beyond being. Precisely the inadequation of word, the inadequation of truth, the inadequation of time and being reveals that which is beyond all words, all truths, beyond time and being, but to be found at the core of each of these. It is found, though, not by analysis, but by living in time, language, and truth, which leads to their dispossession. Such inadequation is the gateway beyond hierarchy.

In such a thinking conjunction and disjunction are thought as glorification: the 'and,' the 'or' which binds or separates are thought from the eschatological vision of peace. Conjoined, disjoined, in their singular being toward the depth of their own being and the being-in-depth of the other, existents appear in this being-toward, this being-joined. Such being-joined escapes all worldly view, refuses thinking in its systematizing effort, but in that refusal invites thinking of a communion beyond predication. That communion of being joined in singular being is a communion inadequate to the joining of one to the other: a communion in and of humility. Such humble thinking listens not to what can and is said, but to what in the saying through its own self-manifestation allows no further movement. Such a halting is not the discovery of truths (because such discovery is only in the movement onward, the 'and' and 'or' of worldly knowledge), but rather the intuition of the nothing in each case singular, but in each case joined with the other. Such a thinking tarries-with the existent in its movement from its origins, always in the world, but signifies itself as a calling of its own name.

Such a calling of its own name is not of the name proper to it alone—proper names are never proper in this sense[5]—but rather of a name which it calls from itself as telling nothing of itself, by simply announcing itself. To tarry with that announcing is to tarry with the existent as that which is not a beginning, but only through which a beginning, an arché, can appear.

Thinking Peace and Violence

Christian life is proclaimed in peace, as peace, yet is so often manifested violently. This is not simply because Christianity promises a peace 'worth' killing and dying for, but also—and more fundamentally—because its proclamation of peace happens as disruption. Christian praise responds to that which punctures the world. For the Christian, in expressing things in the world, the existent finds at the heart of its clear articulations that which disrupts them. This disruption is violent, revealing a nothingness out of which it comes and suggests annihilation. But it is at the same time an instance which calls for peace, which brings a peace through its proclamation of the utterly singular being of all entities. Thinking in such peace is thinking in the face of a void, a night, which is the eternal in the moment, in terms of which all knowledge is empty, but in faithful hearing of which the inner source of all things may be heard. The peace of such attending hearing opens up a place beyond worldly authority, a place from which all the limiting claims of normalization, through which experience is brought back to worldly standards of evaluation and control, can be dismissed. The transforming figure of the Incarnation, the refiguring of past and future in the moment, the sudden overturning in the present unleashes novelty—the 'new heaven and the new earth'—which in living temporality as temporality, as, namely, that which temporalizes time, can disrupt the power of law in the name of justice. The apocalyptical ending of the world, however—and the Incarnation as the intertwining and intermingling of divine and animal, creation as the divine source of all matter, the kairos as the expression in a chronologically situated time and place of divine love, all suggest this—can be met with a love of the least of things in the world, which sees in them a beauty drawing the existent out of itself toward the singular being of the other and the transcendent origin in itself and in all things. Between peace and violence in their intertwining within a world for an existent living its life as unworldly in its being, the becoming apparent of things is a singular manifestation of agapeic origins. Glory as the darkening of the world lets existents appear as singular manifestations of an originating love.

Notes

Introduction

1. This is one reason for the recent philosophical interest in the work of Paul to which the account of Paul offered in the course of this book is indebted. See Agamben, *The Time that Remains*, Badiou, *St. Paul*, Breton, *The Word and the Cross*, and Caputo et al., *Paul Amongst the Philosophers*.

2. See Marion, "Christian Philosophy—Hermeneutics or Heuristics," and Henry, "Christianisme et phenomenologie."

3. Barth: *Church Dogmatics*, vol. 3, pt. 2, pp. 3–6.

4. Central to this question is the issue of the natural desire for god. Theologically, the pivotal figure here (and not only in terms of Catholic theology) was Henri de Lubac, who argues against the positing of a 'pure nature' of man without god and for the reintegration of the natural and the supernatural, the visible and the invisible. He rejects the methodological move of constructs such as pure nature. For one thing, such constructs presuppose a dichotomy of nature and the supernatural, even when theologians go on to deny the actuality of such a dichotomy. Secondly, the hypothesis, though possible, concerns as he says another universe and one which is not constituted by god's call. To place oneself in a universe in which one is not destined to see god is, de Lubac affirms, impossible. He goes on to say that between those two people (the man like me and me myself) there is a difference in nature. In other words, the place to begin in understanding the gratuitousness of grace is in its concrete reality. This concrete reality de Lubac understands as the dynamic of call and desire. The desire to see god is not an accident, but rather is essential to human nature as constituted by god's call. This call is a call to finality, that is, a call to fulfillment of the nature of each person. "As soon as I exist . . . no other finality . . . seems possible for me than that which is now really inscribed in the depths of my nature; there is only one end and therefore I bear within me, consciously or otherwise, a 'natural desire' for it." De Lubac, *The Mystery of the Supernatural*, p. 72. Karl Rahner makes a similar point (although he argues against de Lubac for the limited applicability of a notion of 'pure nature') using the vocabulary of the personal being: "it is precisely the essence of the personal being (his paradox without which he cannot be understood) that he is ordained to personal communion with God in love (by nature) and must receive just his love as free gift." Rahner, "Concerning the Relationship between Nature and Grace," p. 305. It is in the space opened up here, the space of the interpenetration of the natural and the supernatural, that the possibility of a 'Christian philosophy' emerges.

5. I can here only indicate a position on this debate regarding the relation of Plato and Aristotle. What is characteristic of Platonism is the coinciding of metaphysical and theological questions, something which is most evident also in Aristotle's *Metaphysics*. If the metaphysical question becomes one concerning the divine principle of things, and the question concerning god is understood as one which seeks to position the divine in terms of a basic ontological intelligibility in things, then a hierarchical understanding of beings and a teleological account of knowledge and the pursuit of wisdom seem inescapable. Furthermore, the concern with delineation, the defense against contagion (especially of the material and the

immaterial) is pursued in both Plato and Aristotle, as is clear from Aristotle's understanding of substance as separability and thisness (cf. *Metaphysics*, 1029a30). My understanding of the relation of Aristotle to Plato has been strongly influenced by Lloyd Gerson's *Aristotle and Other Platonists*. In this book he argues that Aristotle cannot be coherently read except in terms of his Platonic assumptions concerning the harmony of the world. This is not the standard view, of course. Generally, we are faced with a choice: either Plato or Aristotle. This is a position which is strongly influenced by Jaeger's developmentalist reading of Aristotle. See his *Aristotle*. More recently Martha Nussbaum's *The Fragility of Goodness* emphasizes a strong distinction between the respective projects of Plato and Aristotle.

6. See chapter 2.

7. Cf. Milbank et al., *Radical Orthodoxy*, p. 3.

8. Pickstock, *After Writing*, p. 12.

9. It is of course true that the church fathers themselves recognized the limits to any synthesis of Plato and Christianity, something James Smith shows in a discussion of Pickstock with respect to the Incarnation in Augustine. See Smith, *Speech and Theology*, pp. 175–176.

10. On the question of creation see chapter 5. Creation here is being understood in the Christian sense of creation out of nothing. The account of the origins of the world and the universe (*kosmos* and *ouranos*) in the *Timaeus* is not an account of creation in this sense, but rather of demiurgic making.

11. Smith, *Speech and Theology*, p. 176.

12. By sacred logic I mean a logic of purity and classification. The sacred logic is one which seeks to separate and distinguish, and to prescribe what is out of place. It is a logic based on the anxiety of contagion, understood as defilement. As Mary Douglas points out, such a notion of contagion is dependent on a system, in which the contagious is defined. In such a system 'dirt' is that which is out of place—out of place relative to the system itself. See Douglas, *Purity and Danger*, p. 35. The search for purity here is one which seeks to force experience into "logical categories of non-contradiction" (ibid., p. 162). Plato is a systematic thinker to the extent to which he thinks in terms of relations in which things belong, and the maintenance of this belonging is not achieved by rituals and sacrifice, but by the responsible philosopher.

13. See the account of the chiasmus in the *Timaeus*, 36b.

14. Pascal, above all, has shown the centrality of contradiction to Christianity.

15. For the philosophical significance of such notions of the fall and redemption in Nietzsche, Heidegger, and Wittgenstein see Mulhall, *Philosophical Myths of the Fall*.

16. See Kierkegaard, *Philosophical Fragments*, pp. 28–45.

17. Nietzsche, *Thus Spoke Zarathustra*, p. 162.

18. See Nietzsche, *The Birth of Tragedy*, p. 19.

19. Ibid., p. 21.

20. Nietzsche, *Thus Spoke Zarathustra*, p. 110.

21. In this and the following two sections I will confine myself to that strand of thinking which can be drawn from Heidegger through Levinas and Derrida to Henry and Marion. There are other voices, many other (philosophical and theological) voices, on the issue of the relation of Christianity and more broadly *Judeo*-Christianity with philosophy: names such as Scheler, Benjamin, Jaspers, Mounier, Marcel, Weil, Ricoeur, de Lubac, von Balthasar, Rahner, Chrétien, Lacoste, Caputo, Westphal, Kearney, and many more. These will all figure in the discussions which follow. At this point I wish to draw out the question of world and alterity as it reverberates through the phenomenological traditions as a propaedeutic to a discussion of phenomenality as glory and night.

22. On Heidegger's theological beginnings see especially Kisiel, *The Genesis of Heidegger's Being and Time*, pp. 70–115; van Buren, *The Young Heidegger*, pp. 157–202; Crowe, *Heidegger's*

Religious Origins, pp. 15–66; McGrath, *The Early Heidegger and Medieval Theology*; and Westphal, *Overcoming Onto-theology*, pp. 29–46.

23. There have of course been exceptions to this, such as Edith Stein.

24. See Ward, *Barth, Derrida and the Language of Theology*; Ott, *Denken und Sein*; and Connell, "Against Idolatry," pp. 156–161.

25. On this theme see especially van Buren, *The Young Heidegger*, pp. 159–163.

26. Heidegger, *The Phenomenology of Religious Life*, p. 54.

27. Ibid., p. 104.

28. Cf. Kierkegaard, *Philosophical Fragments*, pp. 111–138, on the disciple at second hand.

29. Heidegger, *Being and Time*, p. 18 / *Sein und Zeit*, p. 21.

30. Ibid., p. 20/22.

31. The attempts by Volpi, Taminiaux, Bernasconi, and others to show the reading of Aristotle underlying the analyses of objective presence (*Vorhandenheit*) and handiness (*Zuhandenheit*), etc., presume this.

32. Heidegger, *Being and Time*, p. 351 / *Sein und Zeit*, p. 383.

33. Ibid., p. 361/396: "historical science strives to alienate Dasein from its authentic historicity."

34. See McGrath, *The Early Heidegger and Medieval Thought*, pp. 11–12.

35. Heidegger, "Essence of Grounds," p. 371.

36. Heidegger, *Four Seminars*, p. 80.

37. Heidegger, "What is Metaphysics," p. 90.

38. Ibid., p. 96 (translation modified).

39. Heidegger, *Contributions to Philosophy*, p. 6.

40. Ibid., p. 161.

41. Ibid., p. 163.

42. Ibid., p. 289.

43. Heidegger, *On the Way to Language*, pp. 9–10. See on this issue Harries, "'Das Ding,' 'Bauen, Wohnen, Denken,'" pp. 301–302.

44. Heidegger, *Four Seminars*, pp. 80–81.

45. See Marion, *The Idol and Distance*, p. 94.

46. Levinas, *Totality and Infinity*, p. 89.

47. For example, Levinas sounds quite Barthian when he states: "The atheism of the metaphysician means, positively, that our relation with the Metaphysical is an ethical behavior and not theology, not a thematization, be it knowledge by analogy, of the attributes of God." Ibid., p. 78.

48. Heidegger, *Being and Time*, pp. 110–111 / *Sein und Zeit*, p. 117.

49. Ibid., pp. 154–155/165. See further my "Reduction, Externalism, Immanence," pp. 389–390.

50. Heidegger, *Being and Time*, p. 151/161 (translation modified).

51. Ibid., p. 137/146.

52. Levinas, *Totality and Infinity*, pp. 77–78.

53. Ibid., p. 78.

54. Levinas, "God and Philosophy," p. 130. In this, Levinas repeats Heidegger's critique of onto-theology, and, also like Heidegger, only addresses a certain type of theology. Arguably, neither Aquinas nor Luther would understand god as the highest being, because for both thinkers god is unknowable and as such separate from the being of the world. See also Westphal, "Hermeneutics and the God of Promise," pp. 79–85.

55. Levinas, "God and Philosophy," p. 131.

56. Ibid.

57. The sometimes shrill oppositions between ethics and ontology in discussions of Heidegger and Levinas have outlived their heuristic value. We need to conceive of this difference phenomenologically in terms of that place in the world where the world becomes undone for Levinas.

58. Levinas, "God and Philosophy," p. 134.

59. Ibid., p. 135.

60. Ibid.

61. Ibid., p. 137.

62. Ibid., p. 139.

63. Ibid., p. 140.

64. Levinas, "God and Philosophy," p. 141.

65. Ibid., p. 145.

66. Ibid.

67. Levinas, *Otherwise than Being*, p. 180.

68. Levinas, *Totality and Infinity*, p. 66.

69. Ibid., p. 79.

70. Derrida, "Violence and Metaphysics," p. 101.

71. Ibid., p. 115.

72. Ibid., p. 107.

73. Ibid., p. 117.

74. Ibid.

75. Ibid., p. 121.

76. Ibid.

77. Ibid.

78. Ibid., p. 125.

79. Ibid., p. 126.

80. See O'Connor, *Profanations*.

81. Henry, "Christianisme et phénomenologie," p. 139.

82. Ibid., p. 142.

83. Ibid.

84. Henry, *I Am the Truth*, p. 71.

85. Ibid., p. 14.

86. Ibid., p. 20.

87. Ibid., p. 23 (emphasis in original).

88. Ibid., p. 25.

89. See ibid., p. 26.

90. Ibid.

91. Ibid., p. 31.

92. Ibid., p. 42.

93. Ibid.

94. Ibid., p. 53.

95. Ibid., p. 55.

96. Ibid., p. 59.

97. Ibid., p. 60.

98. Ibid., p. 71.

99. Ibid., p. 80.

100. Ibid., p. 81.

101. Ibid., p. 83 (emphasis mine).

102. See ibid., p. 84.

103. Ibid., p. 85.
104. Ibid., p. 87.
105. Ibid., p. 88.
106. Ibid.
107. Ibid., p. 91.
108. Ibid., p. 101; cf. Barth, *Church Dogmatics*, vol. 3, pt. 2, p. 48.
109. Henry, *I Am the Truth*, p. 101.
110. Henry, "La verité de la gnose," p. 131.
111. Henry, "Parole et religion," p. 193.
112. See Louth, *The Origins of the Christian Mystical Tradition*, pp. 79–80.
113. The nearest that the authors of the Hebrew scriptures come to such a formulation is in 2 Maccabees 7:28.
114. This is a point which Caputo stressed in his *The Weakness of God*.
115. I shall return to this question of creation in greater detail in chapter 6.
116. Marion, "'Christian Philosophy': Hermeneutic or Heuristic," p. 249.
117. Ibid., pp. 251–254.
118. Ibid., p. 254.
119. Ibid.
120. Ibid., p. 256 (translation modified).
121. Ibid., p. 257.
122. Marion, *The Idol and Distance*, p. 75.
123. See Marion, *God without Being*, p. 8: "The idol and the icon determine two manners of being for beings, not two classes of being."
124. Cf. ibid., p. 7.
125. Ibid., p. 11.
126. Ibid., p. 17.
127. On the following see my "Glory, Idolatry, Kairos."
128. Quoted in Marion, *God without Being*, p. 86.
129. Ibid., p. 88.
130. Ibid., p. 93.
131. Ibid., p. 94.
132. Ibid., p. 17.
133. Ibid., p. 18.
134. Ibid., p. 19.
135. Ibid.
136. Ibid., p. 21.
137. Marion, "The Saturated Phenomenon," p. 104.
138. Ibid., p. 112.
139. Ibid., p. 114.
140. Ibid.
141. Ibid.
142. Plato, *The Republic*, 517a. Quoted in Marion, "The Saturated Phenomenon," p. 115.
143. We shall return to the transcendentals in chapter 1.
144. Marion, "The Saturated Phenomenon," p. 118.
145. Ibid., p. 119.
146. Ibid.
147. Ibid.
148. Ibid., p. 120.
149. Ibid.

150. See Derrida, "Faith and Knowledge," pp. 79–82.
151. On this issue see Lacoste, *Experience and the Absolute*, pp. 23–39.
152. Janicaud, *The Theological Turn*, p. 35.
153. Merleau-Ponty, *The Visible and the Invisible*, p. 149.
154. Ibid., p. 148.
155. Merleau-Ponty, *The Prose of the World*, p. 10.
156. Ibid., p. 14.
157. Merleau-Ponty, *Resumes de Cours*, p. 179: "The unconscious is sensing itself, because sensing is not the intellectual possession of 'that which' is sensed, but the dispossession of ourselves for its sake, openness to that which we have no need to think in order to recognize it [*L'inconscient est le sentir lui-même, puisque le sentir n'est pas la possession intellectuelle de 'ce qui' est senti, mais dépossession de nous-même à son profit, ouverture à ce que nous n'avons pas besoin de penser pour le reconnaître*]." I would like to acknowledge the help of my former student Dr. Pierre-Yves Fioraso in translating this passage.
158. Ibid., p. 178.
159. Ibid.
160. Merleau-Ponty, *The Visible and the Invisible*, pp. 143–144.
161. Ibid., pp. 144/187.
162. Henry, *L'incarnation*, pp. 163–166.

1. Desire and Phenomenon

1. Marcel had something similar in view when he spoke of the double possibility of existence as that of receiving and degrading, of being and having. See Marcel, *Being and Having*, pp. 164–165.
2. Cf. Simone Weil on the catholicity of existence: "We have to be catholic . . . not bound by so much as a thread to any created thing, unless it be to creation in its entirety." Weil, *Waiting on God*, p. 46.
3. In this sense Heidegger is right to say that "beauty is one way in which truth as uncon-cealment comes to presence [*Wahrheit als Unverborgenheit west*]." Heidegger, "The Origin of the Work of Art," p. 32. The question, however, is how to think this relation of beauty and truth. Heidegger is rejecting the classification of truth under logic, and beauty under aesthet-ics (ibid., p. 16). But if beauty is to be understood as a manner of truth, what is characteristic of that manner of truth? In what follows, I will argue that desire responds to the hiddenness in the happening of truth, that beauty is that hiddenness in the presencing of entities. As such, beauty is not so much a manner of the happening of truth as the self-revelation of the thing to a desiring existent.
4. "We call beautiful for the eyes that which *of itself* is able to please those who see it." William of Auverge, quoted in Murphy, *Christ in the Form of Beauty*, p. 212.
5. In Genesis, man is created not to possess creation, but to name it. Cf. on this theme Benjamin, "The Language of Man and Language as Such," p. 64.
6. The term '*existentia*' first appears in the work of Marius Victorinus, a church father who wrote in the fourth century CE. Victorinus defines *existentia* as *prae-existens substan-tia*. After Victorinus it was not until the Thomists of the thirteenth century that *existentia* became a current term. Here the opposition is with *essentia*. In this context the distinction served to mark the distinction between knowing that god exists and knowing what god is.
7. Karl Jaspers expresses this thought, if somewhat obscurely, in his *Existenzphiloso-phie*: "Existence is freedom, but not without transcendence, from which it knows itself to be gifted [*Existenz ist Freiheit nicht ohne Transendenz, durch die sie sich geschenkt weiss*]."

My thanks to my colleague Heike Schmidt-Felzmann for her help in translating this rather cryptic sentence.

8. Cf. Romans 8:1: "the law of the spirit . . . has set you free from the law of sin and death" and 8:9: "You . . . live not by your natural inclinations but by the spirit."

9. See Levinas, "Philosophy and the Idea of Infinity," in Levinas: *Collected Philosophical Papers*, p. 56; on hunger and desire see further Sartre, *Being and Nothingness*, pp. 287–288.

10. Von Balthasar: *Theo-drama*, vol. 5, p. 603.

11. On acceptance and refusal as modalities of existence see further Mounier, *Le Personalisme*, pp. 63–64. This same structure is evident in Heidegger's distinction between authenticity and inauthenticity and Jaspers's distinction between *Dasein* and *Existenz*. Despite the difference between these accounts, the common insight is that existence is a burden on existents which cannot always be borne, but rather is a constant *possibility* which can be accepted or not.

12. For Heidegger, though, this movement of existence is in the end a movement of appropriation—*Eigentlichkeit*. Such appropriation is not egoism, but rather is the 'enowning' of existent and world in the event of being. No place is left here for the epiphenomenon of Judeo-Christianity—the appearance from elsewhere; or rather, there is only place here, but no sense of that which though occupying place is radically out of place, in the world but not of the world.

13. Mounier, *Le Personalisme*, p. 79.

14. We will need to distinguish in this respect between body and flesh, *Körper* and *Leib*, *corps* and *chair*, but I will leave such a discussion until chapter 5 on the Incarnation.

15. Cf. Sartre's famous example of the keyhole voyeur in *Being and Nothingness*, pp. 261–262.

16. Here it is a matter of indifference whether we are speaking of an act of dressing or undressing. Each involves a complex play of desire and need. As Marion puts it: "in order to remain the object of desire, the object strives maliciously not to strip itself too much, nor too quickly—for the stripping nude destroys what is desirable in it, because the stripping nude transforms itself into a simple object," Marion, *The Erotic Phenomenon*, p. 116.

17. Sartre's analysis of grace is important here: through grace the body is clothed even in its nakedness, clothing it with freedom, hence with excess. "In grace the body is the instrument which manifests freedom. . . . Facticity is clothed and disguised by grace, the nudity of the flesh is wholly present, but it cannot be seen. . . . The most graceful body is the naked body whose acts enclose it with an invisible garment, while entirely disrobing its flesh, while the flesh is totally present to the eyes of the spectator." *Being and Nothingness*, pp. 400–401.

18. Levinas, *Totality and Infinity*, p. 256.

19. But such intimacy is never total. The lovers remain outside each other. The theme of love will be pursued further in chapter 6.

20. Cf. Levinas on insomnia: "the Other within the Same who does not alienate the Same but awakens him. . . . It is an awakening that is an exigency or demand," Levinas *God, Death and Time*, p. 209. The following is indebted to Levinas's sustained attempts to think wakefulness. However, in thinking wakefulness as a determinant of existence, the account presented here, while alive to Levinas's warning to think the within "as at the same time outside," seeks to find this wakefulness in the movement 'without' of existence.

21. For Leibniz the difference between slumber and wakefulness is situated in consciousness, the threshold between slumber and wakefulness being that of apperception. See Leibniz's *Monadology*, §23, p. 20. But a self-conscious being can still be a slumbering existent in the sense that the objects of its consciousness are for it no less projections of its needs than the fantasies of its dreams. Desire, not apperception, opens the existent to that which is other and distant from itself.

22. This theme of asceticism is explored further in chapter 5.

23. On the theme of reverence see William Desmond's "On the Betrayal of Reverence."

24. Mounier, *Personalisme*, p. 79: *"L'être personnel est générosité."*

25. For a brief introduction to the problem of transcendentals amongst the scholastics see Murphy, *Christ in the Form of Beauty*, pp. 216–218.

26. Cf. Chrétien, *L'arche de la parole*, pp. 139–140. Marion in his almost disembodied account of the icon may well—by omission if not commission—fall into this tradition. I will address this question in more detail in chapter 5 on the Incarnation, but for the moment we may reflect on the following: "[the gaze] no longer experiences things as transparent—insufficiently weighed down by light and glory—and a last one finally presents itself as visible, splendid and luminous enough to be the first to attract, capture and fill it. This first visible will offer, for each gaze and in the measure of its scope, its idol." Marion, *God without Being*, p. 11.

27. Chrétien, *L'arche de la parole*, p. 107.

28. Pseudo-Dionysius, *The Divine Names*, ch. 4, pt. 7, p. 140.

29. Ibid., ch. 4, pt. 13, p. 145 (translation modified).

30. Aquinas in his "Commentary on Dionysius' Divine Names" states: "form is a certain radiance which comes from the first clarity [*claritas*]; and clarity belongs to the nature of beauty" (quoted in Eco, *The Aesthetics of Thomas Aquinas*, p. 251, n. 125). Aquinas of course does distinguish beauty and goodness in relation to appetite: goodness not beauty was the object of desire. But this understanding of desire as appetite relates desire to utility—to what it is good for—that is closer to need, as I am understanding it.

31. Possibly the subtlest account of this incarnate splendor we have from the medievals is from Bonaventure's *The Journey of the Mind to God*. For Bonaventure to understand god one must follow his traces which are material, temporal, and eternal. We can see god through perceived things but also in them, as he is in them by his essence, power, and presence. The image of the invisible god and the brightness of his glory and the image of his substance exist everywhere in the species (form) of objects. Hence, all things are beautiful and in some way pleasurable.

32. *Critique of Pure Reason*, B526/A598.

33. As Kant says: "the judgment of taste is merely contemplative, i.e., a judgment that, indifferent with regard to the existence of the object, merely connects its constitution (*Beschaffenheit*) together with the feeling of pleasure or displeasure." *Critique of the Power of Judgment*, p. 95.

34. This assumes that interest and need are correlative. As Kant puts it: "All interest presupposes a need or produces one; and as a determining ground of approval it no longer leaves the judgment on the object free" (ibid).

35. See ibid., p. 100.

36. Ibid., p. 101.

37. Kant, *Critique of Pure Reason*, B70.

38. Ibid., B25, A11.

39. Ibid., B26, A13.

40. For Kant the judgment of the sublime is connected to a disturbance of the mind (*Bewegung des Gemüts*), while judgment of beauty assumes a still contemplation (*ruhiger Kontemplation*). Kant, *Critique of the Power of Judgment*, p. 131.

41. Ibid., p. 129.

42. Ibid., p. 139.

43. Ibid., p. 136: the concept of a thing of nature "brings with it a determinate end."

44. Ibid., p. 144.

45. Ibid.

46. Ibid., p. 147.

47. Von Balthasar, *The Glory of the Lord,* vol. 5, p. 600.

48. Husserl, *Ideas Pertaining to a Pure Phenomenology,* vol. 2, p. 199.

49. See Anthony Steinbock's "Translator's Introduction" to Husserl, *Analyses Concerning Active and Passive Synthesis,* p. xlv.

50. Ibid., p. 148.

51. Ibid., p. 162: "Any kind of constituted sense is pregiven insofar as it exercises an affective allure. . . . Affective unities must be constituted in order for a world of objects to be constituted in subjectivity at all."

52. See ibid., p. 166.

53. Ibid., p. 167.

54. Ibid., p. 179.

55. Cf. Bonaventure, *The Journey of the Soul to God,* p. 33: "Desire is the strongest for what attracts the most."

56. "All things are beautiful, in some way pleasurable" (ibid., p. 25).

57. Maritain, *Creative Intuition,* p. 162.

58. Merleau-Ponty, *The Visible and the Invisible,* p. 50.

59. For this reason the attempt, as Merleau-Ponty makes clear, to express faith in constative, propositional statements is a secondary, reflective movement, parasitic on a prior faith. Faith is not for that reason inexpressible, it is rather inexpressible constatively. Again this does not mean that faith is non-linguistic, rather it is fundamental to linguistic communication to bring the silent meaning of the world to expression. I will return to this issue in the next section.

60. Merleau-Ponty, *The Visible and the Invisible,* p. 151.

61. See von Balthasar, *The Glory of the Lord,* vol. 4, p. 14.

62. It is to this that von Balthasar is referring when he speaks of "the identity of Christ's personal consciousness and his mission-consciousness, an identity that has no conceivable beginning." Von Balthasar, *Theo-drama,* vol. 3, p. 268.

63. Ibid., pp. 267–268.

64. This is the meaning of Barth's claim that Christ was the only complete human being. In the terms of this work we can say further that Christ was the only complete existent, the only being in whom being and existence coincided completely. Again, no truth claims are being made here; the *meaning* of the *figure* of Christ alone interests us here.

65. Cf. von Balthasar, *Theo-drama,* vol. 3, p. 178: "The mission of Jesus has no conceivable temporal beginning. But as it unfolds, through historical time, it enters increasingly into history."

66. Ibid., p. 159.

67. Ibid., p. 198. Cf. von Balthasar, *The Glory of the Lord,* vol. 7, p. 400: "the willingness of man to undergo expropriation is called faith."

68. On this theme see chapter 5.

69. Mounier, *Engagement de la foi,* p. 100.

70. This logic of loss and gain is at the heart of what Marion calls the "erotic reduction." See Marion, *The Erotic Phenomenon,* pp. 19–26.

71. There is here an attitude of rupture characterizing the epoché which is fundamentally vocational. See Husserl, "The Vienna Lecture," in Husserl, *The Crisis of the European Sciences,* p. 270; cf. further Mounier, *Engagement de la foi,* p. 202.

72. Origen, *Contra Celsum,* vol. 2, pt. 67, pp. 117–118.

73. Not alone does the aesthetic reveal the ethical here (as von Balthasar suggests), but it is transformed by the religious.

74. Levinas, "Reality and its Shadow," in Hand, ed., *The Levinas Reader,* p. 137.
75. This is an issue to which I will return in chapter 5 on the Incarnation.
76. Cf. von Balthasar, *The Glory of the Lord,* vol. 7, p. 407.
77. In this sense Heidegger's polemos of earth and world (sky) repeats key Platonic structures. See Heidegger, "Origin of the Work of Art," pp. 23–33.
78. In this respect Christianity is closer to Greek myth than to Greek philosophy. In mythology the positivity of self-affirmation was recognized and the hero in Greek tragedy embodied this positivity. The tragic hero affirms the uniqueness of the individual, who is both singular and embodies universal human predicaments. Cf. von Balthasar, *Theo-drama,* vol. 2, p. 47.
79. Pascal, *Pensées,* §423/§243 (French edition).
80. Cf. Paul, 1 Corinthians 1:26: "consider, brothers, how you were called; not many of you are wise by human standards."
81. In recent years Quentin Meillasoux has coined the term 'correlationism' to refer to what he understands as a relativistic account of truth and being from Kant to Heidegger. This is not the place to discuss the merits of his analysis. Suffice to say in this context that an account of truth as correlation of soul and reality is one which is pre-Kantian and indeed prior to modern subjectivism. In fact it is present already in Plato's divided line. See further Meillassoux, *After Finitude,* pp. 5–7.
82. Again here theologically the issue of the natural desire for the supernatural, the chiasmic intersection of both, which the discussion of de Lubac's work brought to the fore, forms the background. As de Lubac puts it: "If . . . the desire [for God] is truly a 'natural inclination,' it is not by that fact a 'sufficient' or 'proportionate' inclination . . . so this desire is unable to strive 'suitably' or 'efficaciously.'" A little later he goes on: "it is the 'light of glory' which strengthens the intellect and thus raises it up to a vision of the divine essence." De Lubac, *The Mystery of the Supernatural,* pp. 111–112.
83. Cf. chapter 6 on creation.
84. Augustine, *On Christian Doctrine,* chs. 1, 3–5, pp. 4–6.
85. Cf. Nicholas of Cusa, *The Vision of God,* pp. 78–79. "For the intelligible it knowth does not sate it, nor the intelligible, whereof it is utterly ignorant, but only the intelligible, which it knowth to be so intelligible that it can never be fully understood—this alone can sate it."
86. "While the animal's life is centric, the human life is eccentric." Plessner, *Die Stufen des Organischen und der Mensch,* p. 291.
87. Heidegger, "Phenomenology and Theology," in Heidegger, *Pathmarks,* p. 43.
88. Pannenberg, in an essay titled "Analogy and Doxology," speaks of the Christian speech about god as indirect. "In the moment in which we grasp by means of a simple event, the totality of reality in which we live and around which our lives circulate, there we experience a work of God in the individual event. . . . The indirectness of speech about God has to do, first of all with the difference between the current, concrete event and the totality of reality experienced therein." In Pannenberg, *Basic Questions in Theology,* pp. 229–230.
89. Cf. Husserl, *Ideas Pertaining to a Pure Phenomenology,* vol. 1, p. 61.
90. Husserl, *Experience and Judgment,* p. 80.
91. Weil, *Waiting on God,* p. 58.
92. Ibid., p. 53.
93. Cf. Chrétien, *L'arche de la parole,* p. 62.
94. Ibid., p. 66: "Silence itself sings, when it is the silence of desire."
95. "Hope is neither expectation nor anticipation, but an opening to what precisely comes from beyond expectation and anticipation." Bloechl, "The Twilight of the Idols and the Night of the Senses," p. 165.

2. Light and Dark

1. Cf. Derrida, "Faith and Knowledge," p. 77.
2. "That region which is mingled with darkness, the world of becoming and passing away." Plato, *Republic*, 508 d7.
3. For this and what follows see *De Anima*, 422b17–424a14.
4. On this issue cf. Derrida's discussion of the mediacy of touch in Aristotle. Derrida, *On Touching*, pp. 17–19.
5. The question of the need for compulsion here is one which is relatively lacking in discussion by Plato scholars. For a useful article on this, which attempts to reconcile this discourse of compulsion with that of eros in the *Symposium*, see Barney, "Eros and Necessity in the Ascent from the Cave."
6. While the relation of the divided line to the other allegories is not uncontroversial, its place between the allegory of the sun and of the cave points to its pivotal position.
7. As Barth puts it: "Faith as response to revelation is not mere opinion or belief as in Plato's divided line, it is knowledge." Barth, *Church Dogmatics*, vol. 2, pt. 1, p. 13.
8. For a classic discussion of this topic see Lovejoy, *The Great Chain of Being*, pp. 61–64.
9. See Turner, *The Darkness of God*, p. 27.
10. See Pseudo-Dionysius, *Divine Names* VII, 2, p. 177: "For the divine intellect does not know by learning about beings in terms of beings; rather from itself and in itself it comprehends beforehand the understanding, knowledge, and being of all beings according to cause."
11. It is instructive that Pseudo-Dionysius, in following the allegory of the cave, displays a resolute intellectualism, such that the journey to god is understood as an ascent of mind, and knowing takes precedence over love. Cf. Turner, *The Darkness of God*, p. 47.
12. The following analysis is indebted to Derrida, as it is indeed to Benjamin. The messianic question which lies at the core of both of their analyses will not, however, become explicit until the next chapter. See Derrida, "Des Tours de Babel," and Benjamin, "On the Language of Man and Language as Such."
13. It seems more likely that the reference to scaling the heavens was meant as hyperbole. On this issue see Alter, *Genesis*, p. 46.
14. See Gowen, *Genesis 1–11*, p. 118.
15. That these phrases mirror the terms used with reference to god's creation in Genesis I and can be understood in terms of human creativity as that which is the image of the divine creation is cogently discussed by Elad Lalipot in his "What is the Reason for Translating Philosophy? I. Undoing Babel." Like Lalipot, I see the dispersal of humanity in the story of Babel not as a punishment, but rather as an account of the origins of diversity. I would like to thank Veronica O'Neill for bringing this article to my attention.
16. Benjamin, "On Language as such and the Language of Man," p. 68.
17. Ibid., p. 155.
18. Merleau-Ponty has done more than anyone to uncover this space of silence. See "Indirect Language and the Voices of Silence."
19. On this theme see Waldenfels, *Bruchlinien der Erfahrung*, p. 33.
20. This relation of touch and sight has been understood differently phenomenologically from Husserl through Merleau-Ponty to Levinas. In Husserl touch has primacy over sight in relation to corporeality and hence sensation generally: a being with only vision would not be an incarnate being, Husserl tells us. But for this very reason sight retains the traditional priority in terms of knowledge: with light we are in the realm of spirit. See Husserl, *Ideas pertaining to a pure phenomenology*, vol. 2, pp. 74–76, 155–159. Merleau-Ponty's attempt to understand vision in terms of reversibility, if it remains incomplete and suggestive, holds

out the promise of irreducible corporeality in experience and knowledge. See Merleau-Ponty, *The Visible and the Invisible*, pp. 138–146. Levinas, finally, sees touch as appropriative, as attempting to break through the distance between self and other. Cf. Levinas, *Totality and Infinity*, p. 191. Cathryn Vasseleu's *Textures of Light* is an excellent discussion of these themes. In the context of the present concerns what is crucial is that understanding is irreducibly visual, but that vision has only the—fallen—illusion of imperiousness, an illusion central to Plato's light allegories.

21. As such Genesis is not an allegory in the self-conscious manner of the cave story.

22. This reflects the nature of thinking itself, the nature that is of the perception of the intelligible. Heidegger expresses this by saying that "thinking views with an ear and hears with an eye." Heidegger, *The Principle of Reason*, p. 48.

23. The use of this term beloved of Monet is not accidental: Monet in his painting shows the way in which light appears not as emanating from a source, but rather as forming so to speak a second skin around things, making them luminous and letting them appear (truth) and shine splendidly (beauty). On this issue see Sallis, *Shades—Of Painting at the Limit*, pp. 44–45.

24. As suggested in Job (38:19), the source of light is a mystery known only to god.

25. Pseudo-Dionysius takes up this same theme: "If some do not share in this light, this is not due to the weakness or slowness of its ability to distribute light, but of a non-openness to sharing light which is due to an unsuitableness to receive light on the part of those not illumined by the sun." *Divine Names*, vol. 4, pt. 4, p. 136.

26. As von Balthasar puts it: "The Christian *epiphaneia* of God has nothing about it of the simple radiance of the Platonic sun of the Good." Von Balthasar, *The Glory of the Lord*, vol. 2, p. 12. Origen quoting John's first letter on Christ as the true light (John 1:9) goes on to say: "but has nothing in common with the light of our sun." Origen, *Contra Celsum*, ch. 1, 2, p. 19.

27. This is not to say that the Christ event is unrepeatable. On the contrary, it is precisely to say that it can be known only in its repetition as an event.

28. See, respectively, Heidegger, *Being and Time*, §44; Heidegger, *Four Seminars*, p. 80; Merleau-Ponty, *The Visible and the Invisible*; and Levinas, "There is: existence without existents," pp. 31–35.

29. I will return to this theme in chapter 4.

30. Gregory of Nyssa refers in this context to smell, taste, and touch. See Gregory of Nyssa, *From Glory to Glory*, p. 209.

31. Otto, *The Idea of the Holy*, p. 16.

32. See John of the Cross, *Dark Night of the Soul*, ch. 1, 9, p. 316.

33. Cf. ibid., ch. 1, 13, p. 327.

34. John of the Cross, in contrast, understands the darkness of god by analogy to the darkness caused to our visual faculty in looking at the sun. In this sense the eyes of faith are closer to those of the body than the intellect. Ibid., ch. 2, 5, p. 335.

35. This will be the subject of an extended discussion in the next chapter.

36. The allusion here of course is to Heidegger's discussion of the Greek temple in the "Origin of the Work of Art," pp. 20–22.

37. John of the Cross, *Dark Night of the Soul*, ch. 2, 4, pp. 334–335.

38. Ibid., ch. 2, 9, p. 346.

39. Pseudo-Dionysius, *The Mystical Theology*, ch. 2, p. 216.

40. Hence, the centrality of hope to which I will return in the next chapter.

41. Lacoste, *Experience and the Absolute*, p. 45 (emphasis in original).

42. Ibid., p. 37.

43. Ibid., p. 43.

44. Pseudo-Dionysius, *The Mystical Theology*, vol. 1, p. 211.

3. Glory and Being

1. As Feuerbach puts it: "Being is founded on the particularity of 'this.'" Feuerbach, *Principles of Future Philosophy*, p. 43 (translation modified).

2. This is of course not an uncontroversial claim and assumes a certain Christological stance. In the context of the concerns of this book, however, all that needs to be accepted is that this is a possible and legitimate interpretation of Christ. For the contrary view among the church fathers see Cyril of Alexandria: "To Eulogius" in Cyril of Alexandria, *Select Letters*, p. 65: "there was no mingling or mixing of flesh and word."

3. As Pseudo-Dionysius puts it: "all things desire it [peace]." *Divine Names*, ch. 11, 3, p. 195.

4. Plato's account of participation depends on such an implication: things by virtue of participating in the forms are understood as being imitations of the forms (*Parmenides* 132d2–3: "this participation they [things] come to have in the forms is nothing but their being made in their image." At the other end of the philosophical tradition, Hegel's movement of sublation (*Aufhebung*) depends on the implication that what is self-identical is the becoming of itself through being-in itself, "since the self-identical, which is supposed first to sunder itself of becomes its opposite, is an abstraction or is *already itself* a sundered moment, its self-sundering is therefore a supersession of what it is, and therefore the supersession of its dividedness." Hegel, *The Phenomenology of Spirit*, p. 101.

5. Heidegger, *Being and Time*, p. 55 / *Sein und Zeit*, 59.

6. Ibid., p. 51/54.

7. Ibid. (translation modified).

8. See Macquarie and Robinson's helpful note in their translation of *Being and Time*, p. 80, n. 3.

9. Heidegger, *Being and Time*, p. 51 / *Sein und Zeit*, 55.

10. Ibid., p. 53/56–57.

11. Ibid., p. 62/66.

12. Ibid., p. 64/68 (translation modified).

13. Ibid.

14. Ibid., p. 64/69 (translation modified).

15. Ibid., p. 67/71 (emphasis in original; translation modified).

16. Ibid., p. 78/83–84 (translation modified).

17. Ibid., p. 78/84 (translation modified).

18. "Previously letting be does not mean first to bring something to its being and produce it, but rather to discover something that is already an 'entity' in its handiness and thus let it be encountered as the being-of its being" (ibid., p. 79/85). As should be clear here, any simple pragmatist reading of these sections is mistaken from the beginning.

19. Ibid., p. 80/86.

20. Ibid., p. 81/87 [translation modified].

21. Ibid., p. 58/61.

22. Ibid., p. 66/70.

23. Ibid., p. 67/71.

24. For an account of this 'logic of failure' see my *The Time of Revolution*, p. 82.

25. Heidegger, *Being and Time*, p. 67 / *Sein und Zeit*, p. 71.

26. Ibid., p. 68/73 (translation modified).

27. Ibid., p. 69/74.

28. Ibid., p. 70/74–75 (translation modified).

29. Ibid., p. 70/75 (translation modified).

30. See Merleau-Ponty, "Cezanne's Doubt," pp. 78–79.

31. Heidegger, *Being and Time*, p. 65 / *Sein und Zeit*, p. 69.

32. "[T]he sensuous this that is meant cannot be reached by language, which belongs to consciousness, i.e., to that which is inherently universal." Hegel, *Phenomenology of Spirit*, p. 66.

33. See Heidegger, *Being and Time*, pp. 65, 330–331 / *Sein und Zeit*, pp. 69, 361.

34. Cf. Agamben, *The Time that Remains*, pp. 24–25: "In pushing each thing toward itself through the as not, the messianic does not simply cancel out this figure, but it makes it pass, it prefigures its end—the passing of the figure of the world."

35. Heidegger, *Being and Time*, p. 111 / *Sein und Zeit*, p. 118.

36. Ibid., p. 115/122.

37. See on this theme Breton, *The Word and the Cross*, p. 42.

38. Von Balthasar, *The Glory of the Lord*, vol. 1, p. 437.

39. Derrida understands the messianic dimension as not depending upon any messianism, as following no determinate revelation, as belonging "properly to no Abrahamic religion," but to be an issue of a "general structure of experience." Derrida, "Faith and Knowledge," p. 56. For Christianity, though, the messiah is an event which has occurred and continues to occur in the hearts of believers. The event of Christ is one which calls for an openness to the world for that which it cannot see, and as such the claim that the messiah has come is a claim that the time of the present is both a time of the messiah as having come and a time of the messiah, in the second coming, as to come. What this suggests is a break with the Husserlian account of time as retention and protention, such that all at once future and past are contained in the one moment, that moment being lived as if everything depended upon it from the beginning to the end. This is possible only if the moment is a way beyond all worldly things, all systems of signs, toward an origin which is precisely nothing, an origin which all things manifest as in excess of what they signify.

40. Cf. Agamben, *The Time that Remains*, p. 76.

41. "The messianic vocation nullifies the whole subject—'it is no longer I that live, but the messiah living in me [1 *Galatians*, 2:20]'" (ibid., p. 41).

42. Heraclitus, *Diels/Kranz* [henceforth DK], 22 B 53.

43. Cf. Psalm 46: 9: "[Yahweh] breaks the bow, he snaps the spear, shields he burns in the fire."

44. Tertullian, *De spectaculis*, p. 255.

45. This is particularly the case with Christianity, which has only one genuine (in the sense of specifically Christian) article of faith: that of the Incarnation, which is not an article of faith at all but rather characterizes faith as openness toward the ultimate unworldliness of a fleshy being.

46. To again quote Tertullian: "The world [*saeculum*] is God's, what is worldly is the devil's." Tertullian, *De spectaculis*, p. 271.

47. In a similar tone William Desmond writes: "The primal 'it is good' . . . celebrates the creation coming to be not out of *polemos*, but out of giving as giving, which releases the gift of creation into its own good." Desmond, "On Peace—Between Philosophy and Religion," p. 326.

48. As part of his ongoing discussion of the Homo Sacer and the politics of 'bare life,' Giorgio Agamben has made an important contribution to the understanding of glory in his recent work *The Kingdom and the Glory*. In this work Agamben argues forcefully that the economic understanding of the Trinity formed a paradigm of government which found expressions in modernity in the separation of powers. Furthermore, as this economy is an economy of glorification, this paradigm is one which contains a strong liturgical element. See Agamben, *The Kingdom and the Glory*, pp. 17–38. While not denying the pertinence of his analysis it seems to me to be a mistake to read this development back into the theological questions

out of which the account of glory arose. The 'glory of the Lord' is a messianic concept (as Agamben acknowledges) and is one which tends to subvert rather than institute government. In this respect Marcel Gauchet's account of Christianity as the religion of the departure from religion (to which Agamben does not refer), that is, the departure from religion as structuring "united social body" to a "regime of duality" (of God and world), seems to me largely correct. See Gauchet, *The Disenchantment of the World,* especially pp. 104–105, 130–144. In developing his account of the "deconstruction of Christianity," Jean-Luc Nancy "presupposes . . . absolute agreement" with Gauchet on this point. For Nancy this points to Christianity's constant movement of self-overcoming, a movement which *is* only as response to that which it cannot capture in itself. See Nancy, "The Deconstruction of Christianity," pp. 142 and 146. In the course of his account Agamben distances himself decisively from the theological aesthetics of glory found in von Balthasar and Barth, to whose work the present volume is indebted. The present work brackets any direct discussion of questions of sovereignty and power, although they are clearly present in the notion of glory. This is justified on the basis of the claim animating this work that 'glory,' understood in terms of *kabod, doxa,* and *gloria,* is a basic phenomenological datum and one which breaks with, while remaining in critical relation to, the mundanity of the political world.

49. DK B 1:29–33. See further Heidegger's account of doxa in Heidegger, *Introduction to Metaphysics,* pp. 108–109. It is striking that Heidegger ignores the biblical transformation of doxa and is able for that reason to conclude his account with the reaffirmation of Nietzsche's claim that Christianity is 'Platonism for the People' (ibid., p. 111).

50. For the following see Kittel, *Theological Dictionary of the New Testament,* vol. 1, pp. 232–255.

51. Von Balthasar, *The Glory of the Lord,* vol. 6, p. 33.

52. Rahner, "The Hiddenness of God," in Rahner, *Theological Investigations,* vol. 13, p. 243.

53. Jean-Luc Marion talks in this context of bedazzlement. See his "Evidence and Bedazzlement," pp. 66–67. Bedazzlement arises when the gaze cannot bear what appears to it. This appearance must be perceived in order to bedazzle. It bedazzles, however, only if seen as a gift of love, and this is only possible through love "which bears all" (1 Corinthians 13:7).

54. Cf. John 1:10; 1 Corinthians 1:21. See the discussion of this theme in Heidegger, "On the Essence of Ground," pp. 112–113.

55. See Pickstock, *After Writing,* pp. 40–42.

56. Girard and Gauchet in very different ways give expression to this withdrawal from the political in Christianity. See further Girard, *Things Hidden Since the Foundation of the World* and Gauchet, *The Disenchantment of the World.*

57. Gauchet, *The Disenchantment of the World,* pp. 101–161.

58. "Our words are not our own property, but His. . . . We use our words improperly and pictorially—as we can now say looking back from God's revelation—when we apply them within the confines of what is appropriate to us as creatures." Barth, *Church Dogmatics,* vol. 2, pt. 1, p. 229. For Barth revelation demonstrates for us the analogical relation of our words and the Word of God. This relation is one between human language and language itself. We see language in this way through faith. When we understand language only cognitively, we mistake it as a system of signs for worldly manipulation, as that which is at hand. See Ward, *Barth, Derrida and the Language of Theology,* pp. 97–102.

59. Cf. Milbank, *The Word made Strange,* pp. 138–139.

60. Kevin Hart puts it well: "no one inaugurates a relationship with God: prayer is always a response, even though it can feel like a response to silence." Hart, "The Experience of the Kingdom of God," p. 79.

61. Kant, *Religion Within the Bounds of Reason Alone,* pp. 102–104.

62. The scriptural writer who speaks most of the gospel, *euaggelium*, the good news—Paul—understood that good news as the death and resurrection of the Christ. In other words, not the message which Christ brought, but the event of divine self-revelation is the crucial thing.

63. Weil, *Notebooks*, vol. 2, p. 520.

64. Ibid., p. 155.

65. This view is echoed in more contemporary times in the work of Karl Barth. We do not know what particular attitude God may have to our fellow creatures and what may be their decisive particularity within the cosmos. Cf. Barth, *Church Dogmatics*, vol. 3, pt. 2, p. 78. Barth goes on to say that for all we know the glory of other creatures may be greater than our own (ibid., p. 138).

66. Within the eschatological view of Christian perception of the world, hierarchy is in principle undone. Cf. 1 Corinthians 15:24: "After that will come the end, when he will hand over the kingdom to God the father having abolished every principality, every ruling force and power."

67. Von Balthasar, *The Glory of the Lord*, vol. 7, p. 64.

68. See Jüngel, *God as the Mystery the World*, p. 77.

69. It is, as Ramsey points out, in humiliation that the glory of Christ is revealed—the humiliation of birth, of the messianic secret, and of death. Cf. Ramsey, *The Glory of God*, pp. 36–45.

70. Caputo, *The Weakness of God*, p. 34.

71. See Barth, *Church Dogmatics*, vol. 1, pt. 2, pp. 110–113.

72. This alone undermines Gnostic readings of Jesus of Nazareth.

73. The centrality of death—its place at the heart of human existence, rather than at the outer margins—is best exemplified in the Gothic cathedral. On entering a Gothic cathedral the believer is symbolically dying. On approaching the church the doorway is elaborate: above it the last judgment is often depicted, yet from the inside the door hardly appears. It is not there to be exited: to exit is an unavoidable accident which is symbolically impossible; symbolically it means a return from the "heavenly Jerusalem," in terms of which the cathedral is built, to the world. On this see Georg Simmel, "Bridge and Door," in *Simmel on Culture*, Frisby et al., eds., pp. 173–175. The Gothic cathedral represents the heavenly Jerusalem, or rather it represents motion toward the heavenly Jerusalem, the force of attraction of that heavenly Jerusalem, the desire and seeking after that which marks the end of the world, a desire for that dwelling of God among mortals which is to come, as John's Apocalypse tells us (Revelations 21:1–2). If entry into such a church is symbolic death, the ritual center, the altar, contains death itself: the mortal remains of a saint.

74. I will return to this in chapter 4.

75. Breton, *The Word and the Cross*, p. 127.

76. This differs fundamentally with the view expressed in the Pseudo-Aristotelian text *de Mundo* that the cosmos appears as the most radiant glory, because perfect. Cf. von Balthasar, *The Glory of the Lord*, vol. 4, p. 222.

77. Von Balthasar, *The Glory of the Lord*, vol. 1, p. 119.

78. Cf. Ramsey, *The Glory of God*, pp. 33–35.

79. Leibniz, *Monadology*, §6, p. 17.

80. Kierkegaard, *Philosophical Fragments*, pp. 90–93.

81. A non-doxological understanding of the world, one which reduces the world to constative sentences, cannot overcome a Cartesian understanding of time as discrete moments in which the future (and the past) are without cognitive content and hence cannot be thought. The Christian understanding of time resembles the Cartesian in the priority it gives to the

moment, and in this respect Bultmann is right to see a similarity between Christian and Cartesian time. But as Bultmann also says the Christian moment is a moment of decision, hence a moment turned toward future and past, but in the light of the transforming power of the moment. See Breton, *The Word and the Cross*, p. 23.

82. Von Balthasar is correct I think in his interpretation of the "Song of Songs" as in its elevation of eros setting up the world as self-sufficient before God. See von Balthasar, *The Glory of the Lord*, vol. 6, pp. 130–137. This view, however, is implicitly challenged by Kearney, *The God Who May Be*, pp. 53–60.

83. See Scheler on the fundamental place of agon in the Greek notion of love—eros: "Even the objects try to surpass each other in a race for victory, in a cosmic 'agon' for the deity." Scheler, "Love and Knowledge," p. 65.

84. Girard, *Things Hidden*, p. 270.

85. See Agamben, "On Potentiality," in Agamben, *Potentialities*, pp. 177–184.

86. See Z. Hayes, "Christology—Cosmology," pp. 51–55.

87. Kittel, *Theological Dictionary of the New Testament*, vol. 1, pp. 93–94.

4. Night, Faith, and Evil

1. Pascal, *Pensées*, §188 (§267 French edition): "The last step that Reason takes is to recognize that here is an infinity of things that lie beyond it. Reason is a poor thing indeed if it does not recognize that."

2. Feuerbach, *Principles of Future Philosophy*, p. 28.

3. As Augustine puts it: "that ineffable light caused us to turn aside our gaze." "On the Trinity," bk. 15, ch. 6, pp. 176–177.

4. See von Balthasar, *The Glory of the Lord*, vol. 6, pp. 41–44.

5. Cf. John 4:13: "Whoever drinks this water will be thirsty again."

6. See Sartre's analysis of the dancer in *Being and Nothingness*, p. 389.

7. Cf. Nicholas of Cusa, *The Vision of God*, bk. 5, p. 20: "Albeit I turn away from Thee when I turn utterly to some other thing, yet . . . Thy never move Thine eyes nor Thy glance [from me]."

8. Von Balthasar, *The Glory of the Lord*, vol. 1, p. 118.

9. Gregory of Nyssa, *The Life of Moses*, vol. 2, §239, p. 116.

10. Cusa, *The Vision of God*, vol. 2, p. 11.

11. Provocation is a key concept in Levinas's later account of the ethical; cf. Levinas, *Totality and Infinity*, pp. 198–201. Responsibility for Levinas arises out of a negativity, a provocation against me and for the other. The other affects me by addressing me, by making a claim on me to which I must respond. This claim need not be verbally articulated; in fact the mute presence of a beggar lays as much claim on me as the bantering approaches of a salesman. Levinas understands the source of such affectedness as the face of the other. The face of the other is not simply that which I can see, but rather that which I cannot see, that which sees, looks upon, me. This face gazing upon me refuses me the luxury of being alone in my world, refuses me a life without provocation. The ultimate provocation, that which lies at the core of all provocation, is the provocation to murder, to annihilate that face which calls me to account for myself. This is the ultimate provocation because it calls forth a violence which is from the beginning futile. The only way I can murder the other is to undermine his very otherness, to reduce him to a merely physical thing, a mass of flesh which I can of course destroy. But gaze of the other is irreducible to such mere physicality and fleshiness. The ambiguity of the face of the other in Levinas's account lies in the fact that it both brings murder into the world and declares its impossibility. The other calls forth the ultimate violence, murder,

while denying me the power to inflict it. The statement, 'thou shalt not kill,' which the other utters without doing so expressly, is in this pre-moral sense as much a dare as an injunction: the other dares me not to kill him; this is the provocation of the other. Where the other is, there can be no peace. This may appear to contradict the inner intention of Levinas's philosophy. Yet, peace for Levinas comes not from the other, but from the I (ibid., p. 304). This is so because violence arises not in the 'I,' not in the realm of the same at all, but precisely through the penetration of the same by the other. If there is an obligation in the being of the other—a claim on me—by the same token there is the invitation to a violation of this claim. This violation is initiated by the other. My powerlessness to kill—understood as an incapacity of my autonomous will—lies in being affected by the initiatory being of the other. My act—or my lack of acting—is a response to this initiation. As such at the roots of responsibility and the ethical is a certain violence of provocation. That which provokes me calls me and does so against myself. At the roots of the ethical is a possibility of profound violence. Love and violence are both rooted in this prior provocation of the other, this prior violence. This assumes an existence closed in to itself, an existence separated from the other. Indeed, this view of existence forms the fundamental beginning of Levinas's analysis. But it is difficult to see how such an existence can be provoked. Stones do not weep, because stones are not toward the other. To be provoked is to be capable of being provoked. This 'being capable,' 'being able,' is existence in its movement. Without existence there can be no ethics. As such the movement of existence cannot be reduced to its worldliness as Levinas does. Furthermore, the movement of existence is a movement of attraction; attraction is the primary provocation. Only a being which is attracted, which seeks beyond itself, whose existence is desire, can be provoked either to violence or to love. The 'peace of the Lord' is rooted in such existence and is always at the same time unsettled by such existence.

12. Cusa, *Vision of God*, ch. 7, pp. 28–29.

13. Cf. ibid., ch. 6, p. 27: "Thy [God's] face cannot be found except veiled; but that very darkness reveals Thy face to be there, beyond all veils . . . as when our eye seeks to look on the case of the sun."

14. Only with the advent of the mechanical clock do we count time at night. Previous to that the hour was always an hour of the light.

15. See the account of the vigil in Lacoste, *Experience and the Absolute*, p. 79: "every ethical duty having been honoured, man gives to the Absolute the time (and thus the being) he might otherwise have given to sleep."

16. Ibid., p. 79.

17. Ibid.

18. Lacoste, "Présence et affection," in Lacoste, *Presence et Parousia*, p. 36: "We open the non-liturgical place, in the strength of our faith, and we agree in advance to nocturnal non-experience in which we content ourselves to know that one is there in whom we believe and to whom we wish to be available." [*Nous ouvrons le non-lieu liturgique, à la force de notre foi, et nous consentons par avance à la non-expérience nocturne dans laquelle nous nous contenterons de savoir qu'un est là en qui nous croyons et auquel nous nous voulons disponibles*].

19. Cf. *Parmenides* 156 d–e.

20. Pseudo-Dionysius, "Letter Three (to Gaius)," in Pseudo-Dionysius, *The Divine Names*, p. 264.

21. Cusa, *Vision of God*, ch. 9, p. 44.

22. Marcel, "Belonging and Disposability," in Marcel, *Creative Fidelity*, p. 49.

23. Pseudo-Dionysius, *Mystical Theology*, ch. 2, p. 215.

24. Ibid., ch. 1, p. 211.

25. See Häring, *Sin in a Secular Age*, pp. 26–34.

26. Marion says of the idol that "it shows that which . . . occupies the field of the visible . . . invests it only on the basis of vision itself." Marion, *God without Being*, p. 26. Such an understanding remains incomplete because it fails to follow the invisible within the field of the visible on the basis of vision. For Marion the idol results from an abandonment of the invisible. But the visible is not without the invisible; the appearance to sight gives only through a withdrawal. The idol does not so much mark the displacement of the invisible (cf. Marion, *In Excess*, p. 68), as it does being fascinated by the immanence of the world reflected in the thing. The invisible in the idol is the invisible of this world, in fact something close to the invisible explored by the later Merleau-Ponty: "the invisible of this world, that which inhabits this world, sustains it, renders it visible, its own and interior possibility, the Being of this being." Merleau-Ponty, *The Visible and the Invisible*, p. 151. The idol expresses the invisible of this world. But things express their own being created. This being created is an invisibility presenting the thing as an expression of its invisible coming into the world.

27. Cf. Blumenberg, *Lebenszeit und Weltzeit*, pp. 80–85.

28. Cusa, *Vision of God*, ch. 13, pp. 59–61.

29. Pseudo-Dionysius, *Mystical Theology*, ch. 5, pp. 221–222; cf. Turner, *The Darkness of God*, pp. 43–45.

30. Such a giving praise is not a giving thanks to God for having created the world; that would be to "love like a whore," as Scheler quotes Hugo de Saint Victor as saying (Scheler, *Ressentiment*, p. 72). As Scheler goes on to elucidate: "We should not love God because of his heaven and earth: we should love heaven and earth because they are God's and because they adumbrate eternal love by means of sensible *expression*" (ibid.).

31. *Dark Night of the Soul*, ch. 1, 10, p. 315.

32. Ibid., ch. 1, 13, pp. 320–327.

33. Ibid., ch. 2, 4, p. 334.

34. Ibid., ch. 2, 5, p. 335. Divine light is darkness to the soul because in its height it transcends the talent of the soul and because the goodness God shows makes the soul suffer its own impurity. Again here the light of God—the glory of God—is being contrasted to the light of the world. In worldly terms divine light is darkness.

35. Ibid., ch. 2, 9, p. 348.

36. Ibid.

37. Ibid., ch. 2, 14, p. 362.

38. Cf. *Ascent to Mount Carmel*, ch. 2, 3, p. 110: "The intellect, *by its own power,* comprehends only natural knowledge" (my emphasis).

39. See further von Balthasar, *The Glory of the Lord*, vol. 1, pp. 1131–1141.

40. *Dark Night*, ch. 2, 16, p. 367.

41. *Ascent of Mount Carmel*, ch. 2, 3, p. 110.

42. *Dark Night*, ch. 2, 21, p. 381. The two other theological virtues (hope and charity) perform similarly with respect to memory and will.

43. See *Ascent to Mount Carmel*, ch. 2, 3, p. 110.

44. Cf. 2 Corinthians 13:3–10. Cf. also von Balthasar, *Glory of the Lord*, vol. 1, pp. 261–264.

45. *Being and Time*, pp. 140–141 / *Sein und Zeit*, p. 150.

46. Ibid., p. 135/144: "Understanding is the existential being of the ownmost potentiality of being of Dasein in such a way that this being discloses in itself what its very being is about."

47. A term of course reminiscent of Kierkegaard, but for Heidegger, too, reason in its ungroundedness points toward the pre-rational. Despite Heidegger's denials that this leap should be understood as a leap of faith, it is difficult to escape such a conclusion. Cf. Derrida, "Faith and Knowledge," pp. 94–95.

48. Kierkegaard, *Fear and Trembling*, p. 66.

49. Ibid., p. 84.
50. Ibid., p. 85.
51. Ibid., p. 88.
52. Ibid., p. 89.
53. Ibid., p. 89.
54. Ibid., p. 78.
55. A peripheral figure in the Synoptic Gospels—simply mentioned as one of the twelve apostles—Thomas appears three times in John's Gospel (11:16, 14:5, 20:24–29). On each occasion he is both uncomprehending and faithful.
56. See on this point Most, *Doubting Thomas*, pp. 69–73.
57. See Bultmann, "Concerning the Hidden and Revealed God," in Bultmann, *Existence and Faith*, p. 30: "God must be a hidden and mysterious God, full of contradictions and riddles. Otherwise our inner life would become static, and we would lose the power to obtain experience from life's fullness."
58. What is provisionally stated here will be developed in chapter 6.
59. On this point see Agamben, *The Time that Remains*, p. 181.
60. Mounier, *Le Personalisme*, p. 6.
61. "It is an astonishing fact that the OT did not develop any word for conscience." Kittel, *Theological Dictionary of the New Testament*, vol. 7, p. 908. The first mention of conscience in the Hebrew scriptures is in the late, Hellenistic-influenced book of Wisdom (cf. 17:11). But clearly that which 'conscience' expresses is closely associated with accounts of the 'heart' in the Hebrew scriptures.
62. Leibniz, *Monadology*, §74, p. 26.
63. Such a living is characteristic of Christian asceticism, as we will see in the next chapter.
64. Descartes, *Meditations*, in the *Philosophical Works*, vol. 2, p. 35.

5. Incarnation and Asceticism

1. Socrates understands death in terms of a liberation of the soul from the body and the uniting of the soul with the forms. The contingency of not just human existence but individual existence also is undone. "If we are ever to have pure knowledge of anything we must get rid of the body and contemplate things by themselves with the soul by itself" (*Phaedo*, 66d5).
2. Still an indispensable work in understanding such a logic of purity and defilement is Douglas, *Purity and Danger*.
3. On this background see Otto, *Die Götter Griechenlands*.
4. Although of course this consequence was and is strongly resisted in much Christological thought, hence the claim made at the Council of Chalcedon that Christ was a true man and a true God but that there was no mixing of these two natures. The point, however, is precisely that such a mixing is possible in Christianity without ending in monstrosity (as it would in pre-Christian thought), precisely because God is nothing of the world, hence not a distinct nature in the world. On this point see Sokolowski, *The God of Reason and Faith*, p. 36.
5. Cf. Milbank, "The Double Glory or Paradox versus Dialectic: On not quite agreeing with Slavoj Žižek," in Milbank and Žižek, *The Monstrosity of Christ*, pp. 110–233.
6. Disgust, which Martha Nussbaum has persuasively argued, is closely linked to anxiety regarding our own animality. Nussbaum, *Hiding from Humanity*, pp. 89–98.
7. Cf. above chapter 1.
8. The 'desert father' John Cassian explicitly compares spiritual struggle to the physical struggles of athletes in the Olympic games. See Cassian, *The Institutes*, p. 125; and cf. Waddell, *Sayings of the Desert Fathers*, p. 14.

9. Think of the metaphors of height, accuracy (bow and arrow), and running in Aristotle.

10. It is impossible to speak of asceticism today without reference to Nietzsche. Nietzsche's attack on asceticism in the third essay of the *Genealogy* is as ambiguous—and is so in parallel ways—as his attack on Christianity and slave morality in the first essay. The crucial issue here is the role of asceticism in the development of humanity. Ostensibly, Nietzsche sees asceticism almost as a ladder which we can now push away. It is not at all apparent that this is possible, for reasons which will become clear in the course of this chapter. More centrally for this chapter's concerns, however, is the place of asceticism in the experience of embodiment: for Nietzsche this is mostly negative; I will argue that—despite its attendant pathologies—a certain ascetics is fundamental to the experience of the body, something which lies at the basis of the central Christian doctrines of incarnation and resurrection.

11. In tackling this theme mention must be made of the later works of Michel Henry. Henry, in his attempt at a "phenomenology of Christ," stresses too the non-dualistic nature of Christian thought on the body and understands Christ also in terms of life. The key idea of Henry's thinking is that auto-affection is the non-differential, immediate relation of the self with itself. On this experience of the self, Henry bases his radical dualism of life and world, opposed as he says to the ontological monism of philosophy from Plato to Heidegger. In his early work *The Essence of Manifestation* Henry allows for no ambiguity on this score: "THAT WHICH IS FELT WITH THE INTERMEDIARY OF ANY SENSE WHATSOEVER IS IN ITS ESSENCE AFFECTIVITY." Henry, *The Essence of Manifestation*, p. 462 (block capitals in original). There are a number of possible approaches philosophically to question this position. Above all, one could start from the question of how such a feeling can be articulated, that is, differentiated, if it is without sense. The language of phenomena of which Henry speaks seems to be an inarticulate language as it knows no difference: it speaks of emotion, but emotion without worldly reference is amorphous, as emotion is always of that in the world. This inarticulable language can say nothing of the world and in consequence is in no way creative. In becoming flesh the Word is auto-affective, but is not of a being with created matter. But in such a case then the glory of this Word is not revealed at all in the world: the event character of Christian revelation is lost or rather, as discussed in the Introduction, becomes accidental. Revelation is of the self to itself, a revelation without worldly intermediary. In such a view the phenomenology of life and Christianity are one and the same. What Henry attempts to capture here is the sense of singularity in Christianity as opposed to the difference and alterity found in the work of Levinas and Derrida. Yet the claim of the present work is that these are not opposed alternatives: the Christian understands the singularity of the existent in its singular, non-worldly relation to its origins; as such, the other existent is present to me in its singular being, but always as a being which remains other to me, excessive in its being, precisely because it is turned away from me in its being, toward its origins not 'of the world.' The living, auto-affective being in this understanding is that being which is at once interior and exterior, at once in the world and not of the world, and lives in that ambiguity. Henry's Christian philosophy is in the end a Gnostic Christianity, which leaves obscure the relation of life to the created world. See especially Henry, "La verité de la gnose." For a critical account of Henry's appropriation of Christianity, cf. Bernet, "Christianity and Philosophy."

12. See chapter 4 above.

13. While John speaks of the word becoming flesh (*sarx*), Paul generally reserves the word *sarx* for the natural attachments of the body. I cannot here go into the different theological assumptions at play here; suffice that for Paul the movement from *sarx* to *soma* is done following the example of Christ as the incarnate God.

14. Jean-Luc Nancy in his own terms expresses the movement of the body: "The body is the return of the 'outside' that it is to the 'inside' that isn't. Instead of being in extension, the

body is in expulsion toward its own 'interior,' right up to the very limit where the sign is abolished in the presence it represented." Nancy, *Corpus*, p. 67.

15. The glorification of the body reveals it as it is precisely in transfiguring it. As Nancy puts it: "the glorious body is either the transfiguration of the extended body or its very figuration, its figuration in malleable clay" (ibid., p. 62).

16. On this see Derrida, *The Animal Therefore that I Am*, pp. 3–5.

17. For an insightful discussion of this theme see Badiou, *St. Paul*, pp. 99–102.

18. On the question of the body in the ancient world and the place of Christianity in that respect see Brown, *The Body and Society*.

19. Ibid., p. 31.

20. What is crucial here is that the goal of Christian ascetics was the transformation, not the simple subjection, of the body. On Clement see ibid., pp. 122–139.

21. See ibid., pp. 306–322.

22. Ibid., pp. 218–219.

23. Cassian, *The Institutes*, bk. 5, ch. 6, p. 120.

24. The faithful were warned to keep animals away from the marriage bed and not to practice animal-like forms of intercourse. See Brown, *The Body and Society*, p. 432.

25. Ibid., p. 93.

26. Ibid., p. 223.

27. On eternity and time see chapter 7.

28. Cf. Heidegger, *The Fundamental Concepts of Metaphysics*, pp. 185–192.

29. What Heidegger terms *'Benommenheit'*—captivation (ibid., p. 239).

30. On this theme see Agamben, *The Time that Remains*, p. 83.

31. See Brown, *The Body and Society*, p. 19.

32. Ibid. Brown reports that the physician Galen believed that if Olympic athletes could be castrated in such a way that their reserves of heat would not be disrupted by the operation, they would be stronger. Such speculations are not simply theoretical either. Some religious cults in antiquity practiced voluntary castration, something not unknown in Christianity either, as the case of Origen illustrates.

33. Cassian, *The Institutes*, bk. 6, ch. 6, p. 155.

34. Cf. ibid., bk. 5, ch. 21, pp. 130–131.

35. Waddell, *Sayings of the Desert Fathers*, p. 109.

36. Nietzsche, "On Truth and Lies in a Nonmoral Sense," p. 21. Cf. a similar thought in Plato, *Republic*, 572b.

37. Brown notes: "seldom, in ancient thought, had the body been seen as more deeply implicated in the transformation of the soul and never was it made to bear so heavy a burden." Brown, *The Body and Society*, p. 235.

38. Cassian, *The Institutes*, bk. 4, ch. 9, pp. 82–83.

39. St. Ambrose, *On Virginity*.

40. See Fink, *Spiel als Weltsymbol*.

41. The allusion here is to Montaigne's famous question as to whether he was playing with his cats or his cats with him. Montaigne, *Essays*, p. 331.

42. See Huzinga, *Homo Ludens*, p. 19: "Play goes beyond the limits of purely biological or physical activity."

43. Gordon Burghardt proposes quite suggestively that the motivation for such play is based in boredom. See his "On the Origins of Play," pp. 33–35.

44. From OE *plegan* "to exercise oneself."

45. Turner, *From Ritual to Theatre*, p. 75.

46. Grimes, *Beginnings in Ritual Studies*, pp. 36–37.

47. Douglas, *Purity and Danger*, p. 10.
48. Lacoste, *Experience and the Absolute*, p. 22: "Liturgy exceeds being-in-the-world and the relation to the earth."
49. Ibid., p. 125.
50. This is a highly contested passage. Cf., for a representative discussion, Donahue and Harrington, *The Gospel of Mark*, pp. 226–231. The authenticity of this saying is contested by many scholars; the extent to which it amounts to a rejection of the Law is also a matter of much discussion. Nonetheless, even if it reflects Mark's theology more than the teaching of Jesus, the affirmation of porosity, the rejection of a discourse of contamination, is striking and in keeping with the reality of the Incarnation which I am tracing.
51. Lacoste, *Experience and the Absolute*, p. 172.
52. As Merleau-Ponty puts it, "desire seeks the outside in the inside and the inside in the outside [*recherché du dehors dans le dedans et du dedans dans le dehors*]." Merleau-Ponty, *Resumes de cours*, p. 178.

6. Creation

1. See von Balthasar, *The Glory of the Lord*, vol. 1, p. 448: "by its very being creation shows that it was not necessary. Creaturely beings, thrown into existence, reveal themselves in obedience to natural necessity; but God creates freely."
2. See Proverbs 8:30: "I was beside the master craftsman."
3. See Matthew 5:48: "Be you perfect as your heavenly father is perfect."
4. Acts of creation are in this sense sacramental: the prayer of consecration in the *Roman Missal*: "which earth has given and human hands have made." See further Wainwright, *Doxology*, p. 24.
5. According to Alistair McGrath, the Christian doctrine of *creatio ex nihilo* was in part a reaction against the "Greek teaching of the eternity of the world" (McGrath, *A Scientific Theology*, p. 160).
6. See May, *Creatio ex nihilo*, pp. 22–25.
7. Ibid., pp. 83–84.
8. "It is not the question of the principle of the cosmos that forms the starting point for the assertions of pre-existence, but these 'sprang from Christological reflection which was enquiring about the ultimate origin of the Christ-event and the ascension to be divine messianic Lord contrasting most strongly with the earthly life ending in death'" (ibid., p. 28). The quotation is from Vögtle. Cf. Sokolowski, *The God of Reason and Faith*, pp. 35–37.
9. Referring to Aquinas's *de Veritate*, q. 18, a. 3, von Balthasar writes: "God's 'voice,' addressing Adam in paradise, is not a sensory phenomenon amongst others, but rather God's presence through grace in the voices of nature and of the heart" (von Balthasar, *The Glory of the Lord*, vol. 1, p. 452). Further on he states in respect of the Incarnation: "What is most familiar to man [his own being and life] is suddenly turned for him into a word and a teaching about God" (ibid., p. 457).
10. See May, *Creatio ex nihilo*, pp. 121–128.
11. Ibid., pp. 57–59.
12. Cf. Tertullian, *Against Marcion*, p. 70: "he showed his stamp in that essence which he derived from God Himself, and in the freedom and power of his will."
13. This motif of obedience to the father is a constant through the Gospels from the account of the tempting of Jesus by the devil (Matthew 4:10) to the eve of his crucifixion (Matthew 26:39; Mark 14:36; Luke 22:42).

14. There are clear echoes here of Isaiah 11:6: "The wolf will lie down with the lamb / the panther lie down with the kid."

15. Von Balthasar, *The Glory of the Lord*, vol. 1, p. 451.

16. Averroes indeed critiques the doctrine of *creatio ex nihilo* in these terms. Cf. McGrath, *A Scientific Theology*, p. 165.

17. Hence there is the possibility that the world would not have been. On this theme cf. Sokolowski, *The God of Faith and Reason*, p. 32.

18. Bergson, "The Possible and the Real," pp. 113–116.

19. This idea finds support in Johann Hamann, who understood creation as kenosis, as penetrating into nothingness. See Betz, *After Enlightenment: The Post-Secular Vision of J. G. Hamann*.

20. This distinguishes the nothing of creation fundamentally from Plato's *khora* and the Derridian appropriation of this term. As Derrida tells us: "She [khora] 'is' nothing other than the sum of the process of what has just been inscribed 'on' her, on the subject of her, on her subject, right up against her subject, but she is not the *subject* or the *present support* of all these interpretations, even though, nevertheless, she is not reducible to them. Simply this excess is nothing, nothing that may be and be said ontologically" (Derrida, *On the Name*, p. 99). The khora is pre-originary in a relation of independence (pp. 124–125) and is "a necessity which is neither generative nor engendered and which carries philosophy, 'precedes'... and 'receives' the effect, there the image of oppositions (intelligible and sensible): philosophy" (ibid., p. 126). Elsewhere Derrida tells us: "Khora is nothing (no being, nothing present), but not the Nothing which in the anxiety of Dasein would still open the question of being. This Greek noun says in our memory that which is not reappropriable, even by our memory, even by our 'Greek' memory; it says the immemoriality of a desert in the desert of which it is neither a threshold nor a mourning" ("Faith and Knowledge," in Derrida, *Acts of Religion*, p. 59). The khora is not the nothing of anxiety which opens up the question of being nor is it the nothing of creation which interrupts that question. As Derrida understands it, the khora is the nothingness of a giving place, anterior to any place taking. It is nothing of any ontological categories, and prior to any difference, an alterity beyond or before any namable difference. Creation, on the other hand, is pre-originary, a giving place anterior to any place, but is a nothing not of 'indifference' but rather of singular gift. Such a singular gift is not prior to the name, but a giving of a name, a name through which an entity is called into being. The nothingness of creation is a personal nothingness, or a nothingness as person. The person is prior to all categories, a non-category, a being infused with nothing. The personal relation is a relation of nothing. In it entities do not fall back into indifference (khora) or insignificance (anxiety), but rather stand forth as entities in excess of their worldly being. Richard Kearney, from a somewhat different perspective, shows the fundamental difference between khora and god in the Christian sense. See his *Strangers, Gods and Monsters*, pp. 200–208.

21. "There is only one God and that God is all-sufficient" (Leibniz, *Monadology*, §39, p. 22). In the *Theodicy*, Leibniz tells us: god is "the substance which carries with it the reason for its existence, and which in consequence is necessary and eternal" (Leibniz, *Theodicy*, §7, p. 127). While Leibniz's god is that of the self-sufficient, mirrored in human form by the Stoic ideal of the apathetic wise man, the nothing into and out of which the Christian god creates is that which surpasses all being, namely, love. As Scheler puts it: "The deity of Greek metaphysics is the ideal of the 'sage' in its absolute form: a logical egoist, a being closed in itself, self-observing, self-thinking. . . . The Christian deity is a personal God who creates the 'world' out of an infinite overflow of love" (Scheler, *Ressentiment*, p. 47).

22. Leibniz, *Monadology*, §6, p. 17.

23. Ibid., §17, p. 19: "There is nothing . . . besides perceptions and their changes . . . that one could possibly find in a simple substance."

24. Ibid., §§7 and 18 (pp. 17 and 19), respectively.

25. Derrida, *Given Time*, p. 13: "It cannot be a gift except by not being present as a gift." On the debate between Derrida and Marion on this issue see Caputo and Scanlon (eds.), *God, the Gift and Postmodernism*.

26. Economy is thus not simply abolished in the gift. Rather, there is in all economy an element of gift to the extent to which the object exchanged always exceeds—qualitatively not quantitatively—the price for which it is sold. In this sense, too, there is always something Eucharistic lurking in every exchange. William Desmond expresses this agapeic moment when he states: "When we give thanks for food . . . we acknowledge the generosity of the giver, just in the act of using it for our own self-survival, self-satisfaction. We are released toward otherness, even though we must consume it. We dignify the instrumental with this reminder of, this gratitude for, what in its being is beyond instrumentalization" (*Perplexity and Ultimacy*, p. 117).

27. In this sense, too, the distinction Marion draws between exchange and love in terms of that which is to be exchanged and its price, Marion, *The Erotic Phenomenon*, p. 79, needs to be relativized. In exchange there is some thing to be exchanged but that thing is 'priceless.' That does not mean that we cannot give it a price: the exchange is only possible if a price is given (whether in the form of barter or money). But the price is never sufficient, because it misses the singular being of the thing exchanged. In that sense while in love there is nothing to exchange, that which is exchanged can be loved. Furthermore, the lack of reciprocity does not mark an absolute difference between economy and love: the act of praise or thanks is structured non-reciprocally: praise does not reciprocate, it rather marks the unsubstitutable, singular being of the person or thing praised.

28. See on this point Osborne, *Eros Unveiled*, pp. 20–22.

29. In the following I concentrate on Luke's account of the beatitudes rather than that of Matthew, because the structure of reversal found in Luke is not present in Matthew, and the emphasis on the non-reciprocity of the lover of enemies is not as strong in Matthew as it is in Luke.

30. Luke 6:20: "fixing his eyes on his disciples he said . . ."

31. See Ricoeur, "Love and Justice," pp. 324–329.

32. Marion expresses this as the nature of love when he states: "he loves at once without waiting for anything in return—neither a real counter-love nor the possibility of conceiving a certain hope" (Marion, *The Erotic Phenomenon*, p. 77).

33. *Summa Theologica*, 2.2, question 23, article 1.

34. For an acute phenomenological analysis of this parable, which though in its implications conflicts with the position being articulated here, see Held, "Ethos und die christliche Gotteserfahrung."

35. In this and other respects Carl Schmitt's reading of the injunction to love one's enemies is distortive. See Schmitt, *The Concept of the Political*, p. 29.

36. Leibniz, *Discourse on Metaphysics*, §36, in Leibniz, *Philosophical Texts*, p. 88.

37. I take Desmond to be indicating this phenomenon also when he speaks of "the creative love of creation that descends to the love of consecrated particularity . . . love of the particular as particular," *Perplexity and Ultimacy*, p. 124.

38. Husserl, *Ideas pertaining to a pure phenomenology*, vol. 2, p. 225.

39. See Barbaras's insightful account in his *Desire and Distance*, pp. 109–114.

40. This is in effect the core of Marion's critique of Husserl. See his "Being and Phenomena" in Marion, *Reduction and Givenness*, pp. 49–53.

41. The term is Levinas's. See his "God and Philosophy," p. 67.

42. On this theme, see my "Love of Enemies for a Lover of Wisdom, or, can a Phenomenologist be a Philosopher?" In a somewhat similar vein James Olthuis speaks of "creatio ex amore." See his "Creatio ex Amore," in Benson and Wirzba, *Transforming Philosophy and Religion*, pp. 155–170.

43. As Marion puts it: "The lover does not scorn reason: quite simply, reason itself goes lacking once love is at issue" (*The Erotic Phenomenon*, p. 79).

44. Leibniz, *Theodicy*, §7, p. 127.

45. Leibniz, *Monadology*, §§36–37, pp. 21–22.

46. Cusa, *Vision of God*, p. 57.

47. See Osborne, *Eros Unveiled*, p. 73.

48. The concepts of anger and provocation have an interesting history especially in legal thought. For a fuller description of both concepts taking account of this history see Horder, *Provocation and Responsibility*. See also my discussion of this theme in my "On Provocation."

49. In this context the question of law is inescapable. Law governs the space between the first and second creation. Its fulfillment in the figure of the messiah is one which is rooted in a messianic promise of justice beyond law. That promise in opening up a messianic time both brings peace to the world, which the world does not know, and puts out of play the worldly constraints on violence, those of law. In the name of justice beyond law, unmediated by law—even then, especially then, when it claims to set up a law which embodies justice—violence without limits is an ever-present option. For this reason there can be no simple movement from the wrathful to the peaceful god within the *Judeo*-Christian scriptures. The questions here are ones which have been tackled in different but related ways by Benjamin, Derrida, and Badiou. A full discussion of this theme would require an engagement not just with these authors but also with Heidegger, in particular his discussion of the Anaximander fragment. Such a discussion goes beyond the scope of the present work, however.

7. Aion, Chronos, Kairos

1. I will not explore the question of time in Greek tragedy, which is itself a vast terrain. In the context of the present work, however, the contrast between Greek and Shakespearian tragedy is in this respect significant: in Greek tragedy the tragedy lies in a fatal flaw in the hero not so much of moral weakness as of the existential condition of temporal existence; in Shakespeare the tragedy is contingent, is related to fatal moral flaws, and in principle the tragic consequences are avoidable up to a decisive moment in Act Three. The contingency of the moment and the manner in which that moment can refigure past and future are fundamentally Christian (and specifically Augustinian) moments in Shakespeare's plays.

2. Cf. Matthew 28:20: "I will be with you always; yes, to the end of time (*aionos*)."

3. Deleuze thinks the difference of aion and chronos in ways too subtle and far-ranging to discuss here. He understands aion as event: "This is the event in its difference in nature from cause-bodies, the Aion in its difference in nature from devouring Chronos" (*The Logic of Sense*, p. 132). Aion further is the "eternal truth of time" (ibid., p. 165). Speaking in a different register, the following analysis wishes to show aion as the truth of time.

4. This thesis echoes that of Gadamer's that play is not metaphorically used of nature, but is rather perhaps primordially found there. Gadamer, *Truth and Method*, p. 105.

5. Ibid., p. 102.

6. On this whole debate, cf. Wohlfart, *Also Sprach Herakleitos*, pp. 134–149.

7. "Play is without 'why'" [*Das Spiel ist ohne 'warum'*] (Heidegger, *The Principle of Reasons*, p. 113).

8. I believe it to be no accident that this character of intensity of play is to be found in the Greek word which characterizes life, *zoē*. On this see Krell, *Daimon Life*, pp. 14–15. This word is formed with the root *za* which has the function of intensification. From this origin *zōon* means 'much being,' being in the sense of emergence and in the sense of losing itself. (Both senses are captured in the German word *Aufgehen*.) Life is the way of being which is characterized by the fact that being is not dispersed, but rather descends into itself and as such rests darkly in itself. In this there appears a lightness which has something godly—I am thinking here of the reference in Plato's *Laws* (903d–e) to god as a draughts-player. In this lightness the in-tensity of play changes over into an ex-tensity, which following Henri Bergson, I wish to characterize as explosivity (cf. Bergson, *Creative Evolution*, p. 102). For a moment the animal appears to swim in the light of the sun, in its movements a world is opened up—a world which happens to the extent to which it shines forth out of the dark core of the play.

9. For a forceful articulation of this argument see Held, *Heraklit*, pp. 438–442.

10. Hence, Kirk, for example, sees no cosmological significance in this fragment; rather he understands aion as the finite human life-time. See Kirk, *Heraclitus*, p. xiii.

11. See Wohlfart, *Also Sprach Heraklitus*, pp. 82–94.

12. Cf. Held, *Heraklit*, pp. 151–161.

13. It has been the practice to interpret this passage in the light of later texts, rather than in relation to the Heraclitus fragment. This is so because of the difficulties interpreting fragment B 52 and because of an assumption that aion can be understood as eternity in Plato, while this seems inappropriate for an understanding of the Heraclitus fragment. But in this way the question of how on the basis of life-time or life-force the philosophical concept of eternity was developed remains not just unanswered, but also unasked. Plato did not radically change the meaning of the word "aion." He did not confer for the first time the meaning of eternity on it, but rather he thought further the thought Heraclitus had already begun.

14. My reading of Plato on this point owes much to Böhme, *Idee und Kosmos*.

15. On this point see Callahan, *Four Views of Time*, pp. 23–26.

16. See, for example, Böhme, *Idee und Kosmos*, p. 82.

17. In this respect the notion of forgetfulness of life which I am using draws on the Husserlian thesis of the forgetfulness of the life-world.

18. For the following see Kittel, *Theological Dictionary of the New Testament*, vol. 11, pp. 197–209.

19. The story of the road to Emmaus exemplifies this, as the kairological figure, Christ, explains in retrospect, in the light of himself, the scriptures—now more past than before, as fulfilled, but past as they could never have been present. In contrast, Greek tragedy and philosophy emphasize the necessity of the past and its acceptance.

20. Cf. Koselleck, "Space of Experience."

21. On this theme see Manoussakis, *God after Metaphysics*, pp. 64–70.

22. On the Christian experience of eternity as alterity in contrast to that of the Greeks see Theunissen, *Die Negative Theologie der Zeit*, p. 370.

23. Kierkegaard, *Philosophical Fragments*, p. 75.

24. Ibid., pp. 95–96.

25. Derrida, "Faith and Knowledge," p. 56. Cf. Derrida, *Spectres of Marx*, p. 74.

26. Derrida, *Spectres of Marx*, p. 56.

27. As Kierkegaard puts it: "If he believes his eyes, he is deceived, for the God is not immediately knowable" (Kierkegaard, *Philosophical Fragments*, p. 78). As for the contemporary who is given the condition by the Teacher, then such a contemporary "beholds his glory with the eyes of faith" (ibid., p. 87).

28. Derrida, "Faith and Knowledge," p. 18.

29. Kierkegaard denies this on the basis that knowledge is either theoretical (knowledge of the Eternal) or practical (pure historical knowledge) (*Philosophical Fragments*, p. 76). This though is to assume that knowledge is governed by a Greek account of time and eternity, in which a Pythagorean harmony characterizes the cosmos. If the moment is an event in the world, then it gives itself to be known, and to be known precisely in an existence which aims toward the singular as such.

30. Cf. ibid., p. 77: "the contradiction of our hypothesis is that man receives the condition of the Moment, the same condition which, since it is requisite for the understanding of the eternal Truth, is *eo ipso* an eternal condition." Further on Kierkegaard notes that the absolute eternal fact can only be a historical fact on pain of contradiction (ibid., p. 125).

31. The difference in the texts of scripture, affirmed from Origen through Augustine to Pascal and beyond, between the spiritual and the carnal meaning of the biblical texts arises at a fundamental level from a situation in which the interpretation of the past has to be explained as being contrary to—often in open conflict with—the perception of that past when present. The claim to superiority of the retrospective reading does not rest simply on a claim to a better perspective or indeed on an anti-Judaism (although both may also be present), but rather on the recognition of the transformative effect of the messianic event.

32. Derrida, *Spectres of Marx*, p. 74.

33. Lavelle, *The Meaning of Holiness*, pp. 24–25.

34. Ibid., p. 23.

35. Ibid., p. 25.

36. Ibid., p. 6.

37. Bloechl, "Response to Lacoste," pp. 110–111.

38. Hölderlin, "Die Wanderung (the Journey)," lines 18–19.

8. Thinking Night and Glory

1. Cf. Manoussakis, *God after Metaphysics*, pp. 57–70.

2. See further Tredé, "Kairos: problemes etymologique," p. xii.

3. Origen makes this comparison in his commentary on the Song of Songs. See on this point Osborne, *Eros Unveiled*, pp. 72–73.

4. Nietzsche, *Twilight of the Idols*, p. 48.

5. See Marion, *Being Given*, pp. 291–293.

Bibliography

For Scriptural References:
The Jerusalem Bible. London: Darton, Longman and Todd, 1990.
The Septuagint with Apocrypha: Greek and English. Edited by L. Brenton. Peabody, MA:
  Hendrickson Publishers, 1985

Agamben, G. *The Kingdom and the Glory: For a Theological Genealogy of Economy and
  Government.* Translated by L. Chiesa. Stanford, CA: Stanford University Press, 2008.
———. *Potentialities.* Translated by D. Heller-Roazen. Stanford, CA: Stanford University
  Press, 1999.
———. *The Time that Remains.* Translated by P. Dailey. Stanford, CA: Stanford University
  Press, 2005.
Alter, R. *Genesis.* London: Norton, 1996.
Ambrose. *On Virginity.* Translated by D. Callam. Toronto: Pergina, 1996.
Aquinas, Thomas. *The Disputed Questions on Truth.* Translated by R. Mulligan. Chicago:
  Henry Regnery Co., 1953.
———. *On Faith and Reason.* Edited by S. Brown. London: Hackett, 1999.
———. *Summa Theologica. Complete English Edition in Five Volumes.* Translated by Fathers
  of the English Dominican Province. Allen, TX: Christian Classics, 1948.
Aristotle. *The Complete Works of Aristotle.* Edited by J. Barnes. Oxford: Oxford University
  Press, 1986.
Augustine. *Confessions.* Translated by G. Wills. London: Penguin, 1990.
———. *On Christian Doctrine.* Translated by D. Robertson. New York: Prentice Hall, 1958.
———. *On the Trinity.* Translated by Garret Matthews. Cambridge: Cambridge University
  Press, 2002.
Badiou, A. *Being and Event.* Translated by R. Feltham. London: Continuum, 2007.
———. *St. Paul.* Translated by R. Brasier. Stanford: Stanford University Press, 2003.
Barbaras, R. *Desire and Distance: Introduction to a Phenomenology of Perception.* Translated
  by P. Milan. Stanford: Stanford University Press, 2005.
Barney, R. "Eros and Necessity in the Ascent from the Cave." In *Ancient Philosophy* 28, 2008:
  pp. 357–372.
Barth, K. *Church Dogmatics.* Vol. 1, pt. 2. Translated by G. Thompson and H. Knight. Edin-
  burgh: T&T Clark 1956.
———. *Church Dogmatics.* Vol. 2, pt. 1. Translated by T. Parker, W. Johnston, H. Knight,
  J. Haire. Edinburgh: T&T Clark, 1964.
———. *Church Dogmatics.* Vol. 3, pt. 2. Translated by H. Knight, G. Broimley, J. Reid,
  R. Fuller. Edinburgh: T&T Clark, 1960.
Benjamin, W. "On the Language of Man and Language as Such." In *Selected Writings,* vol.
  1, edited by M. Bullock and M. Jennings. Cambridge, MA: Harvard University Press,
  2002, pp. 64–78.
Bergson, H. *Creative Evolution.* Translated by A. Mitchell. New York: The Modern Library,
  1944.

——. "The Possible and the Real." In *The Creative Mind,* translated by M. Andison. New York: The Philosophical Library, 1944, pp. 91–107.

Bernet, R. "Christianity and Philosophy." *Continental Philosophy Review* 32 (1999): pp. 325–342.

Betz, J. *After Enlightenment: The Post-Secular Vision of J. G. Hamann.* London: Wiley-Blackwell, 2012.

Bloechl, J. "Response to Lacoste." In *The Experience of God,* edited by K. Hart and B. Wall. New York: Fordham University Press, 2005, pp. 104–112.

——. "The Twilight of the Idols and the Night of the Senses." In Hart and Wall, pp. 156–172.

Blumenberg, H. *Lebenszeit und Weltzeit.* Frankfurt a.M.: Suhrkamp, 1985.

Böhme, G. *Idee und Kosmos. Platons Zeitlehre—Eine Einführung in seine theoretische Philosophie.* Frankfurt a.M.: Klostermann, 1996.

Bonaventure. "The Journey of the Soul to God." In *Mystical Opuscula,* translated by J. de Vinck. Vol. 1 of *The Works of Bonaventure.* Paterson, NJ: St. Anthony Guild Press, 1979.

Breton, S. *The Word and the Cross.* New York: Fordham University Press, 2002.

Brown, P. *The Body and Society.* New York: Columbia University Press, 1988.

Bultmann, R. *Existence and Faith.* London: Meridian Books, 1960.

Callahan, J. F. *Four Views of Time in Ancient Philosophy.* Westport, CN: Greenwood Press, 1979.

Caputo and Scanlon, eds. *God, the Gift and Postmodernism.* Bloomington: Indiana University Press, 1999.

Caputo, J. *The Weakness of God.* Bloomington: Indiana University Press, 2006.

Caputo, J., and Alcoff, L., eds. *Paul Amongst the Philosophers.* Bloomington: Indiana University Press, 2009.

Cassian, J. *The Institutes.* Translated by B. Ramsey. New York: Newman Press, 2000.

Chrétien, J-L. *L'arche de la parole.* Paris: PUF, 2008.

——. *The Call and the Response.* Translated by A. Davenport. New York: Fordham University Press, 2004.

Connell, G. "Against Idolatry: Heidegger and Natural Theology." In *Postmodernism and Christian Thought,* edited by M. Westphal. Bloomington: Indiana University Press, 1999, pp. 144–168.

Crowe, B. *Heidegger's Religious Origins.* Bloomington: Indiana University Press, 2006.

Cusa, Nicholas of. *Of Learned Ignorance.* Translated by G. Heron. London: Routledge and Kegan Paul, 1954.

——. *The Vision of God.* Translated by E. Salter. New York: Dutton, 1928.

Cyril of Alexandria. *Select Letters.* Translated by L. Wickham. Oxford: Oxford University Press, 1993.

Deleuze, G. *The Logic of Sense.* Translated by V. Boundas. New York: Columbia University Press, 1990.

de Lubac, H. *Augustinianism and Modern Theology.* Translated by L. Sheppard. New York: Crossroad Publishing, 2000.

——. *The Mystery of the Supernatural.* Translated by R. Sheed. London: Chapman, 1967.

de Montaigne, M. *The Complete Works of Montaigne. Essays, Travel Journal, Letters.* Translated by D. Frame. Stanford: Stanford University Press, 1971.

Derrida, J. *The Animal That Therefore I Am.* Translated by D. Wills. New York: Fordham University Press, 2008.

——. "Faith and Knowledge." Translated by S. Weber. In *Acts of Religion.* London: Routledge, 2002, pp. 40–101.

——. *Given Time 1: Counterfeit Money.* Translated by P. Kamuf. Chicago: Chicago University Press, 1992.

———. *On the Name*. Translated by D. Wood, J. Leavey, I. McLeod. Stanford: Stanford University Press, 1995.

———. *Specters of Marx*. Translated by P. Kamuf. London: Routledge, 1994.

———. *On Touching–Jean-Luc Nancy*. Translated by C. Irizarry. Stanford: Stanford University Press, 2005.

———. "Des Tours de Babel." Translated by J. Graham. In *Acts of Religion*. London: Routledge, 2002, pp. 102–134.

———. "Violence and Metaphysics." In *Writing and Difference*. Translated by A. Bass. Chicago: University of Chicago Press, 1980, pp. 79–153.

Descartes, R. *The Philosophical Writings of Descartes*. Vol. 2, edited by J. Cottingham. Cambridge: Cambridge University Press, 1984.

Desmond, W. *God and the Between*. London: Blackwell, 2008

———. "On the Betrayals of Reverence." In *Is there a Sabbath for Thought?* New York: Fordham University Press, 2005, pp. 262–288.

———. "On Peace—Between Philosophy and Religion." In *Is there a Sabbath for Thought?* New York: Fordham University Press, 2005, pp. 312–356.

———. *Perplexity and Ultimacy: Metaphysical Thoughts from the Middle*. Albany: SUNY Press, 1995.

Diels, H. and Kranz, W. *Die Fragmente der Vorsokratiker*. Vol. 1. Berlin: Weidmannsche, 1934.

Donahue, J., and Harrington, D., eds. *The Gospel of Mark*. Collegeville, MN: The Liturgical Press, 2002.

Douglas, M. *Purity and Danger*. London: Routledge, 2002.

Eco, U. *The Aesthetics of Thomas Aquinas*. Translated by H. Bredin. Cambridge, MA: Harvard University Press, 1988.

Feuerbach, L. *Principles of Future Philosophy*. Translated by M. Vogel. New York: Bobbs-Merrill, 1966.

Fink, E. *Spiel als Weltsymbol*. Freiburg i.B.: Alber, 2010.

Foucault, M. *The Care of the Self*. Translated by R. Hurley. London: Penguin, 1992.

Gadamer, H-G.*Truth and Method*. Translated by J. Weinsheimer and D. Marshal. New York: Continuum, 1990.

Gauchet, M. *The Disenchantment of the World*. Translated by R. Burge. Princeton: Princeton University Press, 1997.

Gerson, L. *Aristotle and Other Platonists*. Cornell: Cornell University Press, 2006.

Girard, R. *Things Hidden Since the Foundation of the World*. Stanford: Stanford University Press, 1987.

Gowen, D. *Genesis 1–11: From Eden to Babel*. Grand Rapids, MI: Eerdmanns, 1988.

Grimes, R. *Beginnings in Ritual Studies*. Lanham, MD: University Press of America, 1982.

Häring, B. *Sin in a Secular Age*. Garden City: Doubleday, 1974.

Harries, K. "'Das Ding', 'Bauen, Wohnen, Denken' und andere Texte aus dem Umfeld." In *Heidegger-Handbuch*, edited by D. Thomä. Stuttgart, Weimar: Metzler, 2003, pp. 301–302.

Hart, K. "The Experience of the Kingdom of God." In Hart and Wall, pp. 71–86.

Hart, K., and B. Wall, eds. *The Experience of God*. New York: Fordham University Press, 2005.

Hayes, Z. "Christology—Cosmology." *Spirit and Life*7 (1997): pp. 41–58.

Hegel, G. W. F. *Phenomenology of Spirit*. Translated by A. V. Millar. Oxford: Oxford University Press, 1977.

Heidegger, M. *Being and Time*. Translated J. Macquarie and E. Robinson. London: Harper and Row, 1962.

———. *Being and Time*. Translated by J. Stambaugh. Albany: SUNY Press, 1996.

———. *Contributions to Philosophy From Enowning*. Translated by P. Emad and K. Maly. Bloomington: Indiana University Press, 1999.

———. *Four Seminars*. Translated by A. Mitchell, F. Raffoul. Bloomington: Indiana University Press, 2003.

———. *The Fundamental Concepts of Metaphysics: World, Finitude, Solitude*. Translated by W. McNeill and N. Walker. Bloomington: Indiana University Press. 2001.

———. *The Introduction to Metaphysics*. Translated by G. Fried, R. Pold. New Haven: Yale University Press, 2000.

———. "On the Essence of Ground." Translated by W. McNeill. In *Pathmarks*, edited by W. McNeill. Cambridge: Cambridge University Press, 1998, pp. 97–135.

———. "On the Origin of the Work of Art." In *Off the Beaten Track*, edited and translated by J. Young and K. Haynes. Cambridge: Cambridge University Press, 2002, pp. 1–56.

———. *On the Way to Language*. Translated by P. Hertz. London: Harper and Row, 1971.

———. "Phenomenology and Theology." In *Pathmarks*, edited by W. McNeill. Cambridge: Cambridge University Press, 1998, pp. 39–62.

———. *The Phenomenology of Religious Life*. Translated by M. Fritsch, J. Gosetti-Ferencei. Bloomington: Indiana University Press, 2004.

———. *The Principle of Reason*. Translated by R. Lilly. Bloomington: Indiana University Press, 1991.

———. "What is Metaphysics?" In *Pathmarks*, edited by W. McNeill. Cambridge: Cambridge University Press, 1998, pp. 82–96.

Held, K. "Ethos und die christliche Gotteserfahrung." *Archivio di Filosofia* 69 (2001): pp. 247–261.

———. "Heidegger und das Prinzip der Phänomenologie." In *Heidegger und die praktische Philosophie*, edited by A. Gethmann-Siefert and O. Pöggeler. Frankfurt a.M.: Suhrkamp, 1989, pp. 111–139.

———. *Heraklit, Parmenides und der Anfang von Philosophie und Wissenschaft. Eine phänomenologische Besinnung*. Berlin: de Gruyter 1980.

Henry, M. "Christianisme et phenomenologie." In *Auto-donation*. Paris: Beauchesne, 2004, pp. 139–158.

———. *The Essence of Manifestation*. Translated by G. Etzkorn. The Hague: Martinus Nijhoff, 1972.

———. *I Am the Truth*. Translated by S. Emmanuel. Stanford: Stanford University Press, 2003.

———. *L'incarnation*. Paris: Seuil, 2000.

———. "Parole et religion." In *Phénoménologie de la vie Tome IV, Sur l'éthique et la religion*. Paris: PUF, 2004, pp. 177–204.

———. "La verité de la gnose." In *Phénoménologie de la vie Tome IV, Sur l'éthique et la religion*. Paris: PUF, 2004, pp. 131–143.

Hölderlin, F. *Hölderlin Selected Verse*. Edited and translated by M. Hamburger. London: Penguin, 1986.

Horder, J. *Provocation and Responsibility*. Oxford: Oxford University Press, 1992.

Huizinga, J. *Homo Ludens: A Study of the Play Element in Culture*. London: Maurice Temple Smith, 1970.

Husserl, E. *Analyses Concerning Active and Passive Synthesis*. Translated by A. Steinbock. Dordrecht: Kluwer Academic Publishers, 2001.

———. *The Crisis of European Sciences and Transcendental Phenomenology: An Introduction to Phenomenology*. Translated by D. Carr. Evanston, IL: Northwestern University Press, 1970.

———. *Experience and Judgment.* Translated by J. Churchill, K. Ameriks. Evanston: Northwestern University Press, 1973.

———. *Ideas Pertaining to a Pure Phenomenology.* Vol. 1. Translated by F. Kersten. The Hague: Martinus Nijhoff, 1983.

———. *Ideas Pertaining to a Pure Phenomenology.* Vol. 2. Translated by R. Rojcewicz and A. Schuwer. New York: Springer, 1989.

Janicaud, D. *Phenomenology and the Theological Turn: The French Debate.* New York: Fordham University Press, 2000.

Jaritz, G. *Time and Eternity: The Medieval Discourse.* Turnhout: Brepol, 2003.

Jaspers, K. *Existenzphilosophie.* Berlin: De Gruyter, 1964.

Jaeger, W. *Aristotle: Fundamentals of the History of his Development.* Translated by R. Robinson. London: Clarendon Press, 1948.

John of the Cross. *The Collected Works of St. John of the Cross.* New York: Doubleday, 1964.

Jüngel, E. *God as the Mystery the World.* Edinburgh: T&T Clark, 1983.

Kant, I. *Critique of the Power of Judgment.* Translated by P. Guyer and E. Matthews. Cambridge: Cambridge University Press, 2000.

———. *Critique of Pure Reason.* Edited by V. Politis. London: Everyman, 1993.

———. *Religion within the Bounds of Mere Reason.* Edited and translated by A. Wood and G. Giovanni. Cambridge: Cambridge University Press, 1998.

Kearney, R. *Anatheism: Returning to the God after God.* New York: Columbia University Press, 2010.

———. *The God who May Be.* Bloomington: Indiana University Press, 2001.

———. *Strangers, Gods and Monsters.* London: Routledge, 2003.

Kierkegaard, S. *Fear and Trembling.* Translated by A. Hannay. London: Penguin Classics, 1985.

———. *Philosophical Fragments.* Translated by E. & H. Hong. Princeton: Princeton University Press, 1974.

Kirk, G. S. *Heraclitus: The Cosmic Fragments.* Cambridge: Cambridge University Press, 1978.

Kisiel, T. *The Genesis of Heidegger's Being and Time.* Berkeley: University of California Press, 1995.

Kittel, G. *Theological Dictionary of the New Testament.* Vols. 1 and 7. Grand Rapids, MI: Eerdmanns, 1964, 1971.

Koselleck, R. "'Space of Experience' and 'Horizon of Expectation': Two Historical Categories." In *Futures Past: On the Semantics of Historical Time.* Cambridge, MA: MIT Press, 1985, pp. 267–288.

Krell, D. F. *Daimon Life: Heidegger and Life-Philosophy.* Bloomington: Indiana University Press, 1992.

Lacoste, J-Y. *Experience and the Absolute.* Translated by M. Raftery-Skehan. New York: Fordham University Press, 2004.

———. *Presence et Parousia.* Paris: Ad Solem, 2006.

Lalipot, E. "What is the Reason for Translating Philosophy? I. Undoing Babel." In *Translation and Philosophy,* edited by L. Foran. Oxford: Peter Lang, 2011, pp. 89–106.

Lavelle, L. *The Meaning of Holiness.* Translated by D. O'Sullivan. London: The Catholic Book Club, 1954.

Leibniz, G. W. *Monadology.* Translated and edited by N. Rescher. Pittsburgh: University of Pittsburgh Press, 1991.

———. *Theodicy: Essays on the Goodness of God, the Freedom of Man, and the Origin of Evil.* Edited by Austin Farrer. La Salle: Open Court, 1985.

———. *Philosophical Texts*. Translated by R. Francks and R. S. Woolhouse. Oxford: Oxford University Press, 1998.

Levinas, E. "God and Philosophy." In *Basic Philosophical Writings*. Translated by A. Lingis. Bloomington: Indiana University Press, 1996, pp. 153–174.

———. *God, Death and Time*. Translated by B. Bergo. Stanford: Stanford University Press, 2000.

———. *Of God who Comes to Mind*. Translated by B. Bergo. Stanford: Stanford University Press, 1998.

———. "Philosophy and the Idea of Infinity." In *Basic Philosophical Writings*. Bloomington: Indiana University Press, 1996, pp. 47–60.

———. *Otherwise than Being*. Translated by A. Lingis. The Hague: Martinus Nijhoff, 1981.

———. "Reality and its Shadow." In *The Levinas Reader*, edited by S. Hand. London: Blackwell, 1989, pp. 129–143.

———. *Time and the Other*. Translated by R. Cohen. Pittsburgh: Duquesne University Press, 1987.

———. "There Is: Existence without Existents." In *The Levinas Reader*, edited by S. Hand. London: Blackwell, 1989, pp. 29–36.

———. *Totality and Infinity*. Translated by A. Lingis. Pittsburgh: Duquesne University Press, 1969.

Louth, A. *The Origins of the Christian Mystical Tradition*. Oxford: Clarendon, 1981.

Lovejoy, A. *The Great Chain of Being*. Cambridge, MA: Harvard University Press, 1964.

Manoussakis, J. *God after Metaphysics: A Theological Aesthetic*. Bloomington: Indiana University Press, 2007.

Marcel, G. *Being and Having*. Translated by K. Farrer. Westminster: Dacre Press, 1949.

———. *Creative Fidelity*. Translated by R. Rosthal. New York: Fordham University Press, 1964.

Marion, J-L. *Being Given: Toward a Phenomenology of Givenness*. Translated by J. Kosky. Stanford: Stanford University Press, 2002.

———. "Christian Philosophy—Hermeneutics or Heuristics." In *The Question of Christian Philosophy Today*, edited by F. Ambrosio. New York: Fordham University Press, 1999, pp. 247–264.

———. *The Erotic Phenomenon*. Translated by S. Lewis. Chicago: University of Chicago Press, 2007.

———. "Evidence and Bedazzlement." Translated by S. Lewis. In *Prolegomena to Charity*. New York: Fordham University Press, 2002, pp. 53–70.

———. *God without Being*. Translated by T. Carlson. Chicago: University of Chicago Press, 1991.

———. *The Idol and Distance*. Translated by T. Carlson. New York: Fordham University Press, 2001.

———. *In Excess*. Translated by V. Berraud. New York: Fordham University Press, 2002.

———. *Reduction and Givenness*. Translated by T. Carlson. Evanston: Northwestern University Press, 1998.

———. "The Saturated Phenomenon." Translated by T. Carlson. *Philosophy Today* 40 (1996): pp. 103–124.

———. *The Visible and the Revealed*. Translated by C. Gschwandtner. New York: Fordham University Press, 2008.

Maritain, J. *Creative Intuition in Art and Poetics*. Princeton: Princeton University Press, 1953.

May, G. *Creatio ex nihilo*. Translated by A. Worral. Edinburgh: T&T Clark, 1994

McGrath, A. *Nature*. Vol. 1 of *A Scientific Theology*. Edinburgh: T&T Clark, 2001.

McGrath, S. *The Early Heidegger and Medieval Philosophy*. Washington, D.C.: Catholic University of America Press, 2006.

Meillassoux, Q. *After Finitude: An Essay on the Necessity of Contingency*. Translated by R. Brassier. London: Continuum, 2010.

Merleau-Ponty, M. "Cezanne's Doubt." Translated by H. and P. Dryfus. In *The Merleau-Ponty Reader*, edited by G. Johnson. Evanston: Northwestern University Press, 2007, pp. 59–75.

———. "Indirect Language and the Voices of Silence." In *Signs*, translated by R. McCleary. Evanston: Northwestern University Press, 1964, pp. 39–84.

———. *The Prose of the World*. Translated by J. O'Neill. Evanston: Northwestern University Press, 1973.

———. *Resumes de cours, College de France, 1952–1960*. Paris: Gallimard, 1968.

———. *The Visible and the Invisible*. Translated by A. Longis. Evanston: Northwestern University Press, 1968.

Milbank, J. *Being Reconciled*. London: Routledge, 2003.

———. *Theology and Social Theory.*London: Blackwell, 1993.

———. *The Word Made Strange*. London: Wiley Blackwell, 1997.

Milbank, J., C. Pickstock, C., and K. Ward.*Radical Orthodoxy*. London: Routledge, 1999.

Milbank and Žižek. *The Monstrosity of Christ: Paradox or Dialectic*. Cambridge, MA: MIT Press, 2009.

Most, G. *Doubting Thomas*. Cambridge, MA: Harvard University Press, 2005.

Mounier, E. *Engagement de la foi*. Paris: Seuil, 1968.

———. *Que sais-je? Le Personalisme*. Paris: PUF, 1995.

Mulhall, S. *Philosophical Myths of the Fall*. Princeton: Princeton University Press, 2005.

Murphy, F. *Christ the Form of Beauty*. Edinburgh: T&T Clark, 1995.

Nancy, J-L. *Corpus*. Translated by R. Rand. New York: Fordham University Press, 2008.

———. *Dis-Enclosure: The Deconstruction of Christianity* New York: Fordham University Press, 2008.

Nietzsche, F. *The Birth of Tragedy*. Translated by R. Spiers. Cambridge: Cambridge University Press, 1999.

———. *Genealogy of Morals*. Translated by D. Smith. Oxford: Oxford University Press, 1998.

———. *Thus Spoke Zarathustra: A Book for All and None*. Translated by A. del Caro. Cambridge: Cambridge University Press, 1998.

———. "On Truth and Lies in a Nonmoral Sense." In *On Truth and Untruth: Selected Writings*. Translated and edited by T. Carmen. London: Harper Perennial Modern Classics, 2010.

———. *Twilight of the Idols*. Translated by R. J. Hollingdale. London: Penguin, 1990.

Nussbaum, M. *The Fragility of Goodness: Luck and Ethics in Greek Tragedy and Philosophy*. Cambridge: Cambridge University Press, 2001.

———. *Hiding from Humanity*. Princeton: Princeton University Press, 2004.

Nyssa, Gregory of. *From Glory to Glory: Texts from Gregory of Nyssa's Mystical Writings*. Edited and translated by J. Daniélou, H. Musurillo. Crestwood, NJ: St. Vladimir's Seminary Press, 2001.

———. *Life of Moses*. Translated by A. Malherbe and E. Ferguson. Ramsey, NJ: Paulist Press, 1978.

O'Connor, P. *Profanations: Derrida*. London: Continuum, 2010.

Olthuis, J. "Creatio ex Amore." In *Transforming Philosophy and Religion: Love's Wisdom*, edited by B. Benson and N. Wirzba. Bloomington: Indiana University Press, 2008, pp. 155–170.

Ó Murchadha, F. "Glory, Idolatry, Kairos: Marion and Heidegger on the Ontological Differ-ence." In *Givenness and God: Questions of Jean-Luc Marion*, edited by E. Cassidy and I. Leask. New York: Fordham University Press, 2005, pp. 69–86.

———. "Love of Enemies for a Lover of Wisdom, or, can a Phenomenologist be a Philoso-pher?" In *Transcendence and Phenomenology*, edited by C. Cunningham and P. Candler. London: SCM Press, 2007, pp. 404–420.

———. "On Provocation: Violence as Response." In *Violence, Victims, Justifications*. Oxford: Peter Lang, 2006, pp. 201–217.

———. "Reduction, Externalism and Immanence in Husserl and Heidegger," *Synthese* 160, 3 (2008): pp. 375–395.

———. *The Time of Revolution: Kairos and Chronos in Heidegger*. London: Continuum, 2012.

Origen. *Contra Celsum*. Translated by H. Chadwick. Cambridge: Cambridge University Press, 1965.

———. *On First Principles*. Translated by G. Butterworth. New York: Harper and Row, 1966.

Osborne, C. *Eros Unveiled*. Oxford: Clarendon, 1994.

Ott, H. *Denken und Sein*. Hamburg: Evangelischer Verlag, 1959.

Otto, R. *The Idea of the Holy*. Translated by J. Harvey. Oxford: Oxford University Press, 1950.

Otto, W. *Die Götter Griechenlands*. Bonn: Cohen, 1929.

Pannenberg, W. *Basic Questions in Theology*. G. Kelm. London: SCM Press, 1971.

Pascal, B. *Pensées*. Translated by A. J. Krailsheimer. London: Penguin Classics, 1995. French edition: Pascal, B. *Oeuvres completes*, edited by Henri Gouhier. Paris: de Seuil, 1963.

Plato. *The Collected Dialogues of Plato*. Edited by E. Hamilton. Princeton: Princeton Univer-sity Press, 1961.

Pickstock, C. *After Writing*. Oxford: Blackwell, 1998.

Plessner, H. *Die Stufen des Organischen und der Mensch. Einleitung in die Philosophische Anthropologie*. Berlin: Walter de Gruyter, 1975.

Polkinghorne, J. *The Work of Love: Creation as Kenosis*. Grand Rapids, MI: Eerdmanns, 2001.

Pseudo-Dionysius. *The Divine Names and the Mystical Theology*. Translated by J. Jones. Mil-waukee, WI: Marquette University Press, 1980.

Rahner, K. "Concerning the Relationship between Nature and Grace." In *Theological Inves-tigations*. Vol. 1, translated by Cornelius Ernest. London: Darton, Longman and Todd, 1961.

———. "The Hiddenness of God." In *Theological Investigations*. Vol. 13. London: Darton, Longman and Todd, 1973.

Ramsey, A. M. *The Glory of God and the Transfiguration of Christ*. London: Darton, Longman and Todd, 1967.

Ricoeur, P. "Love and Justice." In *Figuring the Sacred*. Translated by D. Pellauer. Minneapolis, MN: Fortress Press, 1995, pp. 315–330.

Sallis, J. *Shades—Of Painting at the Limit*. Bloomington: Indiana University Press, 1998.

Sartre, J-P. *Being and Nothingness*. Translated by H. Barnes. London: Methuen & Co., 1957.

Scheler, M. "Love and Knowledge." In *On Feeling, Knowing and Valuing*. Edited and trans-lated by H. Bershady. Chicago: University of Chicago Press, 1992.

———. *Ressentiment*. Translated by L. Coser and W. Holdheim. Milwaukee, WI: Marquette University Press, 1998.

Simmel, G. *Simmel on Culture: Selected Writings*. Edited and translated by D. Frisby and M. Featherstone. London: Sage Publications, 1997.

Schmitt, C. G. *The Concept of the Political*. Translated by G. Schwab. New Brunswick, NJ: Rutgers, 1976.

Smith, J. *Speech and Theology*. London: Routledge, 2002.

Sokolowski, R. *The God of Reason and Faith*. Washington, D.C.: Catholic University Press, 1995.

Sutton Smith, B., and Kelly-Byrne, D. "The Idealisation of Play." In *Play in Animals and Humans*, edited by P. Smith. London: Basil Blackwell, 1984, pp. 305–321.

Tertullian. *Against Marcion*. Edinburgh: T&T Clark, 1987.

———. *Apology and De spectaculis*. Translated by G. Rendall. Cambridge, MA: Harvard University Press, 1989.

Theunissen, M. *Die Negative Theologie der Zeit*. Frankfurt a.M.: Suhrkamp, 1990.

Tredé, M. "Kairos: problemes etymologique." *Revue des Etudes Greque* 97 (1984): pp. xi–xvi.

Turner, D. *The Darkness of God*. Cambridge: Cambridge University Press, 1995.

Turner, V. *From Ritual to Theatre*. New York: PAJ Books, 1987.

van Buren, J. *The Young Heidegger*. Bloomington: Indiana University Press, 1994.

Vasseleu, C. *Textures of Light: Vision and Touch in Irigaray, Levinas, and Merleau-Ponty*. London: Routledge, 1998.

von Balthasar, U. *Love Alone: The Way of Revelation*. London: Continuum, 1968.

———. *The Glory of the Lord*. Vols. 1–7. Translated by E. Leiva-Merikakis. New York: Ignatius Press, 1982–1991.

———. *Theo-drama*. Vols. 2, 3, and 5. Translated by G. Harrison. New York: Ignatius Press, 1990–1998.

Waddell, H., ed. *Sayings of the Desert Fathers*. London: Constable, 1936.

Wainwright, G. *Doxology*. London: Epworth Press, 1980.

Waldenfels, B. *Antwortregister*. Frankfurt a.M.: Suhrkamp, 1994.

———. *Bruchlinien der Erfahrung*. Frankfurt a.M.: Surhkamp, 2003.

Ward, G. *Barth, Derrida and the Language of Theology*. Cambridge: Cambridge University Press, 1995.

Weil, S. *Notebooks*. Vol. 2. Translated by Arthur Wills. London: Routledge and Keegan Paul, 1958.

———. *Waiting for God*. Translated by E. Craufurd. London: Harper Collins, 2001.

Westphal, M. "Hermeneutics and the God of Promise." In *After God: Richard Kearney and the Religious Turn in Continental Philosophy*, edited by J. Manoussakis. New York: Fordham University Press, 2006, pp. 78–93.

———. *Overcoming Onto-theology: Toward a Postmodern Christian Faith*. New York: Fordham University Press, 2001.

Wohlfart, G. *Also Sprach Herakleitos*. Freiburg i.B.: Alber, 1991.

Index

Abram/Abraham, 50, 74, 77, 79, 131–133, 136, 193

Acosmic, 3, 6, 33, 42

Adam, 13, 103, 126, 144, 150, 161, 164, 166, 299n9

Adiaphoria, 150

Aesop's tales, 64

Aesthetic judgment, 44

Affection, 47, 59, 72, 201. *See also* Henry: auto-affection

Agamben, Giorgio, x, 220n48

Agápe, x, 2, 56, 112, 114, 159, 168, 172–177, 197–198, 200, 203, 205. See also eros; love

Aion, 103, 178, 180–189, 232n2, 232n3, 233n13

Albert the Great, 43

Allure (*Reiz*), 47, 85

Analogia entis, 10

Anaximander, 2

Anger, 67, 134, 176–177

Animal, 150–151, 155–157, 181, 205, 228n24, 233n8; animal play, 155–156, 181. See also *adiaphoria*; animality; desert fathers; play

Animality, 57, 144, 146–147, 151, 154, 156, 157

Anxiety, 61, 75, 85; sacred anxiety, 32, 57, 208n12

Apatheia, 147, 149, 154

Apollo (the Sun-god), 70; and Dionysus, 8–9

Apophasis, 179

Aquinas, Thomas, 42, 43, 116, 141, 159, 170, 199, 214n30

Aristotle, ix, 4–5, 18, 35, 46, 63, 64, 106, 145, 160, 176–177, 180, 185–186, 187, 192, 193, 207n5

Ascetics, 39, 142, 143, 145–149, 150–154, 157–158, 198; and Nietzsche, 227n10. *See also* autarkic; desert fathers

Atheism, 8, 15; methodological atheism (Heidegger), 13, 15, 91

'Athletes of god', 145. *See also* desert fathers

Attention, 39, 47, 59–60, 97–99, 111, 125, 191. *See also* Augustine; Heidegger; Husserl; Weil

Attraction, 34, 40, 41–48, 49, 59, 104, 114, 127, 130. *See also* allure; beauty; mission

Augustine, Saint, ix, 2, 57, 197, 199; concerning time, 190–193, 196

Autarkic, 151, 154. *See also* ascetics

Auto-constitution, 33

Autonomy, 51, 127, 165

Awakening, 47, 51, 213n20. *See also* wakefulness

Babel, Tower of, 75–79, 83–84

Balthasar, Urs von, x, 4, 42, 46, 49, 51, 102, 114, 120, 123, 198, 199

Barbarian, 76–77, 148

Barth, Karl, 3, 4, 10, 15, 21, 25, 27, 198, 215n64, 221n58, 222n65

Beatitudes, 169–170, 231n29

Beauty, 5, 34–35, 40, 48–49, 52–53, 54, 69, 85, 117, 118, 123, 127, 131, 132–133, 157, 159, 168, 201, 205, 212n3, 214n30, 218n23; as transcendental, 41–46, 48. *See also* allure; Aquinas; Chrétien; desire; Pseudo-Dionysius

Bedazzlement, 29, 42, 221n53. *See also* Marion

Being-in, 16, 53, 73, 91, 92–97, 99–102, 113, 119, 125, 139, 204, 219n4; Being-in-Christ (*en Kristoi einai*), 101–102

Being-of, 91–97, 105, 109, 114, 115, 118–119

Being-situated, 129, 130

Being-with, 94, 183, 201

Belief, 36, 58, 67, 72, 74–75, 79, 105, 115, 133, 135, 140, 199, 204. *See also* faith

Benjamin, Walter, 77, 232n49

Bergson, Henri, 165

Betrayal, 200–201

Birth, 23, 49, 139, 189, 196

Blindness, 87, 197

FELIX Ó MURCHADHA is Senior Lecturer in Philosophy at the National University of Ireland, Galway. He is author of *The Time of Revolution: Kairos and Chronos in Heidegger* and editor of *Violence, Victims, Justifications*.

www.ingramcontent.com/pod-product-compliance
Lightning Source LLC
Chambersburg PA
CBHW020403100426
42812CB00001B/174